W9-AEI-754
WITHDRAWN
L. R. COLLEGE LIBRARY

STUDIES IN THE GENESIS OF ROMANTIC THEORY IN THE EIGHTEENTH CENTURY

Studies in the Genesis of Romantic Theory in the Eighteenth Century

By

J. G. ROBERTSON
Professor of German Language and Literature in the University of London

NEW YORK
RUSSELL & RUSSELL · INC
1962

CARL A. RUDISILL LIBRARY
LENOIR RHYNE COLLEGE

809.91
R54s
46,850
April 1964

FIRST PUBLISHED IN 1923
REISSUED, 1962, BY RUSSELL & RUSSELL, INC.
BY ARRANGEMENT WITH CAMBRIDGE UNIVERSITY PRESS
L. C. CATALOG CARD NO: 62—13848
PRINTED IN THE UNITED STATES OF AMERICA

PREFACE

THE present series of studies, which seeks to establish a new starting-point for the evolution of aesthetic values in the eighteenth century, originated in the most trivial of literary 'discoveries.' Some twenty years ago I set myself to solve the mystery why the Swiss critic Bodmer, one of the early continental writers to mention Shakespeare's name, should have called him 'Sasper.' The ingenious phonetic explanations advanced by German scholars, were unconvincing; and I surmised that an eighteenth-century Italian was more likely to have thus maltreated Shakespeare's name than a writer whose mother-tongue was German. Bodmer's Italian source was not very difficult to find, and, although in itself little more than a literary curiosity, it led me to a further hypothesis, namely, that Bodmer and his friend Breitinger might not, as had hitherto been believed, have drawn their ideas on literary aesthetics so much from Addison and Du Bos, as from Italian sources, even that English and French critics might owe some debt in that quarter; that, in other words, the movement which led to the dethronement of the Reason as the chief arbiter in poetic creation, and gave the first place to the Imagination—a movement which, in Germany, inaugurated the rapid development culminating in Goethe and Schiller—is to be put to the credit of Italy rather than ourselves.

In furtherance of the work on Bodmer and Breitinger, which was inaugurated with the *Bodmer-Denkschrift* of 1900, I undertook a series of investigations into the genesis of the Swiss critical theory, and, in particular, copied and collated Bodmer's letters lying in Swiss, German and North Italian libraries. I had hoped, in collaboration with Swiss scholars, to publish a critical edition of Bodmer's early correspondence and certain of his and Breitinger's aesthetic writings; but the war intervened, and the scheme is still in abeyance. Meanwhile, the larger aspect of the question, the influence of Italy on the general critical theory of Europe, as a kind of aftermath of the 'Quarrel of the Ancients and the Moderns,' stirring to life those forces which were subsequently to be designated as 'Romantic,' forced itself on me with cumulative interest.

The object of the present volume is, briefly, then, to show that the Italy which led the critical theory of Europe in the sixteenth century, played again a pioneer rôle at the beginning of the eighteenth; that the conception of the 'creative imagination,' with the help of which Europe emancipated herself from the pincers of pseudo-classicism, was virtually born in Italy to grow to full maturity in England and Germany.

These studies were practically completed before the war; and the spade-work is of considerably older date. I have, however, as will be seen from my footnotes, revised the text of the Italian section in the light of the latest Italian research.

I would take the opportunity of expressing my warm thanks for the kindly and generous aid received from Italian friends, with whom, in many cases, my friendship has been restricted to correspondence; and to libraries abroad, notably the Biblioteca Nazionale in Rome, the Biblioteca Civica in Bergamo, and the Stadtbibliothek in Zürich. At home, the library of University College, London, has been unexpectedly helpful for the study of critical theory; and it need hardly be said that an undertaking like the present would have been impossible outside of Italy, without the unrivalled wealth of the British Museum.

J. G. ROBERTSON

UNIVERSITY OF LONDON
September, 1923

CONTENTS

PAGE

PREFACE v

CHAP.

I. THE FRANCO-ITALIAN CONTROVERSY AND THE ARCADIANS 1

II. GIAN VINCENZO GRAVINA 24

III. LODOVICO ANTONIO MURATORI 60

IV. ANTONIO CONTI 96

V. PIER JACOPO MARTELLI 120

VI. SCIPIONE MAFFEI AND HIS FRIENDS . . . 144

VII. PIETRO DI CALEPIO 164

VIII. GIAMBATTISTA VICO 179

IX. THE INDEBTEDNESS OF FRANCE TO ITALY . . 195

X. ITALIAN INFLUENCE IN SPAIN: IGNACIO DE LUZÁN 219

XI. THE BEGINNINGS OF A NEW AESTHETICS IN ENGLAND: ADDISON 235

XII. ITALIAN INFLUENCE ON AESTHETIC THEORY IN GERMANY 250

CHRONOLOGICAL TABLE 293

INDEX 297

CHAPTER I

THE FRANCO-ITALIAN CONTROVERSY AND THE ARCADIANS

I

IT is one of the more tangible achievements of the vaguely defined science of Comparative Literature that it has lifted the veil from the phenomena of analogous development in literary history. We are no longer content to register the fact that, at certain periods of their history, the literatures of Italy, France, England and Germany passed through identical metamorphoses, and reacted similarly to the same spiritual forces; that great movements like the Renaissance, or Romanticism, moving over the face of Europe, left behind them similar effects on every land; we are beginning now to understand the processes and developments involved in such phenomena; to grasp and formulate, in other words, natural laws of literary evolution. Literature is regarded as a living organism, subject to the laws of growth and decay which all living things obey. Recent studies on the Renaissance, not a few of which draw their inspiration directly or indirectly from Burckhardt's epoch-making work on the Renaissance in Italy, have thrown much light on the spirit of that stupendous movement in its earlier stages. But we are far from having attained equal clearness concerning the latter end, the final metamorphosis of the Renaissance, as it emerged from the 'Quarrel of the Ancients and the Moderns' at the beginning of the eighteenth century. It is to further this object in the fundamental matter of literary theory that the present studies have been planned.

The symptoms of Renaissance development and decay bear a close resemblance in all literatures on which the Renaissance has left its stamp. Like a kind of blight, the phenomenon which is known in Italy as 'marinismo' or 'secentismo,' in Spain as 'culteranismo' or 'gongorismo,' in England as 'Euphuism,' in Germany, quite bluntly, as 'Schwulst,' and which in France is associated with the affectation of the Pléiade, and, more characteristically, with the later extravagances of the 'précieuses ridicules,' spread over Europe and eclipsed the rich achievement of the earlier period, when the light of antiquity had still dazzled Western eyes. The character and intensity of the disease differed in accordance with the conditions prevailing in the various countries; in all, however, it was manifestly due to what might be called a devitalisation of poetry. The spirit of the Renaissance literature had evaporated; the formulas alone remained; and the champions of these formulas devoted themselves with a zeal which often outstripped discretion, to keep them alive by breathing an artificial life into them; they decked them out with a fantastic, often grotesque extravagance, or handled them with an ingenuity which appealed rather to the capricious fancy than to sober common sense. The manifestations also varied according to the intensity with which the Renaissance originally influenced the particular literature, or, having influenced it, in proportion as its power had waned. In England, for instance, almost from the beginning, the Renaissance was assimilated by our national literature, and quickly lost its exotic character: consequently, when the continental disease reached us, taking the form we see in the conceits of *Euphues*, it did not strike us as a symptom of weakness or decadence—nor was it—but merely as a superfluous accessory to our literature, a curious importation from abroad. In France, again, the Pléiade was essentially sound; and later, 'préciosité' played a quite insignificant rôle. The Renaissance movement in France in its earlier stages, instead of reaching exhaustion, as in Italy or Spain, or of being superseded by an anti-classical movement, as in England, gathered strength, and advanced from one triumph to another. The age of Corneille, Racine and Molière, of Boileau, was no age of decadent classicism, but the greatest classic age in modern literature. There was no lack of vitality here, and the encroachments of Italian and Spanish extravagance were easily kept at bay: the 'précieuses ridicules' were merely objects of amused scorn.

But in Italy—and it is with Italy that the present volume is particularly concerned—it was very different; Italy succumbed, and succumbed seriously to the disease. In the seventeenth century the first flush of the Renaissance was a long way off, much farther off than in France; moreover, that movement, which revolutionised European literature as no other since the early Crusades, had in Italy advanced to maturity without disturbing cataclysms; it had been self-contained and independent of outside aid. Italy was looked up to as the exemplar of the Renaissance spirit; she had given other nations models for their lyric, their drama, their romance; she had, with her powerful and original expounders of Aristotle—Robortelli, Vettori, Minturno, Castelvetro, Riccoboni, Beni—imposed upon Europe her theory of poetry. Her writers, indeed, had every reason to be satisfied with their achievement; but they remained satisfied, even when the tide of the Renaissance began to ebb; they were blind to the change that had come; they failed to perceive the insidious encroachment, under the guise of originality, of an unhealthy and decadent literary taste. In the seventeenth century we find them responding with alacrity to the fascinating lure of Marini—a poet the more acceptable by virtue of a wonderful fantasy hardly inferior to that of Ariosto himself—and quite oblivious to the fact that the solid basis of good taste was slipping away from them; that disease and decay were invading their literature, and they, the quondam leaders, were ceasing to be respected in Europe. Protest there was, it is true, but it was ineffectual; it came too early, or it fell on deaf ears. Venturesome predecessors of the 'moderns,' like Tassoni, were not the pioneers of a 'risorgimento' within Italy itself, but rather of the progressive side of that 'Quarrel of the Ancients and Moderns' which broke out in France while Italy was still dreaming of other and remoter things. Thus, looking back on the advance of letters in Italy from the Renaissance onwards, one cannot help thinking that there was something fatal in its very stability. There was no break, as it were, to pull men's minds up, and lead them to take stock of their ideas. No dove descended from heaven to replenish the Grail of the Italian spirit.

Italy's strength in the seventeenth century lay in other fields of intellectual achievement; it was an age of vigorous scientific speculation and discovery. The publication of the epoch-making *Dialogo* of Galileo in 1632 marked the beginning of Italian conquests in the new world of science. This was followed rapidly by the discoveries of Torricelli and Malpighi; while behind these pioneers stood a solid body of educated opinion, interested in the search for scientific truth and represented by such societies as the Accademia del Cimento in Florence, founded under the auspices of Prince Leopoldo dei Medici in 1657. This Academy—the mother of our own Royal Society—was the successor of the famous Accademia dei Lincei, which, in 1630, had suffered an eclipse that lasted for more than a century. And even more important was the first *Giornale dei Letterati*, which began to appear at Rome in 1668, and was modelled on the French *Journal des Savants*[1]. Thus, while in France the literary world was arming for a battle between the authority of antiquity and the rebellious aspiration of the new time, another battle was being fought out in Italy between the ancients and the moderns of science, a battle the issue of which had hardly less far-reaching consequences. It is to Italy we must look for the immediate successors of Bacon, and for the forerunners of the scientific movement which, in England, was to put a new complexion on the eighteenth century. As was only natural, this scientific activity reacted on philosophy and criticism, especially as no hard and fast line had yet been drawn in the seventeenth century between science and literature. Men of letters were at the same time men of science; one might even say that the new movement in Italian aesthetics and criticism would not have been possible at all without the empiricism of the preceding century. But the effects of the reaction were slow in showing themselves, and when they did, they were the reverse of furthering; the scientific movement in its earlier stages was hostile to philosophic speculation; it did not encourage the appreciation of Descartes in Italy—still less did it prepare the way for Vico; it led merely to the uncompromising materialism of Gassendi.

Towards the end of this century of scientific aspiration,

[1] Cp. G. Maugain, *Étude sur l'évolution intellectuelle de l'Italie de 1657 à 1750 environ*, Paris, 1909, pp. 24 f.

Italy definitely lost her leadership in European literature and criticism; her learning became a laboured erudition which spent itself in the compilation of huge compendiums and lifeless catalogues, or frittered itself away in trivial prolixity—a very different thing from the brilliant achievement of earlier scholars like Vettori, Sigonio[1] and Castelvetro. Her erudites now were fascinated by problems of purely external form; they praised or blamed mechanically according to the precepts—unintelligently interpreted—of Aristotle; and with the worship of the letter of Aristotle came, unfortunately, a serious misunderstanding of his spirit. These men could not see that, notwithstanding their preoccupation with form, it was the very formlessness of the 'seicento' that was responsible for Italy's literary undoing. The sterility of their outlook is illustrated by books like the famous *Cannochiale aristotelico* of Emanuelo Tesauro—surely the nadir of Aristotelian interpretation—and by an over-subtle dialogue-literature which indulged in excessive hair-splitting and refused to see poetic theory from a common-sense standpoint. The taste for fantastic thinking, for the 'concetti' of Marini and his followers, became universal, and paralysed all serious literary effort; the Italian theatre lost its self-respect and became divorced from literature, the harlequin, as later in Germany, being allowed to invade the tragic stage[2]. Thus, as the century drew to its close, the aesthetic judgment of Italy seemed to have completely abdicated.

II

Such was the state of things when in the last years of the seventeenth century, the Italian conscience was awakened to a sense of humiliation. This awakening is usually held to have been due to the sting of foreign censure; but there were signs of an earlier revolt in Italy itself. The Church, for instance, had made a stand against the excesses of Marinism; and criticism began to show a healthier moral tone, before there could be

[1] Cp. Maugain, *op. cit.* pp. 85 ff.

[2] English readers will remember Addison's words (*Remarks on Several Parts of Italy; Miscellaneous Works*, ed. by A. C. Guthkelch, London, 1914, II, p. 61): 'I have seen a translation of the *Cid* acted at *Bolonia*, which would never have taken, had they not found a place in it for these Buffoons.'

any question of foreign criticism making its weight felt. Poets like Redi and Buragna celebrated only 'virtuous love'; Maggi and Lemene, both of whom were praised by Muratori in his early years, consigned their amorous poetry to the flames. Martelli gave up writing love-poetry to sing the *Eyes of Jesus*. Especially virulent was the battle round the theatre, which had made itself obnoxious to the Church. The new criticism of the time demanded that the playhouse should be a school of morals; and none, as will be seen, fought more stubbornly for this end than Maffei[1]. Italy must be given all credit for these attempts to reform her literature, and, by her example, to reform that of Europe.

As far as foreign criticism is concerned, it may be said to begin with the Père Bouhours speaking scornfully of the Italian language in his *Entretiens d'Ariste et d'Eugène* (1671)[2]. Boileau, in his *Art poétique* (1674) reflected unkindly, and even harshly, on Italy as the home of bad taste, implying that, in this respect, she was hardly less to be reprobated than Spain[3]. Rapin expressed similar sentiments[4]; Baillet[5], and an ever-increasing chorus followed; and in 1687 appeared the most virulent and damning of all the anti-Italian books, the famous *Manière de bien penser dans les Ouvrages de l'Esprit*, by Bouhours.

The new spirit in literary criticism, which justified France in assuming this standpoint of superiority towards her neighbour, was, no doubt, to some extent bound up with the philosophy and teaching of Descartes. But caution is necessary in estimating Descartes' influence on literature. M. Émile Krantz, in his fascinating study of the aesthetics of Descartes[6], may have been carried away by excess of zeal, when he set up his brilliant paradox that this great thinker, who never wrote a line on aesthetics, was virtually the creator of France's aesthetic canon,

[1] See below, pp. 155 ff., and cp. Maugain, *op. cit.* pp. 236 ff.

[2] See especially the second dialogue ('La langue françoise') and the fourth ('Le bel esprit'). A reprint of this work, edited by R. Radouant, appeared in 1920.

[3] *L'Art poétique*, I, 43 f.; II, 105 f.; III, 209 ff.

[4] R. Rapin, *Réflexions sur la Poétique d'Aristote*, Paris, 1674, *passim*. Cp. G. Maugain, *L'Italie dans quelques publications de jésuites français* (*Bibl. de l'Institut français de Florence*, II, 1). Paris, 1910, pp. 9 ff.

[5] A. Baillet, *Jugemens des Sçavans*, Tome IV, Paris, 1686; the chief references are collected by Maugain, pp. 249 ff.

[6] É. Krantz, *Essai sur l'Esthétique de Descartes*, 2nd ed., Paris, 1898.

and M. Lanson[1] may be right when he claims a more pronounced Cartesianism for the 'moderns' than the 'ancients' in the famous controversy; but I cannot help thinking that there is a deeper connection between Descartes' insistence on the identity of the highest beauty with the highest truth—with its tacit corollary that the Marinesque doctrine of beauty for beauty's sake is vicious and derogatory to good taste—and the ideals of French classicism. Descartes' philosophy does loom behind Boileau's *Art poétique*; and Boileau was, consciously or unconsciously, a Cartesian when he set up the reason as the last tribunal of appeal in literary taste, even if his 'reason' may not be identical with that of Descartes; he is in spirit Cartesian when he insists on clearness and naturalness, and rails against fantasy and capricious artifice. On the Cartesian doctrine of an undifferentiated reason common to all mankind is based the classic dogma of a universal and unchanging taste. Not merely Boileau, but all French criticism at the end of the seventeenth and in the early years of the eighteenth century was, if not openly Cartesian, at least in consonance with that 'manière de bien penser' which Descartes enunciated in his *Discours de la Méthode*. Cartesianism was a factor in the thought of both the 'ancients' and the 'moderns'; and this, as will be seen, is more clearly demonstrated by the Italians than by the French themselves. In France, moreover, the Cartesian stimulus was not allowed to degenerate into that placid acceptance of dogmas, which was fatal to it in Italy; the great literary quarrel might, in fact, be described as to a large extent a controversy concerning the aesthetic interpretation of Cartesianism and its application to poetry.

The attitude of intellectual Italy to Descartes at the end of the seventeenth century is still wrapped in some obscurity[2].

[1] Cp. G. Lanson, *L'Influence de la Philosophie cartésienne sur la littérature française*, in *Revue de Métaphysique et de Morale*, IV, July, 1896, pp. 518 ff. See, however, the chapter on 'Cartesio e il classicismo aristotelico' in G. Toffanin's *La Fine del Umanesimo*, Turin, 1920, pp. 247 ff.

[2] Cp. F. Bouillier, *Histoire de la Philosophie cartésienne*, 3rd ed., Paris, 1868, II, p. 570, and Maugain, *op. cit.* pp. 151 ff. Also G. B. Gerini, *I Seguaci di Cartesio in Italia sul finire del secolo XVII ed il principio del XVIII*, in *Il nuovo Risorgimento*, 1899, pp. 426 ff; and L. Berthé de Besancèle, *Les Cartésiens d'Italie*, Paris, 1920. On the Cartesian influence generally see M. Menéndez y Pelayo, *Historia de las ideas estéticas en España*, 2nd ed., IV, Madrid, 1901, pp. 225 ff.

And lucidly as one of its latest investigators, M. Maugain, has dealt with the question, he has still left uncertainty on some of its aspects. He has, for instance, described excellently the conflict which arose between the new Cartesianism and the scientific and materialistic movement which culminated in Gassendi; but he leaves us unsatisfied in his treatment of the relation between Cartesianism and the philosophy of Italy's greatest thinker, Giambattista Vico—a question that is by no means so simple as some modern Vichians appear to believe[1]. Meanwhile, it is sufficient for our present purposes to note that the chief focus of the new philosophy in Italy was Naples. Here Tommaso Cornelio and Leonardo di Capua had prepared the way; Caloprese, Gravina's teacher, was a Cartesian; and the Neapolitan, Paolo Doria, Vico's friend, in his earlier years regarded Descartes' philosophy sympathetically[2]. It was assuredly not unconnected with these facts that the regeneration of Italian aesthetics went out in large measure from Naples.

But to return to the Père Bouhours and his *Manière de bien penser*, which was mainly responsible for the Italian awakening. From Doncieux's interesting study of Bouhours we gather something of the personality and characteristics of this anything but aristocratic-looking little Jesuit abbé, 'with the massive, rubicund face, the sparkling, intelligent eyes, and the fine, ironic smile.'[3] He was a welcome guest in Mademoiselle de Scudéry's salon, and, as such, had a public familiar with his ideas before his books were written and published. In fact, his literary reputation was made somewhat late in life; his *Entretiens d'Ariste et d'Eugène* appeared in 1671, in his forty-third year; his principal work, the *Manière de bien penser*, not until 1687, his fifty-ninth; he was dead (1702) before the latter book—

[1] See below, pp. 31, 191 ff.

[2] The most eminent of all the Italian Cartesians was, however, a Sicilian settled in Padua, Michelangelo Fardella, on whom there is a recent monograph by G. Candio, Padua, 1904. See also, L. Berthé de Besancèle, *op. cit.* pp. 64 ff.

[3] G. Doncieux, *Un jésuite homme de lettres au 17me siècle: le Père Bouhours*, Paris, 1886, p. 30; also, G. Maugain, *L'Italie dans quelques publications de jésuites français*, pp. 26 ff. M. Doncieux's book has, as frontispiece, a portrait of Bouhours, and there is a less flattering one in Orsi's *Considerazioni*.

which went through two editions before the end of the century, and eleven more in the course of the following century—had expended anything like its full controversial force.

Like most works of literary theory at this time, the *Manière* is written in the form of dialogues. It is, in the main, an anthology from Latin, French, Italian and Spanish authors illustrating the superiority of the classics to the modern literature of Italy and Spain. The interlocutors are of even less account than usual in such works; Eudoxe, the precise thinker of classical tastes, is the mouthpiece of Bouhours himself; he defends 'le bon sens,' 'good' literary practice, as against Philanthe, who loves 'tout ce qui est fleuri, tout ce qui brille,' who prefers the Italians and the Spaniards to the ancients (p. 2).

The first Dialogue deals with 'Des pensées vraies et de celles qui n'en ont que l'apparence,' that is to say, with the just expression of thought, and is the most readable of the four. Truth, Eudoxe insists (p. 9), is 'la premiere qualité, et comme le fondement des pensées,' and 'une pensée est vraye, lorsqu'elle représente les choses fidellement; et elle est fausse, quand elle les fait voir autrement qu'elles ne sont en elles-mêmes.' In answer to Philanthe's objections, Eudoxe points out that there is a great difference between 'la fiction' and 'la fausseté': 'l'une imite et perfectionne en quelque façon la nature; l'autre la gaste, et la détruit entiérement' (p. 10). Philanthe's standpoint, that every nation has a right to its own peculiar tastes, goes down before the universal reign of 'reason' (pp. 41 f.); there is only one 'good taste.' The theme of the second Dialogue, which is much longer, and also duller, is that something more is needed than mere truth in order to make an 'ingenious' thought acceptable; 'et qu'il y falloit ajoûter quelque chose d'extraordinaire qui frappast l'esprit' (p. 78). The remaining two dialogues are mainly taken up with a discussion of such 'embellishments,' which Bouhours classifies under three heads, 'grandeur,' 'agrément,' 'délicatesse.' Dialogue III deals with: 'Les pensées vicieuses dans le genre noble, dans le genre agréable et dans le genre délicat'; and the theme of IV is: 'Que les pensées qui entrent dans les ouvrages d'esprit, doivent être nettes, claires et intelligibles.' Bouhours attempts to distinguish between what is really sublime and what is merely inflated, what is elegant, and what is affected, and, above all, to define that 'délicatesse' which is particularly prone to degenerate into over-refinement and 'galimathias.'

Vous me dîtes hier, says Philanthe, que la délicatesse consistoit en partie dans je ne sçay quoy de mystérieux qui laissoit toûjours quelque chose à deviner. Oui, reprît Eudoxe, il doit y avoir un peu de mystére dans une pensée délicate; mais on ne doit jamais faire un mystére de ses pensées....Le rafinement est la pire de toutes les affectations....Mais souvenez-vous aussi que rien n'est plus opposé à la véritable délicatesse que d'exprimer trop les choses, et que le grand art consiste à ne pas tout dire sur certains sujets; à glisser dessus plûtost que d'y appuyer; en un mot à en laisser penser aux autres plus que l'on n'en dit (pp. 369, 393 f.).

The virtue of the good writer consists rather in knowing what not to say than what to say. In the end, Philanthe is, of course, convinced of the error of his thinking: 'Je sens que la lecture des Italiens et des Espagnols ne me plaira pas tant qu'elle faisoit'; he learns to prefer the 'l'or de Virgile' to 'le clinquant'—Boileau's epithet that had caused so much offence—of Tasso (pp. 392 f.).

Bouhours' book appealed not merely to his friends of the literary salons, but also to all who held sacred the classic taste of France; and there were not wanting admirers who even saw in it a worthy pendant to the *Art poétique* itself[1]. In fact, it is a defence of classic taste against 'préciosité' by a writer who was himself a 'précieux.' Bouhours' critical horizon is extremely limited; and he deals with a very small and even trivial field of aesthetics in his treatise. He is not overburdened with curiosity or imagination; in other words, he was what the polite salons of the time defined as a 'man of taste.' When his biographer sums up his position by saying that he stood between Boileau and Fénelon (p. 224), he is thinking of the wholly good intention that pervades his book; not surely of its individual judgments. Bouhours reprobates, for instance, the 'concetti' or 'vivezze d' ingegno' of the Italians, and the 'agudezas' of the Spaniards (p. 15); he is constantly discovering lapses of taste in Tasso; but this does not prevent him, as Mr Saintsbury has

[1] Cp. Doncieux, p. 231.

noticed[1], from looking up to Voiture as an exemplar of good taste. He argues in all seriousness about the legitimacy of certain similes and metaphors, which to a modern mind is merely trifling; whereas he shows himself quite incapable of discerning between mediocrity and merit in a poet's inspiration, as he does not allow himself to judge it by other than purely 'rational' criteria. Thus, in spite of Addison's warm encomium, of Lord Chesterfield's recommendation of the book to his son, and an undoubted influence it had in moulding 'polite' English taste[2], the *Manière de bien penser* hardly stands reading as a whole nowadays.

Bouhours' attacks on the Italian poets do occasionally, it must be admitted, strike the nail on the head; but the points of attack are unfairly chosen, and his attitude is manifestly inspired by chauvinistic prejudice; he was bound to provoke opposition, even where he could justify himself. The Italians were moved to wrath—a little slowly, it is true[3], possibly due to the fact that no one had the temerity to translate the work into Italian until 1735, and even the translation of the *Entretiens* (1714) omitted from that work its disparagement of the Italian language. Once, however, the insidiousness of Bouhours' challenge to the nation's pride was realised, many pens got to work to meet it. The results of the famous controversy[4] were not merely a spirited

[1] *History of Criticism*, II, Edinburgh, 1902, p. 315. 'Voiture, si je ne me trompe,' says Bouhours (*Manière*, p. 309), 'estoit naturel en tout.'

[2] '*Bouhours*, whom I look upon to be the most penetrating of all the *French* Criticks' (*Spectator*, No. 62); 'I wish you would read this book again, at your leisure hours; for it will not only divert you, but likewise form your taste, and give you a just manner of thinking'; 'I do not know any book that contributes more to form a true taste' (Chesterfield's *Letters to his Son*, ed. by J. Bradshaw, London, 1892, I, pp. 53, 82; cp. also p. 323). The *Manière* appeared in English as *The Art of Criticism: or the Method o, making a right judgment upon subjects of Wit and Learning*. Translated from the last edition of the French of the famous Father Bouhours, by a Person of Quality. London, 1705; it was subsequently adapted by J. Oldmixon as *The Arts of Logick and Rhetorick*, London, 1728.

[3] M. Maugain shows (pp. 253 ff.) that, with the exception of a half-hearted attempt to stand up to Boileau in Menzini's *Arte poetica* (1688), there is no Italian response to French criticism before 1700; but the activity of the Arcadians was, from the beginning, not uninfluenced by Bouhours' attack on Italy.

[4] See F. Foffano, *Una polemica letteraria nel settecento*, in *Ricerche letterarie*, Livorno, 1897, pp. 315 ff., and A. Boeri, *Una contesa letteraria franco-italiana nel secolo XVIII*, Palermo, 1900.

refutation of Bouhours' calumnies, but, what was much more important, a serious effort to remedy the shortcomings which a comparison with French achievement had made apparent.

Amongst those who took upon themselves to defend Italian honour was Giusto Fontanini, whose *Dell' Eloquenza italiana* (1700) is a laborious and not very inspiring justification of Italian literature on encyclopaedic lines; and in the same year Fontanini, in his *Aminta difeso*, vigorously championed Tasso against his detractors, Boileau as well as Bouhours. But much the most eminent of Italy's champions was Muratori. In 1699 this writer defended Carlo Maria Maggi against the attack which Bouhours had made on one of Maggi's canzoni[1], and about the same time, he projected a defence of Italy against Bouhours; but he was forestalled by his friend and patron, the Marchese Gian Giuseppe Orsi, and his own contribution to the controversy, *Della Perfetta Poesia italiana*, did not appear until 1706. It no doubt gained by the delay, which made it possible for Muratori to concentrate his energy on the constructive problem.

The Marchese Orsi[2] was a typical Italian nobleman of literary tastes. He came of an old Bolognese family and was born in 1652. He was well educated and, in 1686, after the death of his wife, travelled in France, making many acquaintances among French men of letters. For a time he was in the service of the Cardinal Rinaldo d'Este, Duke of Modena, but seems to have chafed in this position of subordination and dependence. He returned to Bologna, and the rest of his life was passed between that town and Modena, where he died in 1733. He was a fertile writer of the dilettante type; but he is only now remembered by the famous *Considerazioni nelle opere degli antichi, sopra*

[1] *Vita di C. M. Maggi*, Milan, 1699, p. 173: 'Il P. Bouhours Autore del libro intitolato *La Maniere de bien penser*, ed uomo di singolare erudizione, se l'essere troppo innamorato della gloria de' suoi nazionali gliele lasciasse talora usar con giustizia verso de gl' Italiani, contra de' quali in generale pronuncia egli sovente indiscrete sentenze, solamente fondate su qualche difetto d' alcuni pochi o vero, o da lui immaginato.' Cp. his letter to A. Zeno of July 15, 1701, quoted below, p. 67.

[2] Cp. Muratori's life of Orsi at the end of vol. II of the 1735–6 edition of the *Considerazioni*; also G. Fantuzzi, *Notizie degli Scrittori bolognesi*, VI, Bologna, 1788, pp. 197 ff., and A. Boeri, *op. cit.* pp. 29 ff.

un famoso libro franzese intitolato: La Manière de bien penser dans les Ouvrages d'esprit, cioè la Maniera di ben pensare ne' Componimenti, which appeared at Bologna in 1703.

Like the work which Orsi criticises, his book is in dialogue form; it is also exceedingly bulky. He approaches his real purpose in very leisurely fashion, the four 'dialogisti'—Gelaste, Filalete, Eristico and Eupisto—and the occasion which brings them together, being described in great detail. For the rest, the first five of the seven dialogues contain little but a weary and pedantic reiteration of the ideas and methods which had been deduced from Aristotle by the philological critics of the earlier generation. Orsi had taken care to familiarise himself with the French anti-Bouhours literature[1], and he draws largely upon it. So far, the work is disappointing, and one begins to wonder how it could possibly have had any good effect at all; but the two last dialogues, in which Orsi gets to the real business in hand, come as a surprise. In Dialogue VI he defends Tasso with great spirit, showing skilfully how Bouhours in his obtuseness had fallen into the error of confusing a great poet with mediocrities. And in the last dialogue he takes up the cause of other Italian poets and writers who had been impugned by Bouhours, notably Guarini, Bonarelli, Testi and Pallavicino. At the same time, certain concessions had to be made: Marini, whom the Arcadia repudiated, could not be defended[2]; and it would only have invalidated Orsi's case to try to defend him.

On the appearance of the work, without the author's name, but with a fulsome dedication to Madame Dacier[3], it was re-

[1] In his first Dialogue (p. 14) he mentions Ménage, the Abbé de Bellegarde, Barbier d'Aucour (whose criticism of Bouhours' *Entretiens d'Ariste et d'Eugène—Les Sentimens de Cléanthe*, 1683—is, in particular, laid under contribution ('n'ho frischissima la ricordanza' says his Gelaste), as well as the *Vindiciae nominis Germanici* of J. F. Cramer, one of Germany's replies to Bouhours' taunt that a German could not have 'esprit.'

[2] *Considerazioni*, I, pp. 344 ff.

[3] Madame Dacier was approached through Muratori, who wrote to his friend Boivin in Paris on October 3, 1702 (*Epistolario*, II, Modena, 1901, pp. 606 f.): 'Vengo francamente ad esporvi una mia premurosa preghiera. Per suo divertimento ha un dottissimo Cavaliere, mio gran padrone ed amico, fatta una risposta Italiana al Libro del P. Bouhours, intitolato: *La Manière de bien penser*, ed in essa va egli studiandosi di fare comparire, o l'arditezza o il non perfetto giudizio di cotesto buon Padre, e spezialmente procura di difendere dalla sua censura gli autori Italiani. Di gran racco-

viewed in a liberal and friendly spirit ('con dolce maniera e degna di loro') by the *Mémoires de Trévoux* (February to May, 1705; April, 1706), and this although the journal of the Jesuits was bound to defend Bouhours, who had been one of its regular contributors. Orsi replied in four letters addressed to Madame Dacier; and then his compatriots came to his support with eleven letters. The latter were published at Bologna in 1706, and were subsequently included, together with Madame Dacier's letters, an Italian translation of Bouhours' *Manière* by Gian Andrea Barotti of Ferrara, and the criticism from the *Mémoires de Trévoux*, in the two-volume edition of Orsi's work which appeared at Modena in 1735 and 1736. As the French did not reply to the letters of 1706, the Italians felt that they had won the day, that their literature was finally vindicated. But the controversy went on for some time longer. Count Francesco Montani of Pesaro, whose sympathies were with the French, attacked Orsi in a very lengthy letter, and this called for further discussion, which occupies the greater part of the second volume of the Modena edition. With the appearance of Muratori's *Della Perfetta Poesia italiana* and Gravina's *Ragion poetica*, however, the movement of Italian aesthetics passed from a mere defence against foreign aspersion to a positive and constructive stage.

Nowadays, when we look back on this once famous quarrel, it makes, like most literary quarrels, the impression of having been a very futile beating of the air. We are filled with a kind of wonder at the huge compendium of the controversy, with its page upon page of arid, pedantic discussion of the legitimacy of certain lines and phrases in Italian poets—as

mandazione sarebbe ad un tal libro il nome di chi l' ha composto; ma, pensando la sua modestia di non voler che questo si pubblichi nella stampa, vorebbe egli procurar credito al libro col nome della persona, a cui si vuol dedicare. Egli pertanto ha scelta la dottissima, e chiarissima signora Dacier, per cui ha questo cavaliere grandissima stima (come pure per Mr Dacier) ed a lei bramerebbe di dedicar questa fatica, ov' ella ne fosse contenta. A voi dunque sta l' impetrare la licenza di cotesta virtuosa donna.' Muratori goes on to inform his friend that there will be no ground for offence in the book, and that all the French authors are praised in it. But Madame Dacier had to be assured that even the Père Bouhours would not be maligned, and in view of this and the fact that Bouhours was recently dead, personal criticism was expunged. The letter is also quoted by Maugain, p. 256.

Voltaire wittily, but not unjustly said, 'deux gros volumes pour justifier quelques vers du Tasse'[1]—its childish attempts to set up irrefutable standards of 'good taste.' The letters of Orsi's friends[2] are duller than the treatise itself; but at least Eustachio Manfredi, in what is the most readable of them all, sees the real source of all the pother in Bouhours' contemptuous refusal to allow other nations to participate in the 'esprit' and 'bon goût' which the Frenchman regarded as the peculiar possession of his own[3].

In spite of Orsi's good intentions, which won him the applause and congratulations of all Italy, he cuts, it must be confessed, a much poorer figure as a critic than his antagonist. He has not behind him that tradition of established convictions which served Bouhours so well in place of a reasoned system of his own. His conclusions have no great intrinsic value; for his own culture was not deep enough, nor of the kind to entitle him to an opinion in matters of literary taste. But he is, at least, patriotic; he defends Tasso warmly, and his fellow-countrymen were easily convinced that, his heart being in the right place, everything else was well.

Not merely in criticism, but also in actual productive work, this clash with French classicism was a furthering event in Italian literary history. The controversy overshadows Italian literature in the early eighteenth century, as the Leipzig-Zürich quarrel—which was intrinsically as futile, but in its effects quite as far-reaching—overshadows the German literature of a later period. While the German controversy brought Milton into honour, the Italian controversy made first Tasso and then Dante the pivot round which the national literature turned. Both led to an intensified literary activity. Above all, the interest in the national theatre was revived in Italy; and if Maffei, Calepio, and in the French tongue and on French soil, Luigi Riccoboni, defended the Italian drama by comparing it

[1] *Écrivains français du Siècle de Louis XIV* (*Œuvres*, éd. Garnier, XIV), p. 44.

[2] On these see especially Foffano, *op. cit.* pp. 323 ff.

[3] *Considerazioni*, I, p. 682. On Manfredi, who had a very real sympathy for French literature, see D. Provenzal, *I Riformatori della bella letteratura italiana*, Rocca S. Casciano, 1900.

with the antique to the disadvantage of the French, the attacks of the pugnacious French Jesuit deserve, in the first instance, the credit. Unfortunately, this zeal on the part of the Italians was not persistent; the intention was better than the achievement; and the Italy which these critical pioneers had vindicated before the world—it is disheartening to have to say it—later fell back complacently into line with the ideas of Voltaire. Still, the movement that was ushered in by the Bouhours-Orsi controversy was of very real importance for the literary evolution, not only of Italy herself, but also of Spain, France, and even of England and Germany.

III

So far, I have restricted myself to only one aspect of the awakening of Italy in the beginning of the eighteenth century; a more definitely constructive aspect is to be seen in the activities of the Accademia degli Arcadi, or Arcadia. All the Bouhours controversialists were, however, members of this Academy; and indeed, it forms the background of the whole movement. The history of the Arcadia, which was founded in 1690, has been often told and is generally familiar[1]. Towards the end of the seventeenth century, Queen Christina of Sweden, the daughter of Gustavus Adolphus, renounced her Swedish throne, became a Catholic and fell under the influence of the Jesuits. Before her death in 1689, she had made her palace the centre for a kind of literary revival, with which was associated a good deal of fulsome flattery of herself. It was the coterie that gathered round her which formed itself in 1690 into the Arcadia. The story is told that a number of select spirits of this coterie happened one day to be sitting in the Prati di Castello —'in uno de' luoghi deliziosi, che Roma concede a' suoi felici Abitatori'—engaged in reciting verses, when one of the party cried out: 'Ecco per noi risorta Arcadia!' Thereupon it was resolved to constitute a society under that name, thus linking

[1] Cp. I. Carini, *L'Arcadia*, Rome, 1891; G. Biroccini, *Storia dell' Arcadia*, Rome, 1889; the English reader will find a vivid and picturesque account of the Arcadia in Vernon Lee's *Studies in the Eighteenth Century in Italy*, 2nd ed., London, 1907, pp. 13 ff.; cp. also the Introduction to P. Emiliani-Giudici's edition of Gravina, pp. xxviii f.; and A. Bertoldi, *Studio su G. V. Gravina*, Bologna, 1885, pp. 35 ff.

up their own time with the naive world of Sannazaro[1]. The leading spirits were Vincenzo Leonio da Spoleto and Giovanni Mario Crescimbeni, the latter becoming the first 'custode' or president. Literary academies were in the air; and since, in the previous century, the famous 'Bran' Academy, or Accademia della Crusca, had stemmed the linguistic vagaries of Italian style, before its extravagances were seriously impugned on poetic grounds, progress in literary Italy had been effected by Academies. Why not an academy which should do for letters what the Accademia della Crusca had done for the Italian language? The idea of Leonio and Crescimbeni was received by their friends with enthusiasm: the first meeting took place on October 5, 1690, in the gardens of the Franciscan Padri Riformati of San Pietro at Montorio on Monte Gianicoli; and the fourteen original members led the way by taking upon themselves fantastic pastoral names, the custode calling himself 'Alfesibeo Cario.' Gravina, as 'Opico Erimanteo,' drew up the rules. The emblem of the Academy was a flute of Pan surrounded by a wreath of pine and laurel. Thus arose the famous Arcadia which was to 'renew the sweet studies and innocent customs which the ancient Arcadians cultivated.'[2]

The vogue of the Academy spread with extraordinary rapidity; and in less than twenty-two years the number of 'shepherds' had risen to thirteen hundred[3]. At the height of its fame its meetings took place in the Bosco Parrasio on Monte Gianicolo, which had been presented to the Academy by Don John V of Portugal. Every year, on May 1, the custode solemnly opened the Bosco; and on October 7 closed it with similar ceremony. There were seven meetings annually, six for the 'shepherds'

[1] Cp. F. M. Mancurti, *Vita di G. M. Crescimbeni*, Rome, 1729, pp. 20 f.

[2] Cp. *ibid.*, *op. cit.* p. 21: 'Ella [l'Arcadia] è a guisa di Repubblica Democratica, che sotto il suo dolce dominio quasi tutti i Letterati di Italia, e non pochi Oltromontani accoglie. Niun Protettore, ò Principe ella riconosce, ma un solo Custode, che tutta l' Adunanza rappresenta, e governa; e questo sì onorevole Ministero fin dal giorno della fondazione di quella fu per elezione conferito al nostro Alfesibeo: il quale poi in ogni Olimpiade per tutto l' intero corso di sua vita confermato in tal carica, la rese, e la sostenne sempre con alta sua riputazione, e con sommo vantaggio della Letteratura.' Quoted inaccurately by Emiliani-Giudici, pp. xxxi f.

[3] G. M. Crescimbeni, *Storia dell' Accademia degli Arcadi*, Rome, 1712; London, 1803, p. 6.

resident in Rome, to which they presented their verses; and a final meeting of the entire Academy, at which poetry was read which had been sent in from all quarters. Besides these statutory meetings, there were others of a private and less formal kind. At the beginning of each Olympiad—for the Arcadians reckoned by Olympiads—Olympic games were celebrated in the form of literary competitions. These competitions were of five kinds: theoretical discussions forming the first category; eclogues the second, canzoni the third, sonnets the fourth, and madrigals and epigrams the fifth.

That the Arcadia should have enrolled in its membership practically everyone of literary eminence in Italy—even Goethe was flattered to be elected a member in 1788[1]—is the more surprising when we see how lacking in distinction, critical or poetic, the men were who formed the inner circle of the society. The Abate Crescimbeni, its first president[2], was, no doubt, inspired by the best intentions—he had taken an active part in the work of the pre-Arcadian academies, which was probably a reason why he was elected 'custode' of the new one—but his talent was not of a high order. He wrote a three-volume *Istoria della volgar Poesia* (1698 ff.), which ultimately developed with 'commentarii' into six[3], and a series of dialogues, *La Bellezza della volgar Poesia* (1700), formulating the Arcadian creed. These two books are pilloried by Foffano as examples of the vices of Italian seventeenth century criticism[4]; but this seems hardly fair to them. Crescimbeni is a tedious enough writer, but he handles his language with dignity and skill; and his *Istoria* was for the time—a time when literary history, as we now understand it, was practically non-existent—a useful com-

[1] *Italienische Reise*, Weimar ed., XXXII, p. 217.

[2] Crescimbeni was born at Macerata on October 9, 1683, and educated as a jurist by an uncle in Rome; but to the latter's great disappointment, he turned to literature, and ultimately, in 1705, entered the Church. He died in Rome in 1728.

[3] The *Commentarii* were published in five vols., between 1702 and 1711; the work appeared as a whole with the *Bellezza*, as well as Mancurti's life of the author, appended, in six vols., Venice, 1730. There is a lengthy review of Crescimbeni's works in the *Giornale de' Letterati d' Italia*, VI (1711), pp. 175–261.

[4] *Op. cit.* pp. 207 f. Emiliani-Giudici also calls the *Bellezza della volgar Poesia* a 'noiosissimo libro' (*op. cit.* p. XXXV).

pendium, even if the choice of poets appears indiscriminating and often merely capricious. Crescimbeni's book was the immediate forerunner of Apostolo Zeno's labours, of Gimma's *Idea della Storia dell' Italia letterata* (1723), and of Quadrio's more ambitious work of some years later. The direct line of descent from Crescimbeni to Tiraboschi is not to be ignored.

With regard to Crescimbeni's theoretical treatise, *La Bellezza della volgar Poesia*, it might be claimed that it affords a fairly clear idea of the principles of literary taste which guided the Academy in its early years. The book originated in the practice of certain of the Arcadians meeting every Thursday towards the end of 1697, to discuss, with a view to republication by the Academy, the sonnets of the Tuscan poet Angelo di Costanzo, whom they had selected—a selection which is only one of many testimonies to their lack of real critical judgment—as an antidote to Marini. The edition was abandoned, but Crescimbeni's book undertakes to extract the essence of poetry from four of the sonnets. The verses serve as the loosest of texts, and the discussion is not restricted to the lyric, but ranges over the entire field of poetic art. The first dialogue discusses 'external' and 'internal' poetic beauties, Costanzo being praised for judiciously mixing the two kinds; the second and third, the defects of ancient and modern poets in their use of those poetic beauties, Dante being instanced as a poet who was indifferent to 'external' beauty. The fourth dialogue is concerned with the Greek manner of composition, and how far this may be imitated by the Italians; the fifth with the precepts of tragic poetry, on the example of Crescimbeni's own tragedy *Elvio*, and the adaptation of these precepts to the pastoral. Comedy is, in the sixth dialogue, illustrated by Ariosto's *Suppositi*; the epic, in the seventh and eighth, by Caraccio's *Imperio vendicato*, of which not merely Crescimbeni, but also Gravina had a high opinion. A ninth dialogue, added later, discusses the taste of the eighteenth century in lyric poetry, and weighs the rival merits of the schools of Petrarch and Chiabrera. The conferences are presided over by the daughter of Francesco del Teglia, 'Egina,' who represents the binding element in the dialogues and directs their course. The speakers are Arcadian pastors, among them notabilities like Salvini, Zeno and Martelli; but it is sometimes difficult—I think especially of Martelli, who has the chief share in the last dialogue—to harmonise the opinions placed in their mouths, and still more their manner of expressing themselves, with the writings of the men themselves. Nature and the time of day obtrude less than is usual in dialogues of this kind; but there is that air of leisure which is common to them all; and amidst it these 'shepherds' discourse amiably and courteously, often merely trivially, on the questions of taste that agitated the Arcadian breast. Antagonism to Marinistic artificiality is never allowed to be forgotten[1]; but the language with which that artificiality is discredited, is, it must be confessed, at times hardly to be distinguished from that of Marini himself.

Francesco Saverio Quadrio, of whom it is convenient to say a word or two here, although he belongs to a later period, is a much more interesting personality than Crescimbeni. Born on December 1, 1695, at Ponte in the Valtellina, he was educated by the Jesuits, and subsequently became a priest and teacher of the order in various towns of northern Italy. He devoted himself with enormous zeal to the study of Italian literature, and published in 1734 the first fruits of his study in a work entitled *Della Poesia italiana*, which appeared at Venice under the pseudonym of Giuseppe Maria Andrucci. This subsequently developed into the appallingly learned and voluminous *Della Storia e della Ragione d' ogni Poesia*, which was published at Milan in seven volumes between 1739 and 1759. The encyclopaedic character of this work, which purports to embrace all literatures—often, as in the case of our own and that of Germany, ludicrously inadequate—smacks somewhat of the seventeenth-century compilations, as do also his trivial emphasis of the formal 'kinds' of literature, his mania for classification, and

[1] It is worth quoting what Crescimbeni has to say of Marini in his *Istoria* (ed. of 1730, II, p. 470): '...Al Marini adunque si debbe la libertà del comporre; mentre il bollor dell' ingegno suo, non capace di star ristretto dentro alcun limite, ruppe affatto ogni riparo; nè altra legge volle sofferire, che quella del proprio capriccio, tutta consistente in risonanza di versi, in accozzamento di bizzarrie, ed arguzie, in concepimento d' argomenti fantastici, in affettare il fraseggiamento de' Latini, tralasciato il proprio Toscano; ed in somma in dilettar con finta, e mentitrice apparenza di ricercata, e falsa bellezza.'

extraordinary parcelling out of his materials into 'libri,' 'distinzioni,' 'capitoli' and 'particelli.' But dull and valueless as much of the work is, it is the first presentation of literary fact and theory on what is now called 'comparative' lines[1]; and as such it is not to be neglected.

In the matter of literary theory, which is discussed in his first volume, Quadrio has not much to say that is furthering. His method is eclectic over a wide range of authorities; he marshals opinion, supporting it by bewildering footnotes, and then selects. But this process is apt to result merely in a composite picture of average opinion—an obvious danger of all eclecticism. Such originality of standpoint as Quadrio may have had, is crushed under the weight of his learning. Poetry is to him, as it had been to Gravina, the 'scienza delle umane e delle divine cose, esposta al popolo in immagine, fatta con parole a misura legate';[2] he emphasises the 'giovamento' rather than the 'diletto,' as the purpose of literature[3]; and he is not far enough away from the Bouhours-Orsi controversy to refrain from insisting on the superior excellence of Italian poetry, and especially its freedom from the shackles of Aristotle. But he is obdurately orthodox on the subject of the unities, demanding a day of 'about twelve hours';[4] he accepts the 'people' as the final tribunal of all literary judgment—which healthy revolt against the tyranny of the learned runs through all the Italian aesthetics of the time. But I doubt whether there is anything substantially new in his opinions on literary theory; they are mostly echoes. He is, moreover, sparing in his references to more or less contemporary authorities. Muratori, for instance, is not mentioned at all in his footnotes; nor is Gimma, who was, in some respects, his most immediate predecessor. Martelli is occasionally referred to on matters of dramatic theory; most

[1] Cp. Saintsbury, *History of Criticism*, II, 1902, pp. 542 ff. It must be remembered to Quadrio's credit that he is the first Italian to give any considerable account of Shakespeare, even if that account is merely transferred from Voltaire. It will be found in vol. III, part I (1743), pp. 149 f.; cp. also III, 2, pp. 126, 363.

[2] *Della Storia e della Ragione d' ogni Poesia*, I, p. 2; cp. Gravina, *Ragion poetica*, Book II, Introd. (ed. Emiliani-Giudici, p. 88).

[3] *Ibid.* I, pp. 113 ff.

[4] *Ibid.* III, I, p. 173.

frequently of all, Becelli, who seems to have been a critic after Quadrio's own heart.

Quadrio's life ran by no means the unruffled course we associate with the scholarly ecclesiastic. Whether his engrossing preoccupation with belles-lettres brought him into conflict with his duties to the Church, or whether his faith had been undermined by probing too deeply into the writings of Voltaire, with whom he stood later on terms of friendship, he suddenly resolved—it was in 1744—to throw off the yoke of his priesthood. He fled secretly from Milan to Switzerland; from Zürich he wrote to the Pope, Benedict XIV, justifying his action; and in 1748 he was given permission to become a secular 'abate.' After spending some time in Paris, he obtained, in 1751, the appointment of librarian to Count Pallavicini, governor of Lombardy. When Pallavicini was obliged to leave Milan in 1753, Quadrio retired to a Barnabite convent, where he died on November 21, 1756. One would like to know a little more of the spiritual struggles of this man whose life, we are told, was shortened by bitterness and melancholy. Perhaps this explains his remarkable disquisition on poetic genius which recalls at times Schopenhauer's opinions of a century later[1]; he is modern, too, in the Taine-like insight he shows into the influence of *milieu*, and his insistence on the dependence of psychology on physiology.

But to return to the first Arcadians: their importance lay in the fact that they were alive to the deficiencies of the Italian literature of their time and strove to make them good. Un-

[1] Quadrio's views on genius, to which attention was drawn by G. Marpillero, *F. S. Quadrio e l' uomo di genio* in Cantoni's *Rivista filosofica*, III, Pavia, 1900, pp. 611 ff., are to be found in vol. I, pp. 238 ff. of his work. Cp. especially pp. 244 f.: 'Da queste cose si fa manifesto esser alla Poesia necessario un temperamento di parti ben organizzate, e sane, ma melancolico più tosto, e bilioso: onde la sagacità dell' ingegno, la forza dell' immaginativa, e il prudente giudizio conseguitano....Il color della faccia è in essi traente un pochetto al fosco: e tutto l' aspetto è anzi severo, e truce, che mansueto, ed aperto. Hanno gli occhi proporzionati, e più tosto nella fronte entranti, che sporti in fuori. Che se questi dalle giuste loro misure dechinano un pocolino, ciò è, non alla grandezza, ma alla picciolezza. Le linee, che lor rigano la fronte, e le mani, sono profonde: a le vene hanno essi ampie, e gonfie, il polso veemente, e alquanto duro, il corpo per lo più magro, ed asciutto, e il sonno nè molto abbondante, nè molto grave, ma scarso, e leggiero.'

fortunately, they set about doing so, not by encouraging originality, but by insisting on law and uniformity; and this in itself led back to mediocrity. Imitation was their supreme canon of art; in their lyric, influenced by Costanzo's example, they hankered after the artificial and over-refined Petrarchism of an earlier age. Such progress as the Italian drama made in the early decades of the eighteenth century was achieved, in spite of, rather than as a result of the activities of the Academy. The Arcadians helped to dethrone Marini and to counteract the unregulated taste which he had introduced; but they had only ceremonious proprieties to substitute for that taste; we owe to them—to the first group of the Arcadians, at least—no re-birth of creative work, and not a single poem which Italy has been unwilling to let die. Men like Crescimbeni were incapable of constructing a positive creed; at most, they had a confused conviction that the way out of the slough of 'secentismo' lay in a return to the simplicity of the ancients, that is, in what ultimately took the form of neo-classicism. Thus the significance of the Arcadia—and it is only with the early stage of the Academy I am at present concerned—might be altogether negligible, had it not had among its founders the illustrious thinker and jurist, Gian Vincenzo Gravina.

Chapter II

Gian Vincenzo Gravina

Gravina was by far the most gifted of the inner circle of the Arcadians; indeed, it was a tribute to the hopefulness which the new movement inspired that he espoused it so warmly. But Gravina was never a thorough-going Arcadian; and soon he diverged fundamentally from the precepts of Crescimbeni and his friends. On the other hand, he was entirely in sympathy with the movement which had been inaugurated by Orsi in his attack on Bouhours; he repudiated the claims of the French to be superior masters to the Greeks in the art of the drama; and, if he cherished hopes for a revival of the great traditions of poetry among the moderns, he certainly did not look to France for its fulfilment. But I doubt if he was materially influenced by the anti-Bouhours movement. The principles of his literary aesthetics are to be found, as we shall see, *in nuce* in a little study published in 1692, and he could hardly then have been aware of the significance of the anti-Italian trend in French criticism. If he was influenced at all by the French, it was to the extent of accepting, not being moved to anger by their attitude towards Tasso. Gravina's neo-classicism was, in fact, a direct outcome of his own immersion in the Greek spirit, his abhorrence of 'secentistic' extravagance, and his schooling in Descartes' philosophy. Gravina was the first thinker in Europe to proclaim in unmistakable terms that 'back to the Greeks' doctrine which was to provide the watchword for the later classical aesthetics of the eighteenth century; the first to repudiate the false Aristotelianism which had substituted the letter of Aristotle for the spirit; he was also the first to employ consciously and deliberately Descartes' critical scepticism as a basis for literary aesthetics.

I

Gian Vincenzo Gravina[1] was born at Rogiano—since 1864 called Rogiano-Gravina in his honour—a small town not far from Cosenza in Calabria, on February 18, 1664. His parents were well-to-do, and his education was entrusted to Gregorio Caloprese, a capable classical scholar and thinker of the Cartesian school[2], who, in spite of his great reputation, spent his life in retirement in his native town, Scalea. Caloprese, to whom Gravina was related, regarded his young pupil with a fatherly affection. He inspired him with a healthy dislike for the extravagances of Marini and a love for the classic poets; and, no doubt, the boy received a goodly dose of Cartesianism from his teacher, with whom he read Telesio—also a fellow-countryman in the narrower sense—and Gassendi. Gravina went, well prepared and monetarily assisted by Caloprese, to the University of Naples in 1681, where he was inscribed as a student of jurisprudence.

At first he seems to have been repelled by this subject, in which he was subsequently to become a European authority; and little wonder, for in the hands of the professional jurists, who flourished under the corrupt Spanish rule in Naples at this time, the sordid and mercenary side of the practice of law was chiefly in evidence. Gravina devoted himself by preference to

[1] Cp. G. A. Serao, *De Vita et Scriptis J. V. Gravinae Commentarium*, Rome, 1758; A. Fabronius, *Vitae italorum doctrina excellentium qui saeculo XVIII floruerunt*, Rome, 1769, Decas ii; the biography by G. B. Passeri, in *Opere scelte di G. V. Gravina*, Milan, 1819 (also 1826); P. Emiliani-Giudici in the Introduction to his *Prose di G. V. Gravina*, Florence, 1857; A. C. Casetti, *La vita e le opere di G. V. Gravina* in *Nuova Antologia*, xxv, pp. 339 ff., 600 ff., 850 ff. (February to April, 1874); V. Julia, *Saggio sulla vita e sulle opere di G. V. Gravina*, introductory to F. Balsano, *Delle dottrine filosofiche e civile di G. V. Gravina*, Cosenza, 1879; A. Bertoldi, *Studio su G. V. Gravina*, Bologna, 1885; E. Reich, *G. V. Gravina als Ästhetiker* (*Sitzungsberichte der Wiener Akademie*, cxx), Vienna, 1890; B. Croce, *Di alcuni giudizi sul Gravina considerato come estetico* (*Miscellanea d' Ancona*, pp. 456 ff., Florence, 1901; in *Problemi di Estetica*, Bari, 1910, pp. 360 ff.); F. Moffa, *G. V. Gravina*, in E. Pèrcopo's *Studi di Letteratura italiana*, VII, Naples, 1907, pp. 165 ff.; G. Natali, *G. V. Gravina letterato: discorso*, Rome, 1919.

[2] Vico attributed the diffusion of Cartesianism in Naples to Caloprese and called him a 'gran filosofo renatista' (*Autobiografia*, ed. B. Croce, in *Scrittori d' Italia*, XI, Bari, 1911, p. 19); cp. Casetti, *op. cit.* p. 341, and Maugain, p. 199. On Caloprese see R. Cotugno, *Gregorio Caloprese*, Trani, 1910.

literary studies, especially Latin and Greek, in which his guide was the eminent scholar, Gregorio Messeri. We even hear of two tragedies which he is said to have written, or at least sketched, in those early days, a *Cristo* and a *Santo Atanasio*. But so unintermittently did he pursue his studies in Naples that he became the victim of an obstinate abdominal affection which never left him and was ultimately the cause of his death. Before his student days were over, however, his enthusiasm for the theoretical and philosophical side of jurisprudence had been awakened by the tactful presentation of the subject by the Neapolitan jurist, Serafino Biscardi. Doubtless, too, the eloquence of Tommaso Cornelio had deepened that respect for Descartes with which his first master had inspired him.

In 1689 Gravina, then twenty-five, settled in Rome, living in the house of Count Paolo Coardo, a native of Turin, who was able to bring him into touch with distinguished churchmen and men of letters. Gravina sympathised with the serious movement, which, in spite of the 'précieux' leanings of Queen Christina of Sweden herself, had grown up in her literary coterie, to combat the degenerate taste of the seventeenth century; and in 1690 he was, as we have seen, one of the founders—his patron Coardo was also one—of the 'Accademia degli Arcadi,' his Arcadian pseudonyms being 'Opico Erimanteo' and 'Bione Crateo.' A few years later he was entrusted with drawing up the laws of the Academy, a task which he rounded off with an *Oratio pro legibus Arcadum*.

Gravina's first literary essay, the *Ragionamento sopra l' Endimione*, published in 1692[1], was only in small part a manifesto of the critical views championed by the new Academy. It rails against the degenerate taste of the time, although in a style which is by no means free from the stiffness of the seventeenth century; it shows that lack of a sense for relative values which, with ironic persistency, vitiated all the Academy's efforts

[1] Subsequent editions of Guidi's drama were prefaced by Gravina's encomium, and in a dedicatory poem to Cardinal Albano (later Pope Clement XI) Guidi pays his homage to:

Bione il saggio,
Che di novo intelletto alza la face
Per fugar l' ombre, e per aprire il vero.

to reform literature. For it is nominally a defence—although, it ought perhaps to be added in exoneration of Gravina, a defence inspired by warm friendship—of a pastoral drama by Alessandro Guidi, *Endimione* (1692), the plan and even some verses of which were attributed to the Queen of Sweden; and in those days of easily-satisfied criteria, this 'parto regio,' as, with Marinesque tastelessness, Gravina called it, made no little stir in Rome. Guidi[1] is a poet whose appreciation is now left in the hands of the historians; but I am not sure that we should ignore entirely what Gravina has to say of the *Endimione*. The pastoral is not at all so mediocre as some modern critics would have us believe: its cloying verses have still the power to haunt. The objection to Gravina's claims, however, is that they are lacking in proportion; one resents the imputation that Guidi has produced a work that may be mentioned in the same breath with a Greek tragedy. But the value of his tract does not lie here, but in the fact that it contains in germ the ideas which Gravina subsequently developed in his *Ragion poetica*. These ideas were of far greater significance for the future than anything in Crescimbeni's placid Arcadian dialogues; moreover, they did not at all fit—although the Academy was unwilling to admit it—into the narrow creed of Arcadianism.

On the first pages of the *Ragionamento*[2] Gravina repudiates the restricted outlook of the interpreters of Aristotle; he protests—and it was the first serious protest in Italy—against an aesthetics which was built up on the Aristotelian or pseudo-Aristotelian dicta, and on a sacrosanct classification of 'literary kinds.' He does not care whether the *Endimione* is to be classified as a tragedy, or a comedy, or a tragi-comedy; what matters is that it is an excellent poem. The foundations of criticism, he insists, are to be sought in human reason and in philosophy, not in the 'rules.' Gravina did not perhaps himself realise what a liberating pronouncement this insistence on subjective

[1] Cp. *Poesie d' Alessandro Guidi non più raccolte*, Verona, 1726, with the life of the poet by Crescimbeni, and 'due Ragionamenti (two letters to Maffei) di Vincenzo Gravina non più divulgati.' Martelli, also an admirer, has written a life of Guidi in the *Vite degli Arcadi illustri*, III, Rome, 1714, pp. 229 ff. Cp. I. Carini, *L' Arcadia*, pp. 213 ff.

[2] In the edition of Emiliani-Giudici, p. 251; cp. also p. 264.

judgment in place of traditional authority was. He demands that the ordering and regulating function in literature should lie with the intelligence. Art is an imitation of nature, just as nature itself is like an imprint on wax of the divine idea. But the direct reproduction of life and the world must be tempered by a prudent respect for the examples of antiquity; the imagination must be under strict control. Art, if it will impress us, must have two qualities: novelty ('novità') and marvellousness ('maraviglia'); consequently, the poet is at liberty to go outside nature and depict supernatural things like giants and hippogryphs. The supreme utility of poetry is to raise our souls to the contemplation of the pure and eternal. The domain of poetry includes, not merely the glorification of virtue, of the splendid and the sublime; it must also describe the mediocre and the low; huts and hovels are quite as interesting as palaces, and perhaps more difficult to depict poetically. No man, however great, is without some imperfection, and the heroic must be mingled with the humble and the mediocre. The function of poetry is to transform wise knowledge into sensible images, to express the true under the guise of fiction; poetry is a veil which hides from the eyes of the crowd the dazzling brilliancy of great truths. Here, too, is sounded that paean of praise of Homer and Dante, which gives Gravina an honourable place among the makers of modern opinion of these poets.

As, however, we shall find all these ideas repeated and amplified in the *Ragion poetica*, it is unnecessary to dwell upon them; but it is important to note their presence in this little tract, which, being printed with the play, found its way more rapidly and into wider circles than even the *Ragion poetica* itself. Such ideas were too new and too foreign to the traditional aesthetics of the seventeenth century not to stir up opposition, and if the *Ragionamento sopra l' Endimione* opened up no immediate breach between Gravina and his colleagues of the Arcadia, it was because the poet of the *Endimione* was himself so eminent a personality in the Academy. A year earlier, in 1691, Gravina had already got himself into a veritable wasps' nest by an attack on the casuistry of the Jesuits and the general corruption of the Church; this was in a dialogue entitled *Hydra mistica, sive de corrupta morali doctrina*[1], which he had published in only fifty copies under another pseudonym, 'Priscus Censorinus Fotiscus.' Thus his first taste of fame was mixed with bitterness; he was made the butt of a series of scurrilous Latin satires by a certain Ludovico Sergardi—there is even a story of these having been preceded by a violent scene of personal attack at a meeting of the Arcadia[2]—who concealed himself behind the pseudonym of Quintus Settanus[3]. This controversy left indelible marks on Gravina's sensitive and proud nature.

Gravina's next publication was the *Discorso delle antiche favole* (Rome, 1696), his chief treatise on aesthetics, in so far as it forms the theoretical part of the *Ragion poetica*[4] with which it was subsequently incorporated. It is important to observe that the date at which Gravina launched his most vital aesthetic ideas, was thus not 1708, when the *Ragion* appeared, but 1696. In the same year as the *Discorso delle antiche favole* appeared a collection of Gravina's essays—also a tiny duodecimo—on philosophical and juridical themes (*Opuscula, quae sunt: Specimen prisci juris; De lingua Latina dialogus; De conversione doctrinarum; De contemptu mortis; De luctu minuendo*; to which was added *Pro legibus Arcadum oratio*), mostly written some two years previously. The volume is dedicated to Pope Innocence XII. The most interesting of these essays is the first, which contains in embryo Gravina's theory of the genesis of law in human relations, and formed the basis of his subsequent

[1] Cp. Moffa, *op. cit.* pp. 192 ff. It was probably influenced by the *Lettres provinciales* of Pascal (Casetti, *l.c.* p. 358).

[2] Cp. Moffa, p. 218.

[3] The satires are discussed at considerable length by Bertoldi, *op. cit.* pp. 19 ff., and excellently summarised by F. Moffa, *l.c.* pp. 220 ff. They were published at Amsterdam in 1700 and Lucca, 1783; according to Reich, an Italian translation appeared at Zürich in 1760, but this I have not been able to trace.

[4] The *Discorso delle antiche favole* is a small duodecimo volume of 141 pages, dedicated to Cardinal Boncampagni, Archbishop of Bologna, and with the symbol of the Arcadians on the title-page. Comparing it with the *Ragion poetica*, it begins with the words in chapter I of that treatise 'Siccome l' affermazione contiene' etc. and continues (without divisions into chapters) to the end of chapter XXX. In the *Ragion* there are only two additions within these limits: in chapter I the sentence: 'Onde per quella parte...di vederla intera'; and in chapter XII: 'Quindi appare, che nella scena...le sue operazioni sono d' onestà, o composte o velate.'

examination—in Book II of *De Origine juris civilis*—of the ancient Roman law of the Twelve Tables. Significant, too, for his sympathy with the ideas of the new time is the treatise *De conversione doctrinarum*, in which he praises the humanistic classic culture and the 'modern' philosophy of Telesio, Bruno, Campanella and Descartes[1].

Three years later, Gravina was appointed Professor of Civil Law at the Archiginnasio or Sapienza, the forerunner of the modern University of Rome; and in 1701 he published the first part of his great work on Civil Law: *Originum juris civilis libri tres*. The volume bore the title *De ortu et progressu juris civilis*, and it was followed seven years later by two other parts: *De jure naturali gentium et XII tabularum*, and *De legibus et senatus consultis*[2]. It would be tempting to dwell on the origins and significance of this monumental work, to which one might well apply words similar to those used by Hettner of Winckelmann: like the author of the *Geschichte der Kunst des Altertums*, Gravina was one of the great spiritual navigators of the eighteenth century, who ventured out into an uncharted sea, discovering there undreamt of continents. Finding himself face to face with a confused and confusing mass of empirical laws, he set himself, like a true Cartesian, to make logical order; but in doing so, he introduced a new principle which Cartesianism ignored: he based his order on a study of the organic evolution of law and custom. It is true, he was not altogether a pioneer here, for he had two important Italian predecessors, Alciato and Cuiacio; that he was also indebted to Hugo Grotius is evident, and the first principles of his sociological theory—the progress from

[1] Cp. Moffa, pp. 231 ff.

[2] The first part was printed at Naples in 1701 and reprinted in the same year at Leipzig by J. F. Gleditsch. The latter also obtained, through J. B. Mencke, the right of publishing the remainder of the work in 1708. A second edition appeared at Naples in 1713, with the addition of the chapters *De romano imperio*. The best editions are those of G. Mascovius, Leipzig, 1737, and G. A. Sergio, Naples, 1756. It was translated into French by J. B. Requier, Amsterdam, 1766, 3 vols., under the title *Esprit des loix romaines* (also later editions), and summarised by Scipione Maffei in the *Giornale de' letterati italiani d' Italia*, VI, 1711, pp. 1 ff. (reprinted by Emiliani-Giudici, *ed. cit.* pp. 353 ff.). Gravina himself described Maffei's summary as a 'ristretto che accende d' invidia l' istesso autore dell' opera originale.' An unpublished treatise *De Imperio et Jurisdictione*, was printed by F. Moffa at Catania in 1907.

strife and rapine by way of pact and contract, to social order—are based upon the doctrines of the *Leviathan*. But, as Moffa points out[1], Gravina's idea of society is more modern and more humanely positive than Hobbes's; his solution of the problem of social order lies less in destroying or restricting the power of the individual, than in the delegation of such power to a new entity, the state. The Leviathan has in his conception become a tamer monster.

By virtue of his acknowledgment of the evolutional principle Gravina is clearly the immediate predecessor of Vico—a point that has been somewhat obscured owing to the anti-Cartesian trend of Vico's philosophy[2]; and with the leaven of this idea that human institutions develop according to definite psychological and sociological laws, Gravina vitalised the historical study of jurisprudence long before a similar principle was employed to unravel the orderless accumulations of facts which, down to this time, had passed for political history. Of the significance of Gravina's treatise for the future, it is still less my province to speak; but it may be noted that it left its mark on Montesquieu's *Esprit des Lois*; and possibly, as Cuoco has suggested, on Locke's *Civil Government* and Rousseau's *Contrat Social* as well[3]. For my purpose here it is sufficient to accentuate the essentially progressive nature of Gravina's views.

In 1703 Gravina exchanged his professorship of Civil Law for one on Canonical Law; he appears to have been lecturing on the latter subject for two years previously, and it is doubtful how long he retained the new chair. In 1708, as we have seen, appeared the two concluding parts of his *magnum opus*, and in the same year the critical work with which we are more particularly concerned, *Della Ragion poetica libri due*, Rome, 1708. I deal with this work in my next section.

Meanwhile the gulf between Gravina and his colleagues of the Arcadia, which had been opened by Gravina's *Ragionamento* on Guidi, was rapidly widening; and in 1711 a serious difference

[1] *Op. cit.* pp. 240 f.

[2] Vico may also have been influenced by Gravina's description of the seven ages of man in his oration *De sapientia universa*. The two men became intimate friends in the last years of Gravina's life (see below, p. 190).

[3] See G. Natali, *op. cit.* p. 8.

arose between him and the 'custode' of the Academy, Crescimbeni. The latter had taken steps, in violence of the constitution, to strengthen his own position as president by electing his own friends on the governing body of twelve; on the matter being put to the vote, Gravina and his party were defeated by thirteen to seventy-four. The minority resolved to found a new Academy, and laid claim to the original name of 'Arcadia.' The matter was ultimately brought before the law courts, and the Pope himself intervened. Gravina was obliged to yield, and his new society was christened the 'Accademia dei Quirini.' It was, however, short-lived, and some two months after his death—his former friends having been convinced that he had repented—Gravina's name was again inscribed in the Golden Book of the Arcadians[1].

In 1712 Gravina came forward as a poet with five tragedies, which were written in the brief space of three or four months, between February and May of the year of their publication[2]. The stimulus to dramatic composition would appear to have come from Maffei. On February 20, 1712, we find Gravina writing to him:

> You see how efficacious your views have been; since you wrote to me of your desire to restore the Italian theatre to honour, I have not only encouraged these erudite young men to write plays, but I have also myself, in twelve days during the carnival, written a tragedy entitled *Il Palamede*[3].

His plays were published with a Prologue spoken by 'La Tragedia,' who introduces herself with the proud words:

> Ecco dopo il girar di tanti secoli
> Nel primiero sembiante la Tragedia.

These tragedies are cold, academic productions of which no critic has a good word to say; and it would be hardly possible

[1] See Gravina's letter to Maffei, *Della Divisione d' Arcadia*, 1712, in Emiliani-Giudici's volume, pp. 277 ff.

[2] *Tragedie cinque*, Naples, 1712; Bertoldi quotes an edition of 1717; and a Venice edition of 1740 includes the treatise *Della Tragedia*. The titles of the plays are: *Il Palamede, L' Andromeda, L' Appio Claudio, Il Papiniano, Il Servio Tullio*.

[3] The letter was published by Julia in 1889; it is quoted by A. Parducci, *La Tragedia classica italiana del sec. XVIII*, Rocca S. Casciano, 1902, p. 3.

for the most ardent Gravinian to defend them. The most disappointing thing is not, however, their want of poetic merit, but the fact that their author set so high a value on them. Again, they bear witness to that extraordinary absence of the concrete critical faculty, which had appeared in his excessive praise of Guidi in his first essay. Gravina is clearly an example of the type of mind which, notwithstanding a remarkable faculty for generalising on literary aesthetics, breaks down when brought face to face with the simple problem of the good or bad in individual works. He might well have been characterising himself when he said in the dedication of his *Ragion poetica*: 'è più facile mediocre autore che giusto estimator divenire.' Gravina's mediocrity as a dramatic poet is a characteristic he shares with two other outstanding figures in literary criticism, D'Aubignac and Houdar de la Motte[1]; and his tragedies have fallen into an even better deserved oblivion than theirs. But possibly we do him an injustice in attributing these poetic attempts entirely to a misplaced confidence in his poetic powers. One motive may have been to provide an antidote to modern tendencies of which Gravina could not approve: Martelli's *Teatro italiano*, for instance, had been published in 1710[2]. And Gravina's interesting little theoretical treatise, *Della Tragedia libro uno* (Naples, 1715), was written mainly to defend and justify his own unfortunate excursion into poetry.

Of the latter part of Gravina's life there is not a great deal to relate. Light is thrown on his extensive political activity by the collection of some three hundred letters, dating from 1690 to 1712, to Monsignore Francesco Pignatelli, who subsequently became a Cardinal[3]; but this has little to do with Gravina as an aesthetic theorist. One episode of his later life which has something of romance, must not be overlooked. In 1709 or

[1] Cp. Voltaire's witty remark in his letter to d'Alembert of September, 1753 (*Œuvres*, XXXVIII, p. 125): 'Gravina m'a paru écrire sur la tragédie comme Dacier, et il a fait en conséquence des tragédies comme Dacier, aidé de sa femme, les aurait faites.'

[2] See below, pp. 123, 138 ff.

[3] These letters are in the Biblioteca Nazionale in Naples. See G. Persico Calvalcanti—who promises an edition of them—*L' Epistolario del Gravina* in the *Giornale storico della lett. ital.*, Supplemento i, 1898, pp. 118 ff. The letters have been utilised by Moffa in his monograph.

1710 he happened to be passing through the Piazza di San Silvestro in Rome, and was attracted by a crowd of people near a goldsmith's shop; they were listening to a little boy of twelve, who was improvising verses with the most extraordinary glibness. Gravina was much struck by his gifts and offered him money, which was indignantly refused. But Gravina was not to be baulked; he found that the boy was the son of Felice Trapassi, druggist and macaroni-seller in the Via dei Cappellari, and returned a few days later with the offer to educate him. He wanted to make an orator and jurist of him, not, as his peculiar talent would seem to have suggested, a poet. Thus Bonaventura Trapassi, who was later to be known to the world as Pietro Metastasio, became Gravina's adopted son.

Gravina's old master and kinsman, Caloprese, died in 1714, leaving him his sole heir, and Gravina returned to Scalea; but after a couple of years we find him back again in Rome among the old friends and the old enemies. Meanwhile, his fame as an authority on the history of law had become European, and from Germany, where he had been made known by the Leipzig scholar, Burchard Mencke, who had reviewed his works on jurisprudence in the *Acta Eruditorum*, came the offer of a professorship. But Gravina, whose health was anything but satisfactory—besides the aggravated abdominal ailment, he had trouble with his eyes—was not to be tempted to cross the Alps. On the other hand, a prospect of congenial activity at the University of Turin was opened up to him by the Duke of Savoy, Vittorio Amadeo, and he was about to set out for Turin when he was seized by a violent attack of his old malady. From this attack he never recovered, and on January 6, 1718, he expired in the arms of his adopted son.

Gravina was tall, but bent by his sedentary life and thin almost to emaciation; he was the typical scholar who regarded as lost a day in which he had not spent ten to twelve hours with his books; his life was in his library, over which he placed an inscription, singling out as the five greatest books in the world the Bible, the *Corpus juris*, Plato, Homer and Cicero[1]. His pallid face and sharp eyes marked out the man to whom the search of

[1] Cp. G. A. Serao, *op. cit.* p. 8.

truth was more precious than the care for bodily health. But he is also described as a generous nature who gave willingly of his intellectual treasures, but was unsparing in his attacks on falseness and hypocrisy. One cannot, however, help doubting whether his early years were the best training in character for a man whose life-work brought him more often into antagonism with his contemporaries than into agreement with them; he was not one of these easy-going mediocrities, like his friend Crescimbeni, who could swim with the current. Gravina's education had, least of all, prepared him for the conflicts in which he found himself involved in Rome. He did not readily brook criticism or contradiction; he had his full share of the stubborn, argumentative arrogance of the jurist, and a caustic tongue which made him many enemies. No doubt, there was in Gravina a want of ability to adapt himself to changing conditions. This is seen in the comparatively stationary character of his opinions; and with it came a graver source of weakness, an intellectual vanity and a love of praise, which his enemies were not slow to notice[1]. These less admirable sides of his character are to be seen in the provocative manner of his secession from the Academy of the Arcadians, as well as in the ingenuousness with which he exposed himself to satirical attacks. They are to be seen, too, when, disheartened by the want of favour with which his tragedies were received—tragedies which were to re-establish Greek taste on the modern stage—he spent the last months of his life laboriously translating them into Latin, in order that other nations and other times might give him the credit and honour withheld from him by his own countrymen.

[1] Cp., for instance, Martelli's *Satire*, III (I quote from *Raccolta di Poesie satiriche scritte nel secolo XVIII*, Milan, 1827, pp. 99 f.). After praising warmly his 'divine' gifts as a legislator and his 'aurea eloquenza,' Martelli goes on:

Ma concorrer dovrete in sua sentenza.
    Questo è sol di tant' uomo il peccadiglio,
    Creder che tutta in lui sia la scienza.
Se il loderete, ei vi amerà da figlio;
    E l' udirete, a gioventù fiorita,
    Nè d' applauso mancar, nè di consiglio.

II

'Lassen Sie sich, mein gnädiger Herr,' wrote Winckelmann from Rome in 1762 to his friend Berg in Paris, 'des Gravina *Ragion poetica* anbefohlen sein; lesen Sie dieselbe zehnmal bis zum Auswendiglernen';[1] and Ugo Foscolo recommended it to the Countess Isabella Teotochi-Albrizzi with still greater warmth[2]. In spite of such high eulogy, the *Ragion poetica* has passed, even in Italy, into the limbo of books that are praised rather than read. It does not seem to have been reprinted at all between 1857 and 1921[3].

What Gravina sets out to establish in his treatise is a fundamental basis for poetry. The rules of poetry, he says, change with time and fashion, as do the rules of architecture; but just as, behind the varying fashions of the latter art lie the unchanging laws of geometry, so behind the rules of poetry there must be an 'idea and common reason.' In other words, he seeks a philosophical justification of the rules, and an unvarying

[1] Winckelmann's *Schriften*, Stuttgart, 1847, II, p. 503; and in his *Sendschreiben von der Reise eines Gelehrten nach Italien* (*ibid.* p. 318), he speaks of it as a work 'welches in alle Sprachen übersetzt zu werden verdiente.'

[2] Letter of May 3, 1809, published in the *Memorie e documenti per la storia dell' Università di Pavia*, III, p. 127, quoted by Bertoldi, *op. cit.* pp. 69 f.: 'Leggete, mia cara Isabella, il libro della *Ragione poetica* del Gravina; opera egregia da cui ricaverete mille segni di sapere letterario, pensata profondamente, ragionata finamente, dedotta esattamente, dettata elegantemente. Niuno meglio del Gravina sviscerò i principi morali e politici della poesia degli antichi, nè penetrò quanto lui nei gentili misteri dell' amore del Petrarca. Ma dopo tutte queste lodi al Gravina, vi maraviglierete s' io vi dirò ch' egli antepone il Trissino al Tasso. Leggete voi stessa; quel libro fu scritto per una gentildonna, ed è forse (e senza forse) la più bella arte poetica che abbia il mondo.' Vincenzo Gioberti, too, called it (*Pensieri e Giudici*, raccolti e ordinati da F. Ugolino, Florence, 1856, p. 345): 'il lavoro più perfetto di questo genere che abbia l' Italia.'

[3] The first edition (in quarto) of 1708 was followed in 1711 by a Venice reprint and in 1716 by an octavo edition published at Naples. Subsequent editions appeared at Naples, 1732, at Florence, 1771; Venice, 1829; Bologna, 1830; and there was a London edition, *Dalla Ragion poetica tra' Greci, Latini ed Italiani*, published in 1806 (see below, p. 239). I have also a small Milan edition of 1830. Further, it is to be found in the various editions of *Opere scelte*: Naples, 1756–8; Milan, 1819; Florence, 1826; Milan, 1827; Naples, 1839; and in the *Prose*, already cited, Florence, 1857. The latest reprint of 1921 is edited by G. Natali for the series *Cultura d' Anima* (Carabba, Lanciano). A new edition is promised in Laterza's *Scrittori d' Italia*.

principle on which a science of poetry, modern as well as ancient, may be built up; this is his 'ragion poetica,' something clearly different from the 'ratio' or 'raison' of the older poetics. Gravina's search was in great measure a consequence of his philosophical and legal training; he sought the eternal 'ragione' of poetry, just as, in his great treatise on jurisprudence, he sought the 'ragione' that lay behind the civil law of Rome. And he set out on his quest from a principle that was in antagonism to the theory and practice of the classicists. The latter had insisted on obedience to the letter of the Aristotelian law; he demanded that literature should be free to conform to changing fashions and tastes. Each new generation must adapt the fundamental 'idea' of poetry to its own conditions and needs. The attempt to subject modern poetry to the rules of antiquity is consequently hardly less baneful in its effects than the neglect of the rules altogether. 'As nature is the mother of true things, so the mother of fictitious things is the idea deduced by the human mind from nature; and this idea contains within it all that the mind—whether as understanding or imagination—reproduces' (p. 6)[1].

In his first chapter Gravina proceeds to define, on strictly Cartesian lines, the 'true' and the 'false,' the 'real' and the 'fictitious.' Every judgment, even a negative one, contains an affirmation. A true judgment differs from a false one, in so far as the former contains the entire knowledge of the object judged, the latter only an imperfect knowledge or none at all[2]. An angular tower, for instance, seen from a distance, appears round; we form a false judgment of it owing to our imperfect knowledge. The error arises, not from our imagination forming a picture of the object which has no existence in reality, but from the want of an idea which would exclude the possibility

[1] 'Siccome delle cose vere è madre la natura, così delle cose finte è madre l' idea, tratta dalla mente umana di dentro la natura istessa, ove è contenuto quanto col pensiero ogni mente, o intendendo o immaginando, scolpisce.' The references are to the edition of Emiliani-Giudici.

[2] Cp. Descartes, *Méditations*, IV: 'Toutefois, cela ne me satisfait pas encore tout-à-fait, car l'erreur n'est pas une pure négation, c'est-à-dire, n'est pas le simple défaut ou manquement de quelque perfection qui ne m'est point due, mais c'est une privation ou la manquement de quelque connoissance qu'il semble que je devrois avoir.'

of our imagining the object wrongly. Consequently, when the image of an absent object, or of something which only exists in the future, is not interfered with by some contrary image accepted by our mind as true, the absent or future object presents itself to us as present or already realised—in short, as true. This reasoning is now applied to passions such as ambition and love, which take possession of the mind with peculiar power, and create in it a kind of delirium. The intensity of these passions excludes everything which might indicate the remoteness or even the non-existence of the end or object desired, and our mind accepts the end or object as true and present. 'Whence it happens that men for the most part dream with open eyes' ('Donde avviene che per lo più gli uomini sognano con gli occhi aperti,' p. 8).

The 'efficacy' of poetry (chap. ii) is to assist our imagination in this 'dreaming with open eyes,' by presenting to it a vivid semblance of the true, and further, to protect it from contrary images which may be at variance with the truth expressed by the poet. Our attitude towards the fictitious is thus identical with that towards the true. The response of our mind ('i moti dell' animo nostro') is not in accordance with things as they actually are, or their real qualities, but only with the impression which these external things leave upon it. Thus the poet's imitations of objects have the same effect on us as the objects themselves; the mind accepts the fable as true and real, and the imagination is moved by it as by the impression of a reality. Gravina now proceeds (chap. iii) to discuss the 'probable' and the 'appropriate' ('il verisimile ed il convenevole'), in other words, the means which the poet must adopt in order to keep up the deception which is necessary, if his creations are to make the same impression on the mind as the real objects. What the poet creates must resemble the true, that is, it must be probable, and the expressions he uses must be natural and accurate; in this way the mind is, as it were, turned away from the true, and 'weaves for itself a wonderful enchantment of fantasy' ('s' ordisce un mirabile incanto di fantasia'). Impossible things, which are not 'supported by the might of some deity' ('che non sono sostenuti dalla possanza di qualche nume'), must be avoided, as well as all characteristics not in keeping with the age represented or the person introduced. The consequence of transgressing this rule is to awaken us to the unreal, the fictitious, in the object described. This is the reason why the ancients would not represent on the stage incidents which were separated by months and years; they defined the duration of an action as something not exceeding the time which might be spent by an audience in the theatre, namely, twelve hours. It must be the art of the poet, again, to conceal his art; and in order to prevent his verse appearing artificial, he must occasionally give it the semblance of negligence. Excessive polish has to be avoided, as well as inappropriate elements; for both tend to destroy the enchantment into which the mind is lulled by art. And of all the wise enchanters (chap. iv) Homer is the most powerful and wisest ('il mago più potente e l' incantatore più sagace,' p. 10); he is the supreme poet of the natural. The praise which Gravina bestows upon Homer—he had already singled him out in his 'ragionamente' on the *Endimione*—marks the beginning of a new epoch in the appreciation of Greek poetry[1].

A short chapter (v), 'On the origin of vices in poetry,' repudiates as inconsistent with these guiding principles of poetry, namely, the probable and the appropriate, 'the extravagances of the declamatory school,' the writers of romances, whom it was the chief mission of the Arcadians to discredit. Gravina is not yet, however, finished with the perfections of Homer. In his sixth chapter he discusses the truth of Homer's characters—a truth that avoids the extremes of perfect virtue and unmitigated vice. Neither the perfect nor the unchanging character exists in nature, and those who depict such characters are unable to cast a spell over our imagination, because their creations are not natural.

'Poetry,' Gravina proclaims in his seventh chapter ('On the utility of poetry'), 'is a magician, but a salutary one, and a delirium which dissipates our follies' ('la poesia è una maga, ma salutare, ed un delirio che sgombra le pazzie,' p. 15). Here

[1] Cp. G. Finsler, *Homer in der Neuzeit von Dante bis Goethe*, Leipzig, 1912, p. 98.

lies the significance of the fables of Amphion and Orpheus, who by the music of the lyre could move beasts and stones. It is impossible for the great universal and eternal truths to gain access to vulgar minds, which are almost invariably enveloped in the mist of fantasy; and it is the function of the poets to reach such minds by rendering abstract truth concrete—presenting true things in the form of pictures which will appeal to them. 'Thus men, in becoming delirious, are cured of their follies.' It is the old Horatian doctrine of the 'utile et dulce' which, in spite of Castelvetro's protest, was to dominate Italian and European aesthetics for a century to come. The fables of the Greek mythology were intended to bring home to rude men what philosophy teaches the educated. For although (chap. viii) to the wise man God is one and infinite, to the crowd the various attributes of the Divine Being are represented by different gods. This is the explanation of mythologies that was offered by the fathers of the Church. The first inventors of such fables were the Egyptians from whom the Greeks learned. If mythology was invented by the philosophers to bring home eternal truths to simple minds, it follows that the basis of fables is not the false but the true, that they arise, not from caprice, but from invention, regulated by knowledge; behind their facts and imagery lie great physical and moral laws.

Gravina now proceeds (chap. ix) to define the Fable according to this supposition. It is the 'essence of things,' transformed into terms of human ideas, 'the truth disguised in a popular semblance.' The poet thus reproduces the abstractions of wisdom in visible images; the religion of ancient times was a fabrication ('architettura') of the poets, and for this reason they were regarded as 'divine.' Now it is obvious that the reputation of a poet grows with his power of convincing us that what he tells us is probable, and in order to enhance the probability of their inventions, he combines them with historical facts. At the same time, lest he be convicted of falsification, he avoids recent historical events and takes refuge in the distant past, where everything is vague and shadowy. Thus the poetic fable consists of a true principle attached to vague and remote incidents and persons, which may be altered to suit the exigencies of the truth embodied in the fiction; in other words, alterations may be made in facts in order to exclude 'contrary images,' which might interfere with the doctrine or principle involved. And Gravina sums up this theory of the poet's generalising function by turning again (chap. x) to Homer, who in his *Iliad* makes use of the story of the Trojan War as a medium through which to present the customs of men, the laws of nature, the ordinances of civil government, and, generally, the 'essence of things.' In the same way, the wanderings of Odysseus, in the other epic, are merely the excuse for teaching 'the art and rules for the good conduct of life.'

The eleventh chapter—the most important in the volume—deals with the 'Utility of the Fable.' The purpose of poetic inventions is to bring before the minds of the people the laws of nature and of God, to stimulate religious sentiment and straightforward dealing. This end is the more easily attained in proportion as the invention of the poet approximates to events familiar to the minds of his hearers. But Gravina warns us against accepting what might seem the logical consequence of this statement, namely, that the real and the true would be still more efficacious than the fictitious; it must be remembered that what impresses itself upon our senses is nothing without the reflexion of our mind; for it is only by means of reflexion that a 'cognition' can be arrived at, a universal idea. For what lies near to us and is familiar does not arrest our attention. We take more interest in the phenomena of the heavens than in those of the earth, and we are able to understand other people's souls better than our own. Then again, it is impossible for the mind, observing the full flow of human events, to concentrate itself on what is essential to its purpose. All things which present themselves to our senses, 'bear on their forehead' ('portano in fronte loro,' p. 24) the occasion of knowledge, but, being near to us, they cannot convey to us the truth which lies behind them, just as we cannot read a book held too close to our eyes. The mind is merely distracted by the complexity of images.

On the other hand, when the object has the quality of 'novelty,' it at once arrests our attention; the mind is detached from other images and is forced to observe and reflect on the novel qualities of the object presented to it. Now this quality of 'novelty' appertains to the objects represented by poetry; what in nature is ordinary and valueless, becomes by means of the poet's art, new and unexpected. The mere fact of the objects of nature being reproduced at all in this way excites our wonder. Thus poetry, which by means of various artifices transfers the natural to the domain of the fictitious, lends value to familiar things, gives them the appearance of novelty, and compels us to reflect on them. Moreover, the imitation itself recalls our reminiscence of the real thing, and the comparison of the two implies an examination of their properties; this gives us a pleasure akin to that produced by new knowledge or the recognition of a new truth. For the rest, the imitation has precisely the same effect on us as the real object. The commotion of feelings, even of a painful nature, caused by such an imitation, is always mixed with pleasure when the affect takes place slowly, causing a gentle titillation. In fact, the greatest pleasure arises from emotions which affect our sympathies without distracting us by a sense of personal loss or injury. This is the pleasure we receive from tragedy. In lamenting the sufferings of others, we seem just and upright in our own eyes; the recognition of virtues in ourselves fills us with a pleasure which is superior to all others. Thus the similarity of the imitation with the object imitated is in itself the greatest source of delight and utility.

The remainder of the work may be more briefly summarised. In chapter xii Gravina passes over to a consideration of the various kinds of literature; but here he has little to say that is new. The epic has, of course, the first place, and it bears within it ('porta dentro le viscere') dramatic poetry. We hear once more that the dramatist is restricted to actions which do not last longer than the time an audience spends in the theatre; and we have the familiar distinction that tragedy is a form of dramatic poetry dealing with high personages and momentous political affairs, ending frequently in death, whereas comedy treats private and everyday happenings. Rome, he points out further, did not afford a favourable soil for the drama, owing to the staid and composed temperament of the Romans. Plautus and

Terence were indebted for the characters which they depicted to Greece.

What Gravina has to say of the lyric (chap. xiii) is, like the utterances of all classic critics who exhaust their ingenuity on the epic and the drama, of small importance; the lyric is, in fact, only a minor tributary to the main stream of literary expression in epic and drama. Its function is 'the particular, minute and vivid expression of virtues and vices, tastes and feelings'; it is 'a mirror which illumines human nature by its vivid reflexions'; but it has also a share in promulgating doctrine useful for the regulation of private and public affairs.

We are reminded (chap. xiv) that we must not lay too little weight on popular judgment, because the gold happens to be hidden in the dross. The poet ought certainly not to consider it as a dominating factor, but he cannot succeed without it. He cannot occupy the throne of glory with the people alone, or wholly without the people. Integrity of judgment springs from the eternal and celestial seeds of the true, which are equally distributed among all intellects, but these are—in some less, in others more—shrouded by the darkness caused by the disturbed course of external things. It is, as had been indicated before, the function of poetry to dispel this darkness, which obscures the power of right discernment to be found in all men. In the same chapter Gravina dwells on the advisability of not exceeding a certain measure of praise, otherwise the hearer is estranged from the object praised. The ancients were masters in this respect, for they had a clear sense of the realities of things, that is, of the things themselves.

With chapter xv Gravina passes over from the theory to the history of literature. The various ages of poetry are reviewed, and then the Greek and Latin poets one by one. Homer is once more praised (chap. xvi) as the depicter of human life—in the *Iliad*, as we have seen, of public affairs and political life, in the *Odyssey* of domestic affairs and private life. From Homer he goes on to Hesiod and the tragic dramatists (chaps. xvii–xix), whom he ranks in the order of greatness, Aeschylus, Sophocles, Euripides; then to Aristophanes (chap. xx), who is mainly reproached for having ridiculed Socrates, and Pindar (chap. xxi).

Anacreon, Theocritus, Moscus and Bion are dealt with in chapters xxii and xxiii. The survey of Latin poets begins with Plautus and Terence, and is extended to include the modern Latin poets of Italy. Most noteworthy is perhaps the chapter (xxviii) on Virgil, whose *Georgics* he regards as his best work. He emphasises that poet's dependence on Homer and protests vehemently against Scaliger's insistence on the superiority of Virgil to Homer.

The second book of the *Ragion poetica* deals with the literature of the Italian vernacular; Gravina will show how the same idea or 'ragione' is as applicable to modern poetry as to ancient. If we are to believe the Dedication, it was the Princess di Carpegna who overcame his repugnance to writing about Italian poetry; but the Orsi-Bouhours controversy had obviously also weight with him. Foreigners have formed wrong ideas, he says, about Italian literature; but these wrong ideas have been largely due to the misrepresentations of Italian critics who have not put their literature in the right light. Presumably Gravina has here in mind the spokesmen of 'secentismo.'

The particular interest of the Italian part of Gravina's treatise lies in his warm appreciation of Dante as the greatest of the Italians (chaps. i, iv, ix–xiii)[1]; but his heart is with Ariosto (chap. xvi). His view of Tasso (chap. xviii) is rather in agreement with Bouhours' than with Orsi's; but Antonio Conti hints that the praise of Crescimbeni and Martelli had made Gravina critical[2]. On the other hand, Trissino is, no doubt owing to the fact that his *Italia liberata* was modelled on the *Iliad*, eulogised in chapter xvii as a modern Homer and superior to Tasso and Alamanni. There are also discussions of general matters, such as the disintegration of the Latin language and the rise of the vernacular (chaps. iii, v, vi), the impropriety of rhyme in Italian in view of its absence in classic Latin (chap. ii), and the influence of Provençal literature on Italian (chap. vii). This second part of the *Ragion poetica* has no particular value for aesthetic theory; and even as an essay in critical appreciation,

[1] Cp. F. Balsano, *La Divina Commedia giudicata da G. V. Gravina* (*Coll. di opuscoli danteschi*, vols. XLII, XLIII), Città di Castello, 1879.

[2] A. Conti, *Prose e Poesie*, II, Venice, 1756, p. 263.

it is disappointing. Perhaps that unwillingness, of which Gravina speaks in his dedication, to write on the theme, is the explanation of his perfunctoriness in his dealing with the Italian poets. Apart from his courageous insistence on the primacy of Homer and Dante, the significance of Gravina's *Ragion poetica* lies in its theory rather than in its appreciation of individual poets.

III

Gravina's treatise on Tragedy, *Della Tragedia libro uno*, published seven years after the *Ragion poetica*, contains, in part, a repetition of ideas already expressed in the earlier treatise, in part, ideas drawn from the older commentaries on Aristotle, especially that of Castelvetro. Such value as the treatise possesses, it owes to its critical perspective. It will be convenient to follow the plan I have adopted in discussing the *Ragion poetica*, and first to summarise, as briefly as possible, the ideas set forth in the forty-two chapters of this little book.

Gravina's purpose is to state the principles that must govern an ideal tragedy—of which he fondly believed he had himself given examples[1]—and to show how far the existing Italian drama is from complying with such an ideal. After a dedication to Prince Eugene of Savoy, Gravina considers the two ends of poetry, the 'utile et dulce,' and examines the double function of tragedy in its historical development. He sees in the writer of tragedies the artist who combines in himself the functions of the philosopher, the poet and the musician, and he sets up as the 'true idea' of tragedy, its purpose to transmit to the people the fruits of philosophy and eloquence, in order that they may thereby correct their morals and their speech. He repeats (chap. ii) his previous comparison of tragedy with epic poetry; it stands higher than comedy and is more dignified and perfect, as it is more real, than the epic from which it has sprung. The tragic fable should resemble reality (chap. iii), and the poet is recommended to choose—as Gravina himself had chosen—

[1] Cp. Dedication (ed. Emiliani-Giudici, p. 153): 'Ho voluto con V. A. S. ragionando conferire l' idea antica della Tragedia, di cui con le cinque mie ho rinnovato gli esempi.'

antique personages as the characters of tragedy, and build up round them a truth that cannot grow old. This does not exclude the possibility of a living person being represented in the mask of an ancient. It is well that the people should be familiarised with the life of courts, and that their pity should be awakened by the nemesis which awaits the crimes or weakness of great men. Gravina explains (chap. iv) the 'purgative' power of tragedy, following Castelvetro, by comparing it with the effect of introducing small doses of poison into the human body, which thereby acquires the power of resisting the poison. By frequently witnessing tragic events in the theatre a man grows accustomed to them and thus hardened against them when he meets them in actual life.

Chapter v condemns the work of modern poets who are led astray by their too slavish imitation of the Greeks. Aristotle's treatise is incomplete and gives the impression that the *Oedipus* of Sophocles is the only type of tragedy; this has led too many modern poets to build their tragedies on this model, to the exclusion of Aeschylus and Euripides; it has led to extravagances and monstrosities, of which—one is surprised to learn—the *Pastor fido* is an example. Aristotle deduces the pity we feel for Oedipus from his 'mediocre' character. Gravina, like Corneille, believes that a wrong inference has been drawn from this, namely, that the protagonist of all tragedies must be 'mediocre' in character, whereas such a limitation would exclude several classical dramas. All that is wanted is a subject and characters which correspond to the truth and stir up the emotions of compassion and fear. Further, utility mingled with pleasure must guide the dramatists of the present, as they guided those of the past; but the modern poet should aim at greater variety. In the interests of verisimilitude (chap. vi), the duration of the action represented should not exceed the time spent by the audience in the theatre, but it may be extended to a revolution of the sun. This excludes complicated intrigues, or attempts to present dramatically the entire life of a character. It is also unwise to include, as does Guarini in his *Pastor fido*, developments that require years, in the events of a day. Too complicated fables (chap. vii) are difficult to follow. Aristotle demands (chap. viii) a single event or events linked together to form a unity, a rule against which Guarini again sins. The episodes (chap. ix) must be intimately bound up with the main action. Gravina then sums up the results he has so far reached. When the argument by its distinction and unusual nature attracts the attention of the people; when it is contained within the space of a single day; when the fable is constructed naturally and without apparent artifice; and when it corrects passions, and gives insight into human life—then it will always be worthy of tragedy, whoever the protagonist may be, and whether the end be sad or happy. If tragedy attains its highest end of turning our thoughts from the uncertain vicissitudes of human lives to the Divine bliss that is lasting and unchanging, what does it matter whether the author has neglected precepts which in no wise contribute to the probability and utility of the tragedy? What does it matter where the poet finds his argument, whether it be in history or fable? What authority can prevent him 'di cogliere il bene dove l' incontra'? A martyr, or Christ Himself, may be the subject of a tragedy, in spite of those servile followers of Aristotle who refuse to have anything but a 'mediocre' hero; and we should be deprived of the *Antigone*, the *Oedipus Coloneus*, *Medea*, and many other tragedies, merely because they do not contain a 'recognition.' The simple plots—such as those of Aeschylus—are compared (chap. x) with the involved plots, to the advantage of the latter; but it is admitted that a higher poetic genius is necessary to attain the same end with a simple as with an involved plot.

In chapter xi Gravina turns more sharply against Aristotle, accuses his *Poetics* of lack of order, and other defects already noted by Castelvetro; the latter, he adds, is the only critic of Aristotle who treats him with 'philosophic freedom.' Just as the light of nature herself has been unable to dispel the errors of Aristotle's books on physics, so clear reason, based on examples from ancient tragedy, has shown itself inadequate to set men free from the tyranny of Aristotle's treatise on Poetics. The modern theatre has been stunted and rendered arid by these blind interpreters: and our poets, finding themselves unable to obey the foolish and puerile precepts attributed to Aristotle, have gone to the opposite extreme and broken every law of reason and verisimilitude, of decorum and propriety.

After this outburst, Gravina falls back into a discussion of various points of technique. To unravel the 'knot' without supernatural aid (chap. xii) demands a higher artifice than with it; but the intervention of a deity is not wholly to be condemned; for it reminds the people of Providence. Aeschylus is praised (chap. xiii) as the first poet to narrate revolting happenings instead of representing them. The question of the 'characters' or 'manners' ('costume') represented in a tragedy is dealt with in chapter xiv. This is closely bound up with that of the fable itself; for human events are regulated by 'character': 'il costume è l' organo e lo strumento della favola.' The confusion of modern tragedies in this matter he is also inclined to lay at Aristotle's door, who says that in his time tragedies were without 'costume.' The modern tragedies of Gravina's day are reproached for being entirely chimerical in this respect, confusing sex, age, nation, profession, rank; converting a maid-servant into a queen, a young man into an old, and the like. Every character in a tragedy must express a personality and be true to the accepted 'costume' associated with his rank; only in this way can we foresee his actions. When Aristotle says the manners of a tragedy must be good, he means artistically good, well expressed—again an echo of Corneille; and Castelvetro is wrong when he attempts to show that the protagonist must be morally good. In any case, character (chap. xv) must be probable and natural; for if a certain virtue is not peculiar to human nature, we distrust the value of its acquisition and do not imitate it; if a vice is not human, we do not need to avoid it, for it is without temptation for us. Further, passions are not excited by things removed from nature and the truth; and if the characters described are not natural, we cannot foresee the event: we are like persons in the dark who are suddenly surprised by a great light. The introduction of the unexpected (chap. xvi) is not to be recommended; the tragic event must be gradually led up to, otherwise it will make no impression on us. This is a fault of contemporary poets; they are more anxious to make their events unexpected than the ancients were to prepare them.

Having demonstrated the utility and necessity of 'costume,' Gravina proceeds (chap. xvii) to distinguish three kinds. There is the natural 'costume' which springs from human nature itself; from human relations, such as the love of a father for his sons, or the love we feel to God; or it may be dissociated from reason, such as when revenge is caused by anger, greed by avarice. The civil 'costume' lies in the intercourse of men with one another, involving friendship, loyalty, prudence, justice, or the vices of fraud, strife, hatred and the like. Lastly, the 'domestic costume' is connected with the particular history of some celebrated family or group; it may be, for instance, the genius of a great personage, or the unbridled cruelty of Nero, or it may be the characteristic of a sect, as the indifference of the Stoics. The first of these categories is of no use for the drama. Rustics, whose reasoning powers and characters are weak, cannot, for instance, initiate any action worthy of representation; and the folly of writers of pastoral dramas, like Guarini and Tasso, is patent to everybody. Moreover, Guarini's character-drawing is quite false; he imbues his rustics with the 'costume' of the court. The *Pastor fido* and the *Aminta* are the beginnings of a pestilence in the theatre. Gravina denies the right of these works to be regarded as poetry, for they are not true imitations. It is necessary (chap. xviii) that the poet be acquainted with the nation he introduces into his drama, and not, like the modern Italian poets—here Gravina is, no doubt, thinking of Martelli[1]—represent Greeks and Romans in the 'costume' of modern times. He regards it as a special merit of his own dramas that he endeavoured by long study to attain a correct 'costume.'

Aristotle demands (chap. xix) that the character of a personage should not change, and he blames Euripides for transgressing this rule in his *Iphigeneia*. But there are many cases

[1] Martelli had clearly Gravina in his mind when he wrote in his dialogue *L' Impostore* (see below, pp. 126 ff.), p. 12: 'Si sfogano i secchi Poeti contro i moderni, trovando nell' *Aminta*, nel *Torrismondo*, nel *Pastor fido* gravi difetti, e vi sono. Ma la maggior parte de' loro difetti e sopra de' quali si strepita maggioramente, è il non aver osservate le regole sue, che tutte sono ragioni nate dall' esempio, e dall' applauso comune, e ciò vuol dire, che non han seguitati in ogni lor parte gli esempj, lasciatici, come in retaggio, e in fidecommisso da' Greci.'

where changes are justified by the intervention of a stronger force. Again Gravina takes the opportunity of turning the point of his argument against Tasso, whose treatment of his characters in *Aminta* is not consistent. Modern tragic poets (chap. xx) make it easy for themselves by only dealing with love, and thus deprive our theatre of variety; we have untragic sentimental tragedies and uncomic comedies (again the *Pastor fido* and the *Aminta*). Chapter xxi deals with the introduction of maxims and sentiments, it being, of course, necessary (chap. xxii) to adapt the utterances of personages to their characters, a rule against which Guarini and Tasso offend. Tasso, he says, was more learned and reasonable than Guarini; but his modesty was a weakness and made him unable to resist the corruption of his age, which had renounced the purity and candour of the sixteenth century; too often in his *Aminta* he falls into the common vice of placing in the mouths of shepherds chivalrous sentiments and witty conceits, although these are less frequent and of a less recondite kind than in the *Pastor fido*. But Gravina's chief regret is that the *Pastor fido* and the *Aminta*—especially the latter—have been accepted by foreign nations as the flower of Italian literature. He continues:

But foreigners must not confuse our most learned and erudite men with the courtiers and mercenaries of the Italian States who cross the Alps. They must know that our true scholars remain for the most part in their own country, detained by poverty, which in Italy is the inseparable companion of the greatest geniuses, and the punishment of those who devote themselves to the most cultured studies. With us these studies, instead of being stimulated by rewards, are calumniated and violently oppressed at almost all our courts, except those which dispense rewards on grounds of piety or doctrine (p. 187).

The chapters that follow deal with purely technical matters, xxiii with locution, which leads to a consideration of the excellence of the Greek and Latin languages (chap. xxiv), and the objectionable modern practice of introducing Latinisms and foreign words (chap. xxv). Ought the medium of tragedy (chap. xxvi) to be verse, as Castelvetro required, or is prose permissible, in accordance with the views of Paolo Beni and his followers? Gravina's conclusion is that tragedy must be in verse as a statue must be of marble; but he will not have rhyme. Chapters xxvii to xxxi treat the metre of tragedy, the iambic. Seneca is blamed (chap. xxxii) as being unnatural; and the influence which that writer has had on modern poets is deplored. Chapter xxxiii discusses the part that music plays in the representation. Gravina shares Castelvetro's view that the entire tragedy was accompanied by music on the Greek stage, and not that of Vettori, who held that only the choruses were sung. It is unfortunate, Gravina adds, that Castelvetro is ignored by Dacier—as a matter of fact, he is not—for he throws light on many dark places; but how could it be otherwise when he is neglected by the Italians themselves? Chapter xxxiv considers whether every tragedy should be sung and danced, and Castelvetro's opinion is again defended. In chapter xxxviii Gravina passes to the 'sixth part of quality,' the theatre, and in chapter xl he discusses the parts of quantity. Servile interpreters of Aristotle, he concludes, have reduced the reflexions and counsels of that philosopher to rules, and, as the 'British Democritus,' Bacon, said, the faculties reduced to art become sterile, for art circumscribes them[1]; thus poetry is rendered arid by poetics. Gravina consequently tries to show the primary end of poetry by explaining the 'idea' in the minds of the ancient writers; this he deduces from their knowledge and observation of nature. The opinion of Aristotle is of value only in so far as it is sustained by a deeper 'idea' or 'ragione' behind it. Chapter xli deals with the French tragedies, as some people had complained that foreign writers were exempt from criticism; and Gravina quotes in translation the views of Rapin on gallantry and Dacier's objection to love-intrigues—the former evidently in direct quotation from chapter vi of Muratori's Book III. A brief conclusion (chap. xlii) rounds off the work.

IV

The impressions which Gravina's critical writings leave on the modern reader are strangely mixed. They contain flashes of startling intuition, which have induced some of his critics to

[1] Cp. *Novum Organum*, I, 88 (*Works*, ed. J. Spedding, London, 1887, I, p. 195).

claim him as a pioneer of modern idealistic aesthetics, of Hegel, Schopenhauer and Taine[1]; and, side by side with these, lapses into scholastic pedantries and well-worn dogmas of tradition. But all Gravina's writing is noble and dignified, and adorned with phrases which linger long in the mind; possibly, indeed, it was primarily its style to which the *Ragion poetica* owed its long vitality and the praise that has been lavished upon it.

What is Gravina's place in the history of aesthetic theory? I have already claimed him as the first to formulate the aesthetics of Cartesianism, that is to say, the first to give systematic expression to the attitude towards poetry which is latent in, or deducible from Descartes' philosophy. This is perhaps putting his position too definitely; for it postulates the question how far there is, or can be, an aesthetic philosophy in a system which, as we have seen[2], is essentially hostile to poetic expression as an end in itself. But Gravina's thought was deeply influenced by the stamp which it received at an early stage from the teaching of his master Caloprese; and Caloprese, as is to be seen from the edition of the *Rime* of Della Casa published at Naples in 1694, in which he had a hand[3], showed how Descartes' method of thought could, by means of a fusion with Platonism, or perhaps one should say Plotinism, be made serviceable for aesthetic theory. Cartesian, certainly, is Gravina's insistence on the supremacy of the reason: the business of art is to express what is true; that is to say, poetry must be definitely realistic. This at once set up a barrier against the extravagance of 'secentismo.' He regards with real abhorrence all excrescences of the unregulated imagination, be it in the form of romance or burlesque, incompatible with sound reason, or be it the conceits of Marinism.[4] In all this, it should be noted,

[1] E. Reich, *op. cit.* pp. 32, 73.

[2] See above, pp. 6 f. Also A. Farinelli, *Dante e la Francia*, Milan, 1906, II, pp. 59 ff.

[3] *Rime di M. Gio. della Casa*, sposte per M. A. Severino secondo l' idee d' Hermogene, con la giunta delle spositioni di S. Quattromani, e di G. Caloprese, Naples, 1694. See, for example, p. 129 of that work.

[4] The revolt against Marini in the south of Italy had, however, begun, before Gravina, with Pirro Schettini (1630–78); cp. V. Caravelli, *P. Schettini e l' Antimarinismo* (Reale Accad. di Arch., Napoli: *Atti*, vol. XIV), Naples, 1890.

Gravina's object is not to be distinguished from that of the definitely Cartesian author of the *Manière de bien penser*[1]. Cartesian, too, is, at bottom, Gravina's insistence that behind all manifestations of art there must be a utilitarian, or, more precisely, a moral purpose: poetry must make men wiser and better. In respect of the last-mentioned principle, there was perhaps some vacillation in Gravina's mind, for it was in conflict with Castelvetro's opinion. In the *Ragionamento sopra l' Endimione* he had caught sight, for a moment, of a purely aesthetic purpose[2]; but it was only for a moment, and his mature view of the desirability of combining the 'utile' with the 'dulce' is quite unambiguously expressed both in the *Ragion poetica* and in the treatise on Tragedy. I doubt if Gravina's Cartesianism goes farther than this, or could have gone farther. He sets out bravely from Cartesian distinctions between abstract and apparent truths, and the like; but, a few steps more, and he would inevitably have found himself confronting a blank wall. An art dominated by reason, or enunciating, as its first purpose, 'universal truths,' can have no semblance of life, is, in fact, a contradiction in terms[3].

Fortunately, however, Gravina's rationalism was counteracted by two forces which were of much greater significance for his aesthetic theory: his genuine appreciation of the literature of Greece, and the influence of Castelvetro. Gravina's demand for a return to the Greeks, his unstinted praise of Homer, and

[1] One might even find in Gravina (see above, pp. 37 f.) an immediate echo of the passage (p. 9) where Bouhours makes his Eudoxe say: 'Les pensées sont les images des choses, comme les paroles sont les images des pensées; et penser, à parler en général, c'est former en soy la peinture d'un objet, ou spirituel, ou sensible. Or, les images et les peintures ne sont véritables qu'autant qu'elles sont ressemblantes: ainsi une pensée est vraye, lors qu'elle représente les choses fidellement; et elle est fausse quand elle les fait voir autrement qu'elles ne sont en elles-mêmes.'

[2] Ed. Emiliani-Giudici, p. 253: 'E tali invenzioni non solo ne' poemi sono lodevoli, ma altresì necessarie per la novità e maraviglia che generano; con la quale eccitando l' attenzione, e traendo l' animo dalle terrene cose, lo sollevano sopra se stesso, sicchè si rende più libero e spedito da quei legami, co' quali la natura corporea avvolgendoci, ritarda il nostro volo verso la contemplazione del puro e dell' eterno; essendo questa una delle utilità alle quali è indirizzata la poesia, oltre il raro e nobil diletto che da lei piove.'

[3] Luzán, in introducing the Italian doctrines into Spain, clearly realised this, although he himself favoured 'icastic' imitation. Cp. his *Poética*, I, chap. ix, pp. 42 ff., and below, p. 223.

his elucidation of the simplicity, truth and freedom of the Greek tragic poets, were liberating factors of the first order. They not merely pointed out the way to reform in a literature committed to artificiality; but they also provided a basis for an attack on the mediaeval Aristotelianism which had reduced classic imitation in the seventeenth century to inanition. Gravina's attitude to Aristotelianism was a direct and inevitable corollary of his immersion in Cartesianism, but he makes it throughout clear that the object of his attack is not Aristotle, but his interpreters. He claimed no more than that freedom of judgment in dealing with the *Poetics*, which was so courageously vindicated by Castelvetro. It was unquestionably Gravina's greatest service to his time that he broke the shackles of the false Aristotelianism, which had been responsible for half the evils of the seventeenth century; and the beneficent effects of this liberation are to be seen in all his successors, in Muratori and Martelli, in Conti and Maffei. It is thus not too much to claim Gravina as the thinker who initiated that dominating movement of the later eighteenth century which, in northern Europe, aimed at setting a real classicism, drawn from a first-hand familiarity with the Greeks, in the place of the pseudo-classicism of the later Renaissance. This movement reached its clearest expression in Winckelmann and Lessing.

But Gravina carried his liberating efforts a step further: he demanded not only freedom from the letter of Aristotle, but also the logical consequence of that freedom, the right to interpret Aristotle according to modern needs, and the emancipation of modern literature from the necessity of slavishly imitating ancient models. He asserted, no doubt under the influence of Tassoni, the principle of the relative value of works of literature; the right of judging a poem by the ideals of its own and not of a later time[1]. Thus, although Gravina was by nature cut out to be an 'ancient,' we find him here definitely ranging himself on the side of the 'moderns.'

Apart from these general questions, what may be said on the relation of Gravina to his predecessors? We know of him as an indefatigable scholar whose reading in history and law, in classic

[1] Cp. Moffa, *op. cit.* p. 211.

and Italian literature, was extraordinarily wide. What share had that reading in moulding his aesthetic thought? In dealing with this question it must be borne in mind that his criticism of the *Endimione* appeared in 1692, and his *Delle antiche favole*, in which his fundamental aesthetic principles are already enunciated, in 1696. Now in 1696 not one of the Italian writers who are discussed in the present volume, had emerged into publicity. Crescimbeni's *Istoria della volgar Poesia* did not appear until two years later, and the names of Fontanini, Muratori and Maffei were not heard of until 1700; Orsi's refutation of Bouhours dates only from 1703. Thus Gravina could not be indebted to his Italian contemporaries: he was in advance of all of them.

As for the older writers, it is difficult to state precisely how far Gravina was influenced directly by them. His discussion of the 'new' and the 'marvellous' belongs to the general tradition of aesthetic writing from Longinus onwards; but Pallavicino had stated the doctrine in a form that suggests Gravina's indebtedness to him[1]. Again, Gravina stands in line with Fracastoro's dialogue *Naugerius* in demanding that poetry should express the universal, although Fracastoro arrives at his conclusion by a less direct form of argument[2]. It has already been suggested that Gravina was familiar with Tassoni; there is a further echo of that writer's theory in Gravina's juxtaposition of epics and romances[3], where, however, Gravina is far from sympathising with Tassoni's romantic leanings; but he endorses Tassoni's demand that poets should restrict themselves to the nebulous past which affords the imagination a wider scope than precisely known epochs of history. Gravina had been a close student of Castelvetro, of whom later he speaks with great respect; no doubt also of Tasso's treatise *Del poema eroico*[4], and of the theoretical writings of Trissino.

A more interesting question is as to how far the Gravina of the *Endimione* and the *Delle antiche favole* had taken cognizance of foreign writing on aesthetic questions. The possibility of his

[1] *Trattato dello Stile e del Dialogo*, Rome, 1662, chap. x.
[2] Cp. Conti's review of Gravina, *Prose e Poesie*, II, p. 249.
[3] *De' pensieri diversi*, Venice, 1646. Book IX.
[4] Cp. especially Book III, and Conti, II, p. 260.

having been influenced by Shaftesbury, which need never have been mooted, has been disposed of by Reich[1]: if there is any question of relationship, it was obviously the English writer who was indebted to the Italian; but there is no ground to infer even this. On the other hand, the French 'Quarrel between the Ancients and the Moderns' had been in full swing since 1688, when the first volume of Perrault's *Parallèle des Anciens et des Modernes* and Fontenelle's *Digression sur les Modernes* appeared. But, I doubt if, at this early date, Gravina was sufficiently in touch with the issues of the French controversy to take sides; and his sympathies appear to vary. Indeed, the only point where Gravina came into direct relations with the French Quarrel is in his defence of Homer. Apart from Le Bossu, whose work on the epic Gravina no doubt knew, the French controversy about Homer was a later affair; and instead of Gravina being the debtor here, he may rather have had some influence on French opinion.

In 1708 Gravina, as we have seen, enlarged his treatise on the *Ancient Fables* by adding a survey of Italian literature, and changing the title of the treatise to *Della Ragion poetica*. Crescimbeni and Muratori had led the way by basing the reform of Italian poetry on a study of its history: and there are some signs of indebtedness to Crescimbeni in his estimates of individual poets, and in his views on Provençal influence. To Muratori he owed his discussion, in the section on Dante, of the evolution of the 'volgar lingua' from Latin. His admiration of Dante is a repetition of what Muratori had said in a half-hearted and grudging spirit; but his astonishing eulogy of Trissino seems to be his own. The fact that he could afford, in a period when Tasso was the centre of the international quarrel, to speak so disinterestedly of that poet, and even a little ironically, emphasises that apartness in Gravina's standpoint, which led to his isolation. Gravina seems to have stood aside from the literary turmoil of the day—unless in the quarrel with his own Arcadia; but perhaps just this difference with the Arcadia and his defeat, when it came to a trial of strength, rendered Gravina less inclined to descend into the arena. He makes the

[1] *Op. cit.* pp. 15 f.

impression of being merely an onlooker in the world of letters; he did not regard Bouhours' attack on Tasso as impugning Italy's honour; and the *Ragion* reveals no trace of the tension that was in the air.

The book *Della Tragedia* of 1715 is another matter. Here Gravina does descend into the arena: it is definitely controversial in character, evoked in the first instance by the lack of favour with which his own tragedies had been received. Moreover, he does quote his authorities here; we have as abundant opportunities of discussing his 'sources,' as we had few in the case of his early writings. His championship of Castelvetro is more pronounced; he takes his part against Beni and Vettori on many particular points of Aristotelian interpretation; he knows Corneille, and, as we have seen, he quotes verbatim both Rapin and Dacier.

He had already written of the drama in his first essay, and more superficially in the *Ragion*. When the treatise of 1715 is compared with the views expressed in these earlier books, some changes of standpoint may be observed. The utilitarian purpose of tragedy is more definitely underlined; in the *Ragion poetica* he was still inclined towards the 'mediocre' hero; whereas here he demands the 'perfect' one, being possibly now influenced by the theory and practice of Corneille. Such changes were not for the better. The dependence upon Castelvetro is, however, more clearly marked; he accepts, as we have seen, that critic's interpretation of the 'purgation' of tragedy; and he defends the Castelvetrian unities.

Taken as a whole, and accepting Gravina's standpoint, this little book is not at all an unreasonable treatise on tragedy. His ideal is the simplicity of the Greeks; he demands an antique theme, mythical, or better, historical; but it must not be complicated; the characters must be 'true,' that is, 'verisimilar'; and the work must contain 'instruction' of a moral or civic character. On the whole, Gravina's doctrine is a healthy and reasonable antidote to the artificiality of the Marinistic age, pointing in the direction of common sense and realism: and as such, it may, I think, well be looked upon as a justification of the new type of drama represented by Conti's tragedies, and even of Maffei's *Merope* itself; he was a pioneer—as Martelli in another way—of the European tragedy of philosophical and political ideals which culminated in Voltaire and Alfieri[1]. It is more difficult to explain the relations of the treatise to Gravina's own tragedies, in defence of which it was written. For his theory is very much superior to his practice: Gravina the poet sins grievously against the precepts of Gravina the critic. It is true, his plots are reasonably simple, his characters are either highly virtuous or highly vicious, and he provides moral and civic instruction. But he, no more than any of the other theorists who declaimed against love in tragedy, is able to dispense with it: there are love-plots—attenuated, it is true—in three of his. His ideas of correct milieu and character fall a long way short of the theoretic demands of his treatise. It is thus sheer lack of poetic talent that is responsible for Gravina's failure as a dramatist; the best of theories is no surrogate for inspiration.

A more interesting side of the book of Tragedy is its controversial side. A number of sections bear the heading 'Contro i moderni tragici': but in spite of Gravina's own assertion to the contrary[2], it is difficult to see that he has more modern poets in view than the authors of the *Pastor fido* and *Aminta*, or indeed any other type of drama than the pastoral. If his attack is also directed against Corneille and Racine, it is certainly so veiled as to be unrecognisable, unless in the direct quotations from Rapin and Dacier at the close. Here, again, Gravina seems to me to stand strangely apart from the turmoil and controversy of his time. One might at least have expected —if Martelli's own assertion of Gravina's hostility to him is to be believed—that he would enter into direct polemic against Martelli's dialogue on Tragedy which had appeared two years before, and that Martelli would have been one of the 'moderni tragici' against whom he rails. But beyond the conflict of

[1] Cp. Galletti, *Le Teorie drammatiche e la Tragedia in Italia nel sec. XVIII*, Cremona, 1901, pp. 157 ff., and Moffa, p. 310, who refers to a study by himself, *Raffronto tra il Gravina e Scipione Maffei*, Pozzuoli, 1900, which I have not seen.

[2] Cp. the letter to Maffei in the latter's *Teatro*, ed. by Becelli (Verona, 1730; Discorso prelim. p. ix): 'Nel Trattato, che io già finito *della tragedia*, in lingua volgare, assalisco gli errori comuni e teatrali, particolarmente quelli che nascono delle Tragedie Francesi, benchè ne taccia il nome.'

opinion on the question of the verse most suitable to tragedy, where Muratori differed from him as well as Martelli, I am unable to discover any serious controversy. On the contrary, Gravina and Martelli work to a great extent towards a common end, namely, liberation from the fetters of the Aristotelians.

Croce has made the remark that the best of Gravina's books is their programme[1]. There is some truth in this; the opening of the *Ragion poetica* arouses expectations which the work can hardly be said to satisfy, and every reader feels a certain disappointment when the treatise so soon resolves itself into a collection of detached estimates of Greek, Latin and Italian poets; and its conclusion—which Reich shrewdly thinks may have been a *captatio benevolentiae* addressed to the ecclesiastical powers[2]—where Gravina implies that the supreme glory of poetry is the improvement of the art of eloquence, is a sad descent. Nay more, it would be difficult to say what, after all, is the 'ragione poetica' which Gravina went forth to seek. Does it not rather turn out to be a kind of 'blue flower' which he never succeeds in finding at all? Or perhaps one might say that the value of Gravina's book is rather the consciousness which pervades it that there is such a 'ragione.' No one before Gravina seems to me to have felt as he did the need of such an 'idea.' That need became an insistent demand under the stimulus of the Cartesian metaphysics: and from Gravina and Conti through Du Bos and Batteux, down to Kant and Schiller, the whole aesthetics of the eighteenth century lays itself out to satisfy this demand, to discover a 'ragione poetica' of imaginative creation, to formulate a definition of the beautiful. Here Gravina is clearly a pioneer.

[1] B. Croce, *Di alcuni giudizi sul Gravina come estetico*, p. 458 (*Problemi di Estetica*, Bari, 1910, p. 362).
[2] E. Reich, *op. cit.* p. 66.

Chapter III

Lodovico Antonio Muratori

It is hardly surprising that the life and work of Muratori should not, so far, have tempted any modern scholar to make them the theme of an exhaustive monograph. His single-minded devotion to erudition, can only be monotonous in the telling; and the immensity of his labours and the voluminousness of his writings must necessarily make an intending student pause before embarking on so formidable a task. Any account of Muratori has to be based on the biography by his nephew, Gian Francesco Soli Muratori, which, however, beyond its value as a record of facts, is little more than an unrelieved eulogy. Subsequent lives and studies[1] have carried us little further. Indeed, the one important publication of recent years is the monumental edition of Muratori's Correspondence[2], which provides a veritable panorama of the learned Italy of his time. In the present volume I am fortunate in being only concerned with one side, and a comparatively unvoluminous side of Muratori's activity, his contribution to literary aesthetics. But the importance of this contribution is still—even in Italy—far from adequately realised.

I

Lodovico Antonio Muratori was born of poor parents on October 21, 1672, in the picturesque little town of Vignola, in the Duchy of Modena, some twelve miles to the south of that town. He had hardly learned to read, when the romances of Mlle de Scudéry fell into his hands; and these he devoured with insatiable appetite. This was the beginning of his love of reading. His early schooling took place in his native place, but the unpractical scholastic methods of the old grammarians

[1] *Vita di L. A. Muratori*, descritta da G. F. Soli Muratori, Venice, 1756; further P. Schedoni, *Elogio di L. A Muratori*, Modena, 1818; Tiraboschi, *Biblioteca Modenese*, III and VI; E. di Tipaldo, *Biografie degli Italiani illustri*, VII, Venice, 1840, pp. 1 ff.; S. Brigidi, *Vita di L. A. Muratori*, Florence, 1871.

[2] *Epistolario di L. A. Muratori*, ed. da M. Campori, 12 vols. Modena, 1901–11.

made the Latin grammar neither easy nor attractive to the child. In the autumn of 1685 he was sent to a Jesuit school in Modena, where he made rapid progress. Here he acquired that habit, which remained a dominant one throughout his life, of utilising his time to the last minute. It had been his desire from his earliest years to enter the Church. He was, however, an only son—he had three sisters—and his father was opposed to such a career: but he appears to have been allowed to have his way; and on January 17, 1688, he received his first tonsure from the Bishop of Modena. He threw himself with ardour into his profession, and remained, all his life long, in spite of the fact that his indifferent voice stood in his way as an officiating priest, a good and faithful servant of the Church. He spent three years in the lower schools of the Jesuit fathers, then passed, in 1689, to the public courses in logic. He was extraordinarily industrious, even transcribing books which he could not afford to buy. He devoted much attention to philosophy, in which subject he appears to have gone further afield than was usual in Italian monasteries; and he brought his studies to a brilliant close with a public 'conclusione' on February 4, 1692. Meanwhile, under pressure from his father, he turned his attention to the study and practice of law: and had the benefit of the guidance of Nicolò Santi, Secretary of State to the Duke, and a jurisconsult of some repute. But he soon grew tired both of law and philosophy, and felt the need of a firmer basis of facts than these studies afforded; he was weary, as he said, of repeating merely what others had said.

Literature, no doubt, made a stronger appeal to him, and he spent his leisure in reading poetry and books on poetics. His own tastes here were naturally still those of his time; he shared his contemporaries' love of conceits and 'sentences'; he placed Tesauro, the author of the *Cannochiale Aristotelico*, above all other theoretical writers, whereas he found Petrarch 'dry' and the Petrarchists drier. He, of course, wrote verses, Latin and Italian—the earliest dating from the autumn of 1689—which were the occasion of his being made an associate of the Accademia degli Accesi in Bologna in 1692. His introduction to the poetry of Maggi and Lemene, however, suddenly opened up new horizons: the full tones and vigour of the former, the wide sweep of the latter, taught him to see the vanity and affectation of the 'secentists,' who had hitherto captivated his taste. That he should have found satisfaction in these poets shows from what depths he must have risen. He saw the necessity of acquiring a balanced literary judgment, and devoted himself to the study of the Latin poets, and—in translation—of the Greeks. Quintilian and Libanius were guides to him in his darkness; and even more helpful was the influence of the philosopher Seneca. The Stoic philosophy made a particular appeal to him, and he prosecuted his study of it in Epictetus and Arrian. We know little of the spiritual life of Muratori—even from his more intimate letters, which are strangely impersonal—but from his nephew's words it may be inferred that he found in this philosophy a panacea for many of the ills of life.

But he felt the need of still further extending and deepening his studies; he saw that a knowledge of Greek was indispensable, and he threw himself into it with characteristic energy. In his excursions into ancient erudition he found a helpful master in the learned librarian of the Duke of Modena, Benedetto Bacchini; and ultimately he abandoned the study of law and theology, to devote himself to history and letters. In Modena he had made an acquaintance which was even more important for his future career than Bacchini's, namely, that of the Marchese Orsi who, some years later, was, with his *Considerazioni*, to make so effective a stand against the aspersions of Bouhours. And possibly it was through Orsi that he received, in 1694, an invitation from the Conte Carlo Borromeo to become one of the 'dottori' or librarians of the famous Ambrosian Library in Milan. Several learned dissertations written about this time—one, *De Graecae Linguae usu et praestantia*, the outcome of his study of Greek—had no doubt commended him for this post; and in December, 1694, he received his doctor's degree from the University of Modena.

In Milan, where he settled in February, 1695, he devoted himself with enormous zeal to his new duties, turning especially to the manuscripts of the famous library; the result was two volumes of *Anecdota Latina* (1697, 1698), which gave him a rapidly growing reputation throughout Italy and beyond. His correspondents increased and included Mabillon and Montfaucon—who visited Milan in 1698—in France, and Mencke in Germany; while his labours were lightened by pleasant summer holidays in the Borromean Islands. In spite of the attractions of erudition, he did not, however, lose touch with his own time; and one of the first new acquaintances he made in Milan was that of the poet Carlo Maria Maggi. When Maggi died in 1699, Muratori resolved to repay the debt he owed him for having opened his eyes to a chaster poetic taste, by editing his poetry and writing his life. This, Muratori's first contribution to the criticism of his own literature, appeared in five little volumes in 1700. The *Vita del Maggi* is, however, more a tribute to a dear friend—'Io l' amai teneramente in vita,' he says of him, 'e l' amerò eternamente ancor morto'—than a reasoned piece of literary criticism; he is visibly overawed by Maggi's 'sublime ingegno' and 'vasta mente,' and does not hesitate to extol him as a pioneer of the human spirit comparable to Columbus, Amerigo Vespucci and Ferdinand Cortes![1] At a later date, when confronted with his friend Zeno's criticism and Maffei's more sober estimate, he admitted that he had allowed his personal affection for the man to warp his judgment of him as a poet[2].

And now came the great crisis in life, the only crisis. The Duke of Modena invited him to return to Modena at the same salary which he was receiving in Milan, in the capacity of 'archivista,' the archives in Modena being in a sad state of confusion and disorder. The decision was doubtless a difficult one for Muratori. On the one side, there was the appeal to his patriotism; on the other, he had to give up a congenial post and an incomparable field of scholarly activity. His many friends in Milan, especially Orsi, counselled against his accepting

[1] *Vita del Maggi*, Modena, pp. 2, 91, 109, 111. Maggi—'lo splendor di Milano, il savio Maggi,' as Redi called him—has, however, more merit than modern literary historians admit. Cp. A. Cipollini, *L' Opere di C. M. Maggi*, Milan, 1900.

[2] Cp. Muratori's letter to Zeno, who had taken him to task for his unmeasured eulogy, of September 12, 1710 (*Epistolario*, III, Modena, 1902, pp. 1197 ff.); also the brief *Vita del Maggi* which Muratori wrote for the *Vite degli Arcadi*, I, Venice, 1708, pp. 79 ff.

the invitation; but in addition to patriotic motives, family reasons urged his return: his father had just died, and his three sisters fell to his charge. So he finally accepted, but on the condition that he should have six months to finish the work on which he was engaged in Milan, amongst other things, to complete his edition of Maggi, and also that he should have the title not merely of 'archivista,' but also of 'bibliotecario.'

In August, 1700, he returned to Modena, where it took him some two years to put the Ducal Archives in order, a good deal of his work being undone by the invasion of Lombardy by the French in 1702. That invasion, moreover, suspended his own scholarly activity. He devoted his leisure to a treatise on Italian poetry, *Della Perfetta Poesia italiana*, which appeared in 1706. I discuss this work—his chief contribution to aesthetics—in the following section.

His main activity as a literary critic and theorist of literature lies between 1700, when he wrote the life of Maggi, and 1708, an activity which, as we have seen, was closely bound up with that of his friend and patron, the Marchese Orsi. Muratori had entered the lists as a defender of Orsi, with the letter published in 1707, and with others which purported to come from a certain 'Antonio Lampridi.' With the same object of furthering the rehabilitation of Italian literary taste he conceived the ambitious design, evidently intended to supersede the organisation of the Arcadia, of a Literary Republic of Italy. This is the theme of *I primi Disegni della Repubblica letteraria d' Italia*, which he published in 1703 under a new pseudonym, 'Lamindo Pritanio'—the first three letters of this pseudonym, as of his former one, 'Lampridi,' being, it will be noticed, his own initials. His proposals created a great stir in Italy, and the hierarchy he suggested caused much heart-burning among scholars and men of letters, who believed that they did not, or would not, receive their due. The pseudonymity was carefully concealed, and Muratori enjoyed for a time the situation of unsuspected onlooker. In the end, however, nothing came of his boldly conceived republic. Perhaps instinctively Italy felt that she had had enough of schemes for creating a national literature by collective agencies.

To further his 'Republic' Muratori wrote, still as 'Pritanio,' his *Riflessioni sopra il Buon Gusto nelle scienze e nell' arti*, which was intended—it had been planned as far back as 1701—to facilitate for the younger generation the acquisition of that good taste, which he had himself only attained by long study. The first volume of these *Riflessioni* was published by the Venetian philosopher Trevisano, to whom they were also at first attributed, in 1708: and the second, together with a reprint of the first, in 1715 at 'Colonia,' actually Naples. In 1709 appeared his *Anecdota Graeca*, in which verses of St Gregory of Nazianzus and letters of Julian the Apostate, discovered by Muratori, were published.

Muratori's interest in literary aesthetics from now on gradually slackened, and he devoted himself more and more to purely erudite and editorial labours. Fruits of these were the compilations, *Antichità Estensi* (1717–40), in which, with patriotic zeal, he investigated and unearthed documents bearing on the history of the Ducal house; the monumental *Rerum Italicarum Scriptores*, in twenty-seven volumes (1723–51), a collection of chronicles bearing on Italian history from the fifth to the fifteenth century, and the *Annali d' Italia dal principio dell' era Cristiana sino al anno* 1500, in twelve volumes (1744–9)—to which the *Antichità italiche* are supplementary—a still more laborious compilation, covering geography as well as history, and even enumerating subjects suitable for dramatic treatment by the poets of Italy. Such work, it must be confessed, was in the main mechanical, and consisted in the careful copying of manuscripts and documents; but it could only be achieved by the most extraordinary and self-sacrificing industry. He produced, for instance, the bulk of his *Annali d' Italia* within a single year, a work, which, as one of Muratori's critics observes[1], no one has ever perhaps succeeded in reading in a single year!

In his later years he turned to philosophy, the predominant note in his own thought being antagonism to Locke and the French sensualists. Against Locke he wrote *La Filosofia morale*

[1] C. Belviglieri, *La Vita, le opere, i tempi di L. A. Muratori*, in *Scritti storici*, Verona, 1881, p. 161.

esposata e proposta ai giovani (1735)[1], and, ten years later, his *Delle Forze dell' intendimento umano, o sia il Pirronismo confutato*, a defence of human reason—in which he clearly owed something to Descartes—against Daniel Huet's *Traité philosophique de la Foiblesse de l' Esprit humain*, translated into Italian in 1724. In 1745 appeared also the supplementary work, *Della Forza della Fantasia umana.* This treatise, from the title of which one might infer a contribution to the great controversy concerning the function of the imagination in poetry, which forms the crux of eighteenth-century aesthetics, is disappointing. Muratori did not retrace his steps, and did not resume his early aesthetic studies; he keeps here mainly to psychological questions, and, ignoring the aesthetically productive side of the imagination, endeavours to define its nature and functions as an activity of the brain. He discusses its manifestations in visions and dreams—not forgetting God's use of dreams for the purpose of revealing his will to man—of somnambulism and madness, of magic. But of the function of the imagination as a motive force, not to say *the* motive force in poetry, there is nothing[2]. The pages devoted to this subject in the *Perfetta Poesia italiana*, of nearly forty years earlier, are much more important from the point of view of aesthetics.

For fifty years of an uneventful life Muratori was his Duke's librarian, attending meanwhile faithfully and conscientiously to his ecclesiastical duties as 'proposto,' and dispensing charity. He read and wrote incessantly; but he enjoyed, on the whole, robust health. He had an extraordinarily tenacious memory and mapped out his daily life with the most punctilious and pedantic care, that no moment might be wasted. He himself says: 'Making good use of my time has been the secret of composing my books; and if any one else, endowed by God with like talent and health, and provided, as I have been, with the necessary means of studying, will make the same good use of his time, it will be possible for him to achieve just as much.'[3]

[1] Cp. Maugain, pp. 224 ff.

[2] Cp. L. Ambrosi, *La psicologia della immaginazione nella storia della filosofia*, Rome, 1898, pp. 127 ff.

[3] Soli Muratori, *op. cit.* cap. x (ed. of 1758, p. 157).

As Muratori advanced in years, honours were heaped upon him, and princes sought his friendship; but nothing changed the unassuming modesty and simplicity of his life. It was occasionally disturbed, it is true, by controversies; but none of these in later life was as violent and embittered as that stirred up by the tract *De Ingeniorum moderatione in religionis negotio*, published at Paris in 1714. This even brought upon him an accusation of atheism, although the warm admiration of Pope Benedict XIV was surely a guarantee that such a charge was groundless. But controversy was of the day's work to the eighteenth-century scholar: and, on the whole, Muratori's life may be said to have been relatively smooth and unruffled. The passing of the years was marked only by the making and publication of books. He died in his seventy-seventh year, on January 23, 1750.

II

Muratori's treatise, *Della Perfetta Poesia italiana*, was directly instigated by the attack of the Père Bouhours on the honour of Italy. Its beginnings may be followed as far back as January, 1699, when Muratori wrote to Apostolo Zeno that he was 'ruminating on a work dealing with Italian poetry and language'[1]; and no doubt his defence of Maggi against the French strictures passed on that poet, encouraged the idea[2]. On July 15, 1701, Muratori wrote quite definitely to Zeno:

> I am now working at this plan of mine in the matter of belles-lettres, which I have mentioned to you, being desirous of committing this folly before I turn to my real work. I should like to show what is good taste in Italian poetry, and perhaps I will eventually give my work a proud title, such as *La Riforma della poesia italiana*, or something similar, my object being, not merely to praise and defend, but also to correct our defects for the benefit of the young and posterity. In this connection I am examining the French Parnassus, and perhaps I shall repay, but without impertinence, the impertinences that have been said about us[3].

[1] *Epistolario*, II, Modena, 1901, p. 369. Zeno had himself planned a *Storia de' Poeti italiani*; see below, p. 148.

[2] Cp. *Vita del Maggi*, p. 173, and above, p. 12.

[3] *Epistolario*, II, p. 516.

And Zeno, in his reply of July 23, heartily approved of Muratori's plan:

I confess that I am less touched by your courtesy in imparting to me the idea of your work, than by the pleasure it gives me. *La Riforma della poesia italiana*—a title which you must not regard as arrogant, for great abuses call for more than modest remedies—on which you are engaged, will be a book worthy of you and most useful to everybody. It appeals wholly to my taste, particularly in respect of criticism, which is the most popular study of our day and perhaps the most fruitful. The French are deserving of your lash: Rapin, Bouhours, Saint-Évremond and others have taken too much liberty in setting themselves up as tribunal to judge our authors and our literature, which—to speak without bias—they, for the most part, comprehend little or badly.... Their lyric and epic poets are very inferior compared with ours. For their comic and tragic dramatists, for Molière, Corneille, Racine, I have some respect....[1]

Muratori's original intention was thus to call his treatise *Della Riforma della Poesia italiana*; but exception was taken to the word 'riforma' by some of his friends, as being likely to give offence to contemporary poets[2]; and the title ultimately decided upon was *Della Perfetta Poesia italiana*[3]. It appeared in two volumes at Modena in 1706, that is to say, three years after Orsi's *Considerazioni* on Bouhours' *Manière de bien penser*. The work is long, but it is unavoidable, if I am to justify the claims I would make for Muratori in eighteenth-century literary aesthetics, to describe it in some detail.

The keynote of the book is struck at the outset. There is something divine about poetry: to heaven itself it owes its thoughts. Its noblest function is not, as Gravina would have it, to sugar-coat the pill of wisdom, but 'to dispense the immortal patrimony of glory': the poets render great deeds immortal. Muratori's aim, however (chap. ii), is similar to Gravina's: he will supply men with the means of rightly judging literature, help them to acquire good taste; and this, keeping in view the

[1] A. Zeno, *Lettere*, Venice, 1785, II, pp. 111 f. (quoted in part by Maugain, *op. cit.* p. 255).

[2] *Epistolario*, II, pp. 690, 695 f., 704.

[3] *Della Perfetta Poesia Italiana*, spiegata e dimostrata con varie osservazioni, da L. A. Muratori, Modena, 1706; an edition with notes by A. M. Salvini appeared at Venice in 1724. I have used the reprint of the latter in the series *Classici Italiani*, 4 vols., Milan, 1821.

needs and standards of modern Italian poetry; in other words, he will supplement the fragmentary poetics of the ancients with a treatise representing the modern standpoint. His work is practical, not the compilation of an erudite, and he professes to teach by example. In chapter iii he frankly states that he has been induced to write his treatise in consequence of the contemptuous attitude which French writers like Bouhours, Rapin, Fontenelle, Baillet and Saint-Évremond have taken up to Italian poetry. They had forgotten that bad taste was a universal disease of European literature; they did not see that an improvement had already set in in Italy as well as in France. Muratori's object is thus, by demonstrating what is 'good taste,' to assist the Arcadians in counteracting the 'secentistic' in literature. He then proceeds to give in outline the history of Italian poetry, looking back on the sixteenth century as a kind of golden age, but also hoping that the new Arcadia will make amends for the decadence of the seventeenth. Muratori quotes, it may be noted, unpublished manuscripts—in such things lay his own peculiar glory—and pleads generally for wider scope in the study of literature.

In his fourth chapter he defines the place of poetry in the sphere of intellectual activity; and he leaves no room for ambiguity on this point. 'Poetry is the daughter and servant of moral philosophy, but a less austere daughter than history, and a more pleasing one than rhetoric.' The purpose of poetry from the earliest times has been—and still is—to sing the praises of virtue and the virtuous, and to censure vice and the vicious, in order that people may learn to love the former and hate the latter.

Having laid down this first principle, Muratori now proceeds to examine more closely the 'utile et dulce' maxim, and seems disposed to separate the two functions of the poet. 'In so far as poetry is an imitative art, it has for its end delight; in so far as it is subordinate to moral and political philosophy, its end is to be useful.' This separation of the functions allows, as will be seen, Muratori considerable latitude in considering poetry as poetry. From poetry regarded in itself one seeks delight and delight only; regarded as an art, subject to the 'civic faculty,' it must be useful. Thus, in discussing the reform of poetry, he is able to distinguish between the defects of a poet as such, and his defects as a member of society.

Next comes (chap. v) the all-important question as to what constitutes 'il buon gusto,' good taste, an idea which as Galletti observes[1], Muratori first made familiar to the Italians. This 'good taste' is the power to understand and distinguish the good and the beautiful in poetical composition, as well as in all other sciences, arts and human actions[2]. Muratori suggests a division into 'fecund' good taste, which assists in the creation of works of art, and 'sterile' good taste, by which we merely form judgments on the objects of good taste; or again, into a universal good taste and a particular good taste. The universal good taste is the idea—the 'ragione' as Gravina would have said—of the beautiful, the comprehensive idea which includes all the manifold and changing 'particular' good tastes. It is to arrive at this 'ragione' of the beautiful that Muratori aspires in his present treatise. Good taste, then, consists in respect of poetry (chap. vi), in knowing, distinguishing and appreciating the poetically beautiful; that is to say, it is the ability to judge, in practice as in theory, what is beautiful and what is ugly. But what is beautiful? It is 'that which, when seen, heard or understood, pleases us and excites within us a pleasurable sensation and a love for the cause of this sensation.'

We have to distinguish between 'corporeal' beautiful things and 'incorporeal.' The latter admit of a further division into beautiful things founded principally on the true, and beautiful things founded principally on the good. The beauty of moral virtues is, for instance, founded on the good; this good is

[1] A. Galletti, *Le Teorie drammatiche e la Tragedia in Italia nel secolo XVIII*, Cremona, 1901, p. 20. But Muratori was not without predecessors in Italy. See below, p. 89.

[2] Muratori subsequently elaborated his speculations on the meaning and range of 'good taste' in his *Riflessioni sopra il buon gusto*, written in support of his 'Literary Republic,' and published anonymously in 1708. But it is difficult to see that this inordinately diffuse treatise adds anything essential —at least as far as literary aesthetics is concerned—to the summary statement of the *Perfetta Poesia*. He defines 'good taste' in his later treatise, p. 115: 'Noi per buon Gusto intendiamo il conoscere ed il poter giudicare ciò che sia difettoso, o imperfetto, o mediocre nelle Scienze, e nell' Arti, per guardarsene e ciò che sia il meglio, e il perfetto, per seguirlo a tutto potere.'

clothed with a beauty apprehended by the intellect, and it delights man's moral sense. On the other hand, the beauty of the speculative sciences is founded on the true, and appeals only to the intellect. It must be borne in mind that the true and the good are the two ultimate ends towards which the desires of our intellect and our will strive. The highest end, the vision of God, is perfect beatitude, supreme truth combined with supreme beauty. Just as, in order to preserve life, Nature gives us the desire for food, so the beautiful is the savour of the good and true. But owing to the fall of our first parents in Eden, we are unable to find pleasure in the greatest truths and the greatest beauty; we appreciate only minor ones.

Muratori now studies more particularly the form of beauty founded principally on the true—that is, the beauty which delights our intellect and constitutes poetic beauty. What is the essential and inherent nature of poetic beauty? How does it arise, and how does it differ from the beauty of other forms of truth? Our intellect naturally seeks the true and abhors the false. Two factors, however, may interfere with the search: the intellect may be corrupt and not well regulated, or the truth may be of such a nature as to repel us. Now the beautiful which delights or moves the intellect is the resplendent and attractive aspect of the true, which expels ignorance and causes us pleasure. It may consist in the clearness, brevity, energy, probability, magnificence, etc., with which this truth is represented to our intellect, but not in obscurity, such as is to be found in the poetry of Marini. This 'internal' truth, which forms the essential beauty of poetry, has nothing to do with the senses; Muratori expressly excludes, for instance, the harmony and music of verse, which he regards as a superficial ornament. The distinction is somewhat fine, and also a rather questionable one. One feels that, after all, Muratori's criterion is rather that of utility than aesthetic effect.

Of the three noble arts which appeal to the intellect, it may be said that rhetoric persuades us of the truth, history describes the truth, and poetry tells us what might probably or possibly, be true. It is inherent in human nature that our intellect can only take pleasure in the cognition of the true, or the semblance of the true; but if truth in poetry is to delight, it must be beautiful and not ugly. Thus delight is produced by poetic beauty founded on the true. But as poetry must be of utility to us, as well as afford delight, the definition should be completed by adding that delight is caused by the good as well as by the true.

Poetic truth is to be found in three worlds: the celestial, the human, and the material world. The celestial or superior world comprises things spiritual, *i.e.* the first Cause, the angels, the soul. The third, or inferior world includes all that is formed of matter, while the middle world participates in both the first and the third. These three worlds contain an infinite variety of truths, which may all be the subject of poetry, although the domain of the latter is mainly the middle world. Theology is limited to the highest, mathematics and physics to the lowest, moral philosophy to the middle world.

Thus poetry is distinguished from the sciences by the vastness of its field and by its purpose. Scientists study the true in order to know it; poets in order to depict it and imitate it. The function of poetry is to clothe the true with images, express it by means of sentiments and words, so that the intellect, with the help of the imagination, may grasp it without difficulty and with pleasure. The painter appeals to the external eye, the poet to the internal eye; the former is restricted to the material world, the latter may move in all three. Thus the essence of poetry is to depict; it is consequently an art, not a science. Poetry, again, is distinguished from rhetoric and history, in so far as rhetoric depicts the true, in order to persuade; history describes it as it is, with a view to instruction and utility; whereas poetry represents the true as it is, or ought to be; further, it does so purely with the purpose of depicting, of imitating and causing by that imitation delight, of filling men's imaginations with beautiful, strange and marvellous things.

The end of poetry is thus (chap. vii), in so far as it is a creative art, to delight by means of imitation. Now there are two ways of delighting: either by means of the things imitated, or by the manner of imitating them. In other words, the poet may cause pleasure, either because the things he imitates are new and marvellous in themselves, or because they become so in his hands. Not every truth, but only new and marvellous truths have this power of giving pleasure; common, trivial truths, already familiar, cannot please. Novelty is the mother of marvel, and marvel the mother of delight. The poet has thus two instruments at his disposal: he may either select new and marvellous things to imitate, or he may imitate familiar things in a new and marvellous way. Best of all is a combination of both methods.

If a poet succeeds in filling his verses with novelty, rarity and marvellousness of subject or execution, or of both, he attains what Longinus called the sublime, which is nothing else than the rare and the marvellous. How are such rare and marvellous subjects found, or by what artifice may subjects be made so? The two powers which exercise this function are the 'intellect' and 'imagination'; they are the dispensers of novelty, marvel and delight. Here, in the possession of these faculties, lies the perfection of poets. A vast and acute intellect and a clear, alert and fecund imagination, are the two powers which, in alliance, guide us by different ways, to make our poetic compositions admirable, and with our inventions to enchant the souls of hearers and readers. Happy is the poet who is liberally supplied by nature with them! But happier is he who combines with a great and philosophic mind and a fertile, vivacious imagination a well-balanced and purified judgment! Judgment is the compass whereby spiritual voyagers are guided.

Muratori now turns to consider these three faculties of the soul on which the poetic function depends. Chapter viii deals with the beautiful of material things. It is the poet's function to extract from matter truths little observed by others and never directly presented to our senses by nature. The poet must consequently—if he will awaken wonder and delight—present the objects of the three worlds, not as they ordinarily are, but as they may be, or ought, in a perfect form, to be. The poet, as opposed to the historian, who chronicles things as they are, has to discover, by means of his imagination, the 'eminent' truths of nature; he is the gardener who perfects the flowers. And this process of perfecting, improving on nature, can be carried out in all the four 'parts' of poetry distinguished by Aristotle: in the fable, the manners, the sentiments and the diction.

But this involves us in what, at first sight, seems a paradox (chap. ix). The foundation of poetic beauty is, we are told, the true; but it is the traditional mission of poets to get as far away from the truth as they can, to invent fables, that is, lies. Truth is of two kinds: the truth that is or has been, and the truth which has probably been, might be, or must be according to nature's laws. The first truth is the object of the scientist and the historian, the second the chief theme of the poets. The one is necessary truth, the other verisimilar truth; and the latter brings us as much pleasure as the former. Pallavicino's argument that the only justification for poetry is that it supplies the intellect with sumptuous images, without considering whether they are false or true, is not in accordance with facts. The mind and the imagination may, it is true, outstep the boundaries of the poetically beautiful; they may draw upon the inherently false, or lapse into affectation; but the judgment promptly comes to their assistance and effectually prevents such excesses. If Pallavicino were right, Muratori continues, poets would rush to the extreme of exaggeration, and pay no heed to truth of expression, whereas the highest poetry appeals to the reflecting intellect, and teaches some truth, which has either existed or could possibly exist. After all, the chief thing in poetry is the thought which the poet will express, the image he will conjure up. The external beauty of form in a poet is merely accessory. This was the cardinal fault of Marini and his school; they aimed at beauty of form and neglected the contents.

In his tenth chapter Muratori dealt with the question of the mingling of history and fiction in epic and tragedy. It is the duty of the imitator, who wishes to delight and move, to present objects as nature herself would present them; the more convincing and exact the imitation, the greater the pleasure we receive. There is no need for the poet to base his imitation on actual facts, as far as the pleasure is concerned; and he might equally well spare himself the trouble of seeking out some obscure theme from antiquity. At the same time, epics and tragedies founded on history are more pleasing and admirable than those merely invented. Well-known names, as Aristotle says, render wonderful events more credible, and they also make it easier for the audience to grasp the matter at once. The poet has a certain licence to invent; but he must not contradict established opinions familiar to us from history, such as by making Caesar kill himself. This would be offending against what his audience regards as probable. Existing truths must not be warped; it is in the silent gaps of history that the fictitious may be built up. The writer of comedies, on the other hand, is recommended to invent entirely; he is not concerned with historical truth. Although the poets are thus the inventors of thousands of lies, they do not deceive. It may be wrong to say that what they pretend has happened ever did happen; but it is true that under the given circumstances it might or must have happened; and it is this latter truth of which the poets wish to persuade us.

To fall back on Aristotle's distinction, truth in the three worlds is either universal or particular. The idea of the 'strong man,' for example, is 'universal'; but if we specify Alexander the Great as the strong man, this is a 'particular' idea. The universal truth embraces what is possibly and credibly true; the particular truth is that actually presented to us by nature. Now, the difference between history and poetry is that history describes only the particular truth; while poetry sets out in search of the universal truth and endeavours to reach it, either by taking a particular truth and deducing a universal truth from it, or, proceeding from the universal truth, it endeavours to discover a particular truth in which to embody it. The poet depicts some personage, or some quality, such as disdain, love, generosity, but he does not keep to particular facts, as these are recorded by the historian; he rises to a universal point of view and tries to bring out strange and marvellous aspects which others have not observed. This creative function of the poet is usually called 'inventing'; and it is the special glory of the poet that he is, in this respect, different from the historian. Thus, in describing the taking of Troy, the poet, rising from the particular to the general, must select a method of conquering a city which will appear wonderful and new. He must then descend again to the particular, and describe how the conquest might and could happen. This is 'perfecting nature'—'far eminente la natura,' as Muratori says elsewhere—and gives great delight[1].

The conclusion (chap. xi) which has, so far, been arrived at, is that the function of poetry is to conjure up before our imagination sumptuous, new, noble and wonderful images. But this is not enough. The intellect and judgment must also find some truth in poetry; whether this be real and certain, or merely possible and credible, does not matter. It must be possible to obtain knowledge with pleasure from poetry; and although it may not be practicable to imbue real truth with sufficient marvellousness to give pleasure, it is the business of the poet to seek out possible or verisimilar truth. On the other hand, if he represents things which are clearly false or improbable, he fails, for such things cannot give pleasure to the intellect.

But what truth, it may be asked, whether real or verisimilar, is there in romantic fictions, where things are narrated which never were or never could be in nature, for instance, where trees speak, and the like? To meet this difficulty, Muratori distinguishes between two modes of expressing real or possible truths: one by using purely intellectual images, *i.e.* images such as the intellect directly recognises; the other by dressing up the truth in fantastic images, which the intellect can only apprehend indirectly. For example, a poet may state the simple truth that a poor man is raised to a throne, or he may put it fantastically and say that Fortune became enamoured of the poor man and raised him to the throne.

There is no doubt that the romances contain much that appears improbable to a cultured intellect, such as hippogryphs, enchanted lances and the like; but these poems please and delight. Ariosto will always live in the affection of the world. So Muratori finds it necessary to distinguish between 'popular' verisimilitude and 'noble' verisimilitude. In the noble or higher type, human actions or happenings are brought about by purely human means, without miracles or supernatural aid. The epic poet who introduces beings from the celestial or the lower

[1] One might compare Pallavicino's definition of the end of poetry, *Del Bene*, III, capo 51: 'il far immaginar vivamente oggetti maravigliosi, a ragion si vale di quelle rappresentate minuzie le quali rendono il racconto più che si può, simile al vero.'

world is guilty of making a concession to the unintellectual crowd; and the romances are lacking in nobility. But even Homer makes such concessions; and Muratori has no hesitation in censuring the Greek poet's excessive recourse to divine intervention in human affairs. At the same time, the poetic fantasy cannot be put entirely in chains; poetry does not appeal only to the learned, and the poets must employ popular means to awaken wonder in the people. Thus his conclusion is that, while the use of irrational supernaturalism is not altogether to be avoided, the poet should be as sparing as possible of it; and it should be particularly eschewed in dramatic poetry.

There is, however (chap. xii), one case where fantastic conflicts with the truth are acceptable to the intellect, and permissible; that is, where they are intended to cause laughter. The pleasure we derive from such fantastic extravagances is due to the fact that they are put forward in such a form that the intention of the poet is at once recognisable by the intellect. If, however, the poet puts the impossible and improbable into his poem without being sure that we shall grasp his purpose, then he only causes us annoyance and displeasure. We despise him for his low opinion of us. Examples of this are to be seen in the opera, and even in some tragedies. It is thus, apart from exciting ridicule, the business of the poet to temper the all too marvellous with verisimilitude.

It is demanded that art should perfect nature; but this demand must not be extended to moral matters. The characters of a poem need not be perfect, nor is it forbidden to represent 'mediocre' virtues and vices. If nature shows us the errors of great men and the weaknesses of women, why should the poet be debarred from doing so? Muratori now sums up the argument of his chapter. Be the actions, the things, the personages sublime, or mediocre, or realistic, be the vices, virtues, feelings and characters of the persons strongly marked or only indifferent; should the events have actually happened or be only events that might have happened: the poet must represent these very different things in accordance with their peculiar nature; he must always seek the marvellous, and keep always in view the true or verisimilar. It is in this marvellousness, in this truth or verisimilitude, that the beautiful lies; and these two qualities will assuredly bring delight to the spectator or the listener.

So far Muratori has discussed the beauty of the subject of a poem; he now turns (chap. xiii) to the beauty of expression. A truth, an action, a sentiment, may not be marvellous and extraordinary in itself; but it may become so by the manner of representing it, of depicting it in words. And he proceeds to illustrate this by examples from the Hebrew poets and Homer onwards.

With chapter xiv begins the consideration of the fantasy or imagination—that most fruitful source of marvellousness and poetic beauty. As this is the most important chapter in the work, I deal with it in some detail. Intellect is common to historians and orators as well as poets: fantasy or imagination belongs solely to the poet. What is meant by fantasy? An object presented to the eyes, ears, or other senses, transmits a compendium or image of itself, which, received by the senses, passes by way of the nerves to the brain, where it impresses itself. The power or faculty of the soul which grasps these sensible objects or their images, is the 'fantasia' or 'immaginazione'; it is situated in the 'inferior' part of the soul and may be called the 'apprensiva inferiore'—the 'apprensiva superiore' being the intellect. The business of the imagination is not to judge whether things are true or false, but merely to apprehend them; the business of the intellect is to understand them, and investigate whether they are true or false. In order to form thoughts, these two powers act together, the inferior submitting images and fantasms of objects, which it has in its storehouse, to the superior, without new aid from the senses. Or the inferior faculty may use these fantasms alone to imagine things already apprehended, or to fabricate other fantasms, since it has the power of conceiving new images. The fantasy thus controls the private arsenal and secret treasury of our soul, where so many and so different objects are, as it were, reduced to compendiums. Thus images come from the inferior 'apprensiva'; they are called 'idols' and are set out like so much merchandise in a great square or market, in more or less order—sometimes in disorder—and from these, at one time the fantasy, at another the intellect, swiftly selects appropriate embodiments for its thoughts.

Muratori now proceeds to consider the joint activity of intellect and imagination in creating in us the images, 'idols' and thoughts, which are the materials of our reason. Such images are formed in three ways: the intellect forms them without the fantasy doing more than providing the materials; the intellect and the fantasy work together; or the fantasy achieves everything alone. The first process results in intellectual images, in the reasonings and reflections of the intellect; the third is illustrated by the products of feverish dreams, overstrung emotions, and the like, where the intellect loses that control which, according to Aristotle, it ought to maintain over the imagination. The first class Muratori reserves for discussion in another part of his work; the third has nothing to do with real poetry. Thus his main business is with the second class.

The imagination acting together with the intellect produces images which are either immediately true or appear immediately true to the intellect; an example of such direct truth is the description of a rainbow, or a fight between two warriors. Such images represent a truth brought by the senses to the imagination, and recognised as true by the intellect. Secondly, they may be immediately verisimilar to both imagination and intellect; examples are the scene of the taking of Troy, the arrival of Orestes in Tauris. Or thirdly, images may be immediately verisimilar or true to the imagination, but only indirectly to the intellect. For instance, it may be said that a stream is enamoured of a pleasant country through which it winds slowly; this is a 'fantastic' image which conveys the indirect truth to the intellect that the country is pleasant and the windings of the stream charming. The first two classes of images are simple and natural; the third class might be described as 'artificially fantastic.' Other examples are Fame flying; the birds greeting the dawn with their song.

These products of the imagination are usually described as 'fantasie,' but in order to distinguish them from the faculty of the brain which produces them, Muratori prefers to call them 'immagini' or images. He now investigates the nature of these 'images,' which are the soul of poetry; he shows how the imagination of poets has to obey the intellect, and how the love which the latter has for the true is brought into harmony with the delirium of the fantasy.

Muratori next proceeds to discuss the simple or natural images of the imagination, that is to say, those which are directly acceptable to the intellect as true or verisimilar. The imagination gives us great pleasure when it depicts or represents vividly things distant in time or place; in fact, this is one of the chief functions of poetic art. Perfect imitation gives the greatest delight; and even trivial things, which in nature would escape our notice, appeal strongly to us when imitated. Aristotle has shown that this pleasure arises from comprehending the resemblance between the imitation and the thing imitated. The faculty of imitating in words in order to produce 'evidenza' or 'enargia,' Longinus, in his fifteenth chapter, defined as the end of poetry. Muratori now considers what Castelvetro calls 'particolarizzazione,' that is, the narration of minute details. Homer is superior to Virgil in this art; and Castelvetro, who condemns generalising poets like Virgil, praises Homer. Muratori believes both methods are justified, but is disposed to regard Virgil's as the higher and nobler method, in so far as it appeals to the cultured mind. Tasso follows Virgil in this respect; Ariosto, Homer. Ovid, again, is an unsurpassed master of the art of particularising. Muratori draws attention to the abuse of the Homeric method, in the minute description of irrelevant and tedious things; even Homer himself occasionally errs in this way. There are two ways of describing: either minutely and vividly, so that we leave nothing to be imagined; or by means of suggestion. The latter brings a double pleasure, a pleasure both to our intellect and to our imagination.

In chapter xv Muratori turns to the method of depicting by means of 'artificial fantastic images,' that is, by figures, hyperboles and fantastic images; if judged directly by the intellect these are false, but if reinforced by marvellous and delightful attributes they explain the truths of nature. This type of imagery is the product of the fantasy alone, and it may take the form of a single word (simile or metaphor), a sentence (hyperbole, allegory), a fable or parable, or an entire poem. Looking at these images a little more closely, Muratori distinguishes first those which appear true to the fantasy on the evidence of the senses; for example, the sun going down into the sea, a picture speaking, and the like. But most of these are hackneyed, and if we are to give pleasure, we must discover new ones. Another group of images is made up of those which are directly true or verisimilar, by virtue of their emotional appeal to the imagination. The poetic treasury must have a large stock of these. They are formed whenever the fantasy, stirred by some strong emotion, combines two simple and natural images, and gives them a form different from that presented by the senses. The commonest manifestation of this process is the imbuing of dead things with life. Love is the greatest force in stimulating the fantasy to such images.

A distinction must be drawn (chap. xvi) between what is true according to the intellect and what is true according to the fantasy. Fantastic images containing an inner truth must on no account be called lies. The source of the pleasure we take in these images is that they embody or clothe in sensible form, abstract truths; the intellect takes pleasure in extracting the hidden truth.

Chapter xvii deals with the so-called 'furor poeticus.' The fantasy must be stimulated to create images; but this stimulus is not at our beck and call. 'Poets are born, orators made.' The ancients talked of inspiration by Apollo and the Muses. But Muratori denies that there is anything supernatural in this stimulus, and he quotes Castelvetro's opinion that Plato was merely jesting when he described poetry as a gift of the gods. Enthusiasm is the excitement of the fantasy. The latter may become excited by itself, whence arise ecstasies, visions, dreams, supernatural revelations. But it may also be excited by physical causes, such as feasting, wine, fever, melancholy; or by grief, disdain, love.

These emotions—and Muratori includes not merely the emotions just mentioned, but also all other physical activities, such as esteem, contempt, stupidity, etc.—are the 'movimenti' or 'moti' of the mind. The chief factor in these 'movements' is the fantasy, which may often be so violent as to overpower the intellect. To a poet moved by an emotion things appear different from what they are; the poetic furor increases the majesty of an action, gives novelty to it, and causes delight and wonder to the hearer. Muratori's conclusion is that the 'furor poeticus' may be acquired, if only our imagination has sufficient natural energy to set its fantasms vigorously in motion. If, on the other hand, the imagination has not this innate energy, there can be no question of a 'furor poeticus.' This is what is meant by saying that poets are born, not made.

Chapter xviii deals with the manner in which the intellect or the judgment assists the fantasy. It is not enough that the intellect should recognise indirectly in fantastic images the true or the verisimilar; these must also appear true or verisimilar to the fantasy itself; and the recognition of this truth or verisimilitude is due to the enlightenment provided by the intellect. But when the fantasy believes things to be true or verisimilar, its reasons for doing so are most frequently emotional. This chapter is illustrated from ancient and modern poets.

Chapter xix is mainly an illustrative chapter, giving examples of the delights and ecstasies of the fantasy; while chapter xx shows, with tedious reiteration, the limitations set to the employment of artificial poetic images. They are clearly out of place in prose; and illustrations are given of the reprehensible indulgence in such images by prose writers, and the equally reprehensible intemperance of some poets. Chapter xxi, the last chapter of this book, deals with what Muratori calls 'extended fantastic images,' that is to say, images which are continuous throughout a whole poem, such as the lengthy story of the wooden horse of Troy. In this chapter Muratori refers, too, to the effect of the Christian faith in discrediting the imagery of the ancients; what to the latter appeared as truths acceptable to the intellect, can now only be acceptable as truths to our fantasy. He again takes the opportunity of pointing out defects in Homer, and defending Tasso.

The second book of the *Perfetta Poesia italiana*, which deals with the intellect or 'ingegno,' as the first had dealt with the 'fantasy,' does not demand such detailed analysis. Muratori sums up his theme in the opening pages of the book.

Without going into the philosophy of the matter, he says, the intellect ('ingegno') is in my opinion, nothing more than the active force, whereby the mind collects together and explains the similarities, relations and reasons of things. There are two ways in which the intellect can operate: by penetrating into the heart of things and comprehending their reason, quality and nature; and by collecting together the similarities, correspondences and common ties between the most different objects. He who employs the first method is said to have a penetrating and acute intellect; he who employs the second, a vast intellect. From these two operations are born the most beautiful thoughts and most noble sentiments which adorn poetry (vol. II, p. 5).

The greater part of this book is taken up with the discussion of this programme, defining and criticising, often with ingenious subtlety, often with mere pedantic hairsplitting, the function of the intellect in forming poetic images. The general purpose of the argument is to defend the poets of antiquity, the older Italian poets and Tasso; while Bouhours and the French poets, notably Corneille, come in for condemnation—most of all, naturally, Marini. In chapter v we find a kind of summary of Muratori's conclusions on this function of the intellect. The reflexions of the intellect, which are in reality a 'tacit syllogism,' must, he says, be founded on true or verisimilar premises, that is, true or verisimilar according to the intellect, not according to the fantasy. Secondly, the expression of an idea by a metaphor must not be too daring, otherwise the metaphor becomes cold. Thirdly, when the fantasy has formed some image with a reasonable foundation, the poet must not go on to transfer to it other irrelevant qualities, in which case we merely get conceits. To develop a metaphor with good taste, the metaphorical object should never be regarded as real.

In chapter x Muratori turns to the consideration of the judgment. 'A sublime intellect and a happy fantasy,' he says, 'are the two wings which bear men to excellence in poetry.' But to make proper use of these wings judgment is needed. This is the most powerful factor in one's mind and the noblest virtue. Judgment is a kind of king in our soul. In common life, mediocre knowledge combined with good judgment is better than wide knowledge combined with mediocre judgment. Judgment may also be called prudence, reason itself, or even good taste; and an entire book might be written about it. Judgment is a faculty founded on the study of individuals and particular things; and as these are innumerable, so also are the laws of judgment. Intellect and fantasy are subject to rules, and are controlled by universal and general laws. Not so the judgment, which regulates and defines its conclusions according to the nature of the individuals and the circumstances concerned, employing continually new laws and reflexions applicable only to the particular cases. Judgment may be defined as that virtue of the intellect which instructs us to avoid or pass over all that is inappropriate, or prejudicial to our task; and to select what may be of service to it. It is the insight which discovers, according to circumstances, the extremes between which beauty lies. Variety is one of the most fruitful sources of delight, and judgment teaches us how we may introduce variety. Judgment makes its choice from an infinity of images; it opens to the poet a hundred eyes; it extends his outlook on a hundred sides. Besides eloquence in speech—the daughter of genius and fantasy—we have also eloquence in silence, the daughter of judgment. The virtue of not saying too much is 'fineness of judgment.' The *φιλόκαλια* of the Greeks was a product of judgment.

The remaining chapters of this volume deal with practical questions and with matters of literary criticism: for instance, with the formation of the faculty of judgment, which is acquired with the aid of theoretic writings as well as of great literature. Muratori endeavours to mediate between the extremes of the 'ancients' and the 'moderns'; between the excessive claims for the latter made by Perrault, on the one hand, and the unreasonable attack on 'le clinquant du Tasse' by Boileau on the other. He tries to hold the balance between the rivalry of Homer and Virgil for the highest place in epic poetry. In this controversy, however, Muratori's sympathies are clearly with Virgil; he could not forgive Homer for involving the gods in immoral conduct. From verse he now turns to prose, and discusses the question of style, again expressing his abhorrence of vicious extravagances.

The third volume of the *Perfetta Poesia* in the edition of Salvini may be dealt with still more briefly. There is much repetition in it, *e.g.* on the 'utile et dulce' as the end of poetry, on poetry as a constituent of moral philosophy and politics. Poetry, he says, is 'la figliuola e ministra della filosofia morale, maestra de' buoni costumi, e giovevole alla vita civile'; and again, 'una moral filosofia travestita in abito ameno e dilettevole' (chap. i). He discourses on the defects of poets which militate against their popularity or utility; he dilates on the folly of enamoured poets and the descriptions of 'vile amours' in Marini's verse. But the legitimacy of love-poetry is—in view of the great past of Italian poetry, and especially in view of Dante and Petrarch—a difficult problem for a churchman; he ultimately accepts love-poets as guilty of only a 'malizia leggiera e scusabile' (chap. iii). He even goes further and admits, in discussing the lyric, the justification of a poetry the purpose of which is only to cause delight. He is satisfied if the delight is innocent. Then, after a chapter on the defects due to ignorance and lack of taste, he turns to the modern drama.

The two chapters on the drama and the need for its reform (chaps. v and vi) are mainly interesting as the obvious inspiration of the Introduction to Maffei's *Teatro Italiano*, through which they influenced the revival of dramatic poetry in Italy. Muratori inveighs vigorously against the absurdities of the opera: music must be ousted from the theatre, if the Italian drama is ever to regain its position as a force in literature; and he provides another text for Maffei when he blames the Italian actors for their readiness to sacrifice poetry to buffoonery. He complains of the excessive use of dialect in comedy. He defends the theatre against the attacks of churchmen: 'the theatre may, in a word, become,' he concludes, 'a delightful school of good manners and a pleasant pulpit of moral lessons.'

Muratori's views on the theory and structure of the drama are neither helpful nor original. He points to the necessity of dramatists always keeping Aristotle before them; he demands rigid adherence to the three unities; but, instead of soliloquies, he approves of the modern use of confidants. He would like to see the ancient chorus retained; but is not unfavourable to tragedies in prose. He concludes that, 'although verse may not be absolutely necessary to such compositions, it is, at least, a great aid and ornament.' He agrees with Orsi's recommendation of verses of eleven syllables mingled with those of seven, as a suitable and stately vehicle for Italian tragedy[1]. He warns against the tendency to glorify evil in tragedies—especially evil love—but the Italians are not such great sinners in this respect as the French. He enlarges on the absurdity of love in the French theatre, a criticism which had already been made emphatically by Rapin in his *Réflexions sur la Poétique*[2]. Not that he wishes to see love excluded altogether; but it must be kept within the bounds of verisimilitude. Speaking of comedy, he emphatically condemns Molière, endorsing Baillet's view that Molière is one of the most dangerous enemies of the Church of God. He concludes with the hope that the princes of Italy will abandon the cultivation of the opera and devote themselves to the production of noble and purified tragedies.

From the drama Muratori turns to a less congenial theme, the lyric. The glorification of sexual love which is the dominant theme of lyric poetry, made it difficult for Muratori to approve of it; and what he has to say has little value. He clings still to Maggi and Lemene as models for Italy. He has more sympathy with religious and didactic poetry; even satire is justifiable as long as the Church is held sacrosanct. In this chapter room is also found for praise of the Fables of Lafontaine and for a defence of Dante—inclined to obscurity as he sometimes is—against detractors like Bembo. He concludes with an appeal to his countrymen to remember Quintilian's words: 'Nihil crescit sola imitatione,' and not imitate the ancients servilely.

But courage is needed for such an undertaking. Men cannot hope to make much progress if, dismayed by the glorious careers of the great, they are always, so to speak, hanging on their nurses' apron-strings. They must free themselves, aspire to high things, discover new paths; but in abandoning the ways of their ancestors, they must not let a too ambitious and unwary fantasy bring them to lamentable shipwreck, as so often has happened in the past century (p. 128).

[1] Subsequently, he accepted Martelli's innovation. See below, pp. 135 f.

[2] *Œuvres diverses*, Amsterdam, 1693, II, pp. 186 f. See also below, pp. 211 f.

The remaining chapters of the volume are devoted to a discussion of the Italian language; while volume IV of Salvini's edition contains examples illustrative of the treatise, drawn from the Italian poets.

III

In estimating the value of Muratori's *Della Perfetta Poesia italiana*, its early date must be borne in mind. Aesthetic criticism and literary theory had, in 1706, hardly begun to emerge from the seventeenth-century thraldom of the 'rules,' and we are too apt to forget that Muratori preceded, and did not follow Addison, Burke and Home, Du Bos and Batteux[1]. Viewed in this light, his treatise is a very wonderful achievement: it represents a greater leap forward, and contributed more to the advance of the aesthetic theory of literature than any other work of its time.

In the first instance, Muratori's work has to be regarded as a contribution to the polemical literature evoked by the cynicism of the Père Bouhours. Published three years after Orsi's confutation of the latter, it is a continuation of the controversy opened up by him, or rather, it supplements it on the constructive side. It is a vindication of the Italian poetry of the past; and in consequence, the defence of Tasso, which was common to all the defenders of the honour of Italy, stands in the foreground. Muratori points, if with less sympathy than Gravina, two years later, to the greatness of Dante, both critics having been, no doubt, impressed by Mazzoni's *Difesa di Dante*. Crescimbeni's *Istoria della volgar Poesia* was a monument raised with more or less the same object, the vindication of Italy; and from Crescimbeni Muratori drew, amongst other things, those speculations—also it will be remembered, discussed by Gravina—on the Provençal origins of Italian poetry, which Crescimbeni had based on Jean de Nostredame's *Vies des poètes provensaux*. But there is a vast difference between the unphilosophic, mechanical chronicle of Crescimbeni, compiled according to the ant-like methods of the seventeenth

[1] Cp. A. Rolla, *Storia delle Idee estetiche in Italia*, Turin, 1905, p. 89; also H. Stein, *op. cit.* pp. 310 ff.

century, and the critical account which Muratori presents in his second chapter. Muratori's survey, slight as it is, is an attempt to correlate facts in accordance with a kind of teleological sense of the ultimate end of literary evolution. In his attitude to literary history he combined that scholarly method of scientific documentation—which his friend Apostolo Zeno carried out even more thoroughly—with some inkling of an organic interpretation of history. Crescimbeni had been content to characterise individual writers in an endless procession; Muratori tries to see them not merely with eyes trained by good taste, but also by 'erudition,' which he regards as synonymous with history[1]; he attaches particular importance to original documents. His championship of Italian literature is the more imposing, as he brings to the task his patient habits of research, his boundless knowledge of books, and his astounding capacity for assimilating ideas. Thus the Bouhours controversy must be given some credit for the transformation of the chronicle-history of Italian letters—and in writing about literature Italy was in advance of other lands—into some semblance of living, organic history, a transformation which did not take place in political history until at least a generation later.

In his attitude towards the French critics, Muratori left no stone unturned to understand and appreciate their standpoint; he wrote with fullness of knowledge. He did not oppose them in blind partisanship; for his object was—and herein he differed from Orsi and his friends, who represent only the first militant stage of the quarrel—to show how admitted defects in his own literature might be remedied. He was not merely intent on defending the Italian poetry of the past, and insisting that that poetry need fear no comparison with the achievement of France; but he would also provide practical guidance for the Italian poets of his own time. And the panacea for all the ills of 'secentismo' is 'il buon gusto.' It has been said that Muratori was the first to make the expression 'good taste' a household word in European criticism[2]; but he was not the inventor of the term. Its use to connote a faculty of the judgment would

[1] Cp. Muratori, *Riflessioni sopra il buon gusto*, Venice, 1717, II, chapters iii and iv.

[2] Cp. above, p. 70.

appear to go back to Gracián[1]; Boileau had already made it a catchword in France: and it is the instance to which Bouhours appeals in arraigning the literatures of Italy and Spain. Even in Italy itself, Muratori was not so great an innovator as might appear; for, ten years before the *Perfetta Poesia*, Camillo Ettorri had published at Bologna a work on *Il Buon Gusto ne' componimenti rettorici*[2]. But no doubt after Muratori—and especially after the *Riflessioni sopra il buon gusto*, which appeared two years later than the *Perfetta Poesia*—the word did attain a greater currency.

To pass for a moment from the faculty of 'good taste' to the quality of good taste as it appears in works of art, we have frankly to admit that Muratori has by no means succeeded in shaking himself free from the old 'gusto cattivo.' We have already seen how Crescimbeni occasionally lapsed into the style he set out to discredit, his writings being, after all, no very effectual antidote to Marinism; but even from the *Perfetta Poesia*, Marini might have occasionally drawn justification. The truth is, Muratori, Crescimbeni and the entire Arcadia of the early years, were still in great measure groping in the dark; they had but a vague idea as to what constituted this 'good taste' which was to exorcise the evil. Nor must we forget that the hard and fast lines, which the historian likes to draw between epochs and movements in literary history, are rarely borne out by actual facts and happenings. There is no definite point at which Marinism ceases and the new purified taste asserts itself. The old movement shades into the new; just as, in northern lands, the equivalent of Marinism passed over with no very definite break into admiration for Milton—admiration in the first instance just for Milton's 'Marinism'—and, subsequently, into the passionate enthusiasm for nature of the new time[3]. Muratori might have emancipated himself more completely, had he not, like all the critics with whom I deal in the

[1] Cp. K. Borinski, *Die Poetik der Renaissance*, pp. 308 ff. (quoted by B. Croce, *Estetica*, p. 196).

[2] Unfortunately I only know this work from the account given of it by Croce, *Estetica*, pp. 197 f., and *Problemi di Estetica*, Bari, 1910, pp. 376 ff.

[3] A striking illustration of the transition is to be seen in the Hamburg poet Brockes. See below, p. 249.

present volume, suffered from a strangely ineffective critical judgment where individual works were concerned, from an incapacity to distinguish merit from mediocrity. As Gravina had glorified Guidi, so Muratori set Maggi and Lemene on pinnacles; and his criticism of the great poets of the past, notably Homer, whom, following Scaliger, he regarded as inferior to Virgil, is often trivial and lacking in that 'good taste' by which he lays so much store.

An aspect of the *Perfetta Poesia* which may be dismissed briefly, but is none the less negatively important, is Muratori's views on the individual *genres* of literature. Here, in fact, Muratori reveals his alienation from literature in its concrete forms. I have shown how, in the case of the drama and theatre, he was convinced that something was wrong; but when he attempted to lay down what ought to be done in order to establish the drama on a worthy footing, he failed lamentably. Even Gravina's little treatise on tragedy is more helpful from the playwright's point of view. Muratori's theory of the drama had, in fact, first to be translated into practical terms by Maffei. What is true of Muratori's discussion of this form of poetry is also true of his discussion of other literary forms. He offered no clue as to how the 'perfect' epic was to be written; and the lyric lay from the first entirely outside his sphere of interest. Muratori was, with all his practical aspirations, a theorist of poetry, and a theorist only. Thus the *Perfetta Poesia* failed to justify itself in respect of that function which its author particularly intended it to fulfil, namely, as a guide for the reform of Italian letters. Critics of far less vital significance, like Gottsched in Germany, kept more clearly before them the need of providing an 'ars poetica'; they gave their contemporaries some rules of thumb, whereby poetry might be written. The Italian poets seeking such help from Muratori, must have sought in vain.

But these imperfections and disadvantages are far outweighed by another aspect of Muratori's treatise, its significance in providing a foundation of the aesthetics of literature. Of little help as a guide to the production of 'kinds' of literature, Muratori was yet of inestimable value as an expounder of the basic conditions of poetic creation. He had a well-disciplined, constructive mind; and no aesthetic thinker of his time had clearer ideas—although unfortunately hampered by a redundancy of words and illustration—concerning the factors that go to the production of poetry, namely, the intellect, the imagination and the judgment. To lay bare the sources of Muratori's theory is a task before which the most indefatigable investigator might well shrink. His erudition and reading in this field were no less exhaustive than in that of history and antiquities; he took no step without familiarising himself with all the available knowledge accumulated by his predecessors. That he knew the ancients intimately goes without saying: Aristotle and all his commentators down to Dacier were at his elbow; and amongst these commentators, it was only fitting that Castelvetro, who broke the thrall of the mediaeval Aristotle for Italy, and made a new criticism and a new aesthetics possible, should have had the first place in his esteem. Muratori's chief debt to antiquity is possibly to Longinus—whom Boileau had made a force in modern thought—and to Quintilian, where are to be found the germs of that modern development of which Muratori was a pioneer. His quotations of Latin authorities range from Horace to Saint Augustine and the later Italians, such as Fracastoro; and of his more immediate predecessors, he mentions Cardinal Jacopo Sadoleto, Francesco Molza and Alessandro Tassoni[1]. But the list might be extended to include every one in Italy who had dealt with aesthetic theory. He had especially read and marked the critics of the French 'Querelle': Perrault, Lamy, Rapin, Fontenelle; he knew Le Bossu and Malebranche. Thus in the weft of Muratori's system there are threads of many colours; but he went to work as a constructive thinker for whom his predecessors provided merely the materials.

In dealing with Gravina, I have urged the significance of the Cartesian philosophy for his aesthetics, that significance lying not in concrete details, but in the underlying search for the 'truth' on which Descartes' demolition of the last strongholds of scholasticism was based. Descartes went out to seek a new truth, and in his search revolutionised human thinking; he established his system on a new criterion of reality, and the

[1] *Della Perfetta Poesia*, I, p. 3.

philosophies of the Middle Ages faded into thin air. Now this is precisely the method and achievement of both Muratori's aesthetics and Gravina's. Both thinkers set out to discover the irrefutable 'cogito ergo sum' of poetry; to discriminate between the true and the false, that false which, in the hands of the 'secentists,' had debased the dignity of literature, and reduced it to trivialities divorced from experience. We have seen how Gravina put this search for truth in the forefront of his treatise on the *Ancient Fables*, and it is equally fundamental for Muratori: perhaps indeed Muratori might never have achieved all that the *Perfetta Poesia* stands for, had not Gravina prepared the way for him.

What, then, is truth in poetry? From this question springs the whole *Perfetta Poesia*; the answer to it is the theme of that treatise. And just as Descartes destroyed the illusion that truth lies in what the senses grasp, so Muratori sees that the truth in poetry is no surface appeal to the passive understanding, but something deeper, something, indeed, that may not be superficially true at all. In other words, truth in poetry is verisimilitude. Fracastoro and Castelvetro had already stated this for Italian aesthetics; and Gravina had adumbrated it in his *Ragionamento sopra l' Endimione*. But Gravina never arrived at complete logical clearness on the subject: and it will be remembered how he timidly went back on his first justification of the supernatural in poetry. His *Ragion* is bluntly intolerant of the hippogryphs of romance; Muratori, on the other hand, is more indulgent towards the unreal, for he saw, that it might, after all, be a vehicle for a deeper and more essential truth.

In forming his conception of verisimilitude, Muratori was, no doubt, aided by a predecessor whose influence upon the literary theory of this period has hardly been sufficiently appreciated, Cardinal Sforza Pallavicino[1]. The work of Pallavicino's which mainly comes in question here, *Del Bene*, appeared in 1681. Muratori frequently mentions him[2], and then usually to controvert his opinion; but he was, none the less, one of the

[1] Pallavicino has, strange to say, no place in Saintsbury's *History o, Criticism*; even Croce, I think, does not give him his due.

[2] *E.g. Della Perfetta Poesia italiana*, I, pp. 130 ff., 310 f.

important formative influences on Muratori's aesthetics. We have already seen how Gravina had learned from him[1]; in fact, he was probably responsible for an occasional warping in Gravina's otherwise irreproachable Cartesianism. Not only do Muratori's discussions of the 'verisimilar' seem to me to be traceable to Pallavicino, but possibly even those ideas on the function of the imagination, which are Muratori's most significant contribution to aesthetic theory. He may also have been the source of that democratic conception of literature, which has left its mark alike on Gravina, Muratori, Quadrio, Calepio, and indeed, on all the Italian theorists, that poetry is essentially an art, not for the cultured classes only, but also for the common people.

The first deduction from the insistence on the true and the verisimilar was necessarily disqualification and repudiation of the conceits and strained metaphors of Marinism; that goes without saying. But had Muratori proceeded no further and seen no deeper, the result might have been only a shallow naturalism—there was clearly a danger of this in Gravina—an 'aimez donc la raison,' which would have been as defenceless as Boileau's against the reinstatement of an artificial classicism. Without deeper insight, Muratori would have been merely a reviver of rationalism in poetry, merely a neo-classicist, as he has been so often and so inadequately described. He was a neo-classicist in so far as he protested against the extravagances into which the scholastic classicism of the seventeenth century had degenerated; but if by rationalism or classicism we mean merely lip-service to a superficial truth of appearance, Muratori cannot be claimed as one of its advocates. He helped rather to establish an aesthetic system which foreshadows the movement which was to be known to a much later generation as Romanticism.

The secret of Muratori's achievement as the creator of a new aesthetics lay in the fact that he emphasised the significance of the 'fantasia' or imagination. Muratori had not immersed himself in the spirit of Plato for nothing[2]; and the paralysing tyranny of the letter of Aristotle, which Castelvetro had first attacked, now yielded to a new idealism which, in its essentials,

[1] See above, p. 55.
[2] Cp. *Riflessioni sopra il buon gusto*, I, p. 161.

has its source in the Platonic dialogues. Gravina had also repudiated the tyranny of Aristotelianism; but it is to Muratori the honour belongs of having set up in its place a new positive and reasoned idealism. For the first time in European aesthetics, he established in unambiguous terms the imagination as the essential factor in artistic creation. But the stimulus was not exclusively Platonic; Bacon had already indicated that poetry was the peculiar business of the imagination; Hobbes had also discussed the functions of the imagination; and Muratori's Italian predecessors, such as Pallavicino, had already begun to apply these ideas to literary aesthetics. Descartes, too, deserves some credit for having prepared the way for the new point of view. Had it not been for the Cartesian faith in the spirit as the only reality, Muratori would hardly have dared—paradoxical as it may seem—to claim for the imagination so large a share in poetry. He realised that it was by virtue of the imagination that the poet could penetrate into those regions of higher truth and beauty which were hidden from the ordinary senses; that he could discover that new and marvellous truth which it is the function of art to embody. Boileau and the classicists had demanded the subordination of the imagination, and had set up reason as a bulwark against the untruth inherent in poetic fantasies; Muratori gave the dominating rôle to the imagination. At the same time, he was not blind to the fact that the imagination—and nothing but the imagination—was responsible for the dry rot of 'secentismo'; he realised that the imagination must be held in check by a certain 'je ne sais quoi,' a 'buon gusto.' In the imagination, nevertheless, lies for him the key to a higher truth; it is in no conflict with, and is no enemy of reason. If we are to obtain something higher and more perfect than nature—to 'far eminente la natura'—the imagination is the faculty that must help us to that end.

The insistence on aesthetic truth unites Muratori and Gravina as workers towards a common end, but the points of divergence between the two men are equally significant. Too many modern critics throw together Gravina and Muratori, and label them neo-classicists, without realising the unfairness of this rough and ready association. We in England, remembering Addison, ought to be particularly wary of the use of the ill-defined term neo-classic, which has wrought as much confusion in accurate thinking on critical theory as the word romanticism itself. As a matter of fact, even Gravina rendered so-called neo-classicism a very dubious service; the vital element in Gravina's thought could not be identified with its aims. At the same time, he was a champion of classic ideals, in so far as he opposed—like his essentially neo-classic colleagues of the Arcadia—the extravagances of the seventeenth century. He pinned his faith on the august masterpieces of Greek literature; and the *Ragion poetica* is, in this sense, the final link in the chain of Renaissance Poetics in Italy—the last, as it is certainly the most polished—which looked to antiquity as the one and only way to poetic salvation.

When we turn to Muratori, we find a thinker of a more practical and flexible, a more modern type. He, too, wishes to revive the cultivation of those classic ideals which the perversity of the seventeenth century had obscured; but his extraordinarily wide sympathies excluded, from the beginning, too narrow a predilection for the classic literatures; and moreover, he writes with his eye fixed, not on a hypothetical 'ragione' which lies behind all literary expression, but on the practical measures which he deems effective to achieve a 'perfect Italian poetry.' Associated all his life with Northern Italy, he is far away from the strife that attended the inauguration of the Arcadia, and although he was himself a member of the Arcadia, and dedicated his treatise to a distinguished Arcadian, he often gives the impression that the Arcadia was for him already a turned page. In other words, we find it difficult to believe that the *Perfetta Poesia italiana* was published not before, but a generation later than the *Ragion poetica* of Gravina.

Gravina looks backwards, sets his hopes of reform on the revival of the golden age; Muratori looks forward, and, so far from being a pillar of neo-classicism, he was, of all the critics of his time, the least genuinely neo-classic at heart. No other writer of that age—not Addison, nor the Swiss critics Bodmer and Breitinger, who, as we shall see, drew largely on him, not his Spanish disciple Luzán, or even Lessing himself—had so much to say that was furthering for the anti-classic trend of the eighteenth century.

Chapter IV

Antonio Conti

Of the writers who come within the scope of the present volume, Antonio Conti has been described as a link between England and Italy. He spent over two of the most eventful and impressionable years of his life with us, was imbued with English thought, and translated English poets. Moreover, his personal relations with prominent English people, such as Sir Isaac Newton, Lord Bolingbroke—he was one of the latter's intimates at La Source—the Duke of Buckingham, Brook Taylor, Lady Mary Wortley Montagu, make him a figure of no small interest to English students of the early eighteenth century. But Conti was not the only Italian critic who, at this time, was in touch with English literature: and of his contemporaries, at least A. M. Salvini had a wider sympathy than he for our ideas and our literature; indeed, we have rather to regret that, with his great advantages, Conti should not have been a better interpreter of the English mind than he actually was. For all that was peculiarly English in our literature, or in our opinions about literature, he had, in fact, little understanding; his appreciation of us was rigidly bounded by the canons of French taste. His importance, however, lies, as far as the present studies are concerned, not in his interpretation of either English or French ideas, but in his development of the empiric aesthetics of Gravina and Muratori on metaphysical lines.

I

Antonio Schinella, of the ancient and illustrious family of the Contis, was born at Padua on January 22, 1677[1]. On his

[1] On Conti's life see Ginguené's article in the *Biographie universelle* (IX, 1852, pp. 124 ff.), the introduction (by Giuseppe Toaldo) to vol. II of Conti's *Prose e Poesie*, Venice, 1756; A. Cicutto, *Elogio dell' Abate Antonio Conti*, Venice, 1814; G. Vedova, *Biografia degli scrittori padovani*, I, Padua, 1832, pp. 276 ff.; and especially G. Brognoligo's articles on *L' Opera letteraria di Antonio Conti* in the *Ateneo Veneto*, July, 1893, to December, 1894. I take this opportunity of expressing my indebtedness to these articles, which their

mother's side he was descended from Sperone Speroni, whose manuscripts he possessed; and he was mainly responsible for the edition of that writer's works published at Venice in 1740. We have no definite information about his early years. His education was begun at home and possibly continued in one of the Jesuit colleges in Florence. He seems to have had little ambition for the public career which was, doubtless, open to him; and about 1699 he became a priest in Venice. Even in this capacity he did not aspire to any higher position in the Church, his one wish being to devote himself to the 'contemplazione della verità.'

The Cartesian philosophy burst upon Conti, as on so many leaders of Italian thought at this time, with the force of a new revelation. He himself dated this epoch-making event in his life from a day in the year 1706—he was then twenty-nine—when he overheard the new philosophy being praised in a bookseller's shop in Venice. He thereupon sought out the Abate Fardella, the famous Paduan pioneer of Cartesianism, who happened to be at that time in Venice, and had the *Méditations* of Descartes fully explained to him. He threw himself with ardour into these new studies, and, to gain more freedom, withdrew in 1708 from the active duties of the Church. The mathematical sciences were expounded to him by eminent Italian teachers; and he set himself to master the philosophical systems of Bacon and Leibnitz, of Malebranche and Locke. He was actuated, he tells us, by the desire to reconcile the materialism of Locke with the metaphysics of Descartes; and he wrote at this time a dissertation on the immanent force in matter and spirit, which, however, has not been preserved. His scientific interests led him also to busy himself with the writings of Galileo, Borelli and Montanari; and, at the suggestion of his friend Antonio Vallisnieri of Padua, he published in volume XII of the *Giornale dei Letterati* a dissertation on a book by a certain Francesco Maria Nigrisoli of Ferrara, *Considerazioni intorno alla generazione de' viventi, e particolarmente de' mostri*. This work—it sets up a metaphysical

author, years ago, kindly placed at my disposal. See also, L. Berthé de Besancèle, *op. cit.* pp. 222 ff. The *Lettere scelte di celebri autori all' Abate A. Conti* (including nine from Maffei and four from Muratori) were published at Venice in 1812.

hypothesis of generation which the author attributed to what he called 'seminal light'—was hardly worth confuting; but Conti's long and learned article[1] was looked upon as a vindication of Italian science and philosophy, and gave him a certain reputation. He sent his article to distinguished people, and he included their letters of approval—amongst them, one from Malebranche, who wrote very sensibly: 'Je m'étonne, Monsieur, que vous ayez pris la peine de réfuter cet Auteur,' others from Fontenelle, Coste and Leibnitz—in the edition of his *Risposta alla Difesa del libro delle Considerazioni* etc., which he published at Venice in 1716, with a flattering dedication to Maffei. When in 1713, Conti betook himself to Paris, he found that his reputation had preceded him and prepared for him a warm welcome.

Conti's departure for France—he did not see Italy again for thirteen years—was the turning-point in his life; it was his residence abroad and his close touch with French and English thought that gave his intellectual work, and, more particularly, the phase of it which interests us in these pages, its distinctive mark. In Paris he found time, not merely to pursue his studies, but also to enjoy the social life of the French capital. Conti was nothing if not gregarious; wherever he went he made friends, and he always preferred to acquire knowledge from conversation with men of learning rather than from their books. 'He loved,' says his biographer, Toaldo[2], 'to approach the same truths by different methods, and to see them from all sides; he would drink at the fountainhead and listen to systems and theories from the lips of their authors.' In Paris he made the personal acquaintance of Malebranche—with whom, however, he does not seem to have got on well—Fontenelle, Fraguier, Malézieu, De la Hire, Saurin and others; and he attended regularly lectures and social functions. With his fellow-countryman, Martelli, who had arrived in Paris somewhat earlier, he

[1] *Lettera del Sig. Abate Conte Antonio Conti a Monsignor Illustriss. Reverendiss. Filippo del Torre, Vescovo d' Adria, sopra le Considerazioni ec. del Sig. Nigrisoli* (*Giorn. dei Letterati*, XII, 1712, pp. 240 ff.). Nigrisoli replied to Conti in a *Difesa delle Considerazioni intorno* etc., Ferrara, 1714, a book of 107 pp.

[2] Conti, *Prose e Poesie*, Venice, 1739, 1756, II, p. 20.

discussed the nature of tragedy in the gardens of the Tuileries, and he may even have had some share in the composition of Martelli's famous dialogue *L' Impostore*[1]; in any case, he superintended the printing of that work after its author's return to Italy. It is clear that, as a result of these new friendships, his attention was being directed more and more to literary matters; the 'Quarrel of the Ancients and the Moderns' was beginning to rival in his interests the conflicts of the philosophers and scientists.

Conti spent two years in Paris, and then went to London, the immediate occasion of his visit to England being connected with his scientific interests. On April 22, 1715, a total eclipse of the sun was to be visible in London, and Conti—not debarred by Martelli's warning that the air of London would be prejudicial to his health[2]—joined the contingent of French scientists who crossed the channel.

The day after his arrival he was taken, with his French friend Rémond de Monmort, by De Moivre to visit Sir Isaac Newton, who received him 'very politely.'[3] Newton returned the call, and 'talked at length with Conti on the subject of the Cartesian philosophy,' and showed him his experiments on colours. An invitation to dinner followed, and Newton asked him very pressingly to attend the meetings of the Royal Society; he also proposed to put Conti's name down for membership of that body[4]. Through the Hanoverian Countess von Kilmansegg, Conti was presented to the king, George I, and he was henceforth a frequent guest at court, where, however, he could only talk French, his knowledge of English not yet being

[1] Cp. the letter from Martelli to Conti prefaced to the latter's *Il Cesare*, Faenza, 1726, pp. 35 f.: 'Il che ho io ne' mesi, che godei della vostra dotta e ingenua conversazione in Parigi.... Fu per consiglio vostro, e diciam anche fu colla vostra assistenza, che i dialoghi della Tragedia antica e moderna col titolo d'*Impostore* abbozzai.... Voi foste, che sendo io tornato in Italia, ne faceste uscire da cotesti torchi la prima edizione l'anno 1714.' Conti in his reply (p. 45) dwells on the happy days they spent together in the 'boschetti' of the Tuileries. Cp. below, pp. 126 ff.

[2] *Ibid.* p. 46.

[3] *Prose e Poesie*, II, p. 23.

[4] He was admitted on November 17, 1715: 'Sign. Antoni, Comes de Comitibus, of Venice' ('List of Fellows of the Royal Society,' in Thomson's *History of the Royal Society*, London, 1812).

sufficient to allow of his conversing in our language. What seems to have impressed him most in English society was the universal interest in natural philosophy, even the ladies showing an ability to take part in learned discussions.

Before long, however, he had occasion to remember Martelli's warning; as the autumn of 1715 approached, he was attacked by asthma; and for a change of air, he retired to 'Chinsington,' which proved efficacious against the same complaint in the case of King William. 'It is undeniable,' says Conti's latest biographer, 'that his stay at Kensington marked the beginning of his true career as a man of letters.'[1] He turned from his preoccupation with philosophy and science to poetry, and found that he could write verses with facility. On the model of the Abbé Genest, who had in 1716 composed a poem on the Cartesian philosophy, he wrote some two hundred verses on the philosophy of Newton[2]. He read the Duke of Buckingham's *Essay on Poetry*, translated it, and sent his translation to Muratori, who encouraged him in his literary pursuits[3]. This translation has not been printed, but it is preserved in the sixth volume of his 'opere manoscritte.'[4] He now studied other English writers, Pope, Prior, Swift, translated the greatest part of *Paradise Lost*, as well as Pope's *Essay on Man* and *The Rape of the Lock*[5]. Amongst his cantatas is also a version of *Alexander's Feast* by 'Draide, celebre poeta inglese.' Then he turned his attention to Shakespeare's *Julius Caesar*, which the Duke of

[1] G. Brognoligo, *op. cit.* Second article, p. 337.

[2] This is apparently the philosophical poem which Lord Bolingbroke refers to in a letter of December 26, 1723, to Brook Taylor from Paris (cp. Brook Taylor, *Contemplatio philosophica*, London, 1793, p. 136): 'Since my being here, I have seen very few people; our friend the Abbot Conti but once; and then, he was so much out of order, that my conversation with him was very succinct. He had begun a Philosophical Poem, which will be finished, I believe, long before the Anti-Lucretius of Card. de Polignac. Sir Isaac Newton's System will make the principal beauty of it. He recited the exorde to me, which I thought very fine; I need not tell you that he writes it in Italian.'

[3] *Prose e Poesie*, II, p. 37; Muratori's letter, which is dated August 20, 1717, will be found in the *Lettere scelte* to Conti, pp. 33 ff., and Muratori's *Epistolario*, v (1903), pp. 1889 f.

[4] Cp. G. Vedova, *op. cit.* p. 284.

[5] Cp. G. Zanella, *A. Pope e A. Conti*, in the *Nuova Antologia*, July, 1882, pp. i ff.; repr. in *Paralleli letterari*, Verona, 1885, pp. 63 ff.

Buckingham had already put into a form acceptable to classic taste; but Conti's own *Cesare* was not completed until a later date.

Conti soon grew tired of the country and returned to London, where he threw himself with new zeal into his literary studies, frequenting the houses of the Earl of Pembroke and the Duke of Buckingham. Here the illustrious men of letters of the day were to be met. By his influence he brought Italian scientists and scholars—Muratori among others[1]—into relations with the Royal Society.

By special invitation of the king, he visited Hanover with the court, leaving England in October, 1716. While in Hanover, he dined every day with the king. He had hoped—it was one of his chief objects—to make the personal acquaintance of the great Leibnitz; but he found so much to interest him in Holland and so many new friends there—he visited, amongst others, Le Clerc, Quesnel, and the anatomists Ruysch and Leeuwenhoek—that he was delayed, and only arrived in Hanover on the day of Leibnitz's funeral. His relations with Leibnitz dated back to the previous year, when he had acted as a kind of mediator between Newton and the German philosopher in their controversy concerning the invention of the differential calculus[2]. His anxiety to be impartial pleased neither; but, no doubt, Conti had had too pleasant a stay in England to be able to avoid a bias in favour of the English scientist.

In March 1717, Conti, whose health suffered in Hanover, returned with the court to England, where he remained another year, residing alternatively in London and in the country, especially at Hampton Court. He also visited Oxford and Cambridge. He enjoyed the particular favour of the Princess of Wales, to whom he dedicated the manuscript of a compendium of Descartes' *Méditations*. But his old enemy, asthma, attacked him again, and in 1718 he was obliged, on grounds of health, to return to Paris.

[1] Cp. Muratori's letter to Conti, June 1, 1716 (*Lettere scelte*, p. 80; *Epistolario*, v, pp. 1809 f.). From the list in Thomson's *History of the Royal Society* (see note to p. 99) I find that A. M. Salvini was admitted to fellowship in 1716, Muratori and Orsi in 1717.

[2] Cp. Sir David Brewster, *Memoirs of Sir Isaac Newton*, Edinburgh, 1855, pp. 59 ff.

CARL A. RUDISILL LIBRARY
LENOIR RHYNE COLLEGE

Paris remained Conti's home for the following eight years; and he appears to have been as much *persona grata* there as he had been in England. From now on his interests continued to be philosophic and literary rather than scientific. He found French society still disputing about the merits of Homer. During his first stay he had already declared his sympathy with the 'ancients'; and now, in order better to understand and judge, he set about learning Greek in earnest. He devoted himself particularly to the study of Aristotle's *Poetics*, Plato and the history of ancient Greece; he read Euripides with Hardouin, with whom he seems to have been intimate. Among the too scanty literary remains which Toaldo has selected for publication is an extraordinarily interesting sketch of Greek literature, which, if I am not mistaken, is a tribute to the stimulus of Vico. And his parallel of the beginnings of Greek poetry with the conditions among the American aboriginals[1] is surely one of the first attempts to apply comparative methods to the study of primitive literature.

Conti was much engrossed in these years by the disputes of the 'Querelle,' and, besides the writings which I discuss in the following section, he wrote a dissertation on the state of France between 1700 and 1730, which has not been published. He kept in close touch with French intellectual circles, frequenting the houses of Larochefoucauld and Madame Caylus, whose son, Comte Caylus, author of the *Tableaux tirés de l'Iliade*, was one of his most intimate and faithful French friends. Unfortunately his correspondence with Comte Caylus, by which he laid especial store, has not been preserved. His interest in the theatre was kept alive by Luigi Riccoboni ('Lelio') and his wife, Elena Baletti ('Flaminia'), whom Maffei had recommended to him[2]; and with their encouragement he completed his tragedy, *Il Cesare*.

This, Conti's most interesting play, owed, as we have seen,

[1] *Op. cit.* p. 158: 'Poichè la natura è sempre la stessa nelle stesse circostanze, le stesse disposizioni alla Poesia che si veggono negli Americani moderni, possono ancora concepirsi tra i Greci antichi.' The comparison of the American Indians was perhaps suggested by P. Lafitau's *Mœurs des Sauvages amériquains, comparées aux mœurs des premiers temps*, Paris, 1724.

[2] See below, p. 159.

its genesis to his acquaintance with the *Julius Caesar* of 'Sasper, who may be called the Corneille of the English'; and indeed, Conti has the honour of being the first to mention Shakespeare's name—if only in a mutilated form—in Italian literature[1]. 'Sasper,' he says, had composed a tragedy on the death of Julius Caesar, in which, in spite of many deplorable defects, there is much that is beautiful; and the Duke of Buckingham, well aware of these defects, had written two tragedies on the same subject, a *Caesar* and a *Brutus*. Conti became deeply interested in the character of Caesar, studied the Roman historians, and planned a tragedy of his own. Only, however, a few scenes were sketched at this time; and it was reserved for his actor friends in Paris to induce him to complete it. But even then, his temperamental reluctance to give anything out of his hands, stood in his way; he refused to have the play printed, although it had been read in manuscript and approved by several critics, including Orsi and Muratori. Two years passed, and still *Il Cesare* had not appeared; at last Cardinal Bentivoglio, to whom it had been read in 1718, had it sumptuously printed at Faenza without asking the author's permission[2].

[1] Cp. my *The Knowledge of Shakespeare on the Continent at the Beginning of the Eighteenth Century*, in the *Modern Language Review*, I (1908), pp. 318 ff. As the first edition of Conti's play is rare, it is worth quoting the passage on Shakespeare at length (pp. 54 f.): 'Poco dopo il Duca di Bukingano mi diedi a leggere due Tragedie, che aveva fatte; il Cesare, il Bruto, che propriamente non sono, che il Cesare del Sasper diviso in due. Sasper è il Cornelio degl' Inglesi, ma molto più irregolare del Cornelio, sebbene al pari di liu pregno di grandi idee, e di nobili sentimenti. Ristringendomi quì a parlare del suo Cesare, il Sasper lo fa morire al terzo atto; il rimanente della Tragedia è occupato dall' aringa di Marc-antonio al Popolo, indi dalle guerre e dalla morte di Cassio e di Bruto. Può maggiormente violarsi l' unità del tempo, dell' azione, e del luogo? Ma gl' Inglesi disprezzarono sino al Catone le regole d' Aristotile per la ragione, che la Tragedia è fatta per piacere, e che ottima ella è allora che piace; contenesse ella cento azioni diverse, e trasportasse personaggi dall' Europa nell' Asia, e finissero vecchi, ove cominciarono fanciulli. Così pensava cred' io la maggior parte degl' Italiani del 1600 guasti dalle Commedie Spagnuole; e mi maraviglio, come in quel secolo niuno si sia avvisato di tradurre in Italiano le Commedie e Tragedie Inglesi, colme d' accidenti come le Spagnuole, ma certamente con caratteri più naturali e leggiadri. L' Italia avrebbe se non imparata tutta la storia de i Re d' Inghilterra, che da' loro poeti è stata posta sul teatro, ogni vita di Re dando materia ad una tragedia.'

[2] *Il Cesare*, Tragedia del Sig. Ab. Antonio Conti, nobile veneto. Con alcune cose concernenti l' opera medesima, Faenza, 1726. The prefatory letters are: Conti to Bentivoglio; Martelli to Conti; Conti's reply to Martelli;

He added three prefatory letters, as well as some verses by Frugoni, which seem to have irritated Conti more than the fact of the play appearing against his wishes, for the verses were unfriendly to France. This was in 1726. The tragedy was frequently played and won many friends: Vico and Doria, for instance, regarded it—and that at a time when *Merope* was being enthusiastically applauded throughout Italy—as the best Italian tragedy[1]; and Cesarotti—the Cesarotti who admired Ossian—was astounded by the accuracy with which Conti had reproduced the life of ancient Rome, and regarded the play as superior to Shakespeare's[2]!

Brognoligo disposes summarily of the claims that have been too lightly made in the past of Conti's dependence on Shakespeare's *Julius Caesar*, or on the Duke of Buckingham's version of that play[3]; but there are too many resemblances between the Italian and the English tragedy to be summarily dismissed as mere coincidences or common borrowing from Plutarch[4]. The plot of Conti's tragedy follows the familiar lines suggested by Plutarch, Act i being mainly taken up by a Brutus-Cassius scene, while Calpurnia, who has a dream in Act iv, as in Shakespeare, is developed in a way that recalls the French tradition rather than the English. The play falls off badly towards the end, although hardly for the reason of divided interest, which

also 'Versi del padre Frugoni.' Cp. the review in the *Giornale dei Letterati*, XXXVIII, I (1727), pp. 385 ff., A. Zardo, *Un Tragico padovano del secolo scorso*, Padua, 1884; F. Colagrosso, *La prima tragedia di A. Conti*, 2nd ed., Florence, 1898; Abd-el-Kader Salza, *L' Abate Conti e le sue tragedie* (*Annali della R. Scuola Normale superiore*, Pisa, XIII), Pisa, 1898; also Bertana, *op. cit.* p. 72 ff.; Galletti, *op. cit.* pp. 243 ff.; G. Brognoligo, pp. 321 ff., and L. Collison-Morley, *Shakespeare in Italy*, Stratford-upon-Avon, 1916, pp. 6 ff.

[1] *Prose e Poesie*, II, p. 62.

[2] M. Cesarotti, *Ragionamento sopra il Cesare di Voltaire* (*Opere*, XXXIII, Florence, 1810), p. 310.

[3] *Op. cit.* pp. 323 ff.; cp. also his *Le Imitazioni shakespeariane di A. Conti*, in *Rassegna padovana di storia di lettere ed arte*, I, p. 15.

[4] The Italian play, for instance, opens with the Lupercal, in which Antonio is to run; Flavio and Marullo 'castigate' the people who have decorated the statues of Caesar; Caesar is offered the crown—all this in the first act. One might find also verbal similarities: Caesar says of Brutus and Cassio: 'Di que' lor volti pallidi ed austeri nulla mi fido'; Portia is 'degna figlia di Caton'; 'Io lessi,' says Antonio, 'in certe cedolette, che gli Schiavi trovar nel Foro e in Campidoglio sparse: Bruto, ancora tu dormi?' etc.

Fréret complained of; still less was, as Cesarotti asserted, Shakespeare to blame for Conti's shortcomings. The most significant lesson he learned from Shakespeare did not come from *Julius Caesar*, but from Shakespeare's dramas on English history[1]: he exhorts his fellow-countrymen to write tragedies on themes drawn from Italy's great historical past; and he even proposed the establishment of a theatre where dramas illustrating Roman history should be regularly represented. He felt unable to revise *Il Cesare* to meet Fréret's criticism[2], but after 1742 he wrote several more Roman plays. *Giunio Bruto* dates from 1743, *Marco Bruto* from 1744, and *Druso* from 1748. In the preface to his last tragedy, Conti sums up his work as follows: 'In *Giunio Bruto* I represent the establishing of liberty and the consulate; in *Cesare* the attempt to change the republic into a monarchy; in *Marco Bruto* the effort to restore the republic and its first liberties by killing the tyrant.' Finally, in *Druso* he depicted the age of Tiberius, 'an evil emperor, who reigned amidst a still more evil court.'[3] It is obviously not in this doctrinaire spirit that good tragedies are written. The appeal of Conti's dramas to modern readers is slight, and the opinion of his critics on their relative value varies considerably[4]. I cannot, however, help thinking that *Il Cesare* remains the freshest and most alive; the better construction of the last, *Druso*, hardly makes up for its display of learning and the tedious academic sobriety of its verse. In any case, Conti's plays are much superior to Gravina's: Conti was a poet in spite of his metaphysical cast of mind, and Gravina was not. Indeed, one might

[1] Cp. Preface to *Prose e Poesie*, I, p. [xlix]: 'Gl' Inglesi amano le Tragedie dei loro Re, perchè dai fatti dimestici meglio s' impara che da' stranieri.' Amongst Conti's manuscripts is a 'Discorso relativo alla tragedia di Cesare e ch' egli intitolata Fondamenti storici della Tragedia' (Cicutto, quoted by Vedova, *op. cit.* p. 285).

[2] *Le Quattro Tragedie*, Florence, 1751, pp. 175 f. The version in this later collection is a reprint of the edition of 1726.

[3] *Le Quattro Tragedie*, pp. 453 f.

[4] Dejob (*Études sur la Tragédie*, Paris, 1896, pp. 137 f.) is inclined to give the first place to *Druso*; M. Landau (*Geschichte der italienischen Literatur im 18. Jahrh.*, Berlin, 1890, p. 403) calls it his weakest play; Napoli-Signorelli (*Storia critica de' teatri*, III, Naples, 1790, p. 319) prefers *Giunio Bruto*; Parducci (*La tragedia classica italiana del sec. XVIII*, Rocca S. Casciano, 1902, p. 92), *Marco Bruto*.

sum up his achievement as a dramatist by saying that he succeeded in realising Gravina's theory, when Gravina himself failed. He is rightly regarded as the best Italian tragic poet between Maffei and Alfieri. His views on dramatic theory are to be found in the letter to Martelli prefaced to his *Il Cesare* (1726), in the introductory dissertation to his translation of Racine's *Athalie*, and in the Prefaces to his other plays[1]. On the whole, these opinions coincide in principle with those of his master Gravina[2]; his friendship with Martelli in Paris kept him from falling into any pronounced antagonism to the latter; in fact, he acted as a kind of mediator between Gravina and Martelli. He held that tragedy should aim at Greek simplicity, retaining the chorus, but he would have nothing to do with the theories of the Aristotelians; further, that it should be veraciously historical and instruct the people in civic and moral virtues. He laid particular weight on the accurate reproduction of the Roman character and milieu, even insisting that the actors should dress as Romans[3]; but he regarded it as a function of the poet to introduce a certain amount of idealisation in presenting historical characters. He required the strict subordination of love-plots—he is, in point of fact, sparing of them in his own plays—and he objected strongly to Martellian verse[4]. But he had lived too long in France, and admired Racine too warmly[5], not to have imbibed French sympathies; he is an upholder of the unities, to which he added La Motte's unity of interest: but he also makes the sensible remark that 'one of the great arts of tragedy is to interest the audience in such a way

[1] The fifth volume of his promised works was to have contained a treatise on Tragedy; cp. *Prose e Poesie*, I, Pref., p. [xliii], where he defines Tragedy as 'un esempio credibile d' una sciagura accaduta a persone illustri, ed ordinata ad istruire per via della compassione e del terrore gli uomini dell' età presente.'

[2] 'Conformandomi io a tali saggi precetti non dal Gravina, ma dalla natura, o dell' esperienza, e dalla Filosofia stessa dettati...' (Preface to *Marco Bruto*, *op. cit.* p. 150).

[3] Letter to Cardinal Bentivoglio (*Il Cesare*, pp. 28 f.; *Le Quattro Tragedie*, p. 348). Calepio dilates on Conti's historical truth (*Paragone*, p. 171); Martelli, it may be noted, also demanded historical costume (*Opere*, I, p. 172), as also, following the Italian initiative, Gottsched in Germany.

[4] *Le Quattro Tragedie*, pp. 186 f.

[5] *Ibid.* p. 351. Cp. also Dejob, *op. cit.* p. 131, and below, p. 113.

that it does not think of the time at all.'[1] It is more disappointing to find him clinging to technical pedantries, such as 'liaison,' which do not lend freedom and vitality to his work. On the question of confidants versus monologues, he agreed with Martelli in preferring the latter[2].

In 1725 an acrimonious quarrel broke out between Conti and Newton, who accused him of a breach of confidence in allowing Fréret to see and translate a transcript which Conti had made of Newton's *Chronology of ancient Kingdoms amended*[3]. But in spite of this unpleasant affair, Conti did not cease to be one of Newton's most ardent continental champions.

Even in Paris, however, he was still troubled by asthma, and towards the end of 1726, he returned to Italy. He settled in Venice, and passed the remainder of his life between that city and Padua. He had taken back with him scientific instruments with which he repeated Newton's experiments in Italy; and the literary activity of his later years was considerable. In 1732 he wrote a remarkable, if somewhat obscure, philosophical poem *Il Globo di Venere*. In a dream or vision, he believes himself transported to the moon. He sees a large company of ladies advancing ceremoniously to music towards a stately temple. From one of them he learns that he is not in the moon, but in the planet Venus, in which he 'ripose la sede della bellezza e dell' armonia, e l' orno di tutte le meraviglie astronomiche e fisiche che più sorprendono.' Here he beholds the apotheosis of Antonia Anguissola, wife of Paolo Carrara, who had just died, and whom her husband had invited the poets of Italy to celebrate. In this apotheosis Dante's Beatrice, Petrarch's Laura and Venus-Urania herself take part. In its philosophic aspects the theme of the poem is the Platonic ideas of the beautiful, and is

[1] *Prose e Poesie*, I, Pref. p. [lii].

[2] See below, p. 133.

[3] For this controversy, which stirred up much dust in its day, cp. Brewster, *op. cit.* II, pp. 301 ff.; the introduction to Fréret's *Défense de la Chronologie fondée sur les monumens de l'histoire ancienne contre le système chronologique de M. Newton*, Paris, 1758; and especially Des Maizeau's *Recueil de diverses Pièces sur la Philosophie*, etc., 2nd ed., Amsterdam, 1740, vol. II. Newton's denunciation of Conti and Fréret appeared in the *Philosophical Transactions* in 1726, and Conti's defence of himself is in the *Bibliothèque françoise*, May–June, 1726, pp. 182 ff. Cp. his letter to Brook Taylor of May 22, 1721, *op. cit.* pp. 121 ff.

inspired by the *Phaedon* and *Timaeus*[1]. Still more metaphysical and recondite was to have been *Il Scudo di Pallade*, of which Conti gives the plan in the Preface to his *Prose e Poesie*[2]. He seems to have had in view here a kind of poetic sublimation of the Leibnitzian *Théodicée*; but the poem did not get beyond its beginnings.

Besides this, Conti was an industrious translator; his biographer ascribes to him versions of Anacreon, Pindar, Sophocles, Homer and Hesiod; on Homer, in particular, he compiled a large volume containing 'all that critics and commentators had said in favour of this poet.' From the Latin he translated the *Thebaid* of Statius, Virgil's *Georgics*, some of Horace's *Odes*, and parts of the *Aeneid*, of Ovid's *Metamorphoses*, and of Catullus; from the French, tragedies by Racine, some cantos of the *Henriade*, and the *Mérope* of Voltaire (1744); those from the English have already been mentioned. His contributions to literary theory and aesthetics take the form, partly of elaborate letters; partly treatises, which have been published in a fragmentary form in the posthumous volume of his works. He also wrote an *Illustrazione del Parmenide di Platone* (1743), and a *Trattato dell' Idee d' Ermogene* (1740), suggested by Orsi's *Considerazioni*. It is particularly to be regretted that he never finished a history of philosophy which he planned in 1745.

The sum of Conti's intellectual and literary life is disappointing. He was a man with 'an insatiable thirst for knowledge,'[3] and vast ideas—'un ingegno architettonico,' says Toaldo[4]—he cherished great plans, but had too little tenacity of purpose to bring them to completion. He seemed temperamentally unable to put the finishing touches to anything he wrote, and could

[1] Cp. the Dedication of the poem to Ceratti (*Prose e Poesie*, I, pp. iii ff.); and E. Bertana, *In Arcadia*, Naples, 1909, p. 92; also G. Maugain, *op. cit.* pp. 328 f.

[2] *Ibid.* p. [lix ff.]: 'Poema, che ha per Scena con mondi possibili il mondo creato, per azione l' istruzione specolativa e pratica della sapienza, e per fine la giustificazione della Providenza divina nel governo degli uomini.'

[3] Hardouin said of him (I quote the Italian in *Prose e Poesie*, II, pp. 52 f.): 'In una parola egli accoppiava a una insaziabile cupidità di sapere una singolar penetrazione, un senso vivo e dilicato, un gusto fino, e tutto ciò che può costituire in un tempo un' uomo dotto e un bellissimo ingegno.'

[4] *Prose e Poesie*, I, p. 87.

only with difficulty bring himself to publish a book; volume I of his *Prose e Poesie*, the only one published in his life-time, is announced as the first of six volumes[1]. In his last years he began an autobiography, which is utilised by Toaldo in his introduction to the *Prose e Poesie*. The end of his life was solitary and embittered; he seems also to have been in money straits. In November, 1748, he was struck down by apoplexy, but recovered sufficiently to be removed to his native town, Padua, where he spent the last months of his life. A second stroke, on March 30, 1749, was fatal, and he died on April 6.

II

I have dealt at greater length with the life of Antonio Conti than was perhaps necessary to illustrate the rôle he played in the moulding of Italian aesthetics; but it is a typical and interesting life, and doubly interesting to us owing to his ties with England. It supplies the key, too, to the tragic ineffectiveness of his career, that fateful dissipation of energy over wide intellectual fields which, in the eighteenth century, claimed so many victims.

It was in England, as we have seen, that Conti was first wooed from science to literature, although unfortunately his English friends and associates were all of the classic type of mind. The Duke of Buckingham was not the man to put the case of Shakespeare, or the English attitude to literary aesthetics which an appreciation of Shakespeare involved, before him in the best light. But his studies had not advanced very far when he returned to France; here, during his second residence in Paris, he threw himself with single-hearted zeal into the investigation of literary theory. The starting-point was the controversy concerning Homer which was opened by La Motte's translation in 1714, and at once met by Madame Dacier's defence of antiquity in her *Traité des Causes de la Corruption du Goust*. I nthe following year appeared the Abbé Terrasson's negative but logical development of La Motte's standpoint; and for a time the merits of Homer formed the burning question

[1] He left no less than twelve volumes in his own handwriting of works in manuscript; the contents of these volumes is enumerated by Cicutto (see Vedova, *op. cit.* pp. 284 ff.).

of the day in French criticism. At this time and under the stimulus of this controversy, Conti wrote two letters on the rival claims of the 'ancients' and the 'moderns'; from these is to be seen his attitude to the 'Quarrel,' as it stood about the year 1719.

The first of these letters[1], in French, is to a Madame Ferrant, and is dated August 13, 1719, some months, be it noted, after the publication of Du Bos' *Réflexions critiques sur la poésie et sur la peinture*. I am doubtful, however, whether Conti had read Du Bos. The main points of his letter are as follows. It opens with a discussion of the distinctive qualities of verse and prose. On the question whether a poem might be written in prose, Conti takes part with the 'ancients' against Fénelon and La Motte: 'Les discours poëtiques sont les discours les plus figurés, les plus passionés, et les plus armonieux dont une langue soit capable'; 'le caractere qui distingue la poësie de la prose en toutes les langues, c'est la mesure fine et constante des vers' (p. lxxxviii). Poetic pictures must be an imitation of beautiful nature—nature including not only what really exists, outside of us, but also 'tout ce à quoi les hommes d'un certain Siecle et d'un certain pays ont donné l'existence' (p. lxxxix), supernatural beings, such as angels and demons, that is, 'caracteres réels par hipothêse.' With regard to the real characters, Conti warns against the creation of monsters of vice and virtue; in respect of the supernatural, he agrees with Shaftesbury that pagan deities are tedious to the modern reader, and insists on the purely relative value of religious beliefs for purposes of poetry. Thus the supernatural world of Milton—and he refers here to 'the beautiful description of Mons. Addison'—makes a warmer appeal to us moderns than the pagan mythology. 'Tant il est vrai,' he concludes, 'que le Dieu des Juifs et des Chretiens peut fournir d'infiniment plus belles et plus grandes Images que les Idoles du Paganisme, et que la Poësie Orientale est infiniment plus noble que la Latine et la Greque' (pp. xcv f.). Needless to say, the object of poetry remains for Conti, as it had been for Gravina and Muratori, the combination of the 'utile' and the 'dulce': 'Si je puis instruire et plaire en même

[1] *Prose e Poesie*, II, pp. lxxxv ff.

tems, pourquoi m'amuserai-je à plaire seulement?' (p. xcvi). Finally, he discusses the respective merits of Ariosto and Tasso, and reproaches the French writers, especially Boileau and Bouhours, for their adverse criticism of Tasso. The latter part of the letter deals with matters that have less immediate bearing on literature.

The second letter to Maffei[1] is undated, but, as is to be seen from its contents, was written about the same time. It is also in French, and contains, after a preliminary discussion of ancient history, a more complete discussion of 'le caractere et les maximes de l'Ecole moderne,' as they are to be found in the writings of Fontenelle and La Motte. Here Conti ranges himself quite definitely on the side of the 'ancients.' He dismisses Fontenelle's *De la Pluralité des Mondes* as unoriginal, but approves of the *Dialogues des Morts*. He is, however, particularly concerned with Fontenelle's new work, the *Discours sur la Nature de l'Eglogue*. Fontenelle insisted that the theme of a poem is of the first importance: it must be something 'ce qui est beau, grand, nouveau, ce qui interesse, touche, surprend: en un mot il faut peindre la belle nature' (pp. cxiii f.), which is quite in agreement with Muratori. But Fontenelle, Conti goes on, neglects the equally important question of the manner of the imitation. This leads to a statement of his views on the importance of the form, and, in opposition to La Motte, he shows no favour to the paradox of poetry in prose. If not everything, form is, at least, a very important factor. 'La poësie,' he says (p. cxvii), 'n'est pas moins peinture que musique. Imiter est representer si vivement les objets, qu'ils fassent sur nous les mêmes impressions qu'ils feroient si nous les voyons en eux mêmes.' This being so, poetry must 'renoncer aux termes abstraits, aux reflexions, au bel esprit, en un mot, à tout ce qui fait voir l'auteur, et non pas les choses qu'il imite.' In other words, it must be objective and impersonal: it must imitate in such a way that we obtain the same impression from the imitation as we should receive from the reality. This had been, of course, Gravina's conclusion: and, like Gravina, Conti points to Homer as the highest example.

[1] *Op. cit.* II, pp. cviii ff.

The conclusion to which Conti comes is that La Motte, Fontenelle and their partisans are deficient in taste.

De là vient qu'ils ont introduit dans les belles lettres l'esprit et la methode de Mr Des-cartes, et qu'ils jugent de la poësie et de l'eloquence independemment des oreilles et des passions, comme on juge des corps independemment des qualités sensibles. De là vient aussi qu'ils confondent le progrès de la philosophie avec celui des arts. (p. cxx.)

This view is rather surprising as coming from a critic like Conti, whose own poetry is permeated by Cartesianism, as that of the most Cartesian of French writers had never been. As a matter of fact, we find him later repudiating the opinion.

In spite then of some wavering, Conti, in the period of his residence in Paris, took his stand with the French 'ancients.' Where he does not quite see eye to eye with them, it was due to the influence of the thinker to whom he looked up all his life as a master in these matters, and whom he now recommends to French readers, Gravina. We have just seen how he appealed to Gravina's authority for the naturalistic imitation of nature, based on the practice of Homer: and again, when Conti asserts (p. cxxi) that poetic beauty is relative—a much more serious divergence from the 'ancient' doctrine, and indeed, an actual echo of Perrault—he is repeating an idea on which Gravina insisted, namely, that every age has its own ideals of beauty, and that consequently, as Fénelon had said, the beauty of Homer is a beauty for Homer's own time. More or less dependent on this assumption is Conti's attitude to a controversy which ran, more or less, through all the European criticism of this period, the question of the legitimacy of the 'miraculous.' The Greeks and Romans had been liberal in their toleration of miraculous motives in their poetry, and the view of the 'ancients' of the early eighteenth century was that the practice of modern literature in this respect should not go beyond their example. It is here that Conti, claiming with Desmarets a superiority for the 'mirabile cristiano' over the 'mirabile pagano,' ranges himself with the enemy[1]. This, as we have seen, had been taken over by Gravina, from the Italian pioneer of the 'Querelle,' Tassoni;

[1] Cp. the letter to Mad. Ferrant, pp. xciii ff. and below, p. 115.

and no doubt Conti's sympathies for a Christian art had been strengthened by the deep impression made upon him by Milton —although he did not think that Milton managed the 'mirabile' well—and by the *Athalie* of Racine[1].

Brognoligo distinguishes two irreconcilable phases in Conti's views on literary aesthetics: an 'artistic' phase, contained in the documents which we have just been examining: and a 'metaphysical' phase in the fragmentary writings on Imitation, Poetic Fantasms, on the dialogue of Fracastoro and in the letter on Beauty to Caratti[2]. Opposed the two phases may be, but I doubt whether Brognoligo is right in emphasising the inconsistency of the two points of view; the second seems to me rather a legitimate and natural evolution of the opinions held in the first.

Conti continues to maintain in his *Trattato dell' Imitazione* the principle that poetry is an imitation of nature[3]; but he endeavours now to establish the principle on a more satisfying basis than the crudely realistic interpretation of 'imitation' with which he had been previously satisfied, and the merely formal distinction of poetry of his first phase. He has first to distinguish imitation, as applied to words, from imitation in the other arts. He now defines imitation as nothing but 'rappresentar in guisa le cose che facciano su gli organi de' sensi e su l' animo impressioni analoghe a quelle che faceano in loro stesse' (p. 124). In the development of this new point of view the influence of Muratori's *Della Perfetta Poesia italiana* seems to me to have been a decisive factor.

The *Trattato de' Fantasmi poetici* is obviously a continuation

1 'L' Atalia del Racine, la miglior tragedia, che nel Secolo di Luigi XIV siasi composta' (*Le Quattro Tragedie*, pp. 351 f.). His translation of *Athalie*, with an introductory Dissertation, is to be found in *Prose e Poesie*, I, pp. cxliv ff.

2 *Op. cit.* Third article, p. 155.

3 *Trattato dell' Imitazione* (*Prose e Poesie*, II, pp. 109 ff.). Unfortunately, Toaldo gives only a very brief summary of the 'cento e più fogli' on this theme which Conti left; the manuscript is, however, preserved in the eleventh volume of his 'opere manoscritte' (Vedova, p. 286). In the Preface to the first volume of *Prose e Poesie* Conti reproaches his predecessors with not having worked out the idea of imitation, which he there defines as follows: 'Tutte le bell' arti convengono nell' imitazione come in un' idea comune, la quale non perde mai nè la sua natura, nè le sue proprietà per quanto si varino le materie, gli stromenti, ed i modi dell' arte' (p. [xx]). Here we might find *in nuce* the programme of Batteux' work.

of that on Imitation. As imagination is the mother not merely of poetic fantasms, but of those of all other imitative arts, he proposes to define more exactly the kind of imagination peculiar to the poet. History, eloquence, poetry, he says, are all alike the reproduction of 'fantasms': history is restricted to true fantasms: eloquence may be extended to verisimilar fantasms; while poetry may go still further afield and include in its legitimate range possible fantasms. Poetry is a more intense form of expression than either history or eloquence: its descriptions are more alive; its emotions more intense; its imagery more highly coloured[1]. The definition of poetry cannot, however, be restricted to the method of imitation; much more important is the matter. And now (p. 130), quite on Muratorian lines, Conti distinguishes: (i) a 'poetry of images,' that is to say, a poetry that reproduces true or real things ('che corrisponde alle pitture de' ritratti') existent or historical; (ii) a 'poetry of idols,' a poetry which reproduces things not in themselves true, but which are an imitation of true things; and lastly (iii) a 'poetry of spectres,' which deals with wholly imaginary things that correspond to nothing in reality. Thus there are three forms of poetic representation: that of the true, of the true combined with the imaginary, and of the verisimilar with the imaginary. As an example of the first group, Conti cites the poem of Lucretius; of the middle group, the *Georgics* of Virgil (or at least part of them); while of the third and most genuinely 'poetic' group of all, the *Iliad* and the *Aeneid*. *Paradise Lost* would presumably also be a good example. Obviously, there is but one end to which all this metaphysical theorising tends, and that is to setting up the religious or metaphysical poem as the highest form of poetic art.

Conti is in agreement with Fracastoro and Piccolomini in asserting that poetry imitates universal things, that is, expresses the typical, not the concrete; while history and eloquence are restricted to particular things. And this was also essentially Gravina's and Muratori's view[2]. Philosophy, it is true, also

[1] 'La Poesia confrontata all' altre due arti non ha che maggior evidenza nelle descrizioni, maggior energia negli affetti, maggior pompa nelle figure, e studio maggiore nella scelta e collocazione delle parole' (*ibid.* p. 128).

[2] Cp. above, pp. 40, 75; and Conti's dissertation on the *Ragion poetica* of Gravina (II, p. 249).

deals with universals; but it does not imitate them or attempt to reduce them to 'sensible images.' It is this use of 'sensible images' which characterises poetry. There is no longer any question of the poet 'imitating nature,' describing things as they are, as he had demanded in 1719; nor is verse the distinguishing characteristic of poetry. Conti has now tacitly abandoned his Gravinian objection to that claim, on which Fénelon and later La Motte insisted, that poetry may be written in prose[1].

In practice there are considerable limitations to the field available for the poet: these limitations are summed up in the word 'convenienza' or 'convenevolezza,' 'appropriateness' (pp. 131 ff.). Theoretically, the whole knowable universe is open to the poet: in practice, the imitation must be appropriate to the object imitated and to the idea which has to be expressed: and the business of the poet, it must be borne in mind, is to give delight. He is debarred, for instance, from representing mathematical truths or too complicated scientific theories; he has to select, and to make use of only such images as embody appropriately his idea. It is the first object of poetry to give pleasure, and, owing to the natural sloth of man's mind, it attains this end rather by the depiction of verisimilar than true things. The poet must keep in view the tastes of those to whom he appeals. There is much in the ancients and in the romances of the sixteenth century which appealed to the age for which they were written, but which we moderns have a difficulty in appreciating. And on this ground Conti justifies what he calls the greater 'convenienza artistica' in modern eyes, of the Christian 'mirabile,' compared with the pagan 'mirabile.' The purely symbolic use of mythology is another matter, and is, under certain circumstances, permissible.

And now Conti turns to consider the nature of beauty. What is beauty? Is it a result of the artistic representation of the fantasms, or is beauty inherent in the fantasms? In other words, is beauty a quality of form or of matter? Light is thrown on Conti's views on this question by his discussion of Fracastoro's

[1] Cp. letter to Mad. Ferrant, p. lxxxvii; also G. Brognoligo, *op. cit.* Third article, p. 168.

dialogue *Il Navagero, o sia della Poesia* (*Naugerius, sive de poetica*)[1]: and, best of all, by his letter to Ceratti, President of the University of Pisa[2], which, with the *Trattato de' Fantasmi*, is Conti's most important contribution to aesthetics. Indeed, one cannot help thinking that had this letter—not to speak of the other fragmentary studies we are considering—been published when it was written, instead of not until 1756, it would have accelerated considerably the development of the science of aesthetics. Here, in this analysis of aesthetic pleasure, Conti laid the foundations of a philosophy of art[3].

The letter is supplementary to the dedication to Ceratti of the *Globo di Venere*. In Muratori's fashion he proposes to discuss beauty under three heads: the beauty of man and living creatures; the beauty of inanimate things visible on earth or in heaven; and the beauty of virtue. He dwells at great length, and with the citation of many authorities, on the beauty of the human form. It is sufficient, however, to turn at once to Conti's definition of beauty, which has clearly been influenced by Crousaz' *Traité sur le Beau*[4]. Beauty, he says, is 'la varia proporzione delle parti e de' colori soavi uniformemente espressa ed animata dalla grazia e nobilitata dalla venustà' (II, p. clxii). Beauty is a relative idea, a mingling of corporeal and incorporeal elements. So far as it is physical, it may be identified with qualities appreciable by the senses; in so far as it is incorporeal, with the idea of justice or virtue. He dwells on the need of variety as an element that gives pleasure, and of uniformity as an element that tends to concentrate attention and interest on the object. Beauty is unity in variety; in other words, variety and uniformity are the essential elements of the pleasure which the mind receives from beauty; but not the actual cause of that pleasure. Aesthetic pleasure is an intellectual pleasure, the pleasure which every operation of the reason brings us (pp. clxv f.). Here, clearly, is a corner-stone of the new science of aesthetics that was to be; and these contributions of Conti's may justly be claimed as the most important which Italy had so far made to the building up

[1] *Prose e Poesie*, II, pp. 242 ff.
[2] *Ibid.* pp. cxli ff.
[3] Cp. A. Rolla, *op. cit.* p. 120.
[4] See below, p. 203.

of such a science. His speculations are no mere empirical guesswork, but based on a study of the question in all its aspects. Conti was familiar with all that had been thought on it from Aristotle to Descartes, Wolff, and even to 'Mylord Sasfburis' and that 'matematico scozzese' who masquerades in his pages as 'Utchtsonio.'[1]

Thus like his master, Gravina, Conti sought a poetic 'ragione'; and indeed his system is a tribute to the germinative force of the *Ragion poetica*. But for Conti the poetic 'ragione' takes the form of a definition of beauty. And beauty is truth; the end of poetry—here, too, he is faithful to Gravina's teaching—is the expression of the true. But in the later, metaphysical period of his thought, he sought the truth in the universal or typical, and rejected realistic imitation as an unworthy function of poetry. The accusation of inconsistency which has been brought against Conti, seems to me to be more apparent than real. What in fact happened was that, in his quest for the 'ragione,' he abandoned his earlier conclusions, not as wrong, but as immaterial. His interest in poetic expression has become exclusively a metaphysical one. It is the 'ragione' behind the work, and the 'ragione' only, that now interests him, that is to say, the theoretic essence of poetry; the outward form has become a matter of indifference to him; he is, in fact, no longer interested in poetic expression as such. This, I think, explains that peculiar lack of partisanship on Conti's part, which leads him, at heart an 'ancient,' to regard the French 'moderns,' with tolerant sympathy.

And what is Conti's ultimate conclusion? 'Poetry,' he says, 'is the art of making a system of artificial fantasms in the highest degree delightful, by means of objects and words, and by the manner of presenting them.'[2] This definition, says Brognoligo[3],

[1] *Prose e Poesie*, I, Pref. pp. [ix f.].

[2] *Dissertazione sopra la Ragion poetica del Gravina*, II, p. 265; or more fully in the Preface to *Prose e Poesie*, p. [xxvii]: '...inferisco non esser la Poesia, che un sistema di fantasmi sommamente dilettevoli, rappresentativi di cose umane e divine, talora con allegoria, ma sempre con entusiasmo ed armonia, espressi ed applicati dalla facoltà civile ad insegnare la verità e la virtù. Quest' idea è complessa, ma include in sè la materia, la forma, il modo della Poesia, e la sua cagione finale.'

[3] *Op. cit.* Third article, p. 177.

is complete, for it includes form and substance, and covers the whole field of poetry; for in 'highest delight' are comprehended all delights, also what is beneficial and helpful. Indeed, as the 'highest delight' of the soul must be something permanent and durable, it must do more than merely give pleasure; to be worthy of the name, to be 'in the highest degree delightful,' it must fulfil some end of practical utility[1]. Thus the old artistic theory of his first period has given place to a metaphysical theory: the end of poetry is moral; it must embody the highest truth, that is, metaphysical truth. Clearly Conti has travelled a long way since he protested against the introduction of abstractions into poetry. He now insists that poetry should preferably imitate just these abstractions. But to leave it at this, would be to do him less than justice. Although the highest type of poetry is, in his opinion, philosophic or religious, he expressly excludes the didactic poem; he is quite aware that the exclusive pursuit of the ideal he has set up would restrict poetry to an audience of learned men and scientists.

Conti's not very lucid criticism of Gravina is regarded by Brognoligo as another change of front on the part of this evasive thinker. But here again, I am inclined to think that no change of front is implied or intended on Conti's part. He asserts in this essay on his master that poetry is a 'system of fantasms' composed with a view to causing delight; but this does not mean, as Brognoligo infers, that he now denies all metaphysical purpose to poetry; but rather that he is, like Muratori, concentrating for the nonce his attention on one side only of the function of poetry. In fact, just in this definition of the function of poetry Conti again clearly shows his indebtedness to the *Perfetta Poesia italiana*.

In conclusion, I would plead that the unfortunately broken and imperfect record of Conti's development as a thinker is mainly responsible for the impression of inconsistency and vacillation which his modern Italian critic has received from his work. We can ill spare what was to have filled out the six

[1] 'Nel sommo diletto s' include ancora l' utile e il giovamento, perchè il sommo diletto deve esser durevole, nè altro che le cose giovevoli lasciano in noi tal diletto' (*ibid.* p. 266; cp. also *Fantasmi*, p. 131).

volumes of Conti's original plan. Not merely would they have made his development clear to us; but they might also have afforded us a system of aesthetic thought chronologically in advance of that of Baumgarten and the Halle school, and nearer than theirs to the aesthetics of Kant and Schiller. Conti's history of France from 1700 to 1730, which is preserved in manuscript[1], would, no doubt, also throw valuable light on the progress of the great movement in French intellectual life which still awaits a definitive interpretation. But even with our knowledge, based on the fragments Conti's editor has published, we can form some idea of his development, from the time when he emerges as a champion—with, it is true, important reservations —of the French 'ancients,' to that when he stands out as an uncompromising idealist, outside the pale of the 'Querelle,' as a thinker who, from the Pisgah-height of his wide knowledge, caught a glimpse of a new promised land of aesthetic theory. This development seems to me neither inconsistent nor incomprehensible: it is merely obscured by the lack of the connecting links. Might not one claim that Conti went through a process of development, not unsimilar to that which is familiar to us from the later eighteenth century, when the great Germans passed from a realistic 'Storm and Stress' to poetic idealism and to the disinterested pursuit of beauty in the classic age of Weimar?

Two reasons militated against Conti's having the influence on his successors which the originality of his aesthetic theories would have justified: the unfinished nature of his writings, and the fact that they were only published in a fragmentary form after the middle of the eighteenth century, when Conti was himself several years dead.

[1] *Saggio storico-politico sullo stato della Francia dal* 1700 *sino al* 1730 (in vol. x of the manuscripts). Cp. Vedova, *op. cit.* p. 286.

Chapter V

Pier Jacopo Martelli

I

In a mild, late seventeenth-century way Pier Jacopo Martelli might be said to have been born in the purple. His portrait[1] reminds one of an old Renaissance aristocrat; and there was a glamour round his life, tempered although it was by a certain bourgeois domesticity, that recalls the men of letters of the spacious Italian age. As a writer, he is by no means unattractive, although one's estimate of him may be modified by the suspicion that the 'clinquant' in his talent and achievement sometimes outweighed the solid metal. As Conti had been a link between Italy and England, so Martelli is the most conspicuous Italian representative of the French outlook on literature. But to say, as is usually said, that he was a mere 'ambassador of France' in Italy is to underrate his efforts, which were directed, no less than those of the other writers dealt with in the present volume, to the realisation of a 'perfect Italian poetry.'

Born at Bologna on April 28, 1665, Martelli belonged to the older generation of the men of Italy who inaugurated the

[1] An extraordinary sonnet, signed 'A. D.' no doubt 'Aci Delpusiano,' Martelli's friend, Eustachio Manfredi, which is attached to his portrait in vol. II of the Bologna edition of his works (1735), describes him:

Agil gamba, agil fianco, agile imbusto,
    Buon color, fronte aperta, occhio amoroso,
    Sottile il labbro, un sotto l' altro ascoso.
    Naso lungo aquilin, fra 'l grande, e il giusto.
Venerabile il tergo, il passo onusto;
    Alta la testa, il portamento arioso;
    Parlar soaue, ed atteggiar uezzoso,
    Franzese l' aria, e Spagnoletto il fusto.
Vn conuersar giocondo, un naturale
    Affaccendato disinuoltamente
    Di grand' impegno, e di ripiego eguale,
E il carattere in uolto di una mente
    Piena d' alti pensier; fra quai preuale
    La gran tranquillità del non far niente.

eighteenth century[1]. He came of good family, and his father, Giambattista Martelli, was not merely a connoisseur of pictures, but also a learned man, who shared to the full the newly awakened interest in philosophy, natural science and medicine. But the home in which young Martelli was brought up, was, notwithstanding, a sincerely religious one; and the religious stamp remained with him all his life[2]. He received his early education from the Jesuits; and at an early date he turned from medicine, the profession for which he was intended and which he abhorred, to theology, and afterwards to jurisprudence. Meanwhile poetry —and remembering the early date, it need hardly be said Marinistic poetry—became a dominant interest. He began by writing love-verses inspired by Catterina Torri ('Amarilli') whom he married in 1694[3], and a long poem, *Degli Occhi d' Amarilli*; but in his religious zeal he subsequently, like his contemporary Maggi, repudiated his 'amorous verse' and, at his father's instigation, committed the *Occhi d' Amarilli* to the flames. In its place he wrote and dedicated to his wife *Degli Occhi di Gesù*; but across this poem fell the shadow of his father's death in 1700[4]. Indeed, it is a kind of poetic tribute to his father, whose shade, like a Beatrice, conducts the poet through an earthly paradise. The poem is in *ottava rima* and still shows traces of the conceits of the seventeenth century. The hardest task which confronted all the writers of this time was to shake off the pernicious influence they set out to combat; and to none was it harder than to Martelli. But in spite of this, Martelli's lyric poetry merits, it seems to me, as high a place as anything he later achieved. It is like coming upon an oasis in

[1] A brief *Vita di Pier Jacopo Martello scritta da lui stesso sino all' anno* 1718 was published by Calogerà in his *Raccolta d' Opuscoli scientifici e filologici*, II, Venice, 1729, pp. 275 ff. This is reprinted in the edition of the *Femia sentenziato*, by P. Viani, Bologna, 1869; and also, brought to a conclusion, by G. Fantuzzi, *Notizie degli scrittori bolognesi*, V, Bologna, 1786, pp. 332 ff. Another biography will be found in the *Giornale de' Letterati d' Italia*, XXXVIII, 2 (1733), pp. 148 ff. (*Elogio di Pier Jacopo Martello*); reprinted, with some alterations, as Introduction to the Bologna edition of Martelli's *Opere*, 1735. See also A. Fabronius, *Vitae Italorum*, V, Pisa, 1779, pp. 259 ff.; and Carini, *op. cit.* pp. 286 ff.

[2] Cp. G. Maugain, *op. cit.* p. 237.

[3] Cp. M. Carmi, *Pier Jacopo Martelli: Studi*, I, Florence, 1906, p. 92. It is to be regretted that these studies on Martelli have not been continued.

[4] *Opere*, Bologna, 1735, VI, pp. 1 ff. See *Proemio*.

that desert of Arcadian verse, the nine volumes of *Rime degli Arcadi*, edited by Crescimbeni, to light upon the sincerely beautiful poetry (vol. II) in which he pours out his heartfelt sorrow at the death of his six-year-old child Giambattista ('Osmino'), who—at least so the father believed—died as the victim of two quarrelling doctors, 'a dove torn by two cruel hawks.'[1] But this was not the side of his literary work which Martelli wished to be taken seriously. Like all the Italian writers who are considered in the present volume, he first became a man of letters with a serious purpose under the stimulus of Bouhours' taunts. Caught up by the wave of revolt against the conceits of Marini, he soon learned to look to Dante, Petrarca and Boccaccio as the guiding stars of Italian poetry: and he resolved to rehabilitate his literature by cultivating the more abstract lyric and the epic. Orsi first directed Martelli's attention to the drama as the field on which the conflict with France might most advantageously be fought out; and it is not to be overlooked that Eustachio Manfredi[2], who, alone among the supporters of Orsi, had a sympathetic word to say of the great dramatists of France, was one of the intimates of Martelli's youth. Martelli himself felt attracted by tragic poetry, and he shared the indignation of Orsi and his friends at seeing the 'literary' Italian stage dominated by translations of French tragedies[3]. He set about his reformatory task systematically, as Gravina did, or Maffei: he equipped himself by studying the Greeks in translation[4], and—in spite of his scorn of 'the proud, foreign nation'—the French dramatic poets. I doubt if an irresistible impulse or inspiration lay behind Martelli's late-born dramatic activity: it was part

[1] *Opere*, Bologna, 1735, VII, p. 75.

[2] Cp. above, p. 15. Martelli refers to Manfredi's letter to Orsi in his dialogue *Del verso tragico* (*Opere*, II, p. xxxix).

[3] *Vita*, *Opere*, I, p. vii; also *Giorn. de' Letterati*, XXXVIII, p. 155: 'Arse di scorno in vedere il Teatro Italiano occupato da straniera e superba nazione, senza che l' Italia, toltinc alcuni originali per l' antichità, e per alcune poco osservate bellezze, venerabili, avesse che opporre ad essi.'

[4] E. Bertana (*Il Teatro tragico italiano del sec. XVIII prima dell' Alfieri*, p. 21) unnecessarily restricts Martelli's study to Euripides. Cp. *Vita*, p. viii: '...indi ricominciò da capo a rileggere le greche tragedie, che di Sofocle, di Euripide, e d' Eschilo ci rimangono.' By his own confession (*Esamina dell' Euripide lacerato*, *Opere*, VII, p. 250) Martelli did not know Greek: 'Io non vanto di possedere la Greca lingua, siccome giurerei quasi, che molti di coloro, che se ne vantono, non la posseggono.'

of a deliberately conceived plan to assert Italy's claims beside those of France and to wipe out the insults of Bouhours. In 1697, at the age of thirty-two, he was appointed to the honourable position of 'chancellor' or secretary to the Senate of Bologna; in 1707 he became a professor of 'humane letters' in the University, and in the following year went to Rome as secretary to the Bologna Embassy. Before this date—the year of the publication of Gravina's *Ragion poetica*—we know that he had already written several tragedies.

From now on Martelli lived a full literary life. As an Arcadian, 'Mirtilo Dianidio'—he had been obliged to drop an 'l' as the name 'Mirtillo' had already been appropriated—he was a welcome guest at the meetings of the Academy, and he was on friendly terms with everyone in Rome worth knowing from Pope Clement XI, in whose particular favour he stood, downwards. In 1709 and 1710, when he was forty-five, he established his position as a leading man of letters by the publication of two volumes, which blazed his fame through Italy. The first contained his *Degli Occhi di Gesù*, which had already been published at Bologna two years before, his *Canzoniere*, a curiously prophetic dialogue on human flight, and some *Sermoni della Poetica*, possibly suggested by Chiabrera, but surprisingly modern in tone and in sympathy with advanced French thought, especially Fontenelle's. Chiabrera has a share with Guidi in his warmest eulogies. The second volume contained the fruits of his dramatic activity (*La Perselide*, *Il Procolo*, *L'Ifigenia in Tauris*, *La Rachele*, *L'Alceste*, *Il Gesù perduto*, *La Morte di Nerone*) and an important *Discorso sul verso tragico*.

In 1713 came the great opportunity of Martelli's life. The Pope induced the Senate of Bologna to consent to his accompanying the papal nuncio, Monsignor Pompeo Aldrovandi, on a mission to Paris. The journey was one of Renaissance splendour. A distinguished company of Eminences and noblemen embarked at Livorno on a galley of his Royal Highness of Tuscany in March, and sailed to Genoa. Here Martelli seems to have been received with honours, and in return he wrote a sonnet in praise of the city[1]. From Genoa they proceeded by way of

[1] *Vita*, pp. xxi f. See *Canzoniere* (*Opere*, VII), p. 240.

Ruffo, the Pope's legate at Bologna, to obtain redress. Martelli wrote a dignified and not exactly repentant account of the whole quarrel[1], and in his letter to Conti, which introduces the latter's *Cesare*, he inserted a eulogy of *Merope*. In spite of the fact that he had more than his share of detractors and enemies, he was not combative by nature, and he was unwilling to let literary differences degenerate into personal animosities. This is particularly noticeable in his relations to his chief antagonist Gravina; their friendship was not broken by the fact that they stood in opposite camps in the battle of the 'ancients' and the 'moderns.'

Martelli's later years were overshadowed by sorrow. In November 1726 he lost a dearly loved daughter, Virginia, wife of Giuseppe Pozzi, a distinguished doctor and scholar of Bologna; and he fell into a deep melancholy from which he never recovered. His literary career virtually closed with *Il Femia*, but among his papers was found an interesting unfinished epic planned on a generous scale, dealing with Charlemagne's campaign against the Longobardi[2]. He died on May 10, 1727, at the age of sixty-two; and with the death of his only surviving son five years later the family became extinct.

II

In what we are told of Martelli's princely journey from Rome to Paris in the spring of 1713, there is no mention of a mysterious fellow-traveller, of whose presence on the ship Martelli's imagination alone took cognisance, and who was to give the voyage significance in the history of Italian criticism.

Not long after the ship puts out from Genoa, Martelli, deserting for a time the brilliant company on the poop, finds in the bow of the ship a little hunchback of apparently some seventy years of age. Curiosity tempts him to enter into conversation with this odd stranger, who stammers badly. The hunchback declares himself, in fact, to be no other than the 'master of those

[1] *Della ritirata del Femia, lettera inedita*, published by Viani, *op. cit.* pp. 139 ff.

[2] Cp. *Vita*, p. xl. *Il Carlomagno*, Poema inedito di P. J. Martelli. Notizia per A. Restori, Cremona, 1890.

that know,' Aristotle himself. From his father, the physician Nicomachus, he had inherited, he says, the secret of a wonderful elixir of life, a single draught of which has the effect of sinking him in a sleep of some days, and when he awakes, of prolonging his life for a hundred years. But now the flask is empty and Aristotle has lost the art of refilling it; he is enjoying his last century of life.

Martelli is incredulous, and smiles at the hunchback's efforts to convince him. He regards him quite frankly as an impostor, but good-humouredly taking him at his own valuation, he plies him with pertinent questions.

If you really are Aristotle, he asks, what have you been doing in all these centuries? Have you been writing new books, and, if you succeeded in turning out three hundred in seventy years, how many thousands have you written by this time—especially as you have had the advantage of that 'facil troppo invenzion tedesca,' printing? (p. 8).

The 'false Aristotle' is hard put to it by such a question: he can only say he was so aghast at the manner in which his interpreters had maltreated his books that he felt little temptation to add to their number. However, nothing is gained by banter, and Martelli accepts his new friend for what he pretends to be; they agree to discuss the subject that Aristotle had made peculiarly his own in his *Poetics*, the nature and the laws of dramatic poetry.

This ingenious fiction provides the outward form of Martelli's famous dialogue, *L' Impostore: Dialogo sopra la Tragedia antica e moderna*. It would seem to have been begun on the journey, but was, no doubt, mainly written after Martelli's arrival in Paris. It was published in Paris in 1714, with a dedication to the Dauphin, afterwards Louis XV[1], and it appeared in Italy in the following year in a revised and extended form.

Martelli has not been given all the credit he deserves for the framework of his dialogue: it differs materially from the controversial literature of the 'Querelle' in France or Italy,

[1] There is a copy of this edition in the British Museum. A review of it appeared in the *Giornale de' Letterati*, XIX, 1714, pp. 387 ff., where it is described as containing many errors, but these do not seem serious. The Dialogue is printed in vol. I of the *Opere*, Bologna, 1735.

and it is difficult to point to a model that might have served him[1]. The form afforded excellent opportunities for an irony of the biting Renaissance type: and Martelli is not slow to take advantage of them. He disarms criticism by treating his Aristotle frankly as an impostor, but he is always ready to forget the fraud, and accept him, making him a covert advocate of his own 'modern' ideas[2]. Occasionally, the arguments which Martelli puts into the mouth of the 'false Aristotle' are clumsy; and he is often—this is perhaps the most obvious weakness—made to accept after too easy a word-duel the Martellian standpoint. The style, too, is heavy and involved, and not at all in keeping with the sprightliness of the fiction; but, in spite of this, *L' Impostore* is much the most readable dialogue of its time.

In its final form *L'Impostore* is divided into six 'Sessioni,' but the edition of 1714 contained only the first four[3]. As I have already indicated, Dialogue I takes place on board the ship between Genoa and Savona, and closes with the arrival in harbour towards evening. It deals with general aspects of the quarrel between the 'ancients' and the 'moderns,' and more particularly with the 'fable' or plot of tragedy. 'You have seen the Greek tragedies on the stage,' he says to Aristotle (p. 9), 'what do you think of the tragedies of our day?' But before he allows him to answer this question, he obscures the issue by asking him what steps he would advise to be taken in order to silence those persons—he has obviously Gravina in mind—who 'praise only the Greeks

[1] Galletti suggests (p. 85), with considerable plausibility, that Martelli may have found a model for his 'gobbo' in the Abbé Pons, a quick-witted hunchback who fanatically championed the moderns, especially La Motte, in the French literary cafés. He refers to P. Dupont, *Houdar de la Motte*, Paris, 1898, pp. 188 ff.; see also Sainte-Beuve, *Causeries du Lundi*, XIII, pp. 141 ff. The introduction of Aristotle as a character in a dialogue was of course not new; he appears, for instance, in Fontenelle's fourth *Dialogue des Morts* and in Boccalini's *Ragguagli*. Cp. particularly Aristotle's apology for himself in Book I, chapter xxviii of the latter.

[2] Martelli's partisanship of the moderns had already shown itself in the *Sermoni* of 1709, where, notwithstanding his faith in Horace and Boileau, he is clearly influenced by Fontenelle's *Digression sur les anciens et les modernes*. Cp. Galletti, p. 65.

[3] A comparison of the two editions shows that the earlier one was subjected to a careful stylistic revision. Five or six pages were added to the first dialogue; two to the second; and the third was less changed. The fourth dialogue was rounded off with what now forms the conclusion of the sixth.

and believe that the only glory it is possible to attain to is that of resembling them like a shadow.'[1] The question of changing fashions in the drama is introduced by Martelli asking his hunchback why, if he is really Aristotle, he is not attired in Greek costume. And if he has adopted eighteenth-century dress, why should that century be expected to have the same taste in drama as the age of Pericles. He points out other signs of progress, *e.g.*, the great improvement in food since the days when primitive Greeks lived on acorns. And if French tragedy pleases better than Greek tragedy, it is not owing to a degeneration in manners, for the Greek drama describes more barbaric social conditions, even delighting in unnatural crimes such as incest. Martelli repeats Perrault's argument about nature and reason being the ultimate criteria, not Greek taste and Aristotelian theory. He points out that, however excellent the Greeks were, the Italian painters, sculptors and architects of the Renaissance had also great achievements to their credit. 'Aristotle' sets up no real defence; but, without yielding his ground, he expresses his disapproval of those fanatics who see excellence only in the antique and who imagine that by imitating the latter they are giving the modern world Greek tragedies. He recalls to Martelli a meeting in Rome at which Gravina gave a reading of his *Papiniano*, a tragedy 'in cui s' affetta l' antichità.' 'You laughed,' he says, 'at a gray-haired hunchback who cried out "oh bello" at every word, and that was I' (p. 16).

Aristotle admits that modern tragedies like Martelli's own have an advantage over Gravina's, in so far as, when represented on the stage, they please the people. This criterion—the approval of the people—would not, Martelli replies (p. 18), be acceptable to Gravina. To which the hunchback rejoins that the people may not be always good judges of poetic work in general; but they certainly are of dramatic works; and the Spanish drama is quoted in support. This point of view, that the people constitute the highest tribunal in dramatic taste is, as we have seen, something of an axiom in the Italian criticism of the time. Although virtually a corollary of Corneille's in-

[1] *Opere* (1735), I, p. 10. 'Non vogliono, che si possa più conseguire, altra gloria, che quella del somigliarli come ombra corporea.'

sistence that the end of tragedy is to give pleasure, it may be regarded as a specifically Italian contribution to the dogmas of the moderns. Castelvetro would seem to have been responsible for it in the first instance; Maffei, following Muratori, accepted it; it became a corner-stone of Calepio's doctrine; and in France La Motte, possibly under the influence of the Italians, adopted it[1]. From Calepio it passed, by the mediation of Bodmer, to Germany, and may even have facilitated the acceptance of the tragedy of common life in Northern Europe. The thread of Martelli's argument, however, becomes somewhat confused. The people, he says, admittedly show a preference for romantic and intricate plots. This is all very well in comedy, but not in tragedy, as intrigues are inconsistent with the dignity of personages in high places. The French prefer simple plots. But Martelli, and with him his hunchback, distinguish between fantastic intrigue-plots of the Spanish type and the kind of complications to be found in Greek tragedies. The 'false Aristotle' is made to point out that it is not inconsistent with the dignity of the tragic hero to experience terrible misadventures and to fall by sudden misfortune, the problem being rather to reconcile the dignity of tragedy with the introduction of incidents which prevent it degenerating into the dullness of the 'simple' plot (pp. 24 f.). And here Martelli lights on a thought which has been rightly claimed as throwing its shadow very far indeed into the future. Instead of outward happenings, such as physical 'recognition' and the like, there may be moral or spiritual recognition, and tragedy may 'reveal in a soul a passion quite contrary to one which was there a short time before.' Deficiency of intrigue is made up for by this conflict of inner emotions and sentiments (p. 26). This may be only a deduction from the art of Racine; but it is the first clear expression of such a deduction; it contains the germ of that psychological drama which was not to arrive at maturity until the middle of the nineteenth century[2].

Next morning Martelli and his hunchback disembark on the mole at Savona, and the second dialogue takes place in that town. Its subject is the three Unities. The standpoint of Martelli,

[1] See below, pp. 209 f.

[2] A. Galletti, *op. cit.* pp. 89 f.

who knew something of the Spanish drama, is clearly liberal; he believes that an audience is not so easily offended by the non-observance of the rules; and he makes his 'Aristotle' fail to refute him. Aristotle is obliged to be apologetic, if not for himself, at least for his commentators. He says that in his *Poetics* he advised the observance of the unities and raised them to the dignity of rules, because he saw them respected in the work of his contemporaries. But he admits the justice of the 'modern' argument that, if tastes and habits change, the rules may also change. The Unity of Action he holds to be legitimate and necessary, because 'pity and terror,' which it is the business of tragedy to excite, lose in intensity when they are spread over several objects (p. 30). As for the Unity of Time, Aristotle repudiates the rigid doctrine attributed to him by his commentators, and cites the eleventh chapter of the *Poetics*, where he says an action should be limited to the period of a day 'more or less.' He points not merely to the Spaniards, but also, following Corneille, to the shortcomings of the ancients themselves. The Unity of Place, Aristotle says, he has discussed in his treatise, but not in the fragment of it that has been preserved; thus he has more freedom to express himself about it now. His view is that the place of the drama

> should be one, but composed of several parts, as the body of its members. It should be such that the personages of the drama are able to go and come from one part to the other of the locality in which the action takes place in time to allow the action to be terminated in little more or less than a day (p. 38).

The question is then discussed as to how the various parts of the scene are to be represented. Should they all be brought before the spectator simultaneously by a division of the stage? Is it preferable to change the scene? Or ought Corneille's solution of the difficulty to be adopted of choosing an 'indifferent' locality? The 'false Aristotle' holds to the view that the changing of the scenes, of which he finds traces in the Greek dramas, even though the Greek theatre was not so far advanced technically as that of the modern Italians, is the lesser evil[1].

[1] In spite of his bold theoretical standpoint, Martelli showed in practice a preference for the deceptive place-unity of Corneille. He was a little

In connection with the discussion of the unities Martelli's 'Aristotle' has recourse to an ingenious argument of metaphysical subtlety. His long experience (pp. 34 f.), he says, has made him sceptical of the idealism of the philosophers, who, recognising the inferiority of all created things to the idea of them, would raise these things to the perfection of the idea. But the natural deficiencies of the human mind make such perfection unattainable and undesirable. If individual things were to correspond exactly to the ideas, they would all be identical: imperfection is thus the mark of individuality. Plato, in one of his dialogues, has attempted to plan a perfect republic; but no state directed by men ever could correspond to such a plan; and the same may be said of the perfect orator whom Cicero has imagined in his *Brutus*.

As a philosopher, I confess that I have not entirely eradicated in myself the error of my colleagues; I repent of having attempted to conform tragedy to the idea which I had of it, by imitating those examples which approximated most to the idea.... One must not desire from a thing the perfection, which would destroy it. A tragedy which conforms to all the unities will, no doubt, be perfect and most marvellous, but anything that oversteps the limits of the possible is monstrous and chimerical. The rigorous unity of place is one of those perfections which is inconsistent with verisimilar representation; and therefore he who aims at such perfection is looking for the impossible (pp. 36 f.).

This sums up Martelli's whole attitude to the Aristotelian *Poetics*.

Liberal as Martelli's views on the subject of the Unities are, I am doubtful whether Galletti is right in claiming a higher originality for this dialogue than for the first. As a matter of fact, the edifice of the strict unities had begun to crumble in the seventeenth century under Corneille's compromises and Ménage's dissection of Terence; and possibly Martelli, in coming to France, found among his 'modern' friends many who looked at the question from his own liberal standpoint.

afraid of those 'che una fisica unità di luogo superstiziosamente richiedono' (Preface to *I Tamingi*, *Opere*, III, p. 373). Cp. also that to *Il Perseo in Samotracia* (V, p. 46), and to *L' Euripide lacerato* (VII, p 249); and Galletti, *op. cit.* p. 100.

But he deserves the credit of having brought the whole controversy to a clearer focus than any of his predecessors. This was his undeniable merit. The liberating tendency of his views is at once noticeable, not merely in Italian tragedy, but also in Italian theories of tragedy; and, a little later, they were to have, as will be seen, an interesting reverberation in France[1].

At the close of the Dialogue Martelli and his hunchback return to the ship, and no further opportunity of continuing the discussion offers itself until the vessel arrives at Toulon. Here the third Dialogue takes place. Three matters are discussed in it: the question whether confidants or soliloquies are to be preferred; the introduction of love into tragedies; and the 'katharsis' of the emotions by pity and terror. Martelli's 'Aristotle,' although he concedes frankly that the French and Italian poets are superior to the Greeks in the art of constructing a drama, condemns the artifice of the French, whereby the action is developed with the help of confidants; he prefers soliloquies, of which he finds examples in the *Orestes* and *Helena* of Euripides. The French view is that soliloquies are a sign of madness: but surely it is less natural that important personages should confide their most intimate secrets to others?[2] Moreover, we need not think of a soliloquy being spoken other than in a low voice; it is merely a convention that the actor should deliver it loud enough to be heard by the audience. The soliloquy depicts the mind of a personage with a sincerity which might obviously be wanting even in dialogue with a confidant. 'One gets a glimpse, as through a little window, into the soul of the speaker' (p. 53). All this is in harmony with the emphasis which Martelli laid on the psychological action of a tragedy in his first Dialogue.

On the question of the introduction of love into tragedies (pp. 58 ff.), Martelli is in a more difficult position. His Aristotle proposes a kind of compromise. 'With the Greeks,' he says,

[1] See below, pp. 212 f.

[2] His words are (p. 52): 'Pretendono i Franzesi, che sia da pazzo lungamente dialoghizzar con sè stesso; ed inventano attori, che chiamano confidenti, con cui interamente possa aprir l' animo suo un traditore, un amante, una virgine, da che (dicon' essi) nasce più verisimiglianza in chi rappresenta, e più diletto in chi ascolta.'

'love was treated in a more natural and straightforward way, without intrigues'; amorous emotion they regarded as more suitable for the lyric than the drama. The moderns have, on the other hand, their religion, which spiritualises passion. When the expression of love is too subtle and refined, it is not suited for stage-presentation; moreover, 'when it invades the human soul, it weakens and unnerves it, taking all heroic grandeur from it.'[1] He shows the bad effect of love in *Mithridate* and *Phèdre*. 'You moderns exalt love, where love has a place, and where it has no place, you introduce it unseasonably' (p. 66). Martelli in his own person is less equivocal in his defence of love; to him it is an antidote to that aridity under which, he alleges, ancient tragedy suffers. He could not help seeing that theorists, like Gravina, who regarded love as a source of weakness in great political tragedies, had justice on their side: he even himself wrote a tragedy, *Il Procolo*, without either love or female characters; but, on the other hand, popular taste demanded love-plots, and, like Gravina, as well as Voltaire and many another, he bowed—not, perhaps, unwillingly—before this demand. In his views on the tragic purification or 'katharsis' Martelli is quite in agreement with the French 'modern' party.

> When I wrote my *Poetics*, says the hunchback, I wished to imply with this word exactly what the Abbé Fraguier understood, when he interpreted my words: 'Tragedy raises by means of pity and terror the spectator above these passions, sets him free by the use of fictitious objects from the sadness which devours him, just as melancholy music takes away our melancholy.'[2]

Martelli looks at the 'katharsis' in an entirely practical way; it is part of the moral or didactic purpose of tragedy. Men being inclined to ambition, to great power, to revenge, tragic terror frees them from the first two passions, and pity from the third. The emotions are thus 'not really purged, but the soul is purged of the emotions' (p. 70). The world, however, has changed since the days of the Greeks. The poets of our time cannot be inspired by themes depicting the miserable end of ambitious

[1] In his preface to *Il Perseo in Samotracia* (*Opere*, v, p. 42), Martelli compares passion in the drama to ivy on a tree; he repeats the metaphor here (p. 68).

[2] Page 70. Where Fraguier makes this statement I am unable to say.

tyrants; for in the beneficent age of Pope Clement VI and the glorious reign of Louis XIV—and here in the first edition the text (pp. 66, 67) appears in gold lettering!—tyranny does not exist, and monarchy is a fount of glory and wellbeing for the nations. The theatre is thus obliged to seek its examples outside politics, in the moral life and in the conflict of passions, if it will teach the highest duty of man, and show virtue rewarded and vice punished.

At Toulon Martelli loses sight of his hunchback; he sees nothing of him in Marseilles, or in the course of the four and a half days' journey to Paris. But in Paris they meet again after a performance of Racine's *Iphigénie*, with which Martelli has been greatly delighted; the 'gobbo' invites him to accompany him to the Café des Poètes. This is the scene of the fourth Dialogue, which is devoted to the form of verse best suited for tragedy. To some extent it is a repetition of the *Discorso del Verso tragico* of 1710[1], reinforced with new arguments. In that *Discorso* Martelli had passed in lengthy review the Italian tragedy of the past and its metrical forms, to arrive at the conclusion that the lack of a suitable vehicle was the chief source of its weakness. The French, whose language is naturally more prosaic than Italian, had achieved an unquestioned success with their alexandrine. The problem before him was thus to find for the Italians a metre as effective and as well adapted to their needs, an antidote to the excessive lyricism of Italian speech. He feels that it is just the prosaic qualities of French which make that language so well suited for tragedy, and it is owing to the lack of these qualities that Italian loses its hold on realities. With an almost modern insistence Martelli holds that dramatic dialogue must be, above all things, natural and realistic.

Martelli first made the experiment of bodily transferring the alexandrine to Italian by rewriting some scenes of his first tragedy *La Morte di Nerone*; but he found that the rhythmic effect attained thereby was by no means the same as in French. The next step was to find an equivalent. In the writings of

[1] Galletti gives a detailed analysis of his earlier dialogue, *op. cit.* pp. 65 ff.

Chiabrera, whose birthplace at Savona he had reverently saluted[1], he tells us he found recommended a scheme of seven-syllabled verse which that writer called 'giambici dimetri scemi.' From two of these lines he formed a fourteen-syllabled verse, 'un verso capace, tardo e però maestoso, e niente nuovo all' orecchio Italiano, se nelle sue parti considerar lo vogliamo'; and he had the satisfaction of being able to point to its use in the fourteenth century in a canzone by Ciullo d'Alcama. These fourteen-syllabled Martellian verses admit of considerable variety; by the use of 'sdruccioli' (*i.e.*, the two halves ending in dactyls), they could be extended to sixteen syllables, or by elisions reduced to twelve. Masculine and feminine rhymes did not need to alternate with French monotony; and half-verses of seven feet were admissible. The metrical effect was, after all, not so very different from that of the seven-foot metre of the old Italian tragedy, such as the *Canace* of Speroni. It is, however, difficult for a modern reader to see how such a metre can be superior to the 'endecasillabi sciolti' as a counterweight to the lyric quality of Italian; one would rather expect the contrary effect.

The new verse was received with scant sympathy by the critics; it was regarded, in fact, as nothing more than a copy of the French alexandrine[2]; and a reflexion of Martelli's disappointment is to be found in the later dialogue. He now enlists the services of his 'false Aristotle' to support him, and displays considerable ingenuity and subtlety in the arguments by which he makes Aristotle defend so un-Greek a thing as rhyme. Italian, being deficient in the rhythm which the ancients possessed, is obliged, he says, to have recourse to rhyme in order to make verse distinguishable from prose! And, to prove his case, Aristotle quotes Virgil, and in doing so, accentuates the Latin in a way that makes it incomprehensible to the hearer (p. 84).

[1] Cp. Martelli's *Opere*, II, p. xlv.

[2] See review in the *Giornale dei letterati*, v (1711), pp. 257 ff.; Galletti also refers to a letter of E. Manfredi in *Lettere famigliari di alcuni bolognesi del sec. XVIII*, Bologna, 1820, I, pp. 17 ff. Muratori approved of it: see his letter to Martelli of June 11, 1710, and to Conti of August 20, 1717 (*Epistolario*, v, 1903, pp. 1889 f.). Chiari and G. Gozzi employed the metre; and even Goldoni, who did not like it, wrote plays in it because he found it was popular.

The whole controversy does not seem of very vital importance in these days, but it was one which created some stir in literary Europe at the turn of the seventeenth and eighteenth centuries. Galletti, noticing Martelli's appeal to the precedent of English and German usage, has hazarded the suggestion that Martelli had some knowledge of Dryden through Magalotti, who had translated, but not published, Dryden's essays, and of Opitz's theory through some such channel as that available to Muratori[1]. However this may be, we have here an early expression of a controversy on which Milton, as a representative of rhymeless verse, was to rise into fame on the continent, and which was still very much alive in German literature when Klopstock emerged at the middle of the century.

The fifth and sixth Dialogues, which take place at Paris and Versailles, deal with extraneous forms of dramatic representation, the employment of music in melodrama and opera—of which Martelli is a warm defender—and with the ballet. They thus hardly come within the scope of the present studies. Finally, after witnessing a performance of *Médée* in the gardens of the Tuileries, Martelli is walking with his mysterious friend when the latter takes leave of him: '"Amico, a rivederci." Così mi disse: ed entrato fra quelle scene, che formano quivi il teatro, mi lasciò solo; nè mai o nelle Tuillerie, o altrove ho potuto più rivedere il nostro Aristotile, o siasi il nostro Impostore.'

In estimating the value of Martelli's *Impostore* it has to be borne in mind that all that so far had been written in Italian on the new standpoint towards the drama consisted in the few perfunctory pages in Muratori's *Della Perfetta Poesia italiana* some paragraphs in Gravina's *Ragion poetica*, and Maffei's juvenile *Osservazioni sopra la Rodoguna*. *L' Impostore* was published in the same year as Gravina's treatise on *Tragedy* and Maffei's *Merope*; and it was more than ten years before the next contribution to dramatic theory appeared, Maffei's introduction to his *Teatro italiano*. Eighteenth-century tragedy in Italy, says Bertana, begins with Martelli; he might with equal right have added eighteenth-century theory of tragedy.

[1] Galletti, *op. cit.* pp. 110 ff. If we are to look to English sources at all, Martelli's views are more like an echo of Daniel's *Defence of Rhyme* (1603).

III

It is difficult to approach Martelli's dramatic work without prejudice, a prejudice due partly to the general mediocrity of dramatic writing in Italy in his time, and partly to the almost unanimous condemnation of his critics. And yet, while frankly admitting that no indulgence to Martelli can galvanise him into a genius, I cannot help thinking that his work as a dramatic poet stands in need of some rehabilitation; his own countrymen are too hard on him[1]. In more than one respect, Martelli stands out from among the other writers included in the present volume. He may not have been a born dramatist; he came, as has been already indicated, to the theatre, like Gravina and Maffei, by the way of theory, not of irrepressible inspiration; and he came to it comparatively late in life. But he was an initiator of new ideals, which were to play an ever increasing rôle in the dramatic poetry of the eighteenth century. His Italian eulogists quote an opinion expressed about him—by an Italian, however—in the *Mémoires de Trévoux*; that 'few of our tragic poets equal him.'[2] This statement, it seems to me, admits, at least, of a modified endorsement.

It is difficult to establish a chronological sequence for Martelli's dramas, of which he tells us[3] he wrote twenty-five, fourteen of these being tragedies. He brought several completed plays with him to Rome in 1707, of which we know *La Morte di Nerone*, in 'endecasillabi sciolti,' to have been the earliest; but when he began to write we have no means of knowing; and equal uncertainty prevails in respect of his subsequent work. Even the test of internal evidence does not help much, for there is little that may be called development in his dramas. The most convenient method of classifying Martelli's works is according

[1] See especially A. Parducci, *op. cit.* pp. 167 ff., and Bertana, *op. cit.* pp. 19 ff.; the most suggestive criticism of Martelli as a dramatist is to be found in Ch. Dejob, *op. cit.* pp. 107 ff. E. De Marchi, *Lettere e Letterati italiani del sec. XVIII*, Milan, 1882, pp. 248 ff., also writes of Martelli with some sympathy; on the other hand, G. Guerzoni, *Il teatro italiano del sec. XVIII*, Milan, 1876, does not deign him worthy of mention at all.

[2] Cp. Fantuzzi, *op. cit.* p. 341; *Elogio* (*Opere*, I), p. xxxiii. See below, p. 200.

[3] *Apologia dell' Autore a chi legge* (*Opere*, IV, p. 5).

to subjects. The largest group is that of tragedies on Greek subjects, his *Edipo tiranno*, *Edipo coloneo*, *Ifigenia in Tauris*, *Alceste*, *Arianne*, *Elene casta*, *Perseo in Samotracia*. *Il M. Tullio Cicerone*, *Il Q. Fabio*, and *Procolo* are Roman dramas, although the last mentioned might perhaps better be classed as a 'martyr drama' of the type of *Polyeucte*; the first and the last are leavened with a considerable dose of Bolognese patriotism. His *Sisera*, *Rachele*, *Davide in Corte* are Biblical dramas: *L' Adria* is a romantic, although not particularly dramatic eulogy of Venice: while *La Perselide* and *I Taimingi* might be conveniently labelled exotic.

L' Ifigenia in Tauris is perhaps his most acceptable tragedy, as it was the one which, in Riccoboni's hands, found most success on the stage, at Verona, Vicenza, Padua, Venice and elsewhere. Apart from unpleasant lapses into Marinesque conceits, and its lyric effusiveness and puzzling obscurities, it is quite a readable play and well worth study as a consistent and sustained attempt to modernise an ancient theme. Martelli is, according to his lights, a realist, especially in his handling of the action of his play. Nothing that happens must be without an adequate motive—nothing left to chance or coincidence; there must be no effects the causes of which are obscure. To Martelli's mind a Greek drama leaves too much to the imagination: he is not, for instance, satisfied with the proofs which Euripides provides that Orestes is the brother of Iphigeneia; he introduces much circumstantial evidence to strengthen it; and in order to exonerate the heroine's ignoble deceit of the king—an abiding crux for all modern adapters of the Iphigeneia theme—he converts Thoas into a cruel tyrant and a rebel against the gods. All this leads to much childish and often transparently obvious detail, to additional characters and *staffage*, which we would willingly be spared. Another form his realism takes is an endeavour to circumvent the supernatural, be it in motive or in happenings. In his *Ifigenia* the oracle is deprived of all effective force; and in his *Alceste* he goes so far as to cut out the character of Death altogether. Alcestis induces her doctor to administer poison to her that she may thus sacrifice her life for her husband. The doctor gives her a sleeping-draught, and she is buried in a vault, from which Hercules, on the doctor's hint, rescues her! One may smile at such perversions; but they are, after all, quite in accordance with the methods necessarily employed by all modern poets in handling classic themes. There is not one European poet of the eighteenth and nineteenth centuries from Martelli to Alfieri, from Crébillon and Voltaire to Goethe and Grillparzer, who has not in his own way rendered the sagas of antiquity more palatable to his audience by similar although, it may be, less radical changes. If Martelli was cruder than his successors, it must be remembered that he preceded them.

Martelli's realism shows itself in a more advantageous light in its application to character. He probes deeper; he gets further away from the statuesque, generalised figures of the classic drama[1]: he introduces a modern problematic element into figures like Iphigeneia, Orestes and especially Pylades. Here, it seems to me, Martelli is no unworthy precursor of the drama of our day. His psychological subtlety may be but a reflexion of the delicate spiritual realism of Racine; but it is of a more modern cast; it brings Martelli nearer to nineteenth-century romanticism than seventeenth-century classicism. As his poetic theory culminated in his emphasis of spiritual conflict in the drama, so it is just in this spiritual conflict, based on a realistic psychology of character, that his peculiar significance as a dramatic poet lies. One disadvantage of realism of detail in presenting character and motive is that it abridges the distance which separates the poet's own time from the heroes of antiquity; it reduces the latter, so to speak, to ordinary men, when their words and actions are measured by the standards of everyday life. Martelli's Iphigeneia is quite as modern and un-Greek in her mentality as Goethe's. Or, to put it another way, an insidious middle-class element has unconsciously asserted itself and undermined the grandeur of these heroes of the old world. No doubt, Martelli goes too far in this direction. His Iphigeneia is spoiled by the introduction of unworthy comedy elements—especially her love for Pylades—which make her a distant ancestress of

[1] He rightly claims (Dedication of *L' Alceste*, *Opere*, II, p. 270) that his characters are more varied than those of the French stage.

Mr Bernard Shaw's Cleopatra; his *Rachele* makes still more dangerous concessions—it is, in fact, a kind of French *ingénue* comedy[1]. But I would contend that all this is in the direction of a liberation of tragedy from the fetters of a too rigid classicism. Greater poets than Martelli have made experiments; and they, too, have failed, if less disastrously, to avoid the pitfalls; perhaps these are at bottom not to be avoided at all. No man is a hero to his own valet; and it is difficult to distinguish between hero and valet when both speak the same 'natural' dialogue.

Martelli's psychological adventures often lead him into strange and untrodden paths. The reader constantly lights upon scenes which, in their emotional complexity or psychological delicacy, might not be out of place in a tragedy of Hebbel's; he finds a flouting of the laws of construction, an overstepping of polite convention, which would do credit to a rebel romanticist[2]. Occasionally this originality degenerates, it is true, into a mere indulgence in the bizarre; but again, an infusion of the bizarre was not the worst thing that could have happened to the convention-ridden classical drama of the early eighteenth century.

The literary historians are somewhat at variance as to which of Martelli's plays are his best. On the whole, there is most unanimity about *L' Ifigenia*; but *L' Alceste* and *Il M. T. Cicerone* are also singled out for commendation. Something might, I think, be said for Martelli's oriental plays, *La Perselide* and especially *I Taimingi*. The way to this type of play had, of course, been pointed out by Racine with his *Bajazet*; and the heroic novel of the seventeenth century had suggested the exotic background. But it was one thing to write oriental plays like *Bajazet*—or, in Italian literature, Bonarelli's *Il Solimano*, the obvious model of *La Perselide*[3]—plays in which the exoticism was little more than a superficial varnish, an affair of names, and another to apply to such themes the conscious realism of Martelli's method. In composing *I Taimingi*, for instance, a

[1] Cp. Bertana, *op. cit.* pp. 29 ff.

[2] Dejob is suggestive on this point. Of the examples he quotes I note especially the interesting love-scene of the dying lovers at the end of *La Perselide*.

[3] The names of several characters in the two plays are identical.

drama on a Chinese theme, Martelli read all the books on China he could obtain; and when the play was finished, he said it could only be represented if the actors appeared in masks, as no European could look like a Chinaman[1]. He prints the Chinese proverbs, which he quotes, in inverted commas to show the reader that he did not invent them. Well may Dejob say, 'a little more and he would ask our pardon for not having written the piece in Chinese!'[2] Still, with it all, Martelli does achieve 'atmosphere'—as Conti had also achieved it in his Roman plays. After the artificial unrealities of the heroic novel, he has shown that exotic themes can be treated in a manner which does not merely awaken smiling incredulity.

The older critics, deceived by the French sympathies of Martelli, glibly dismissed him as an imitator of Corneille and Racine[3]; but even a cursory perusal of Martelli's tragedies shows how ill-founded is such an imputation. His 'imitation' reduces itself, on closer examination, to the adoption of a handful of motives from the French classical poets[4]. I would see in him less the heir of the seventeenth century than a precursor of the later eighteenth. His choice of themes, his delineation of character, especially his skill in handling subtle spiritual conflicts, and his widening of the scope of tragedy to include modern religious and political problems point, as will be seen from a subsequent chapter, forwards, not backwards.

As everywhere in the international controversies of the 'Quarrel of the Ancients and the Moderns,' we find in Italy conflicting cross-currents. The path of progress here, as in France and England, lay, doubtless, in allegiance to the modern side; but not always. Gravina, a stubborn 'ancient,' had, as we have seen,

[1] Proemio (*Opere*, III, p. 373): 'I nostri Taimingi dimandano, non d' esser rappresentati, ma d' esser letti, perchè, chiedendo più oltre, riporterebbero dagl' Istrioni una tanto giusta, quanto risoluta ripulsa. Due sono le ragioni di questa difficoltà: l' una si è negli Attori, e si è l' altra negli uditori. E per parlare primieramente de' primi, bisognerebbe, che recitassero mascherati alla maniera degli antichi Istrioni.'

[2] Cp. Dejob, *op. cit.* p. 127.

[3] A. Saviotti, *L' imitazione francese nel teatro tragico di P. J. Martelli*, Bologna, 1887. I have not, however, been able to see this study.

[4] Dejob, *op. cit.* pp. 116 f., instances *La Perselide, Il M. T. Cicerone, I Taimingi*, as showing slight traces of French influence. Cp. also Bertana, *op. cit.* p. 28.

much to say that was wise and furthering for the future; while Martelli, a thorough-going 'modern,' left less mark on the advance of Italian letters than other less 'modern' of his contemporaries. There were, in fact, two controversies which incontinently cut across each other in Italy; in the 'ancient *versus* modern' controversy, the triumph of the 'modern' side was in the best interest of progress; but in the national controversy of French *versus* Italian taste, the latter case was better maintained by a championship of the 'ancient' side. The espousal of 'modern' doctrines implied necessarily an acceptance of the new French taste; but such emulation of France ran counter to the national spirit in Italy, which had writhed under Bouhours' taunts. Moreover, the Italians believed, and were right in believing, that the highest interests of their literature were bound up with national 'classic' traditions which had come down unbroken from Roman times.

Martelli, the champion of the 'moderns,' was consequently reckoned to the enemy; his good intentions were discounted, because he appeared to advocate imitation of the French; he was regarded as more hostile to a regenerate Italy than Gravina, whose 'ancient' sympathies in large measure neutralised his good intentions. And yet there is no doubt that Martelli stood on the right side; he had suffered under the French depreciation of Italian poetry; he was as zealous a champion of the honour of the Italian theatre as Muratori or Maffei. Where he erred, if err he did, was in trying to judge fairly and dispassionately. He did not consider it necessary for Italy's honour to repudiate Boileau as a poetic law-giver[1], or to hold up Corneille as a bungler. On the contrary, it was his dream and his ambition, as he said in the Dedication of his *Teatro italiano*, just to do for Italy what Corneille had done for France[2]. The misfortune was that he was no Corneille; his talent as a poet was inadequate to the demands he put upon it.

[1] Cp. *Sermoni* (*Opere*, VI), p. 211. The Dialogue *Il vero parigino italiano*, which, however, is concerned more with taste in architecture than in literature, is an essentially fair comparison of the genius of the two nations (cp. Dejob, pp. 115 f.). The most interesting thing in it is Martelli's warm praise of Ronsard (*Opere*, V, pp. 359 ff.).

[2] Dedication to the Senate of Bologna (*Opere*, V), p. xi.

CHAPTER VI

SCIPIONE MAFFEI AND HIS FRIENDS

I

OF all the names that appear in the present volume that of the Marchese Scipione Maffei is most familiar to students of literature outside of Italy. His *Merope* may not be one of the great plays of the eighteenth century; but Voltaire, and, at a later date, Lessing, helped to render it one of the most famous. Maffei's magnificent work on the antiquities of Verona made a directer appeal to the antiquarian mind than Muratori's more heavily ballasted tomes; and his controversies with foreign theologians like Basnage and Pfaff, were more widely known than Gravina's fundamental contributions to the science of jurisprudence.

The Maffei family[1], which could boast of many distinguished names in the service of the Church and of letters, came originally from Bologna or Volterra to Verona, where Scipione, the youngest of five sisters and three brothers, was born on June 1, 1675. He was his mother's favourite child, and his early training lay in her hands. He was then sent for five years to a College of the Jesuits in Parma, where he received the usual education of an Italian nobleman. We hear especially of his skill in writing Latin verses, and an oratorio on the 'Passion of the Virgin,' written in 1694, has been preserved[2]. On his return from Parma he did not allow the attractions of Verona society to interrupt his studies and literary interests; and in 1697 he visited the principal cities of Italy. In Milan he made the acquaintance of

[1] I. Pindemonte has written a life of Maffei which was originally published in A. Rubbi's *Elogi Italiani*, vol. XII, Venice, 1782; subsequently reprinted as an introduction to the edition of Maffei's works published at Venice in 1790, and later. I quote from the edition (with notes), published at Verona, in 1784. Cp. also E. de Tipaldo, *Biografia degli italiani illustri*, VIII, Venice, 1841, pp. 7 ff., and Teresa Copelli, *Il Teatro di Scipione Maffei*, Parma, 1907, pp. 17 ff.

[2] Cp. P. Rossi, *Le Liriche di Scipione Maffei*, in *Studi Maffeiani*, Turin, 1909, p. 663.

the poet Carlo Maria Maggi, whose rehabilitation was to be Muratori's first literary task, and about whom that critic and Maffei were subsequently to differ. In Genoa he familiarised himself with the works of Chiabrera; and shortly afterwards, in Rome, he became a member of the Arcadia under the flamboyant name of 'Orilto Berenteatico.' At a meeting in 1699 he read a Latin poem of his own. From Rome he paid a brief visit to Naples, and returned to Verona by way of Florence.

Towards the end of the same year we again find him in Rome taking part, with his brother Alessandro, in the celebrations of the Jubilee. This second visit seems to have been decisive for his literary interests. He had brought with him an oratorio, *Il Sansone*[1]—in addition to his other many-sided interests he was a musical connoisseur, and played the violin—but his verses were sharply criticised in literary circles. He saw the error of those Marinistic tastes to which he had hitherto leaned; and threw himself with avidity on the great Italian poets of the past, especially Dante, of whom he had previously been ignorant; his poem on the birth of a Prince of Piedmont[2] is plainly influenced by Dante. In a subsequent canzone on the death of a Bavarian prince[3], he struck a more original note; and it was even prophesied of him at this time that he would one day give Italy a good tragedy[4]. His stay in Rome was both fruitful and happy; and his interest in scientific questions—when he revisited Naples, for instance, he made, at some risk, the ascent of Vesuvius—rivalled that in literature. Fresh honours and favours were showered on him in Florence by the Grand Duke Ferdinando; but he returned to Verona in 1710 and set seriously about the task of reforming Verona's taste in literature. To this end he put together a cento of poems in which, as in a mirror, the Veronese literary world might see the errors of its past.

His first prose work *Osservazioni sopra la Rodoguna*[5], occasioned by a performance of Corneille's *Rodogune* in Verona in the

[1] *Rime e Prose*, Venice, 1719, pp. 83 ff.
[2] *Ibid.* pp. 1 ff.
[3] *Ibid.* pp. 9 ff.
[4] Pindemonte, *op. cit.* p. 7; see also F. A. Zaccaria, *Storia letteraria d' Italia*, XIV, Modena, 1759, p. 282.
[5] *Rime e Prose*, pp. 165 ff.

summer of 1700, was a protest against the excessive adulation of the French poet by Maffei's fellow-townsmen. Another literary undertaking of this time was more like a lapse into the fatuities of 'secentismo,' namely a hundred *Conclusioni D' Amore* (1702)[1], in imitation of Tasso, which he read before the Accademia Filarmonica. According to Pindemonte, these *Conclusioni* were to have formed part of a collection covering the entire domain of moral philosophy[2].

Maffei's plans for educating the taste of his native town were interrupted by a year or two of very active and even adventurous life. The War of Succession broke out in 1701, and Maffei's brother was a general in command of Bavarian and French troops. Maffei was a neutral; but he offered himself as a volunteer and resolved to join his brother. He proposed to cross over to Bavaria by way of Bolzano (Bozen), a dangerous undertaking, which failed owing to the treachery of a peasant who offered to act as his guide; and it was not until 1703 that he succeeded in reaching his brother by way of Friuli, Styria and Carinthia. In the course of the campaign he narrowly escaped death from a cannon ball at Donauwörth, and in Munich he saved his brother—who had been appointed Governor of the town—from the hands of an assassin.

After his military experiences, we find Maffei in Venice, where his hopes of being taken into the service of the state were disappointed; he also declined an invitation to write the official history of the war, on the ground that he had not had an opportunity of familiarising himself with its events from the beginning. He returned to Verona and resumed his interests in literature. Possibly the germ of his subsequent critical work is to be found in his talks in Venice with Bavarian and French officers, whom he sought to convince that lyrics could be written in Italian which were no less graceful and more musical than those in French. In Verona he founded a colony of the Arcadia, with himself as vice-custodian, inaugurating it with a historical survey of Italian poetry[3], in which he defended the Italians against the reproach that they were responsible for seventeenth-century

[1] *Rime e Prose*, pp. 21 ff.
[2] Pindemonte, p. 9.
[3] *Rime e Prose*, pp. 136 ff.; *Opuscoli letterari*, Venice, 1829, pp. 17 ff.

extravagance. He censured the Italian poets, however, for not having taken more vigorous steps to hold this extravagance in check. In this connection he wrote in the form of a letter, his *Giudizio sopra le Poesie liriche di C. M. Maggi* (Venice, 1706)[1], in which he disapproved of Muratori's excessive praise. He followed up his criticism with a poem of some hundred stanzas in varied metres which, according to Pindemonte's description, was an exceedingly fantastic, not to say Marinistic production—an allegorical journey to the moon—into which he wove, amongst other apparently irrelevant things, his own experience of the war. It is perhaps no great loss that this poem has not been preserved.

Meanwhile Orsi's refutation of Bouhours appeared in 1703; Muratori's *Perfetta Poesia italiana* in 1708. This brought Maffei's plans to a focus. He shared the resentment of literary Italy at the false light in which Italian letters had been placed, and, together with Apostolo Zeno and the physicist Vallisnieri, he conceived the scheme of an Italian journal, a *Giornale dei Letterati d'Italia*, the sixth of its name, which was to serve as a counterweight to the *Mémoires de Trévoux*. He succeeded in obtaining the cooperation of the leading literary men of Italy and introduced the new venture with a preface on periodical literature in general[2].

In the early years the chief burden of editing the *Giornale* fell on the shoulders of Apostolo Zeno[3]. Zeno was born at Venice on December 11, 1668. He came of a family, an ancestor of which had been sent to Crete in the thirteenth century as a representative of the state of Venice. He lost his father in infancy, and at an early age showed precocious talents. At seventeen he had written a poem, *L'Incendio Veneto* (1686); then, repelled by the aridness of philosophy, he interested himself for a time in mathematics, ultimately to find his *métier* as a

[1] *Rime e Prose*, pp. 138 ff.

[2] Reprinted, *Rime e Prose*, pp. 185 ff.; *Opuscoli letterari*, pp. 29 ff. Cp. G. Bolognini, *Sc. Maffei critico e giornalista* (*Studi Maffeiani*, pp. 533 ff.); also L. Piccioni, *Il giornalismo letterario in Italia*, Turin, 1894, p. 84.

[3] There is a life of Apostolo Zeno by G. B. Baseggi in E. de Tipaldo, *Biografia degli Italiani illustri*, VII, Venice, 1840, pp. 25 ff.; also F. Negri, *Vita di Apostolo Zeno*, Venice, 1816. His *Lettere* were published in six volumes, 2nd ed., Venice, 1785.

dramatic poet. His first play, *Gl' Inganni felici* (1696), was well received; the Emperor Leopold became his patron and treated him with great generosity. A second play, *Il Temistocle* (1696), carried his fame to Germany and won the interest of the Prince of Ansbach. In 1708 he directed the celebrations at the accession of the Duke d'Este. Besides being a poet, Zeno was, like all the leading men of his time—with whom he carried on a vast correspondence—a scholar of antiquarian leanings. He was collaborator on the *Galleria di Minerva*, the forerunner of the *Giornale de' Letterati*, and he was the chief editor of the latter publication for nine years. In 1718 he accepted an invitation to Vienna as Ducal Librarian, where he remained till 1723. The rest of his life—he died on November 11, 1750—was spent in Italy. Of his learned work mention must be made of a *Dissertazione sopra le Biblioteche antiche* (1697); and in 1698 he collected unedited ancient Italian poetry, and compiled *Annotazioni sopra il Vocabolo della Crusca* (published 1705). He set to work on a great *Storia de' Poeti Italiani*, which, however, was forestalled by Crescimbeni in 1698[1]; thus, although his first volume was finished, it was never published. One of his last tasks was an edition of Fontanini's *Biblioteca dell' Eloquenza italiana* published after his death in 1735. His labours were indefatigable, in spite of persistent ill-health, the traces of which are plainly visible in the portrait which forms the frontispiece of his *Lettere*. As a dramatist, his chief successes were won with the musical dramas *Il Euristeo*, *L' Andronico*, *Il Giangir*, *La Semiramide*, *Lo Spartaco*.

From the point of view of literary criticism, Zeno's *Dissertazioni Vossiane* and *Annotazioni alla Biblioteca* of Fontanini are of most importance. Although it may be too much to claim Zeno as the initiator of a new method of criticism[2], there is no doubt that he did an invaluable service in lopping off the pedantic excrescences of the old scholastic methods; he strengthened the vital side of critical scholarship, perhaps, indeed, achieved more

[1] See letter to Crescimbeni of April 12, 1698 (*Lettere*, Venice, 1785, I, p. 18; cp. also pp. 44, 61 f., 103, 116).

[2] Cp. L. Menghi, *Lo Zeno e la Critica letteraria*, Camerioni, 1901, pp. 10 f., 85 f.

in this direction than even Muratori, who suffered under the leisurely diffuseness of the seventeenth-century tradition.

Maffei's *Giornale*, of which the first number appeared in 1710, does not strike us now-a-days as a very successful rival to the French reviews; and there was probably some justice in the hostile criticism of a certain Antonio Bernardi, which incensed Maffei as coming from an Italian[1]. Like its models, it suffers from a polyhistoric attempt to cover all fields of knowledge. But its avowed purpose was to represent the Italian standpoint, and to draw attention to the work of Italian scientists and men of letters, and so far it succeeded[2]. The *Giornale* lived for twenty-six years. When it came to an end, Maffei brought out a new review in its place, under the title *Osservazioni letterarie* (6 vols. 1737–40), which is even more a misnomer in the modern sense of 'literary'; for, with the exception of a criticism of Fontanini's *Eloquenza italiana* and Calepio's *Paragone*, the contents of these six volumes are what we should now call strictly scientific. Not without justice Muratori called it an 'opera principalmente fatta dall' autore per lodar le sue cose, e quelle dei Veronesi, e per far guerra a chi è d' umore differente dal suo.'[3]

During the years in which Maffei was preoccupied by the *Giornale*, we find him in various parts of Italy, in Padua, then in Florence, where he obtained permission to dedicate the review to the Grand Duke of Tuscany; in Lucca for reasons of health, and finally in Rome. Here he published a work, the result of strenuous research, which brought him fame, or perhaps one should say notoriety, throughout Italy: *Della Scienza chiamata cavalleresca* (published 1710)[4]. His thesis was to prove the barbaric origin of the code of chivalry, and his purpose to discredit duelling as a primitive and degrading custom. This work had been preceded some years earlier by a shorter treatise,

[1] *Lettera ad un cavalier erudito sopra i tre primi tometti del nuovo Giornale de' Letterati.* Attention was called to it by the *Mémoires de Trévoux*, May, 1713, pp. 839 ff.

[2] Much information about the journal is to be found in Zeno's letters, II, pp. 15 ff.

[3] Letter to Gori, August 6, 1740 (*Epistolario*, x, p. 4030), quoted by T. Copelli, *op. cit.* p. 36.

[4] *Opere*, Venice, 1790, vol. XIII.

La Vanità della scienza cavalleresca (1706), which, in turn, seems to have grown from an episode in the author's unpublished allegorical poem. His opinions won favour with the Pope, Clement XI, who offered him inducements to settle in Rome. But a little later he was again in the north; he went to Turin to try to win back the marquisate of Farigliano, to which his family laid claim. He failed in his suit; but he turned his visit to good account by studying the manuscripts and inscriptions in the Turin library[1].

It is at this point—Maffei had reached his thirty-eighth year—that his interest in the theatre seems to have awakened. Together with the actor Luigi Riccoboni, he set about the reform of the Italian stage, his efforts culminating in the tragedy of *La Merope*, written in two months and performed on June 12, 1713, in Modena. With the production of this play Maffei became for a time the most famous man of letters in Italy, and to the outside world the most famous Italian. For *Merope* was carried abroad by translations into French, English, German, Spanish, Russian and even, as Maffei mentions with pride, into Serbian; it became still more famous through the imitation of Voltaire, the latter's controversy with Maffei, and the commentary on that controversy by Lessing in his *Hamburgische Dramaturgie*. The critical estimate of the play has varied much and itself provides an interesting chapter in the history of literary appreciation. Welcomed with enthusiasm on its first appearance, it remained in Italian and foreign eyes—one thinks of Goldsmith's high opinion[2], and Lessing's declaration of its superiority to Voltaire's imitation—the typical example of Italian tragedy. With the advent of Alfieri the wind changed; Alfieri was indignant that it should be regarded as the one and only Italian tragedy[3], and since then, there has been a danger of its being unduly neglected. There is no doubt that Maffei scored over his contemporaries by virtue of the simple and yet

[1] See letter to Apostolo Zeno of June 26, 1711, printed in the *Giornale de' Letterati*, VI (1711), pp. 449 ff.

[2] *Present State of Polite Learning* (*Works*, ed. Cunningham, London, 1854, II), p. 20.

[3] *Autobiografia*, IV, chap. ix (*Opere*, Turin, 1903, I, p. 170); cp. also his *Parere intorno alle sue tragedie* (*ibid.* III, pp. 253 f.).

solid construction of his play, and by the vitality of his characters. There is a more direct semblance of life in *Merope* than in the often hybrid plays of Martelli; and there is more of the modern outlook in it than in the Roman tragedies of Conti. In metrical respects, it successfully established the 'endecasillabo sciolto' as the metre of the Italian stage.

The resounding achievement of *Merope* stands alone in Maffei's career. Riccoboni, who joined him in his efforts to give Italy a national theatre worthy of her, speaks of him being engaged on a second tragedy; but it never saw the light. His dramatic works comprise, besides *Merope*, two comedies of small value, *Le Ceremonie* (1728) and *Il Raguet* (1747), and two oratorios *Lo Zelo di Fineo* and *La Fida Ninfa* (1732), the latter the revision of an early work[1]. This disappointing sequel to so promising a beginning almost justifies the view that *Merope* sprang from no real poetic impulse, but was rather the calculated effort of a theorist who would give an object-lesson to his reformed stage.

Maffei's interests—and again, his life moves parallel with those of other writers I have dealt with in this volume—were polyhistoric. He had time, while engrossed with the reformation of the Italian stage, to study problems of hydraulics; and when the triumph of *Merope* was ringing through Italy, he was busy writing, as the result of his observations during a thunderstorm, his essay *Della Formazione dei Fulmini*[2]. But Maffei turned rather to erudition than to science; and he soon found himself involved in a controversy that was theological rather than philological. Christoph Pfaff had discovered in the Turin Library some Greek fragments which he attributed to Irenaeus. These seemed to foreshadow the Reformation; and Maffei came forward as a defender of the Catholic church by disputing Irenaeus's authorship. In pursuance of this end, he plunged

[1] Maffei's dramatic works, with the exception of *Lo Zelo di Fineo*, which will be found in *Rime e Prose*, pp. 91 ff., are published in vol. XII of the *Opere*, Venice, 1790. The many editions of *Merope* will be found enumerated in F. Doro's Bibliography in the Appendix to the *Studi Maffeiani*, Turin, 1909, pp. ii f. Signorina Copelli's book gives an excellent estimate of Maffei as a dramatist.

[2] *Rime e Prose*, pp. 330 ff.; cp. E. Bertana, *Arcadia*, pp. 6 f.

into recondite questions of church history, and studied with such zeal that his eyes suffered under the strain. From theology he turned to antiquarian questions, especially in relation to his native town. The results of this study of manuscripts appears in the learned *Trattato degli Anfiteatri* (Verona, 1728)[1], and the magnificent monument to his native city, *Verona illustrata*[2], which appeared in 1732, the author's fifty-seventh year.

On August 26, 1732, Maffei left Verona to visit France[3], where he was received with all honours and made a member of the Académie des Inscriptions. Amongst papers on more recondite themes which he read to that body, was a *Ragionamento in difesa del pensare italiano, ossia della qualità dei sentimenti usati dagli Italiani nel comporre*, which could not have been much to the taste of its members[4]. After spending nearly three years in France, he proceeded (May, 1735) to England. Voltaire wrote to Thiériot in London, describing him as 'the Varro and Sophocles of Italy';[5] and all doors were open to him. The Prince of Wales welcomed him warmly, and promptly had his translation into Italian of the first book of the *Iliad*, which Maffei presented to him, sent to the printers (1736). Lord Burlington gave him a copy of his *Fabbriche antiche designate da Palladio* (1730); Lord Oxford also presented him with MSS., amongst others, one of Vitruvius. In Dr Richard Mead's collection he studied a rare manuscript of Greek epigraphs, which William Sherard had brought from Smyrna, and he copied inscriptions in the Hans Sloane collection, now the British Museum. He was elected an associate of the Royal Society and the Society of Antiquaries. Lords Dupplin and Coleraine took him to Cambridge where Bentley invited him to dinner, an occasion which evoked a jest in a note to Pope's *Dunciad*, where a *De Compotationibus academicis*, is ascribed to 'the learned Scipio Maffei.'[6] In Oxford he was received with even greater honours. The degree of Doctor of Laws was conferred on him; and, as his biographer tells us, he was able

[1] *Opere*, vols. x, xi. [2] *Ibid*. vols. iv–ix.
[3] Cp. *Studi Maffeiani*, pp. 326 ff. [4] Cp. T. Copelli, *op. cit*. p. 35.
[5] Letter of July 24, 1733 (*Oeuvres*, ed. Garnier, xxxiii, p. 364).
[6] A. Pope, *Works*, ed. by W. Elwin and W. J. Courthope, iv, London, 1882, p. 201.

to hear his praise in the Latin oration without blushing, because he could not understand the English pronunciation of the language. Algarotti, Voltaire's friend, was present on this occasion. Maffei's acquaintance with England was extended to Winchester, Salisbury—including, of course, Stonehenge—and Portsmouth; but his warmest memory was associated with his visit to Pope in Twickenham, Pope being at that time contemplating a translation of *Merope*[1].

He left England on August 3, 1736, and crossed to Holland, where he made the acquaintance of Gronovius, Burmann and Boerhavius. He then travelled by way of Namur, Brussels, Regensburg and Vienna, to Venice, a journey which, as far as the learned world was concerned, was a triumphal progress. In Venice he renewed his ties with his old friend Zeno. On his return to Verona, Maffei found that his fellow-townsmen had set up a bust to him: 'Al Maffei ancor vivo,' which he modestly had removed[2]. His literary activity and his preoccupation with science—he possessed, for instance, the first electrical machine in Verona—remained as great as ever. As he grew older, however, he seems to have acquired an unfortunate faculty for making enemies. He stirred up much opposition with a treatise *Dell' impiego del denaro* (1744), and his work *De' teatri antichi e moderni* (1753)[3] is the precipitate of a still more acrimonious controversy with the Dominican, F. D. Cóncina, who had a grudge against him. Cóncina attacked him with rancour in his *De spectaculis theatralibus*, maintaining that the theatre was the highway to perdition, and Maffei an enemy of good morals. Maffei contented himself with correcting the ignorance of the ancient theatre displayed by his adversary, and affected to regard the personal attack more in sorrow than in anger. It must, however, be confessed that his defence of the modern theatre in his *Teatri antichi e moderni*, which is essentially a work of erudition, is not very whole-hearted[4]. The day of Maffei's

[1] Cp. Pindemonte, *op. cit.* pp. 51 f.

[2] Voltaire refers to this in his famous letter to Maffei prefacing his own *Mérope*. There is a photograph of the bust in the *Studi Maffeiani*, p. 464.

[3] *Opere*, I, pp. 109 ff.

[4] Cp. T. Copelli, *op. cit.* pp. 46 f. The controversy between Church and theatre in the eighteenth century has many ramifications in the theological literature of the time.

interest in the living theatre was past; the poet of *Merope* had been stifled by the erudition of the antiquary. In the spring of 1754 Maffei's health began to fail, and he died of asthma on February 11, 1755.

The Italian critics of the eighteenth century name Maffei and Muratori together. Cardinal Quirini called them 'i due sostegni della nostra letteratura'; Apostolo Zeno, 'i due primi uomini d' Italia'; and Tiraboschi mentions them in the preface to his last volume as pursuing the same end[1]. They had a common desire to vindicate Italian letters; they worked hand in hand for the realisation of a 'perfetta poesia italiana.' But both men succumbed to the superior attraction of scholarship and antiquarian research, and poetry was soon relegated to an inferior place in their lives. Muratori was the more profound student of literary theory, while Maffei sought to reform by practice, to purify the theatre and give dramatic poets an example to imitate. 'Voi siete,' said Muratori three days before he died, 'il campione più vigoroso e coraggioso della letteratura in Italia.'[2] In the theory of literary creation Muratori had the loftier, more far-reaching ideas; but in the estimate of individual literary works Maffei had, as a man of the world, the sounder and saner judgment. His eulogist cannot resist reminding us that Muratori applied the epithet 'divine' to Maggi and denied it to Homer; while Maffei 'overthrew the altar of Maggi and venerated Homer supremely.'

II

Maffei's contributions to the subject of the present volume represent almost as small a fraction of his collected writings as we found to be the case with Muratori's.

His *Osservazioni sopra la Rodoguna, tragedia francese* (1700), is an immature and youthfully exuberant attack on Corneille's drama, written before the patriotic movement in Italian letters had properly emerged. *Rodogune*, he says, contains atrocious and inexcusable crimes which cannot possibly awaken pity; and it is at variance with history. But offences against the probable

[1] Cp. Pindemonte, p. 112.

[2] In a letter of January 20, 1750, quoted by Soli Muratori, *Vita di L. A. Muratori*, Naples, 1758, p. 169.

are more serious in poetry than those against the true; and much in *Rodogune* is highly improbable. The exposition is defective, and there are grave faults in the character-drawing. When, however, Maffei turns to dramaturgic theory in general, he is plainly still far from reasoned convictions on the subject. The *Osservazioni sopra la Rodoguna* stands by itself; for during the first decade of the eighteenth century Maffei manifested no interest in either the drama or the theatre, being then mainly occupied with preparations for the *Giornale dei Letterati*.

In 1711 Luigi Riccoboni, the leader of a company of actors who were playing in Verona, approached Maffei with the request that he would give them something to act which he regarded as of poetic value. Maffei was much struck by Riccoboni's readiness to serve the ends of literature, as well as by the ability of his company; and hopes awakened in him of reforming the Italian theatre with their aid. He readily acquiesced and looked out some old and new tragedies, some of them in verse, which had at that time fallen into disuse on the stage[1]. The undertaking was full of promise, and he made an appeal to the principal writers of Italy to support it by providing plays. Martelli had anticipated the appeal, and such of his tragedies as were playable were incorporated in the new repertory; and it was, as we have seen, under this stimulus that Gravina made his ill-advised appearance as a dramatist[2]. But the triumph of the enterprise was the production of Maffei's own *Merope*, without which neither the old Italian plays nor Martelli's would have carried the reform very far.

It was thus to further the establishment of a national theatre on the historical side that Maffei drew from obscurity the Italian tragedies included in his *Teatro Italiano, o sia Scelta di Tragedie per uso della scena*[3]. This collection, the first of its kind, had,

[1] Preface to the *Teatro italiano*, I, p. xii. Cp. also Maffei's *De' Teatri antichi e moderni*, pp. 4 f.

[2] See above, p. 32.

[3] The plays which Maffei reprinted are: Vol. I (1723): Trissino, *La Sofonisba*; G. Rucellai, *L' Oreste*; Orsatto Giustiniano, *L' Edipo Rè* (tragedia di Sofocle); Pomponio Torelli, *La Merope*. Vol. II (1723): Tasso, *Il Rè Torrismondo*; Bongianni Gratarolo, *L' Astianatte*; Muzio Manfredi, *La Semiramide*; Ansaldo Cebà, *Le Gemelle Capovane*. Vol. III (1725): Prospero Bonarelli, *Il Solimano*; Ansaldo Cebà, *L' Alcippo Spartano*; Carlo de' Dottori, *L' Aristodemo*; Cardinal Delfino, *La Cleopatra*. The nature of the collection

the editor tells us, three objects in view: 'to make known our best works of this genre; to reprint works that have become extremely rare; and to introduce the Greek form of tragedy with stable chorus and no division between acts and scenes.'

It was necessary, both for the honour of our nation, and the information of other nations, that the Italian theatre should be seen for what it really is. It will be no small advantage if this edition succeeds in disabusing Europe of its belief that our language is not as happy in dramatic poetry as in the epic and in the lyric; that we possess nothing of distinction in this genre except some pastorals; and that tragedies and comedies are only to be found in France. It is not our intention here to defraud in the least the French authors of the praise which is their due; but it is also not right that the Italian theatre should be judged by farces, not written by poets, but composed for the most part by the actors who play them[1].

The introduction to the collection is an *Istoria del Teatro e difeso di esso*, and Maffei's most complete pronouncement on the subject of the drama[2]. He begins by giving a sketch of the rise of the theatre from the confusion that settled upon it after the passing of the classical literatures; he discusses briefly the church plays, the encroachment of the vernacular on Latin; and urges the importance of Mussato and Trissino as the pioneers of a higher order of drama. In the fifteenth century the study of Greek gave a new impetus to the development of dramatic poetry, as is to be seen from the *Sofonisba* of Trissino, 'a cui il bell' onore non dee invidiarsi d' aver inalzate le nostre scene sino a emulare i famosi esemplari de' Greci' (p. iv). In all this achievement—and Maffei with patriotic pride loses no opportunity of putting in the best light the work of Veronese writers—Italy was more than sixty years in advance of France. The rich promise of the fifteenth century was, however, destroyed by two disintegrating forces. The first of these was the introduction of music and the rise of the opera; the second the employment of dialect and masks in comedy, and the consequent

was limited, Maffei tells us, by his desire to publish only plays suitable for public representation; this is the reason why the tragedies of G. B. Giraldi, of Dolci, and *Il Cieco* by Adria were not included; Tasso's *Aminta* is also omitted as being unsuited for the theatre.

[1] *Teatro italiano*, I, Preface, pp. xv f.

[2] It is reprinted in Maffei's *Opuscoli letterari*, Venice, 1829, pp. 67 ff.

substitution of prose for verse. Notwithstanding the success of his friend Apostolo Zeno's musical plays, Maffei, like Saint-Évremond, condemns a form of drama in which the poet is necessarily of inferior importance to the musician. Amongst the best comedies of this time he singles out the *Calandra* of the Cardinal da Bibiena, and the *Ramnusia* of Aurelio Schioppi, a Veronese. He mentions, too, the growing taste for 'Intromesse.'

After describing his own and Riccoboni's share in the reform of the theatre, he explains the object of his collection. He then turns to general questions. First, there is the moral purpose of the theatre; its importance as an educational factor. Some churchmen have maintained that the theatre should be suppressed altogether, as subversive of morality; but Maffei recalls the close ties of the ancient Greek theatre with religion, and brings up an effective battery of defence from ancient authors. The controversy is one to which he was to return in later life. Next, he deals with the deficiencies of the actors. The comic actor in Italy has too long acted without artistic restraint, inserting foolish words of his own which have brought Italian comedy into disrepute. In fact, thanks to the present system, or lack of system, almost all the members of a theatrical company are held in contempt by educated people. Proper instruction in the art of acting is thus, above all things, necessary; the actor must learn how to recite—in the theatre there must be neither declaiming nor arguing; he must not allow himself to get excited and noisy, and, at the same time, avoid becoming languid, or speaking monotonously or too quickly. He should read the play in presence of some one who understands the poet's intentions. Maffei illustrates these precepts with reference to his own *Merope*. He returns to the inherent falsity of the opera; and to the bad taste that demands prose instead of verse. He condemns the senseless introduction of love into tragedies—a usage not to be found among the Greeks—and ridicules the 'Monsieur' Ulysse and 'Madame' Andromaque of Racine. He objects to the continual constraint of rhyme, as leading to monotony and narrowing the freedom of the poet. For, above all, naturalness of diction is to be aimed at.

This, as will be seen, is a little treatise on what, after Lessing's time, came to be known as 'dramaturgy,' prefaced by a historical introduction; but its originality is not, when one comes to look into it, very great. The historical outline is of the slightest; and the rest of the contents is mainly suggested by what Muratori has to say on the drama in his *Perfetta Poesia italiana*. Muratorian, too, is the line of defence which Maffei takes up in face of the antagonism of the Church to the theatre. On the other hand, Maffei had himself been alive to the weak points of French tragedy, ever since he had attacked *Rodogune* in his youth; and there was plenty of support for his criticism in Gravina and Martelli. Where Maffei is most original is on the practical side: in the purpose of his collection of plays, and in the demand he makes for the proper education and equipment of the actor. That a nobleman and a scholar should have condescended to join hands with actors in the reform of the theatre was, in itself, a most significant feature in Maffei's effort; but it is safe to say that he would hardly have had the courage to take such a step had not Cardinal Richelieu directly interested himself in the reform of the theatre in France, or, following Richelieu's example, Cardinal Borromeo in Italy[1]. The beginning of the modern theatre as a serious institution dates from the projects of reform drawn up by D'Aubignac at Richelieu's instigation. Muratori had been visibly impressed by this interest of the great Cardinal in the theatre; and Muratori's reference to it[2] might well have stimulated Maffei to undertake the reform of the Italian theatre.

It is very questionable how far Maffei's collection of old Italian plays justified its purpose; indeed, it would have been without a parallel in theatrical history, if this attempt to create a non-existent theatre with the aid of old plays—not one of which had the slightest prospect of appealing to the audience which applauded *Merope*—had met with success. It is noticeable, moreover, that Riccoboni's references to the reform are pitched in a lower key than Maffei's; the practical man of the

[1] Cp. L. Riccoboni, *Histoire du Théâtre italien*, Paris, 1728, I, p. 58.

[2] Cp. *Della perfetta poesia*, III, pp. 78 f. 'Laonde,' Muratori concludes, 'riman tuttavia un bel campo da coltivare a chi volesse in tutte le sue parti correggere e migliorar il teatro.'

theatre—and of a theatre which had hitherto subsisted on quite 'unliterary' popular farces—must have been very dubious of antiquarian experiments. In later years, when Riccoboni, under religious influence, had turned his back on the theatre, he wrote rather bitterly about Maffei. He published a letter to Desfontaines in the letters *Observations sur les écrits modernes* in 1737, in which he said:

Il me proposa de faire un essai des Tragédies Italiennes du 16me siècle. Je lui répondis qu'on m'avoit dit qu'elles étoient mauvaises, et que je n'avois jamais voulu les lire. Il se mit en fureur; il me soutint qu'elles étoient excellentes, et que la seule *Sophonisbe* du Trissin valoit mieux que tout Corneille et Racine. Je lus et examinai cette Tragédie, et comme pour bien des raisons je ne trouvai pas qu'on pût la joüer dans l'état où elle étoit, il se chargea de la diviser par Actes, et d'en retrancher l'inutile. Il fit la même chose de la *Cléopatre* du Delphino, de l'*Oreste* du Rucellai, du *Torrismond* du Tasse. J'eus la complaisance de les joüer avec bien de la peine, et avec une grande dépense, dont le nombre des Spectateurs, qui n'étoit pas considerable, ne me dédommagea pas; et malgré l'intérêt, que chacun y prenoit pour la gloire de la Patrie, Corneille et Racine triumphoient toujours[1].

This criticism is in so far unfair, as Maffei had scrupulously endeavoured to give the great French drama its due; but after allowance has been made for Riccoboni's change of mood, there is considerable truth in his condemnation of the *Teatro italiano* as a measure of practical utility.

When Riccoboni went to try his fortunes in Paris in 1716, he carried with him a letter from Maffei to Antonio Conti, which speaks of him and his wife in the most generous terms:

Luigi Riccoboni and Elena his wife are my friends in more than an ordinary sense, for their characters are very different from what is usual in their profession; they are not wanting in nobility, except as regards their birth, which is, none the less, excellent. Of their good will I could not say enough. They have been the sole instrument by which I have achieved some reform of our Italian theatre,

[1] Vol. VIII, Paris, 1737, pp. 89 f., quoted also by Pindemonte in a note (*op. cit.* p. 121). It called forth a *Lettera ammonitaria a Lelio commediante che sta in Parigi*, Venice, 1737 (quoted by Maugain, p. 274) by Maffei's loyal friend, G. C. Becelli, but certainly inspired by Maffei himself.

having induced them to act our good old tragedies, of which we had almost no knowledge or memory[1].

And indeed, Luigi Riccoboni and Elena Baletti, who, amongst her other accomplishments, was a capable Latin scholar, deserve a place of honour in the history of the European theatre. No actor of the eighteenth century had a more liberal and humane view of the theatre than Riccoboni; none had so wide an outlook.

Born in 1675 at Modena, and the son of a celebrated actor, he won fame under the name of 'Lelio.' The great moment of his earlier life was when, with Maffei's cooperation, he agreed to substitute written plays for the improvisations of the *commedia dell' arte*. But he had a much more disheartening and uphill task than one might infer from Maffei, who won easy laurels with his *Merope*. Riccoboni realised that his reform would go for nothing, if he could not carry it out in the theatre-metropolis of Northern Italy, Venice. He made the attempt and failed; Venice declined to applaud *La Scolastica* of Ariosto; her love for romance and the *commedia dell' arte* proved too strong for Riccoboni. He took his failure much to heart; and it made him the more ready to shake the dust of Italy from his feet and accept the invitation of the Duke of Orleans to re-establish the Théâtre italien in Paris. From 1716 to 1729 he was the leader of the Italian actors here; and, with the exception of a brief return to Italy in 1729, Paris remained his home until his death in 1753. Riccoboni is the author of more than twenty plays, and he translated Racine's *Andromaque* and *Britannicus*. His *Histoire du Théâtre italien* (2 vols. Paris, 1728, 1731), unsatisfactory compilation as it is, remained the most authoritative account of the Italian theatre for Europe until as late as Lessing[2], and in his *Réflexions historiques et critiques sur les différens théâtres de l'Europe* (1740), where, by the way, Shakespeare is not forgotten, he made a first attempt towards a comparative history of the theatre. In a short poem, *Dell' Arte rappresen-*

[1] Pindemonte, Maffei's biographer quotes the letter (p. 120) in order apparently to refute the gossip which insinuated that Maffei had been in love with Riccoboni's wife. There is a hint of this also in Martelli's *Femia*.

[2] Lessing translates most of it into German in his *Theatralische Bibliothek* (1754).

tativa (London, 1728), he dealt, in six 'capitoli,' with the art of the actor; and in his *Observations sur la Comédie* (Paris, 1736), he railed against Molière as subversive of good morals, a view which, it will be remembered, Muratori shared. His last book was *De la Réformation du Théâtre* (Paris, 1743, and again, 1767); but, by this time, Riccoboni had renounced the stage, and viewed it with very hostile eyes[1].

Beyond the brief spell of Maffei's reformatory activity with Riccoboni, his *Teatro italiano* and *Merope*, Maffei has little more claim on our attention in these pages. In later years he returned, in consequence of Cóncina's attacks, to his defence of the theatre; but that controversy was, as we have seen, theological and erudite, rather than practical.

III

One after the other, the writers who form the subject of the present volume have been set up by Italian critics as representative of a definitely modern attitude to literature; and in point of fact, Gravina, Muratori, Martelli, Conti, are all, in one aspect or another, in antagonism to the neo-classic doctrine of their time. In the wide interpretation of the word Romanticism, they have a claim to be regarded as its 'precursor.' The description 'precursor of Romanticism' was, however, more particularly applied by Bertana, nearly thirty years ago, to a writer who may be briefly dealt with in the present chapter, Giulio Cesare Becelli[2]. Becelli was Maffei's most loyal henchman. Born in 1683, he was also a native of Verona. He became a Jesuit priest, but obtained a dispensation allowing him to marry, and he settled down to a studious literary life in Rome. He seems to have been hard put to it to make a living, and had to eke out his scanty resources by teaching, and preparing the books of others for the press. He died in 1750[3].

The work of Becelli's which is here mainly in question, *Della*

[1] Cp. F. Righetti, *Studj sull' arte drammatica*, I, Turin, 1834; N. M. Bernardin, *La Comédie italienne*, Paris, 1902, pp. 180 ff.

[2] E. Bertana, *Un precursore del Romanticismo* (*G. C. Becelli*) in *Giornale storico della lett. ital.* XXVI (1895), pp. 114 ff.

[3] Cp. G. M. Mazzuchelli, *Gli Scrittori d' Italia*, II, Brescia, 1760, pp. 606 ff.; E. de Tipaldo, *Biografia degli italiani illustri*, VII, 1840, pp. 481 ff. Also N. Tommaseo, *Dizionario d' Estetica*, 4th ed., Milan, 1867, I, col. 99 ff.

novella Poesia, cioè del vero genere e particolari bellezze della Poesia italiana, libri tre, Verona 1732, is a most readable and even fascinating book; standing by itself, it might well justify Bertana's high claim for it; but, considered together with the large body of literary criticism from which it sprang, its originality is not great. It sets forth no new truth or idea; but merely underlines and emphasises what others had already said. In fact, its chief value is as a kind of supplement to Maffei. Nothing in it, at least, is in contradiction with what we know to have been Maffei's aesthetic creed.

In summing up the work, Bertana shows that it turns round two fundamental ideas: that the modern literatures of Europe in general, and of Italy in particular, are no less rich and no less noble than the ancient classic literatures; and that modern writers, who have quite as many new and praiseworthy things to say as the Greeks and Latins, must be allowed to break away deliberately from the rules and example of the ancients. The imitation of the ancients, Becelli says, is not in the least necessary. Many of our modern writers have produced magnificent original works, notwithstanding the deep-seated conviction that all the treasures of our poetry must necessarily come—and have actually come—from the fountain-head of Greece and Rome. In a later work, *Esame della Rettorica antica e uso della moderna* (1735–39), Becelli's views on the relation of the ancients and the moderns stiffened into a less tolerant dogma. His antagonism to antiquity became biassed by religious prejudices, and he set up a narrowly 'christian' rhetoric in place of that of the ancients. But the *Novella Poesia* is an eminently fair statement of the case for modern literature.

Italy is lacking, he says at the outset, in courageous assertion of her strength and literary genius. We Italians, who possess so sweet and graceful a modern poetry, have neglected to study its various kinds, its rich qualities and singular beauties. We appear rather to be ashamed of ourselves; we weakly concede its origin to have been Greek or Latin, and are content to play the rôle of imitators, if indeed such a rôle can be described as anything else than slavery.

This cowardice he believes to have been a serious source of weakness and loss to Italian literature. This is the burden—

often unnecessarily reiterated—of the entire work; all the rest is merely corollary or deduction. In his first book he deals with the forms of composition which, for good or for evil, the Italians have in common with the ancients; and in the second with kinds of poetry which are not represented in Greek and Latin literature, such as religious poems, romances, pastorals, farces, and literature in dialect. Finally he discusses, and with a fullness and an understanding rare in the literature of the time, the lyric.

Obviously, we have in the *Novella Poesia* merely an exposition of views, differing only in their confident tone, from what had already been said by the 'moderns' in Italy; but the late date of Becelli's work amply accounts for his advance. The claim for the independent development of modern literature was as old as Gravina, and had been a more constant element in Italian theory, than in French; and Becelli's views on the drama, especially on such matters as the unities, had been already expressed by Martelli. If Becelli is more outspoken than Martelli, it may be because he had read La Motte's *Discourses*, which appeared two years earlier.

CHAPTER VII

PIETRO DI CALEPIO

IN the foregoing studies Martelli and Conti have respectively been presented as links between France and Italy and England and Italy; in both cases it was a question of the fertilisation of Italian thought by foreign ideas. Calepio, the subject of the present chapter, forms a tie between Italy and Germany; but, inasmuch as the Germany of the first decades of the eighteenth century was intellectually too poverty-stricken to have anything to offer her neighbours, Calepio represents, not an influence of Germany on Italy, but rather a bridge across which Italian ideas found their way to the north. This is the justification for his inclusion in the present volume. Although his book comparing French and Italian tragedy lacks distinctive originality, it has the stamp of personality and a sense of style which give it an honourable place in the theoretical literature of its time; and it helped, to an extent which has not yet been adequately realised, to mould German critical ideas from Gottsched and Bodmer to Mendelssohn and Lessing.

I

Count Pietro dei Conti di Calepio sprang from an ancient and noble family which had long held possessions in the valley of Calepio near Bergamo[1]. He was born on January 13, 1693, and, as he showed precocious talents, was, at the age of seven, taught Latin by some priests. He became subsequently a scholar of the Collegio di S. Antonio in Brescia, where, until his seventeenth year, he had a distinguished career. Here he mastered Greek as well as French. As he was to administer the family estates, he was sent by his father to Rome, in order that he might gain some knowledge of law. This gave him the oppor-

[1] I have gathered my biographical data from the 'Vita dell' Autore scritta dal Conte Marco Tomini Foresti,' and prefaced to the Venice edition (1770) of Calepio's *Paragone*, pp. iii ff. There is a portrait of Calepio as frontispiece of this edition.

tunity of his life. For, without neglecting his legal studies, he threw himself with zeal into the rich and varied intellectual life the city offered. He became a member of academies there, attended their meetings and made many friends, no doubt coming into personal contact with both Gravina and Martelli[1]. From erudite studies in the ancient languages to literary composition the step in those days was not a great one, and we hear of sonnets and canzoni by him that circulated among his friends in manuscript; he even attempted two tragedies, a *Perdicca* and a *Seleuco*. Subsequently, having, as he tells us, a low opinion of these plays, he destined them to the flames, but his father's pride stayed their destruction for some years[2]. Another production of this Roman period has, however, been printed, namely, an *Apologia di Sofocle contro le censure del Signor di Voltaire*, *con alcune Annotazioni sopra la traduzione dell' Edippo di Orsato Giustiniani*. It dates probably from 1723 or 1724, after the appearance of the first volume of Maffei's *Teatro italiano*, which made the Italian *Oedipus* accessible. The *Apologia* was warmly recommended for publication by A. M. Salvini; Caspar von Muralt wrote a long letter in support of it; and it was at a later date printed in Switzerland[3]. It is, however, a rather slight production, in which Sophocles is defended against Voltaire's strictures in his *Lettres sur l'Oedipe*. Calepio shows that Voltaire did not know the real Sophocles at all, but was content to base his arguments on the translation of Brumoy; and that much of Voltaire's censure of the Greek poet was due to a misunderstanding of the conditions under which ancient tragedy was performed.

After leaving Rome, Calepio resolved to widen his intellectual horizon by visiting France, where he perfected his knowledge of the language and made acquaintances among men of letters. During his stay here he wrote, apparently at the suggestion of Caspar von Muralt, letters *Sopra il Carattere degli' Italiani*,

[1] Cp. A. Galletti, *op. cit.* p. 222.

[2] Cp. *Paragone*, ed. of 1770, p. v.

[3] Calepio sent the manuscript of the *Apologia* to Bodmer—it is now in the Zürich Stadtbibliothek—who published it in his *Sammlung critischer, poetischer, und andrer geistvollen Schriften* (St. III, pp. 37–74), Zürich, 1742.

which were planned as a kind of counterpart to the *Lettres sur les Anglois et sur les François* by Muralt's relative, L. B. von Muralt. The manuscript came into Bodmer's hands, and was sent by him to a 'gentleman of Lausanne,'[1] who, without Calepio's knowledge, translated, annotated and published it in the *Bibliothèque italique*[2]. Regarded as a counterpart to Muralt's famous *Lettres sur les Anglois et sur les François*, this series of essays on the Italians is disappointing. They make but dry and tedious reading which is hardly enlivened by the apologetic and explanatory notes of the French translator, who signs himself 'N. D. J.' The opening letter (vol. III, pp. 208 ff.) is the best. As a forerunner of Montesquieu, Madame de Staël and Taine, Calepio reviews the peoples of Europe in a comparative spirit, and shows how their characteristic developments have been influenced by climate.

> L'*Italie* se trouve placée en des Climats qui, tenant un milieu entre les extrêmes, jouissent des prérogatives de l'un et de l'autre.... Cette situation donne aux Italiens un Caractére tempéré, qui participe de la fierté et de la douceur, de la timidité et de la hardiesse, avec un tour d'Esprit qui se proportionne à toutes sortes d'Etudes (p. 214).

He deals first with the 'external' qualities of the Italians, then with their manners and social characteristics; lastly, he discusses their studies. Unfortunately, this final section, which might have been the most interesting, is perfunctory and disappointing. Paolo Doria is highly praised; his *Vita civile* is not only exempt from the errors of Hobbes, but 'on peut dire qu'à certains égards, Doria a quelque chose de plus parfait que Grotius et Pufendorf.'[3] All the writers discussed in these pages—Orsi, Gravina, Muratori, Maffei, Vico—are passed in brief review supplemented by the more detailed notes of the

[1] Bodmer wrote on the last page of the manuscript (Zürich Stadtbibliothek, Bodmer MSS., Fremdes, I, 39): 'Habe dieses Msc. an Herrn Seigneux nach Losanne gesandt, der es übersetzen und der "Bibliotheca Italiana" beydrucken liess' (L. Donati, *Bodmer und die italienische Literatur, Bodmer-Denkschrift*, Zürich, 1900, p. 256).

[2] *Lettres de Monsieur *** sur le Caractère des Italiens, Bibliothèque Italique*, III (October, 1728) to X (April, 1731). The Italian original is in the Zürich library.

[3] Vol. III, pp. 239 f. and V, p. 254.

translator; and the author finds an opportunity to extol the virtues of the people of the 'Territoire de Bergamo.'

A letter written by Calepio about this time, or somewhat earlier, in which he replied to a criticism of Tasso, was published in a German translation. This is evidently *Tasso's Jerusalem vertheidigt*, which appeared in the *Freymüthige Nachrichten* of Zürich in 1750[1]. His most important work, however, is the *Paragone della Poesia tragica d' Italia con quella di Francia*, which, his biographer implies, was written while the author was still on his travels. He sent his manuscript to Bodmer, who was, as he says, 'della novità e bellezza di tale opera rapito,' and had it published at Zürich in 1732, without the author's name[2].

Calepio returned home somewhere about 1728, married and settled down on his estates. About this time, too, he became acquainted with Bodmer through Caspar von Muralt; and although the two men never met, they carried on a correspondence which lasted from 1728 until 1761, that is to say, until shortly before Calepio's death. A number of the letters, as will be seen[3], were utilised by Bodmer for his *Briefwechsel von der Natur des poetischen Geschmackes* (Zürich, 1736). Bodmer interested Calepio in German literature, notably in 'Clopstoc's' *Messias*. Calepio translated samples of the epic (from the French translation), and, as appears from the correspondence, sent them to the *Novelle della Repubblica letteraria*, published in Venice[4]; but the manuscript was lost on the way.

[1] Vol. x, pp. 14 ff. It was reprinted in the *Archiv der schweizerischen Kritik*, 1768, pp. 115 ff. Cp. Donati, *l.c.* p. 291, who regards it as Bodmer's own.

[2] On January 20, 1731, Bodmer wrote to Calepio: 'Je me félicite sur l'achèvement de l'Examen de la poësie Tragique, après lequel je soupire si long temps. Mais afin que ma satisfaction soit entière, je vous supplie de me permettre la lecture de cet ouvrage, qui ne peut être que rempli de rares connoissances et de nouvelles lumières....Au reste je souhaiterois d'avoir assez d'ascendant sur Vous Mr. pour Vous persuader de publier Votre dissertation; Je suis peut être plus que personne en état de Vous servir pour cet Effet; ayant à ma solde une bonne imprimerie qui dépend de moi. J'attend sur cela Vos ordres, si Vous entrez dans mes pensées ce sera moi qui corrigerai les Epreuves' (from an unpublished letter in the Biblioteca Civica in Bergamo).

[3] See below, pp. 265 ff.

[4] A note in the number of the *Novelle* of November 22, 1749, is worth quoting: 'Con Lettera di Zurigo si rileva, essere uscito in lingua Alemana un raro e pregevole Poema, lavorata sul gusto di quello Inglese del famoso

Calepio's later life seems to have been fully occupied by the manifold duties that fell to him as administrator, judge and deputy for the town of Bergamo; but, in spite of this, his literary and scholarly interests did not die down. He kept up a large correspondence, not only with Bodmer and Caspar von Muralt, but with distinguished Italian contemporaries, including Eustachio Manfredi, A. M. Salvini, Domenico Lazzarini, Scipione Maffei and Crescimbeni[1]. Of his later labours there is a hint in the correspondence with Bodmer that he planned a continuation of Maffei's *Teatro italiano*; his biographer mentions that he assisted the Accademia della Crusca with its Dictionary; he interested himself, like Maffei, in antiquarian research and ancient inscriptions; and he defended his *Paragone* against the criticism of Salio. His death took place on February 26, 1762.

II

The *Paragone della Poesia tragica d' Italia con quella di Francia*, which Carducci has described as 'one of the best, if not perhaps the best among the old Italian books on the aesthetic theory of the theatre,'[2] is a concise, clearly reasoned, systematically arranged little study. It is not altogether free from irritating repetitions; but it succeeds in concentrating the entire argument in seven chapters, each of these being divided into a number of 'articoli.'

The treatise was, as we have been, published anonymously

Milton: senonchè l' Autore Tedesco, che si dice essere il Sig. Clopestoc, prendendo un soggetto differente da quello del *Paradiso perduto*, o sia della disgrazia dell' Uomo, in questo si fa vedere la di lui salute e Redenzione; onde il Poema viene intitolato *Il Messia*. Noi stante il giudizio d' un Cavalier Alemano addottrinato, per le bellezze peregrine che trovansi in questo nuovo Poema, speriamo di vederne presto nella nostra Italiana favella un opportuna Traduzione.' Cp. Donati, *l.c.* pp. 254, 305. When Bodmer learned that Quadrio was writing a general history of literature, he got Calepio—who, however, did not share Bodmer's enthusiasm for the *Messias*—to inform him about Klopstock. In mentioning the latter, Quadrio refers to Bodmer (*Storia e Ragione d' ogni Poesia*, VII, p. 284).

[1] Calepio's biographer says (p. ix) that his eldest son, Count Galeazzo, made a collection of his father's correspondence; but this has not been published.

[2] *Il 'Torrismondo' di T. Tasso*, in *Nuova Antologia*, January 1, 1894, p. 19 (quoted by Bertana, *op. cit.* p. 90); now in *Su L. Ariosto e T. Tasso* (*Opere*, XV), Bologna, 1905, p. 513.

by Bodmer, the author fearing, as Bodmer said in his Latin Preface to the 'ingenuous reader,' the controversy in which the book would be sure to involve him. In the dedication of the book to his Swiss friend, Calepio says that his object is to treat at more length and in more detail the theme broached by Maffei in the preface to his *Teatro italiano*. He begins by laying down concisely the plan of his work, which is arranged on Aristotelian lines. It falls into two halves, a general part, in which the 'spirit' of the tragic fable is considered under the three headings: the character of tragic fables, the 'peripeteia,' and the episodes; and a second part dealing with the 'body' of the fable, *i.e.* 'costume,' 'sentence,' style and metre. Calepio's method—theoretical statement followed by examples drawn from the dramatic literature of Greece, France and Italy—is familiar to us from the Italian critics already considered. He writes with warm conviction, and is almost too anxious to guard against the view that his attitude to French tragedy is prompted by a petty patriotic desire to press the claims of his own countrymen. His reading in French and Italian tragedy, as well as in Greek, is unusually wide.

Opening with the well-worn assertion that the end of poetry is to guide men by way of delight to virtue, he proceeds at once to discuss Corneille's theory and practice, this being one of the avowed objects of his investigation. He opens the attack on Corneille by accusing him of pretending to follow Aristotle and, when he finds that his own plays are not strictly Aristotelian, adapting and interpreting Aristotle—'s'accommodant avec Aristote,' as Corneille puts it—to suit his purpose. He holds, for instance, that Aristotle did not consider both fear and pity necessary to tragedy, but fear *or* pity—a view which cannot be maintained. Again, Aristotle does not approve of well-known persons being killed; Corneille twists this round in order to save his *Cid*, *Cinna*, etc. He has created no genuine tragic heroes; his characters, in fact, are better suited for the epic, in so far as they awaken only fear, or only compassion and admiration. Corneille regards 'delight' alone as the end of tragedy, and from the pleasure a tragedy gives, the success it meets with, he infers its merits.

In the second article of chapter I Calepio interprets Aristotle's definition of the end of tragedy as 'il purgar con piacevolezza lo sregolamento delle passioni per mezzo della compassione, e del terrore' (p. 9). He accepts Corneille's and Dacier's interpretation, the 'purification of *all* passions,' not merely, the like passions. The best means of effecting this is by representing a good character who is plunged into misery. Aristotle, it is true, was opposed to admitting a person of eminent virtues as a hero of tragedy, but Calepio is inclined to justify such a hero, because, from the Christian standpoint, no one is exempt from some defect. With his own *Cid* in view, Corneille maintained the suitability of the immaculate hero in tragedy; but Calepio ingeniously points out that it was not merely the passion of Rodrigue and Chimène, but also the revenge which Rodrigue takes for the affront offered to his father that sets the catastrophe in motion. Corneille endeavoured to defend his argument by urging that the *Oedipus* of Sophocles did not purge at all; but Calepio shows that there is a misunderstanding here between the temporary ἁμάρτημα, or accidental fault, and the lasting μοχθηρία, or vicious habit. Thus both Dacier's attempt to defend the *Oedipus* of Sophocles by attributing violence, pride and temerity to him, and Terrasson's theory[1] that Sophocles only wished to enforce the moral that a man cannot avoid committing a crime if the gods have destined him to commit it, are alike wrong. Calepio now proceeds to review the tragedy of Greece, and shows that it on the whole agrees with Aristotle's standpoint. In this respect (Art. 3) the Italians conform more to the Aristotelian principle of tragedy than the French, who have been misled by the laxity of Corneille; the former (Art. 4) are superior in the 'substantial dignity of the tragic fable'—the tragic event. Corneille's heroes are all more or less defective; they awaken in us only pity or fear; or heroism and love take the place of true dramatic passions. Racine has given us only two perfect tragedies, *Phèdre* and *Britannicus*; for the rest, he falls into the errors of his predecessor. Common to both is the transference of the tragic passion to secondary characters.

The conclusion to which Calepio comes in this important

[1] See his *Dissertation critique sur l'Iliade*, Paris, 1715, I, p. 175.

section of his book is that the French might be said to have invented a type of drama, which is not tragedy, but—after Corneille—'dramma eroico'; whereas the Italians have adhered more strictly to tragedy. The chief defect of the latter is their overfondness for fictitious arguments and fictitious personages; the Greeks rarely dispensed with the prop of history, or at least of pseudo-historical tradition.

Calepio's second chapter deals with the Aristotelian περιπέτεια, or 'Reversal of the Situation.' The 'peripeteia' is rendered beautiful, and efficacious in awakening fear and pity, by three qualities: marvellousness, recognition and suffering ('maraviglia, riconoscenza, passione'). The first of these arises from the unexpectedness of the danger to which the hero is exposed, when, for instance, it comes from relatives or friends. This is the only form of the marvellous which tragedy, in contrast to epic poetry, requires. The French poets have not, however, paid much consideration to it; Corneille is content if his heroes awaken admiration, although this leads to a confusion of the tragic hero with the epic hero. It is a serious mistake, for admiration does not contribute to the essential end of tragedy; indeed, it rather obscures it. The 'double tragedy,' of which *Merope* is an example, where the bad die and the good are freed from their misery, has also been defended by the French, as teaching by example; but this has really nothing to do with the real end of tragic poetry. The use, again, of 'recognition' (ἀναγνώρισις)—*e.g.* a person, who is believed to be dead or far distant, appearing unexpectedly under a fictitious name—which the Italian poets have commonly observed, has been (Art. 2) disregarded and neglected by the French as inappropriate to tragedy. Corneille defends the French practice on the ground that 'recognition' destroys the opportunity for pathetic sentiments, and that it adds little to the force of the catastrophe to learn who the persons are against whom the hero has sinned. But Corneille might be answered by saying that, although 'recognition' does not affect the final pity, and is, in this respect, not essential, the end of a tragedy is apt to fall off in interest when the conflict of passions in the body of the work is over. 'Recognition,' by increasing the marvellous, counteracts this defect and makes the 'peripeteia' more moving. While the French seem to have erred here, one could wish that the Italians had shown a more compassionate interest in their heroes. The Italian hero is ignorant of nothing; no surprise is in store for him; and consequently the Italian plots are lacking in variety.

With regard to the third element (Art. 3) necessary to the efficacy of the 'peripeteia,' 'passione' or 'patimento,' the following three aspects have to be considered: the nature of the suffering; how compassion for the suffering may be effectively awakened; and what must accompany the suffering in order that it may produce the proper effect on the spectator. The French are not so strict in looking for the misfortune of the hero in historical events, such as death, loss of states, etc.; indeed there is a difficulty in doing so, because one rarely finds the suitable hero associated with the suitable disaster. The second point, effective preparation with a view to awakening compassion, is also, in practice, neglected by the French. Finally, care ought to be taken that the force of the final emotions is not dissipated, or our interest weakened by the sufferings of subordinate characters or by the introduction of extraneous motives, as, for example, excessive cruelty. In this respect the French are again great offenders, as is to be seen in such examples as Corneille's *Rodogune* and Racine's *Iphigénie*. It has also to be noted that the emotions of the subordinate characters are more efficacious in awakening a response in the spectator, just as the chorus was entrusted by the ancients with the function of expressing sympathy. Here again the Italians deserve the palm over the French.

Chapter III deals with the episodes, which (Art. 1) ought to be sparingly introduced into tragedy, the business of this form of poetry being to delight by awakening pity, not, as in the case of the epic, by multiplicity of events. The Greeks, in their natural love for simplicity, did not need theoretical guidance on this point; and the Italians have followed them, although their tragedies are not free from superfluous monologues. There is no doubt (Art. 2) that the episodic digressions introduced by the French poets lend a peculiar grace and charm to their tragedies without weakening the tragic force of the primary action, while the Italian episodes are too often irrelevant. Calepio, however, would like to see a stricter treatment of the episodes than he finds in French tragedy; he objects to dialogues between personages who are spectators rather than actors in the drama, and to confidants; he disapproves of the interpolation of mere accidents in the fable. These things militate against the unity of the action. Many authors, again, sin in the matter of time, owing to Corneille's demand that the fable must be kept strictly within the limits imposed by the unities. This is excusable in the representation of events which, in actual history, are spread over a long period, as the only alternative would be to exclude them altogether from the theatre; but it is another matter with invented plots, which ought not to be allowed to transgress. It is also objectionable for an episodic digression to overshadow the tragedy, to dwarf the primary intention, or to destroy the necessary unity of plot. Finally, Calepio takes exception to the kind of intrigue which is to be found in the French episodes. Article 3 deals with the introduction of love into tragedy, which Corneille had regarded as indispensable. Allowance must, of course, be made for the temperament of the nation and the conditions under which French tragedy is represented; but there are obvious dangers in the introduction of love episodes; they are apt to weaken our interest in the chief tragic event.

Chapter IV is concerned with the utility of various artifices which the French employ in the arrangement and form of their tragic representations, or, in modern phrase, with the technique of tragedy. Herein lies the great superiority of the French over the Italians; in this respect both Greeks and Italians are clumsy. Subjects ought to be avoided which require long monologues and explanations; these are invariably tedious to the audience; the excessive use of confidants in the French drama is also to be deprecated, and the recourse of the French dramatists to dreams is as objectionable as the Italian use of oracles. Nothing is to be said against the introduction of prologues, unless they are employed merely to evade difficulties of construction. The French are (Art. 2) much the superiors of the Italians in the skilful and natural introduction of incidents, while they recognise that the chorus is an incongruous anachronism. The Italians might also learn from the French (Art. 3) the art of making the catastrophe depend on essential elements of the fable, not on mere casual happenings. In other matters (Art. 4) the French are to be imitated; for example, in not allowing any actor to appear who does not quickly make himself known, in keeping the principal personages on the stage most of the time, and in supplying natural motives for the entrances and exits of the characters. This leads Calepio to touch on the difficulties of the unity of place, and he finds much to praise in the ingenuity of Corneille and Racine. In the matter of diction (Art. 5), the French avoid the tedious narratives of the Italians and succeed in placing the audience in possession of vital facts without being unnatural; the same is true of their use of soliloquies. Lastly (Art. 6), the superiority of the French is plain in the arrangement, variety and naturalness of their scenes, and in their abolition of the chorus. He concludes this chapter (Art. 7) by pointing out that the French have succeeded in all these things, because they have studied the pleasure of the people for whom they write, while the Italians are too intent on imitating antiquity.

Chapter V deals with the observance of the rules concerning 'costume' or character. The tendency in France is (Art. 1) to lay more stress on 'character' than on the essentials of tragedy. The first point Calepio takes up (Art. 3) is the 'moral tendency.' Le Bossu does not allow every 'good' to be the end of poetry, but only the 'poetical good,' that is to say, an attribute which is applicable alike to the morally bad and the morally good. Similarly, Corneille explains—and Calepio agrees with him—the 'good' in a tragic personage, not as a virtue worthy of our sympathy, but as a 'caractère brillant,' whether virtuous or criminal. Evil characters are, in his opinion, capable of tragic greatness, the proof being that, without them, the great tragedies of literature could not exist. His best argument, which he had made use of in an earlier chapter, is based on Aristotle's *Ethics* III, 15, where the 'vicious habit' is distinguished from the 'accidental fault'; but Aristotle had no intention of destroying the prerogative of the perfect tragedy to serve the end of good morals, which is after all the worthiest end of art.

Corneille's theory ends in practice in a play like *Le Menteur*, which renders vice attractive. Racine, it has to be noted, is, in this respect, more careful. Corneille claimed for his own time certain moral ideas which, he said, the ancients did not sufficiently recognise, such as the castigation of moral evil and the recompense of virtue, but, in so doing, he spoke in ignorance of the ancient tragedies. Corneille believed he was an innovator in writing tragedies the object of which was to bring before the people models of virtue; but this is not a function of tragedy at all, but of the epic. In tragedy it only confuses the spectators, or it makes them fanatics. Racine is more reasonable in this respect, and on this account La Bruyère, borrowing Aristotle's judgment on Sophocles and Euripides, says that Corneille forms men as they ought to be, Racine as they are; but it would be truer to say that Racine forms them as they ought to be and Corneille often as they cannot be. In regard to all these matters, the Italians are not (Art. 3) deserving of much praise; too often they do little more than show virtue oppressed.

Calepio now turns (Art. 4) to 'decorum,' to which the Greeks paid less attention than Seneca. The French sin, as he had already pointed out, by introducing too much love; Racine's Alexandre is an example, and Thomas Corneille's Essex 'dies of despair rather than of greatness of soul.' Another French error is to give too much prominence to the women of the tragedies, and too little to national or local colour. Amongst minor errors might be mentioned those in respect of age; children, such as Britannicus, speak with a wisdom beyond their years. In their blind imitation of the Greeks, the Italian poets have offended (Art. 5) most against the majesty of their tragic personages. With regard to the third element of 'costume' (Art. 6), the French are not careful to maintain verisimilitude; they introduce irrelevant love-episodes, and ennoble their characters too much. At the same time, they possess in a higher degree than the Italians, and even the Greeks, the art of character-drawing. In respect of historical truth, the French have no tragic writer equal to the Abate Conti. Finally (Art. 7), in the matter of full and vivid pictures of the milieu of the play, the French can claim no superiority over the Italians.

Chapter VI deals with style. The French show to advantage, compared with the older Italian writers, who indulge too much in 'concetti' and prolixity; but it is not so clear whether they are superior to the modern Italians, such as Gravina, Martelli and Conti. Corneille sins too often against his own rule that the language of drama should not be as inflated as that of the epic. On the whole, there is a want of adaptability in the French tragic style. Chapter VII, finally, deals with metre. Neither the Italians nor the French possess a metre which compares in tragic dignity with that of Greek tragedy; but the Italians stand at no disadvantage in comparison with other modern peoples. Calepio is himself in favour of the combination of the endecasillabo with the ettasillabo; and he does not approve of Martelli's reform. With the exception of Maffei, the Italians are too slavish imitators of the ancients. In conclusion, he claims no perfection for the Italians, who are still too close imitators of the ancients; but he has shown that they are superior in many respects to the French. The best way to arrive at perfection would be by the judicious combination of the good features of both nations.

III

The starting-point of the *Paragone*, as Calepio himself tells us, was the Preface to Maffei's *Teatro italiano*, just as his juvenile essay in dramatic criticism had been suggested by the publication of Orsatto Giustiniano's version of the *Oedipus tyrannus* in the first volume of that work. Indeed, one might regard the passage from Maffei which is quoted above (p. 156), as the germ of Calepio's treatise. It is, in any case, clear that Maffei was the chief inspirer of Calepio's criticism; and in his discussion of Corneille's *Rodogune* we also find occasional echoes of Maffei's youthful *Osservazioni* on that play. Outside Maffei, the only Italian critic whose influence is to be found in the *Paragone*, is Muratori. Both Gravina's and Martelli's treatises on tragedy he no doubt knew; but I cannot see that he was materially indebted to either of them in writing his own book.

Of Calepio's French sources, much the most frequently used is Dacier's translation of the *Poétique d'Aristote*; here he found justification for his criticism of Corneille's interpretation of Aristotle; and, once at least, he went beyond Dacier, namely, in his attack on Corneille's explanation of the use of the disjunctive conjunction in the definition of tragedy: 'fear *or* pity.' With La Motte's heresies he does not seem to have become familiar until after he had written his own work; he discusses them only in an appendix to the *Paragone*. In the main, Calepio agrees with the new theories; he appreciates what La Motte has to say on the vexed subject of the unities, and also, needless to say, his objection to the excessive use of love motives in tragedy. Only in one point is he distinctly opposed to La Motte: he maintains, as a disciple of Maffei, the inadmissibility of prose as a medium of tragedy.

Maffei, as we have seen, reviewed the *Paragone* in his *Osservazioni letterarie*. He is, on the whole, a warm admirer, but one has the feeling that he might have been warmer—for he agrees with everything—had Calepio not, in his studious efforts to be 'fair' to his opponents, deprecated certain aspects of Maffei's *Merope*. This evidently caused resentment on Maffei's part, and his notice is largely a defence of his own tragedy[1]. The *Paragone* was, however, the theme of a voluminous attack by a young poet, Giuseppe Salio, whose tragedy *Temisto* had been slightingly spoken of by Calepio. Salio's volume is considerably larger than the *Paragone* itself—he did not know who was the author of the book he criticised—and bears the title: *Esame critico intorno a varie sentenze d' alcuni rinomati Scrittori di cose poetiche, ed in particolare dell' Autore del Paragone della Poesia tragica d' Italia con quella di Francia*, Padua, 1738. Much of the treatise is irrelevant to the *Paragone*, and what is in the form of direct criticism is based on the conviction that Greek tragedy is unapproachably excellent, and modern tragedy not to be compared with it; on the absolute justification of both chorus and unities; and on the canonical value of Aristotle's *Poetics*. He is prepared to accept no compromise, a standpoint which leaves little room for any real discussion.

[1] There is (Donati, *l.c.* p. 306) among the Bodmer papers in Zürich a çopy by Calepio himself of a long letter which he wrote to Maffei defending his standpoint.

Nevertheless, Calepio replied, although his reply did not appear in print until both Salio and Calepio himself were several years dead. His *Confutazione di molti sentimenti disposti da Giuseppe Salio nel libro intitolato Esame critico*, etc., appeared in the edition of the *Paragone* which was published in 1770 (pp. 223 ff.). Calepio's standpoint in this criticism is not essentially different, as far as I can see, from that of the *Paragone* itself; but Galletti is perhaps right in finding less equivocation in Calepio's defence of the moderns against the ancients. He quotes Calepio's words: 'Se tutti avessero tenuto il Capo chino a questo giogo (*i.e.* the imitation and rules of the ancients) l' Arte Tragica sarebbe ancora nella sua infanzia.'[1]

In conclusion, there is little or no originality in the *Paragone*; and it contains a very considerable admixture of the pedantry of the seventeenth-century schools—classification of 'decorums' of 'characters,' the weighing and balancing of moral and artistic ends—which makes much of it tedious now. But, this apart, the treatise is carefully planned and concise; Calepio has good judgment. He has the ability and courage to discriminate merits in plays, the serious defects of which were grave enough to justify their condemnation by any tribunal of 'good taste.' It matters little that there should be elements in fifteenth-century Italians which are superior to what we find in Corneille in the seventeenth, if their plays are forgotten; but Calepio's recognition of such elements is in itself a proof of his critical independence. Moreover, the little book acquires distinction by its steady insistence on certain great principles, such as respect for the excellence of Greek tragedy, and impatience with the 'accommodating' Aristotelian criticism of the French. Calepio has no hesitation in proclaiming the unnaturalness of French tragedy, and he has a firm faith in the possibilities—and here his hopes, like Maffei's and Martelli's, are directed to Italy—of a purely modern tragedy, which shall be free from slavish imitation of the Greeks.

[1] *Paragone*, ed. of 1770, p. 227; cp. Galletti, *op. cit.* p. 233.

Chapter VIII

Giambattista Vico

Rigault devotes the concluding chapter of his work on the 'Querelle des Anciens et des Modernes' to Vico; the greatest of the Italian thinkers is thus presented to us by him as a kind of culmination of the 'modern' movement. This fact, taken with Croce's claim[1] for Vico as the founder of the modern science of aesthetics, behoves us to examine very carefully his share in the evolution of critical theory.

In spite of an admirable little book on Vico by Flint, written nearly forty years ago[2], our interest in Vico in this country has never been great; and, apart from Michelet's labours in popularising him in France, nearly a century ago[3], it cannot be said that he has been much studied there; while in Germany, which had more reason than any other land to know Vico's work and thought, he has been still more neglected[4].

I

Giovanni Battista, or Giambattista Vico was born at Naples, on June 23, 1668[5]. His father, Antonio Vico, who represented the 'Frohnatur' in his parentage, was a bookseller in a small way; his mother, Candida Masullo, was the opposite in temperament and inclined to melancholia. Unfortunately, Vico inherited more from his mother than from his father, although

[1] B. Croce, *Estetica*, 2nd ed., Milan, 1904, pp. 223 ff., and his *Filosofia di G. B. Vico*, Bari, 1911. For the bibliography of Vico see Croce's *Bibliografia Vichiana*, Bari, 1911; and its continuation in *La Critica*, vols. xv ff.

[2] R. Flint, *Vico* (*Philosophical Classics for English Readers*), Edinburgh, 1884; 1901. Cp. C. E. Vaughan, *G. B. Vico, an Eighteenth Century Pioneer* (*Bulletin of the John Rylands Library*), Manchester, 1921.

[3] J. Michelet, *Principes de la Philosophie de l'histoire*, Paris, 1827; reprinted in *Oeuvres choisies de Vico*, Paris, 1835, 2 vols.

[4] The best German work on Vico is still that by the Viennese philosopher, Karl Werner, *G. B. Vico als Philosoph und gelehrter Forscher dargestellt*, Vienna, 1879.

[5] See Vico's own Autobiography: *Vita di G. B. Vico scritta da se medesimo* (I quote from the edition in the *Scrittori d' Italia*, Bari, 1914). Cp. also the works by Croce and Flint.

he himself ascribed his moody temperament to an accident. At the age of seven he fell downstairs, and received such a serious cerebral percussion that he was unconscious for five hours, and the doctor declared that he would either die of the injury or become weak-minded. Neither prediction came true, although his convalescence extended over three years. As a boy, he showed phenomenal talents, easily outstripping all his schoolfellows. Nothing but his mother's anxious consideration for his health could restrain him; he was, as he says himself, 'spiritosissimo e impaziente di riposo.' He plunged into logic and philosophy, guided by a Jesuit teacher, Antonio del Balzo, who introduced him to the writings of Petrus Hispanus and Paolo Sarpi. At length, however, caught in the perplexing web of scholasticism, he grew discouraged, and for a time gave the whole matter up. The revival of the 'Accademia degli Infuriati,' which caused some stir, had a stimulating effect, and brought him back to his studies. He returned to philosophy again, and, partly at the hand of a new Jesuit teacher, Giuseppe Ricci, a disciple of Duns Scotus, but a Zenonist at heart, and partly on his own account, he once more attempted to unravel the enigmas of scholastic metaphysics. Ricci brought to his attention Francisco Suarez' *Metaphisica*, and he spent a year in studying it.

A single visit which he paid to the university, led to metaphysics being ousted by a new study: jurisprudence. Here again all he asked from his teachers was the first impetus; this received, he instinctively followed his own bent. He was preeminently, as Caloprese called him, an αὐτοδιδάσκαλος. From the first, he seems to have viewed law from a wider point of view than other scholars; seen it as but one weft in a varied and intricate texture, of history, language, literature, ethnology—in short, of humanity. In a marvellously brief time he had mastered the principles of civil and ecclesiastical law, and although only sixteen years of age, and without any kind of certificated qualification, he was permitted to defend a case which had been brought against his father. He won the case, and the encomium of both the judge and his opponent. But this was his one and only attempt at legal practice. The procedure of the courts was repugnant to him, and his delicate health—he was threatened with consumption—would not have stood the wear and tear of such a profession.

A chance conversation with the bishop of Ischia, Geronimo Rocca, who was struck by young Vico's ideas on the study of jurisprudence, resulted in his being invited to act as tutor to the bishop's nephews, sons of Domenico Rocca, Marchese di Vatolla, who was a lover of poetry and a kindly patron of literature. From 1685 to 1694, nine happy years, Vico lived in the retirement of Vatolla, situated amidst beautiful surroundings near Cilento, in the province of Salerno. Combined as this healthy life was with plenty of leisure and access to an excellent library nothing could have been more favourable for Vico's physical health and spiritual growth. He threw himself with his accustomed ardour into the study of literature, reading alternately the Latin and Italian classics; and he arrived at conclusions to which the Bouhours controversy and the activity of the Arcadians had been gradually leading Italy, namely, that, judged by the standards of antiquity, she had seriously fallen from her high estate. From poetry he passed back to his first mistress, philosophy. He found that Horace in his *Ars poetica* laid weight on the moral basis of literature, and from Horace he turned for confirmation of this idea to the Greek moralists. In these years, too, the idea of evolution seems to have taken hold of him; he sought to explain languages, literatures, religion, institutions, by tracing their growth from their sources and earliest forms. He endeavoured to find the bedrock of Roman law in the ethical systems of the Greeks and of Cicero; and behind all these quests, to arrive at clear ideas on the development of the human race.

He had been attracted by Plato rather than by Aristotle; but both thinkers he saw as yet only darkly through the glass of scholasticism. Plato was to him Plato in the neo-platonic interpretation of Marsilio Ficino; Aristotle he only knew from the distortions of Averroes and Suarez. Of particular importance was his first introduction to Descartes, although, unfortunately, through the very misleading medium of the *Fundamenta physicae* of Heinricus Regius, which Descartes himself had repudiated. The only gap in his prodigious universality of knowledge was natural science and especially mathematics, for which Vico seems to have had no talent or interest; the 'pons asinorum' of Euclid he declined to cross.

In 1694 Vico returned to Naples, where he spent the remaining fifty years of his life. He himself describes in his *Autobiography* the conditions he found in Naples: the degeneracy of literary taste, which, no doubt, appeared to him the more appalling after his long communion with the masters of literature in the library at Vatolla; the encroachment of Cartesianism and empiric science on philosophy, and the consequent neglect of the historical sciences. Vico makes no secret in his *Autobiography* of his antipathy to Descartes and to the Cartesian method, which discouraged the study of poets, historians and orators: 'Descartes prefers to them,' he says, 'his metaphysics, his physics, and his mathematics, and thus reduces literature to the knowledge of the Arabs' (p. 25). But the French philosopher had an eloquent pleader in Gravina's master, Caloprese, who, he himself tells us, loved Descartes much; and at this time Vico was 'bound by an intimate and noble friendship' to another thinker, whose sympathies were, at first at least, with Descartes, Paolo Matteo Doria[1]. No doubt, one reason for Vico's antipathy was that he, with his strong religious bias, saw in Descartes a serious danger to the authority of the catholic faith, a fear which Doria shared. The Church had itself taken the initiative in the matter by placing the writings of Descartes on the Index in 1663[2]. Possibly, too, in his earlier period, Vico, confusing the materialism of Gassendi with Cartesianism, found here another reason for repudiating Descartes. And yet, in spite of his antagonism, Vico's system does not really clash with that of Descartes; his idea of historical evolution may have nothing in

[1] *Vita*, p. 25: 'Questo gran cavalliere e filosofo fu il primo con cui il Vico potè cominciare a ragionare di metafisica; e ciò che il Doria ammirava di sublime, grande e nuovo in Renato, il Vico avvertiva che era vecchio e volgare tra' platonici.' Cp. F. Bouillier, *Histoire de la Philosophie cartésienne*, 3rd ed., Paris, 1868, p. 370; G. B. Gerini, *Gli Scrittori pedagogici italiani del sec. XVIII*, Turin, 1901, pp. 41 ff. Also F. Tocco, *Descartes jugé par Vico*, in the *Revue de métaphysique et de morale*, IV, 4 (1896), pp. 568 ff., and above, p. 8.

[2] Twenty-six years after the publication of the *Discours de la Méthode*, thirteen after Descartes' death! (Bouillier, *op. cit.* I, pp. 466 f.).

common with Descartes' metaphysical idealism, which wholly ignored the historical factor, yet the one system might be reasonably regarded as supplementary to the other. The *Méditations*, no less than the *Scienza Nuova*, is a defence of the spiritual and the unseen against the levelling matter-of-factness of the new physical sciences. And even if Vico himself never grasped or admitted this kinship, his immediate successors recognised it, when they found themselves confronted by a mightier than Gassendi, by John Locke. It is the common foe, materialism, which links up Cartesianism and Vichianism, and brings Vico into relationship, as an aesthetic theorist, with Gravina and Muratori.

But to return to Vico in Naples. He felt himself a stranger in his own land; and a stranger he remained[1]. All his life long, indeed, he suffered from the uncongenial surroundings and adverse circumstances in which he was placed. His only means of subsistence, his pen, was hampered by the apathy of the public; and he had often, for his daily bread, to descend to the degrading business of writing orations and poems to order. He had some hopes of obtaining an official position as town-clerk; but these were disappointed. Subsequently, however, in 1697, he was made professor of rhetoric in the university on a very small salary, 100 scudi (about £20). Notwithstanding this pittance, he married at the end of 1699 a dowerless Neapolitan, Teresa Caterina Destito, who could not even write her name. She brought him a family of four sons, one of whom died in infancy. His activity as a university teacher is represented in his works by the various inaugural lectures which he held between 1699 and 1708. These, and especially the last, *De nostri temporis studiorum ratione*[2], foreshadow the doctrines which reached maturity in the *Scienza Nuova*. The influence of Bacon is apparent in these addresses; and it is to be seen in Vico's first independent philosophical work, with the Baconian title, *De antiquissima Italorum sapientia* (1710)[3]. This fragmentary work—only the first of three books was completed—

[1] Cp. *Vita*, p. 22: 'Per queste ragioni il Vico non solo viveva da straniero nella sua patria, ma anche sconosciuto.'

[2] *Opere*, ed. G. Ferrari, Milan, 1835, II, pp. 1 ff.

[3] *Ibid.*, II, pp. 47 ff.

is more than a foreshadowing of the *Scienza Nuova*; it is a kind of first rough draft of it. Here we find the plan, based on the *Cratylus* of Plato, of establishing the etymology of Latin words pregnant with philosophical meaning; here is the adumbration of Vico's quest for the origins of Italian philosophical doctrines in an ancient Etrurian sect which came from Egypt—a theory combated in a respectful polemic in the pages of the *Giornale dei Letterati*[1]. Of deeper philosophic significance is Vico's insistence that language is a product of the fantasy, and that truth, so far from being an absolute entity, is created by the mind. In this last doctrine might we not find a link both with the relativity of Descartes and the idealism of the great German philosophers of the end of the eighteenth century?

Vico's next book was a life of an eminent Neapolitan, Antonio Caraffa (*De rebus gestis A. Caraphaei*), who had acquired in the service of the Austrians notoriety for unscrupulous cruelty. Vico's task was undertaken to order and for a remuneration of a thousand ducats (about £150); and although it bears on it the stamp of a prescribed panegyric, it contains much of interest. It was the means of bringing together Vico and Gravina in an intimacy which lasted through the remaining two years of the latter's life. Still more momentous was it for Vico's future, for the preparation of the book led him to make the acquaintance of Hugo Grotius's *De jure belli et pacis*. This was to Vico's mind like the crystal that brings solidification to the super-saturated solution; Grotius's dream of universal, harmonious law founded on the study of the past, suddenly brought order into his ideas, and provided him with the key to the maze of his own thought. In his first zeal he proposed to publish a new edition of Grotius's work with a commentary of his own; but he shrank from the accusation of heresy which, he felt sure, this undertaking would bring upon him. The stimulus of Grotius's thought is to be seen in Vico's inaugural university discourse of 1719, in his *De universi juris uno principio et fine uno* (1720) and *De constantia jurisprudentis* (1721)[2], works which, as Flint says (p. 34), 'could of themselves have entitled him to be ranked among the greatest of the philosophical jurists of

[1] *Opere*, II, pp. 108 ff.

[2] *Ibid.* III, pp. 1 ff., 157 ff.

Italy.' Again, we might regard these writings as early drafts of the *magnum opus*. The first lays down the principles of Vico's philosophy of law, with special reference to Roman jurisprudence; the latter part of the second, which is entitled *De constantia philologiae*, adapts this philosophy to the universal problems of human knowledge. The foundations of 'philology,' which for Vico is the science of humanity, are sought in language, in mythical beliefs, in primitive poetry; and on these foundations he shows what his masterwork was to achieve, how a new science, wide as the history of civilisation itself, could be reared.

Notwithstanding the acknowledged merit of these treatises, Vico was overlooked when the chair of jurisprudence, with its salary of 600 ducats, became vacant in the university. In spite of this disappointment, he was not discouraged; he laboured on at the great work of his life, which ultimately appeared in a first edition at Naples in 1725 under the title: *Principj di una Scienza nuova intorno alla natura delle nazioni*.

On November 25, 1725, Vico wrote to his friend B. M Giacchi:

> Since I completed my great work, I feel that I have become a new man. I am no longer tempted to declaim against the bad taste of the age, because in denying me the place I sought, it has given me time to compose my 'scienza nuova.' Shall I say it? I perhaps deceive myself, although I am most unwilling to do so; the composition of the work has animated me with a heroic spirit, which places me above the fear of death and the calumnies of my rivals. I feel that I am seated upon a rock of adamant, when I think of that law of God, according to which the esteem of the wise renders justice to genius[1].

With the *Scienza nuova* Vico's life culminated. No sooner was the first edition out, than he set about remodelling it, and a second, very much altered, appeared in 1730; a third was published shortly before his death in 1744. All the rest of his life was, in fact, devoted to this work; and the little he wrote outside of it in his later years has comparatively small interest. From the point of view of the present studies, an oration *De mente heroica* and a brief estimate of Dante are most worthy of notice[2].

[1] Flint, *op. cit.* p. 35; *Opere*, VI, p. 33.
[2] *Opere*, VI, pp. 46 ff., 124 ff.

As far as outward recognition is concerned, Vico's life was infinitely pathetic and tragic; he lived in obscurity; his fame was entirely posthumous[1]. Nor had he any compensation in his domestic life, which was full of sorrows and afflictions. One of his daughters was an imbecile, and a son became a vagabond and a criminal; but another daughter made a small name for herself as a poet, and another son, Gennaro, succeeded his father in the chair of rhetoric at the university[2]. When, with the accession of the Bourbons—Carlo II appointed him his historiographer at a salary of 100 ducats a year—fortune began to smile upon him a little, it was too late; his life was rapidly declining. He ultimately fell a victim to cancer of the throat and mouth, and died after a long and painful illness, on January 23, 1744. Ill fortune followed him literally to the grave; for at his funeral there was an unseemly quarrel as to whether the monks of St Sofia or the professors of the university should carry the bier, and for a time it was left standing on the public street.

II

Vico is a thinker who, like Spinoza, exerts a growing fascination on those who give themselves unreservedly up to him. At first, the foreign reader of Vico is repelled; it needs some courage to study him. His uncompromising 'italianità' stands in the way; as Flint says, he was as typically Italian as Bishop Butler was English[3]. Moreover, his language and style present peculiar obstacles. This great Italian had so immersed himself in Latin that his handling of his own native tongue suffered; his Italian has neither the style of Gravina nor the lucidity of Maffei. Or perhaps we might more justly put it another way, and say his thought lay mostly too deep for the facile Italian style which had been moulded, for good as well as for evil, by a century of 'secentismo.' The *Scienza Nuova* is—it must frankly be confessed—a very difficult book to comprehend; Monti well described it as 'like the mountain of Golconda, covered with

[1] Cp. R. Cotugno, *La sorte di G. B. Vico, e le polemiche scientifiche e letterarie dalla fine del XVII alla metà del XVIII secolo*, Bari, 1914, pp. 195 ff.
[2] See G. Gentile, *Studi Vichiani*, Messina, 1915, pp. 147 ff.
[3] Cp. Flint, *op. cit.* p. 4; also G. Gentile, *op. cit.* p. 92.

rocks and full of diamonds.'[1] It is a work which renders up its secret unwillingly; and yet the further one penetrates into its 'arcana coelestia'—and the task has been rendered inviting by not a few brilliant Italian scholars of our time, who, under the leadership of Benedetto Croce, have devoted themselves to its elucidation—the more engrossing becomes the study.

The *Scienza Nuova* is one of the strangest, as it is one of the deepest works of the eighteenth century. It repels us often as a mere farrago of mediaeval philological quibbling and mouldy scholasticism; at another moment, it fascinates us with its wonderful intuitions on the evolution of things human and divine, on the ways of God the man, which, even without awaiting proof, our mind jubilantly hails as necessarily true. It is a key to the history of humanity, a vast compendium of the psychology of nations. It is a book that puts the sorest strain upon our patience; and yet, if we but persist, we are magnificently rewarded. No work of its century contains more that is now effete, but certainly none contains more far-reaching truths. Not even the great German mystics of earlier centuries penetrated with such self-confidence into the holy of holies of the invisible as Vico; none saw the fate of humanity unrolling itself, in accordance with law based on a sublime necessity, from so lofty a height as he. I have already mentioned Spinoza; again, Spinoza and Vico might be named together as the two thinkers of modern Europe who have best right to the title 'Mehrer des Reiches,' enlargers of the kingdom of the spirit. For the work of both has been, not a putting in a new light of things known, and thoughts already thought, but the conquest of new spiritual territories from the darkness of the Unknown.

The *Scienza Nuova* may be read in three forms, a first edition of 1725, which is, no doubt, the easiest and pleasantest to read. In his later editions Vico has become a contemner of literary graces, and flings his knowledge at us in axioms and enigmatical disquisitions which impair the attractiveness of his work. For our purpose, however, it is advisable to take the book in its

[1] Cp. V. Monti, *Della necessità della eloquenza* (*Opere*, 3rd ed., Naples, 1851), p. 231.

final form[1], if only because the first edition is still lacking in that exposition of the poetic wisdom of Homer, which is an essential factor for these studies. I cannot here offer an adequate analysis of this wonderful work, a task, as Flint recognised, which is peculiarly difficult owing to the prodigality—often in the most apparently irrelevant connections—with which Vico throws out his ideas; I only deal with it in so far as it has bearing on the theory of literature.

There are five books in the *Scienza Nuova* in its final form. The first deals with the Principles of the New Science. Vico's aim is to unravel the origins of universal history; he goes back behind Grotius and Pufendorf, and establishes a sequence of prehistoric human evolution. He postulates three great ages, a divine age, a human age, and finally an age which has entered into the full consciousness of law. The proof of the existence of these three ages is largely a matter of philological criticism, Vico using the word 'philology' in a very wide sense to embrace the whole spiritual record of a people. In the earliest age the imagination is supreme; reason is weak; man, out of fear, invents his gods, whom he devoutly worships as the masters of his individual fate. Human aspiration finds its expression in religion; primitive speech—in its beginnings merely an imitation of natural sounds—is poetry, not prose; and writing is hieroglyphic. The first thinkers are poets or poet-theologians. This age gives place to an age of heroes; then comes a period of social distinctions; and with it the clash of antagonistic interests in war. Writing, too, begins to develop from the hieroglyphic stage. Finally, in the third period the supremacy of the imagination yields to that of the intelligence; conceptions of duty and political responsibility spring into being. Pictures no longer suffice to express thought; for the new ideas are essentially abstractions. After these general considerations Vico goes on to an exposition of law, custom and government; but this does not concern us.

The second book bears the title 'Della sapienza poetica,' 'Of poetic wisdom.' The earliest ages had no definite scientific

[1] *La Scienza nuova giusta l' edizione del* 1744, a cura di F. Nicolini (in *Classici della Filosofia moderna*, XIV), Bari, 1911.

CALL No.
809.91
R543
DATE
DO NOT WRITE IN THIS SPACE
AUTHOR
TITLE
Studies in the genesis of romantic theory in the eighteent century
NAME
COLLEGE P. O. BOX NUMBER

beginnings of
on of the world
purpose of this
nd first formed
logic and ethics;
; their interpreta-
to them by nature,
is an investigation
ians, who were the
nan race—a wisdom
based on reason and
gination. The divine
ment of this wisdom;
ng the knowledge, the
e future. This second
er of a universal history

uestion: who was Homer?
ng of human evolution to
m. He combats the tradi-
tially a philosopher. The
tically believed, an instruc-
interpretation of the infancy
de to the practical conduct of
maturity. Homer is thus not
bol of the Greek people giving
utterance to ... ry. This third book is a combination of the metho... lite scholarship—discussions of the age of Homer, based on the evidence of the text of the *Iliad* and *Odyssey*—with the metaphysical hypotheses enunciated in the earlier book.

In Book IV Vico takes up the thread he had dropped. He proceeds to unravel the history of nations, the evolution of forms of government, of manners, of language and law. In his last book he sets forth a grandiose conception of the cyclical evolution of the human race, the turning of the circle which brings back again in the history of all peoples—transformed, it may be, beyond recognition—the divine age and the heroic age. Here he reaches a hand to Campanella in the past, and may not we add also, to the future, to the latest of the great European thinkers, the philosopher of the 'ewige Wiederkehr,' Friedrich Nietzsche?

The chief magnificence of this wonderful cosmogony for our present investigation lies in the rôle it ascribes to the imagination, or fantasia. Vico recognises the imagination not merely as a function or factor in man's spiritual life; but also, in a much larger sense, as the embodiment of an epoch. Man in his first stage lives in his imagination, not in his intellect; to use the German phrase of a much later date, which may possibly through obscure channels have been influenced by Vico's intuition, primitive man is 'naive,' not 'sentimental.' Moreover, the imagination is, in Vico's thought, an active, creative force; it is not merely the provider of the materials, the 'sumptuous images,' with which, as in the Muratorian system, genius works; it is genius itself. Vico's definition of the function of the imagination as a collective force in the early stages of human evolution, might well have formed the groundwork for a whole system of aesthetic thinking. Unfortunately, however, he went no further; he provided the initial stimulus, laid the foundations, and left it for others to build upon them. It fell to a very different type of thinker, Baumgarten, not to Vico, to give the eighteenth century its first system of aesthetics.

Thus it is difficult to fit Vico into the line of aesthetic thought which I have been trying to trace in these pages, namely, the establishment of a conception of poetry based on the supremacy, not of the reason, but of the imagination. 'Of his contemporaries,' says Croce, 'Vico probably knew the writings of Muratori, whom he cites by name, and of Gravina, with whom he stood in personal intercourse; but certainly, if he read the pages of the *Perfetta Poesia italiana* and of the *Forza della Fantasia*, he must have been very dissatisfied with the treatment there of the imagination, to which he himself ascribed such great importance.'[1] I cannot help thinking that there is an injustice here. No doubt Vico realised—as neither Muratori with his conception of the 'fantasia' as a kind of handmaiden of the intellect, nor Gravina with his retrograde confusion of Homer and the dispensation of

[1] *Estetica*, pp. 236 f.

wisdom—the peculiar province of poetry. That the imagination represents a phase, and is a great positive factor in the evolution of man; and that the 'wisdom' of Homer is not the wisdom of the moralist, of the lawyer, or of the statesman, but 'poetic wisdom,' are, one might say, truths for all time; and Vico's discovery of them will always rank with the greatest deductions of philosophy. But these ideas may be seen gradually emerging in Vico's earlier writings, such as *De nostri temporis studiorum ratione* and *De antiquissima Italorum sapientia*, from a basis, after all, not very far removed from the aesthetics of Gravina[1]. And had Vico come to grips with the function of the imagination in concrete aesthetic production, he would, I believe, have been forced into a position not very much at variance with that of Gravina and Muratori; in other words, he would have recognised the necessary cooperation of the fantasy with the intellect, a cooperation obviously excluded in his primitive age. As it is, his application of the conception of a dominating, creative imagination to later epochs has not got beyond controversial *aperçus*; at no time does he seriously face the problems of poetic inspiration and production in his own time. The ultimate conclusion of Vico's thinking, as it finds expression in the maturity of the later *Scienza Nuova*, is one beside which the aesthetic philosophy of Vico's Italian contemporaries may be but the dogma of a definite age—and a dogma based, moreover, on faulty conceptions of the mechanism of the mind; but even dogmas discarded by later generations have their significance in the history of ideas. No one would compare a moment the prolix erudition of Muratori with the soaring philosophic genius of Vico; but what Vico claimed for the imagination and Muratori's detailed discussion of its peculiar function in poetry are not surely mutually incompatible things. Vico deals with the abstract and the metaphysical, Muratori with quite concrete questions, leading up to the creation of a 'perfect Italian poetry.' Is there not ample room for both?

[1] Cp. R. Cotugno, *op. cit.* pp. 158 f.

of modern Homeric criticism. It is, however, doubtful whether Vico was aware of D'Aubignac's work[1].

In the same way, it seems unfair to Gravina, to deny that his epoch-making—for it was epoch-making—discovery of Dante had not some influence on the younger thinker; the very fact that the latter compares Dante's conception of 'commedia' with Aristophanes' seems to point to this. Lastly, although I am unwilling to press the question of indebtedness too far, may we not see something of a foreshadowing of Vico's own theory of the origin of poetry in the eighth chapter of Gravina's *Ragion poetica*, on the 'Origine dell' idolatria,' or in the Preface to Gravina's second book, which sets forth how 'in its origin poetry is the science of things human and divine, converted into fantastic and harmonious imagery'?[2]

p. 281). Cp. G. Finsler, *Homer in der Neuzeit von Dante bis Goethe*, Leipzig, 1912, pp. 208 ff., and V. Bérard *Un Mensonge de la Science allemande*, Paris, 1917, where Wolf's lack of originality is rather unnecessarily and acidly emphasised.

[1] Cp. Finsler, *op. cit.* p. 110.

[2] Ed. Emiliani-Giudici, pp. 17 ff., 87 f.

Chapter IX

The Indebtedness of France to Italy

The task of appraising the European value of the aesthetic movement in Italy at the end of the seventeenth and beginning of the eighteenth centuries is surrounded with peculiar difficulty. Nowhere is this more so than in the case of France; for, throughout the greater part of the 'Querelle des anciens et des modernes'—that veritable Thirty Years' War of literary controversy—France and Italy were so intricately bound up with each other where questions of literary theory were concerned, and ideas were so bandied backwards and forwards, that the honour of initiation and the share of each country in the development of an idea are often impossible to determine with exactitude. The Italian writers were intimately familiar with the French critical literature from Le Bossu, Boileau, Perrault, to Du Bos; while the French had a wider knowledge of what was being written in Italy from Tassoni[1] onwards, than they are generally credited with. Bouhours himself, who stirred up so much trouble by his attack on Italian taste, cannot be accused of having done so from lack of knowledge of what he was writing about. The interlacing of opinion is particularly noticeable in the criticism of Homer and of the relative values of Homer and Virgil, matters which formed such important pivots in the controversy; it is a particularly delicate task to discriminate here between the giver and the receiver. We are, moreover, at a disadvantage in not yet possessing an adequate account of the critical theories of the 'Querelle'; for, useful as Rigault's admirable work on the controversy[2] still is—and few

[1] E. Schiffer, *Tassoni in Frankreich*, Berlin, 1915, endeavours, however, to disprove that writer's share in the moulding of the French 'modern' doctrine. Not, I think, convincingly; but the fact that such a view may be defended shows the difficulties that confront the investigator.

[2] H. Rigault, *Histoire de la Querelle des anciens et des modernes*, Paris, 1859. It has been unfortunately long out of print. Cp. also H. Gillot, *La Querelle des anciens et des modernes en France*, Paris, 1914, which, however, is more concerned with the earlier stages of the quarrel.

academic monographs have enjoyed such long vitality—it is just his presentation of the critical theory which stands most in need of revision.

The problems, however, become simpler towards the end of the 'Querelle,' which alone falls within the scope of these studies. This, as will be seen, was in great measure due to a certain unwillingness on the part of the French—no doubt, a heritage from the Bouhours controversy—to lend an ear to the Italians. They failed to realise what the other great literatures of Europe were meanwhile realising, that the new aesthetics which emanated from Italy provided a powerful weapon to bring the tedious quarrel to a close, and to initiate an epoch of literary development, more modern than the most ardent of the old 'moderns' had dreamt of. Before, however, considering these questions, it will be useful to ascertain exactly to what extent the writers discussed in the preceding pages were known in France.

I

The French had considerable opportunity of familiarising themselves with the doctrines of Gravina. As early as 1706 his treatise on the *Ancient Fables*, the essential part of the *Ragion poetica*, was translated by G. Regnauld. Although this translation does not seem to have attracted much notice at the time, Gravina's name was becoming rapidly familiar in the learned journals through reviews of his works on jurisprudence[1]; and when the *Ragion poetica* appeared, it had a better chance of being appreciated abroad. In point of fact, both the Leipzig *Acta Eruditorum* and the *Journal des Savants* noticed it in the year of its appearance[2]; but they merely give arid descriptions of it. These notices were compensated for by a very full and attractively written *résumé* of Gravina's book which appeared in the *Journal littéraire* of the Hague in 1718[3]. The reviewer

[1] See especially the detailed reviews in the *Journal des Savants*, November, 1701, pp. 375 ff.; 1707, Suppl., pp. 456 ff.

[2] *Acta Eruditorum*, October, 1708, pp. 504 ff.; *Journal des Savants*, November, 1708, Suppl., pp. 432 ff.

[3] *Journal littéraire*, 1717, IX, 2 (published in 1718), pp. 243–84. In the *Mercure de France* of December, 1714 (p. 2177), there had been a brief note on Gravina's tragedies.

emphasises particularly the importance of Gravina's estimates of Homer and Dante, while he corrects his lack of appreciation of Tasso by referring him to—the Abbé Terrasson! He concludes:

La réputation de M. *Gravina*, à laquelle ce Livre répond très bien, a été encore un puissant motif qui nous a porté à entrer dans ce grand détail. On peut dire qu'il n'est gueres possible de trouver un Ouvrage plus rempli d'esprit et d'éloquence que celui-ci; on peut dire même qu'il y en a de beaucoup trop. Une même proposition s'y trouve souvent exprimée par cinq ou six pensées, plus belles les unes que les autres, qui paroissent s'étouffer mutuellement (p. 282).

He thinks that, writing in Italian, Gravina has adopted 'la pompe et les fleurs' characteristic of that tongue, while, in the medium of Latin, 'il parle avec la dignité des anciens Orateurs.' He also reproaches Gravina for his metaphysical obscurity. The article, appearing in so cosmopolitan a review as the *Journal littéraire*, must have done much—I may recall what the same journal achieved in spreading the fame of Shakespeare on the continent—to make Gravina as a writer on literary aesthetics known to the world outside Italy. The article was, moreover, translated not long afterwards into German[1].

For a second time Gravina was brought prominently before the French reading world by Requier's translation of the *Ragion* in 1755[2]. This translation was very liberally noticed in the French press, led by a review—which is ascribed to the translator himself—in the *Journal étranger*[3]. After paying an enthusiastic tribute to Gravina's work on the origins of civil law as a 'production immortelle, où brillent à la fois le génie, l'érudition, le goût, l'ordre et la clarté,' the reviewer speaks with even greater warmth of the *Ragion*; one might have believed, he says,

qu'il ne s'est appliqué toute sa vie qu'à l'étude de la Poësie. Ses préceptes sont si sages, si vrais, si lumineux, qu'ils peuvent être

[1] See below, pp. 251 f.

[2] *Raison ou Idée de la Poésie*, trad. par J. B. Requier, 2 vols., Paris, 1755. According to the *Journal des Savants*, March, 1740, pp. 168 f., the Comtesse Caylus had also made a translation of the *Ragion*.

[3] *Journal étranger*, August, 1755, pp. 213 ff. Also, *Année littéraire*, 1755, v, pp. 26 ff.; *Mémoires de Trévoux*, July, 1755, pp. 1882 ff.; August, 1756, pp. 1025 ff.

regardés comme autant de regles sûres, pour quiconque est né avec du génie, sans le secours d'une heureuse éducation (p. 214).

From this time on Gravina is frequently quoted as an authority on aesthetic questions in French books and articles; but it was obviously too late—thirty years after the appearance of Du Bos' *Réflexions critiques*—for his theories to be regarded otherwise than as of merely historical interest. On the whole, Gravina's reputation as a critic outside his own land stands highest as a discoverer of Dante.

It was hardly to be expected that the French, who had regarded it as their peculiar mission to reprove the Italians for their lapses from good taste, should have been very ready to listen to Muratori's elaborate exposition of 'il buon gusto'; Bouhours' polite conversations were more to their taste than Muratori's wordy tomes. At the same time it may seem a little surprising that Muratori's chief aesthetic treatise, *Della Perfetta Poesia italiana*, should never have been translated into French, or, indeed, into any other tongue. Yet there was perhaps no great temptation to translate it, at least in its entirety. It deals ostensibly with problems of Italian poetry; and even the general aesthetic principles it discusses are inconveniently dependent on Italian illustrations. Possibly the German and Spanish way of rewriting Muratori's treatise, and providing new illustrations drawn from the literatures of the adapters, was more effective than any literal version could have been. A more serious obstacle to translation lay, however, at Muratori's own door, namely, the tedious verbosity and lack of proportion, which made the *Perfetta Poesia italiana* so unattractive, when, with something of Gravina's conciseness and style, it might easily have been the most influential work on literary aesthetics of the early eighteenth century.

At the same time, the fact remains that the *Perfetta Poesia* did not receive the attention it deserved from the learned press of Europe. One searches the pages of the *Journal des Savants* in vain for a notice, although about the time the *Perfetta Poesia* appeared, that review had plenty to say about Orsi's reply to Bouhours. It also drew attention to the *Riflessioni sopra il buon gusto*, without, however, being aware that Muratori was its author[1]. The *Mémoires de Trévoux*, which had taken a still greater interest in the Orsi-Bouhours controversy, could only spare five pages for the most perfunctory of notices[2]. This conspiracy of silence is difficult to account for. Muratori's name was familiar enough to the learned world; for no writer of his time had a fuller share of the reviews in the learned press. One might have thought that anything he published would have been sure of consideration, although possibly the very importance of his historical and antiquarian works, which were reviewed at great length, put his contributions to aesthetics into the shade. But the real reason may have lain deeper. Muratori was possibly suspected by the French of having gone too far; even the most advanced of the 'moderns' may have regarded his claims for the imagination as dangerous licence, and viewed his book, not as a corrective of the bad taste of Marinism, but as Marinism itself in a new and insidious guise. In testing the French pulse of the early decades of the eighteenth century in these matters, it has to be remembered that the translator of the *Spectator* omitted Addison's criticism of *Paradise Lost* as something too extravagant to be laid before French readers. It is thus hardly a paradox to say that France did not have Muratori's aesthetic doctrines presented fairly to her until the appearance of the eulogistic and detailed analysis of the Spanish *Poética* of Luzán in the *Année littéraire* of the forties[3]. Thus the same fate befell Muratori's fortunes in France as had befallen Gravina's; he was too late in becoming known.

Antonio Conti, again, might have been a very real force in French aesthetics, had his reluctance to bring his ideas to paper not stood in his way. None of the Italians I deal with had so many friends in France as Conti; and no Italian book received a warmer welcome than the first volume of his *Prose e Poesie*. Between December 1739 and March 1740 the *Journal des Savants* devoted three long articles to this work, which were

[1] *Journal des Savants*, January, 1710, pp. 17 ff. It was not until 1739 (p. 376) that the *Journal* discovered Muratori's authorship of the book. A synopsis, without criticism, of Muratori's *Della Forza della Fantasia* appeared in 1746, pp. 252 ff.

[2] *Mémoires de Trévoux*, October, 1707, pp. 1824 ff.

[3] See below, p. 231.

clearly intended to whet the appetite of the French public for the six volumes of Conti's works, which were so rashly promised in the preface to the first one[1]. These volumes were not forthcoming, and the enthusiasm of the reviewer of 1740 was forgotten when the second, posthumous volume of *Prose e Poesie* appeared in 1756. In any case, the fragmentary and unsatisfactory form in which Conti's ideas on literary theory are here gathered together by his editor, was hardly likely to impress French opinion.

The most famous of all the writers of this circle in the eyes of Europe was, no doubt, Maffei: he was a celebrity, to meet whom, as Lord Chesterfield told his son, it was alone worth going to Verona[2]. There was no lack of discussion of his works in the literary journals, the *Journal des Savants* reviewing practically all of them. Voltaire's imitation of Maffei's *Merope* and the, for Voltaire, discreditable controversy that arose over it, made Maffei easily the best known dramatic writer of Italy to the French. On the other hand, his ideas for the reform of the theatre, which, as will be seen, meant—partly directly, and partly through the mediation of Riccoboni—so much for Germany, could teach nothing to France, from which they had, in fact, in the first instance come. At most, the French showed some interest in the plays of his *Teatro italiano*[3].

I cannot find that Martelli's dialogue, *L' Impostore*, was, on its first appearance in 1714, discussed at all in the French reviews; but it is almost incredible that this work, published in Paris and dedicated to the French Dauphin, could have escaped attention; moreover, Conti, who sponsored it, would surely have done his best to make it known. In the notes from Italy of the *Mémoires de Trévoux* of June 1718 there is a mention of the second edition (p. 1141):

> Monsieur Martello, que peu de nos Poëtes tragiques égalent, feint, dans ce petit ouvrage, qu'Aristote lui apparoit et s'entretient avec lui des régles de la tragédie, et de la maniére dont les Italiens les

[1] *Journal des Savants*, 1739, pp. 723 ff.; 1740, pp. 75 ff., 164 ff.

[2] *Letters*, ed. by J. Bradshaw, London, 1892, p. 228.

[3] The *Teatro italiano* was reviewed in the *Journal des Savants* of January, 1729, pp. 74 ff., and again in January, 1747, pp. 19 ff.; it was also noticed by the *Mémoires de Trévoux*, August, 1736, pp. 733 ff.

observent. L'ouvrage est d'un maître de l'art, qui sans s'asservir aux opinions, a formé son goût sur la nature, et l'a reglé par la raison[1].

But Martelli's more advanced ideas on the drama gained entrance into France through his fellow-countryman Riccoboni. Inadequate as Riccoboni's *Histoire du Théâtre italien*—written to refute D'Aubignac's contemptuous reference to the Italian theatre—may be, it was the means of familiarising France and the rest of Europe with Italy's dramatic literature; and, appended to the first volume, which appeared in 1728, is a *Dissertation sur la Tragédie moderne*, which shows plainly the influence of Martelli's *Impostore*. The importance of this *Dissertation* for French dramatic theory I discuss below. Meanwhile, it has to be noted that Riccoboni's work was widely read and extensively reviewed in the French journals[2].

Calepio's son said that his father's *Paragone* attracted much attention in France; but I can find no evidence of this. In Germany, as will be seen, it certainly had some influence; but the opinions and controversies of the treatise were either too familiar to the critical world, or too out-of-date by 1732, to awaken much interest in France.

While Gravina, Muratori and Maffei were fairly familiar names in the European journals of the eighteenth century, one looks almost in vain for that of Vico. None of the great thinkers of the world had, either at home or abroad, so long and hard a struggle for recognition as he[3]. Leclerc in his *Bibliothèque ancienne et moderne* drew attention to him; and the *Mémoires de Trévoux* reviewed the *Scienza Nuova* in 1727[4]; but there is little more[5]. The *Journal des Savants* ignored this, the greatest

[1] There is also an announcement of the edition in the *Mercure de France* of November, 1723, p. 956. Cp. further, June, 1724, II, pp. 1387 f. For Voltaire's knowledge of Martelli see below, p. 216.

[2] *Mercure de France*, September, 1728, pp. 2027 ff.; *Journal des Savants*, December, 1728, pp. 659 ff.; *Mémoires de Trévoux*, December, 1728, pp. 2237 ff.

[3] See especially the work by R. Cotugno, already cited. Also 'La Fortuna del Vico' in Croce's *Filosofia di G. B. Vico*, pp. 283 ff.

[4] Cp. B. Croce, *Bibliografia Vichiana*, pp. 43 f.

[5] Croce apparently overlooks a lengthy review of *De nostri temporis studiorum ratione* in the *Journal des Savants* for 1710, pp. 589 ff. Vico is also mentioned in a note in the *Mémoires de Trévoux*, November, 1714, p. 2029.

Italian work of its age, entirely. And yet, notwithstanding such neglect, Vico's ideas seem to have penetrated, by ways it is difficult to trace, into European thought. As far as France is concerned, Montesquieu's *Esprit des Lois* is generally recognised as the first work which shows the influence of Vico; he was introduced to Vico's writings by Antonio Conti, and probably purchased the first edition of the *Scienza Nuova* when in Naples in 1729[1]. He also expresses his indebtedness to Gravina; in fact, his 'esprit des lois' is practically a 'ragione' in Gravina's sense. But it is difficult to believe that Montesquieu was the only Frenchman of the earlier eighteenth century who was influenced by Vico; frequently one comes upon ideas in the writings of this time which seem an echo, if only faint, of the solitary thinker of Naples. I think particularly of the Abbé Massieu's *Défense de la Poésie*, prefaced to his *Histoire de la Poésie françoise* of 1739. Obviously, however, it was just those parts of the *Scienza Nuova* which deal with aesthetic doctrine, that were slowest to find their way abroad[2]. Not until 1827 was Vico really introduced to France, namely, by Michelet, who published in that year his abridged translation of the *Scienza Nuova*[3].

II

In view of the small interest which France took in the Italian aesthetic theorists, it is hardly surprising that their ideas had but small influence on French opinion. By the time the effects of the Bouhours attack reverberated in France, the larger issues of critical theory had been disposed of; and the protagonists of the 'Querelle' were mainly engaged in bickering over the Homeric question. It will be remembered with what keen interest Conti followed the French quarrels over Homer; and Italian opinion, especially Gravina's striking plea for the supreme greatness of that poet, had, no doubt, some weight; but this was, after all, only a side issue of the new aesthetic theory.

The main reason, however, why the aesthetic doctrines of the

[1] F. Lomonaco, *Vite degli eccellenti italiani*, III, 1803, p. 127; but cp. *Bibliografia Vichiana*, pp. 44 f., and supplement to that work, 1907, p. 9.

[2] B. Croce, *Estetica*, p. 244.

[3] See above, p. 179.

Italians left so little impress on the French mind is to be sought in their anti-Cartesian tendencies; for in France most of the systematic writing on aesthetics in the early eighteenth century was definitely pervaded by Cartesianism. The first French work of this character was the *Traité du Beau* (Amsterdam, 1715) by the half-German, half-French writer, J. F. de Crousaz, professor of philosophy and mathematics at the university of Lausanne, and subsequently at Groningen in Holland. Crousaz goes out from Cartesian premises: he follows strictly the cautious Cartesian method: 'Je ne passerai point à une seconde pensée, sans avoir bien établi la précédente.' Proceeding by the method of psychological analysis, he aims at a metaphysical definition of the 'beautiful'; it is 'unity in variety,' 'the relation of all the parts of an object to the whole.' Cartesian, too—and Leibnitzian as well—is the *Essai sur le Beau* by the Père André, which appeared in 1741, although it had been written some ten years earlier[1].

Such attempts to form an abstract conception of beauty had an important bearing on the evolution of the modern science of aesthetics; and it has already been seen how Crousaz appealed to a mind like Conti's; but they owed, and could have owed nothing to the essentially empiric aesthetics of Gravina and Muratori. However furthering the Cartesian method might be in establishing an abstract theory of the beautiful, it led to no practical and fruitful doctrine; the Baumgarten-Meier school of aesthetics in Halle was definitely anti-Cartesian in its origins. Before France had freed herself from the influence of Descartes in aesthetic matters, it was too late for her to derive benefit from the Italians with whom we are concerned. Still, it is to be noted that the next generation of writers on literary theory, notably Marmontel[2], were still able to read Gravina, and possibly also Muratori, with profit.

Fortunately, however, the Cartesian theorists did not have it all their own way; and by far the most important contribution which France made to the aesthetic thought of Europe in this period, came from the pen of a secular abbé, who approached

[1] Cp. É. Krantz, *Essai sur l'Esthétique de Descartes*, Paris, 1898, pp. 311 ff.
[2] Cp. Marmontel's *Poétique françoise*, Paris, 1763, I, pp. 6 ff., 83.

his subject through other than metaphysical avenues, and more in the spirit of the Italians: the Abbé Du Bos.

Jean Baptiste du Bos[1] was a native of Beauvais, where he was born on December 21, 1670, being thus about a year and a half older than Addison. Of an old and wealthy middle-class family, he inherited an anti-aristocratic bias; but otherwise, he was a remarkably level-headed type of French common sense in a century which admired, above all things, the 'reasonable' man. It was one of his conspicuous merits that he pled earnestly for the rights of genius against the tyranny of the reason; at the same time, he was not easily swayed by enthusiasms; and on this account, no doubt, his words carried the greater weight. He enjoyed an excellent classical education, partly in his native town, and from 1686 on, in Paris. He made up his mind at an early age to enter that profession—or surrogate for a profession—which had so much attraction for the man of literary tastes in France and Italy in the eighteenth century, that of abbé. Not, however, being of noble birth, there were difficulties in the way of his speedily attaining his end; he was obliged to go through a complete course of study at the Sorbonne. He became *maître-ès-arts* in 1688, and then entered the theological faculty, from which he received the *baccalauréat* in 1692. This spectacle of Du Bos, who had not—as we know him at least—the convictions of an ecclesiastic, devoting himself to theological studies in order to gain purely worldly ends, does not make a pleasant impression; but his exoneration is that it was the general custom of his time and country.

Free from the Sorbonne, he turned his attention to the study of antiquities, and in 1695 published his first book, *Histoire des quatre Gordiens*, a quibbling and paradoxical attempt to prove the existence of a fourth Gordian emperor. A more considerable historical work, *Histoire de la Ligue faite à Cambray*, appeared in 1709; and later in life, in 1734, he published an *Histoire critique de l'établissement de la Monarchie françoise dans les Gaules*. But in his early days his heart was in the literary

[1] The admirable study of Du Bos by A. Lombard, *L'Abbé du Bos, un initiateur de la pensée moderne*, Paris, 1913, has rendered the older monographs on Du Bos superfluous.

world, and he was fortunate in being introduced to the salon of Ménage, then a very old man. This led to his becoming one of the contributors to the *Ménagiana*, which, without much reason, gave him some reputation. He also made the acquaintance of Bayle. In the summer of 1698 he paid his first visit to London, and spent the autumn of that year in Holland. In the following year he was again for several months in the Low Countries; and in the latter part of 1700 he set out for Italy, travelling by way of Turin and Florence, to Rome, and returning in the following year by Venice and Milan. In all these journeys it seems not unlikely that he was entrusted with diplomatic missions, although his main object was to gain a knowledge of foreign lands and peoples. It is interesting to remember that he and Addison were in Italy at the same time.

Like most of his compatriots, Du Bos found much to admire in England, which he revisited in 1702; he praised our freedom, our political life and our intellectual achievements. And while he shared the French opinion that the literary products of our classicism were more to our credit—he translated some scenes and possibly the whole of Addison's *Cato* (1716)—he was less superiorly disparaging of our 'national' literature than other French visitors like Voltaire. His chief intellectual debt was to Locke, whose acquaintance, as well as that of other English celebrities, he had made. It is hardly likely, however, that he met Addison. In 1722 Du Bos was elected perpetual secretary of the Academy, and he died in his native town on March 23, 1742. Du Bos was a typical abbé of the eighteenth century, and essentially a *bel esprit*. He had a tenacious memory, was interested in very mundane things—was, like Martelli, a warm admirer of the opera—and spiced his opinions with a delicate sardonic irony.

The only work of Du Bos' which interests us here is his *Réflexions critiques sur la Poésie et sur la Peinture*, which appeared in two volumes at the beginning of 1719, although in its first form it may have been written as early as 1710. A third volume on the theatrical representations of the ancients was added in 1733. The importance of Du Bos' quite unsystematic treatise lies, it may be said at once, in his development of the aesthetics of sensibility, and his antagonism to the domination of reason in art: in so far, he was at one with the forward movement in Italy. He had begun as a Cartesian and a 'modern' disciple of Perrault; but his development led him to take a more catholic view of literature as the expression of humanity; and in the course of the years he found himself more in sympathy with the defenders of the ancients. But his own defence was obviously of a new kind; he succeeded in reconciling his admiration for the classics with his theory of emotionalism as the real basis for artistic expression. In fact, Du Bos, actually a fighter on the side of the 'ancients,' might be said to have brought the weary quarrel to a close, not by assisting one party to victory over the other, but by discovering a new principle which wiped out the old antagonism. He introduced a germinative idea into aesthetic thinking, undreamt-of by the old quarrellers, which provided a fresh starting-point. The influence of Bayle and the sensualistic philosophy in his youth had been fundamental; and they paved the way for the strong appeal which Locke made to him. That Leibnitz, whose writings he certainly knew, could have influenced his aesthetics, is not easy to see; for Du Bos was not a philosopher, nor did he believe in philosophic systems; his attitude to aesthetic problems was never anything but descriptive and empiric. In so far, his aesthetics is distinctly one-sided; he does not deal with the production of art, but merely with the impression which the work of art makes, the emotion it calls forth, and the pleasure it causes, the influence it has upon mind and conduct. This restriction to the subjective aspect of art—and it may be noted that in defining the 'purpose' of art, he inclines to the 'dulce' rather than the 'utile'—afforded him little opportunity of taking advantage of the Italian theories, with some of which he was certainly familiar. His work was rather supplementary to theirs, and it was welcomed as such by the later Italians, like Calepio. Du Bos laid weight, with Fontenelle, upon the importance of climate for poetry, a doctrine that had been elaborated in Italy; and his justification of the use of the 'merveilleux' in poetry had already been urged by Gravina[1], although, like Gravina himself,

[1] *Réflexions*, I, chap. xxviii; *Ragion poetica*, I, chap. vii. Cp. above, p. 112.

he may have been drawing on the older French statement of the problem. In Du Bos, too, we find an echo of the very significant claim of the Italians for the creative imagination: but again, we must remember that he was familiar with the *Spectator*[1], where the doctrine reappears.

In his interpretation of Aristotle, Du Bos did, however, go back directly to Italian opinion; and Gravina—he refers to both his tragedies and his book on tragedy[2]—is repeatedly quoted as an authority. He refutes Gravina's view that the declamation of Greek tragedy was musical, a view which had been espoused in France by the Abbé Vatry[3]; but the definition which he gives of the purging of the passions was, as Lombard has pointed out[4], Gravina's and Castelvetro's before him, namely, that it ameliorates the intolerableness of our emotions by teaching us to accustom ourselves to them, just as we are enabled to resist a poison by taking it in small doses. Du Bos does not mention the *Ragion poetica*; but I cannot help thinking that his conception of aesthetic pleasure—more especially the kind of pleasure which a tragedy causes in us—has been influenced by the very significant eleventh chapter of Gravina's treatise. It is less easy to prove that Du Bos had studied the *Perfetta Poesia italiana* of Muratori; he nowhere mentions it, but his latest critic suggests that his views on the nature of literary sentiment have a Muratorian flavour, and that his condemnation of *Bérénice* was suggested by Muratori's criticism of that play[5].

III

There is ample evidence of the influence of the older Italian interpreters of Aristotle on French dramatic theory; and Dacier, whose translation of and commentary on the *Poetics* were authoritative for this time and long afterwards, had studied carefully all the sixteenth-century commentators. Of these he

[1] There are quotations from the *Spectator* in the *Réflexions*, I, chap. xxxiii, xxxiv, xlii and xlvi.

[2] *Réflexions*, I, chap. xliii, xlvi; II, chap. xxxii; III, chap. v. A review of the work in the *Année littéraire*, December, 1755, p. 204, draws attention to Du Bos' indebtedness to Gravina.

[3] *Ibid.* III, chap. v; Gravina, *Della Tragedia*, chap. xxxiii. See above, p. 51, and Lombard, *op. cit.* p. 284.

[4] Lombard, p. 207; see above p. 46.

[5] *Ibid.* p. 279.

gave the palm to Vettori; he, the 'ancient' in the quarrel, could not naturally approve of the heresies of Castelvetro. In spite of this, however, there is no doubt that by his anti-Cornelian polemic in his edition Dacier did much to break the rigidity of pseudo-classicism, and thus encourage the cultivation of a more modern type of tragedy.

The most revolutionary contribution to dramatic theory of this time is, however, the famous 'paradoxes' of Houdar de la Motte[1]. It has always been something of an enigma that this writer, whose own dramatic work shows no craving for greater freedom, no rattling at the cage bars of convention, should, in the prefaces which he provided for his plays in 1730, have come forward as the champion of the most remarkable literary heresies. Born in 1672, and educated by the Jesuits, he belonged in every respect to the older generation; he was essentially a writer of the seventeenth, not the eighteenth century; and, except for his paradoxes, he remained faithful to it in theory and practice. In 1692, at the age of twenty, La Motte made his *début* at the Théâtre italien with *Les Originaux, ou l'Italien*, the failure of which he took very much to heart; then we find him writing operas in emulation of Quinault, and in 1707 he published a volume of *Odes*. In 1710 he was admitted to the Academy, that conservative and 'ancient' body having been, doubtless, misled by the modest tone of the writings which they accepted as his passport; but La Motte was to prove a disappointment. In the following years he came forward, under Perrault's inspiration, as an aggressive 'modern'; although, being a skilful diplomat, he succeeded in retaining the goodwill of both Boileau and Fénelon. It was, however, in the atmosphere of the cafés that his genius and audacity flourished; a brilliant talker and controversialist, he was for years a leader of those literary reunions, which played a part, which, both earlier and later, had been played by the salons. The particular café over which La Motte presided was the Café Gradot[2].

From operas and odes La Motte turned his attention to

[1] The substance of these pages has already appeared in my short article, *Sources italiennes des paradoxes dramatiques de La Motte*, in the *Revue de littérature comparée*, III, 3, pp. 369 ff.

[2] Cp. P. Dupont, *Houdar de la Motte*, Paris, 1898, pp. 9 ff.

Homer, and in 1714 published his notorious version of the *Iliad*, abbreviated to twelve cantos and in very un-Homeric verse; and in 1719 appeared his *Fables*. More important than his works were his apologies for them and the controversies in which they involved him. With the *Odes* of 1707 he published a lengthy *Discours sur la Poésie en général et sur l'Ode en particulier*; with his *Iliad*, a *Discours sur Homère*. La Motte's Homeric heresies and his outrage on the *Iliad* roused indignation in 'ancient' circles, and Madame Dacier, as their spokesman, attacked this interloper—who was not ashamed to admit that he was unable to read Greek—with a fulminating treatise under the grandiloquent title of *Discours des Causes de la Corruption du Goust*. La Motte replied with a suavely polite volume, *Réflexions sur la Critique* (1715).

The real value of all this critical writing is small. In the controversy with Madame Dacier, La Motte, no doubt, had the better part of the argument; but his opinion is fatally vitiated by his inability to realise wherein the poetic quality of Homer consists. It was of little avail to prove that the 'ancients' were wrong, if it could only be done by enumerating the defects and faults of Homer. La Motte failed to pronounce the liberating word, namely, that such arguments had nothing to do with the matter at all, and that the Homeric epics must be judged, not by the dogmas and standards of any particular school, but as imaginative poetry. La Motte was as incapable of doing this as any of his opponents; he was oblivious to the qualities that make epic poetry great[1]. From the first *Discours* one thought, however, stands out in relief, that the business of poetry is to please, and not to instruct[2]. It was an opinion which, under Castelvetrian influence, Corneille had already tentatively advanced. But there is nothing tentative about La Motte's assertion. Poetry must give pleasure, not to the learned only, but also to the people. Unfortunately, however, the kind of pleasure

[1] Lemoyne's *Saint Louis* and Desmarets' *Clovis* he pronounced, for instance, to be 'much better than the *Iliad*' (*Oeuvres*, Paris, 1754, III, p. 103) —modernism indeed!

[2] *Ibid.* I, pp. 16, 21: 'On voit que son unique fin est de plaire...l'utile qu'on ajoute ne sert qu'à rendre la proposition équivoque; à moins que, sous ce nom vague d'utile, on ne veuille aussi comprendre le plaisir, qui est en effet un des plus grands besoins de l'homme.'

which he seems to expect from poetry is not of a very high order; and he felt it a little derogatory to poetry that it should have so trivial an end as pleasure of any kind. To the poet himself the satisfaction that poetry brings is 'la gloire'; in other words, it ministers to his vanity[1]. Barren as all this theorising was, it had at least one helpful consequence; it freed French poetry from the irksome restraint of having to imitate the ancients; it cancelled the arbitrary rules that had been deduced from their practice. Not that La Motte disdained 'rules' altogether; he only demanded modern ones[2].

In 1721 La Motte turned his attention to tragedy. He had hitherto, he tells us[3], been discouraged by the enormous difficulties of this form of literature; but the popular success of Voltaire's *Oedipe* seems to have ultimately provided the stimulus. In 1721 appeared *Les Machabées*; in 1722, *Romulus*; in 1723, *Inès de Castro*, and finally, in 1726, *Oedipe*. La Motte's older critics imply that his method was that recommended by Le Bossu for the composition of an epic; first select an abstract problem, and then search the pages of history for a subject suitable to illustrate it[4]. This seems to me less than just to La Motte. His choice of subject was mainly guided by what might be called legitimate literary factors. Emulation of Racine sent him to Biblical history, and possibly he had even a nearer model for his *Machabées*; Romulus had been a favourite opera-theme on the Italian stage, and not a little of the dross of the opera style still clings to La Motte's tragedy; while for the story of Inez de Castro it is difficult to believe that he went straight to the *Lusiadas*, but rather knew something of the earlier tragedy by the Portuguese poet, Antonio Ferreira. But the main point for us is that he shows little inclination to put into practice in these plays the innovations he advocates in his preliminary discourses. There is a mild introduction of spectacle in *Romulus*; his *Inès de Castro* turns round the motive of conjugal love, in spite of the classic prejudice against it; and in *Oedipe* he has sought very tentatively to apply his ideas on the 'unity of

[1] Cp. Dupont, *op. cit.* p. 233.
[2] *Oeuvres*, IV, pp. 43 f.
[3] *Ibid.* IV, pp. 23 ff.
[4] D'Alembert in his *Éloge*, quoted by Dupont, p. 59.

interest.' There is also some attempt to involve the confidants in the action, and to reduce monologues[1]. But otherwise, La Motte's plays depart in nowise from the classic norm.

It has not hitherto been noticed that La Motte's dramatic paradoxes owe something to Martelli's dialogue, *L' Impostore*, which, it will be remembered, was first published in Paris by Conti in 1714. But I am doubtful whether La Motte had an immediate knowledge of the dialogue; its ideas came to him rather through Riccoboni's *Dissertation sur la Tragédie moderne*, appended to the *Histoire du Théâtre italien*. The resemblance of La Motte's views to Martelli's has not escaped the latter's Italian critics[2]; and it has been explained on the assumption that Martelli imbibed La Motte's opinions during the months when he came personally into contact with him in Paris[3]. It is, however, out of the question that, as early as 1714, La Motte should have held such opinions, especially as there is so little trace of them in the tragedies which he only began to write seven years later.

In his first discourse La Motte discusses the introduction of love into French tragedies:

> Nous n'avons presque point de Tragédie qui marche par d'autres ressorts; et les étrangers ne nous épargnent pas là-dessus le reproche d'uniformité. J'avoüe que nous mettons quelquefois de l'amour dans les sujets qui y résistent le plus; et il y a aparence que nous ne nous corrigerons pas aisément de ce défaut[4].

His apology is that a tragedy must please, and as ladies are largely represented in the audience, a love story is preferred; and indeed, such stories also appeal to men. His discussion of love in tragedy had been immediately prompted by Riccoboni's *Dissertation*; for at the close of his second chapter Riccoboni censured La Motte himself for introducing love into a sacred tragedy:

> Peut-on croire que dans une Tragedie sacrée l'amour profane de *Polieucte* partage l'interêt de l'action! dans la Tragedie des *Machabées*, le jeune *Machabée* aime une Païenne... (pp. 269 f.).

[1] Cp. P. Dupont, *op. cit.* p. 275.

[2] Cp. A. Galletti, *Le Teorie drammatiche e la tragedia in Italia*, I, Cremona, 1901, pp. 91 ff.

[3] If *L' Impostore* (*Opere*, Bologna, 1735, I, pp. 75 f.) is to be trusted it was in the Café des Poètes that Martelli met La Motte in 1713.

[4] *Oeuvres*, IV, p. 31.

And in the following chapter he says:

> Cet amour Romanesque occupe ordinairement les trois quarts de l'action des Tragedies Françoises...ces Scenes de tendresses n'ont servi qu'à ralentir l'action de la Piéce, à la refroidir, et à rendre les Heros moins grands....On pense generalement en France qu'une Tragedie sans amour ne plairoit point aux Dames Françoises[1], qui font le sort des Théâtres à Paris (pp. 271 f.).

Martelli had also realised the weakening effect of excessive love-intrigue in tragedy, but apologetically sanctioned its introduction as an antidote to the 'aridity' of Greek tragedy[2].

With Martelli and Riccoboni La Motte objects to confidants; but, unwilling to dispense with them altogether, he proposes to avoid their disadvantages by making them participate in the action of the play. As an alternative, Martelli had frankly preferred monologues, even although these might lead the audience to doubt the sanity of the speaker[3]. La Motte in the preliminary discourse to his *Inès de Castro* says:

> Où trouveroit-on dans la nature des hommes raisonnables qui pensassent ainsi tout haut! qui prononçassent distinctement et avec ordre tout ce qui se passe dans leur coeur! si quelqu'un étoit surpris à tenir tout seul des discours si passionnés et si continus, ne seroit-il pas légitimement suspect de folie? (p. 280).

La Motte compromises by conceding only very short monologues; and he advises poets to avoid them as much as possible.

The most interesting of La Motte's paradoxes concerns the unities. The unity of place he regards as often leading to offences against 'vraisemblance,' and a direct hindrance to the appreciation of a drama; in the same way, he objects to actions of obviously long duration being cramped into an artificial unity of time; this only makes them ridiculous. Again, in spite of the fact that there had already been protests against these two unities—which his sixteenth-century Italian commentators had imposed upon Aristotle—by G. de Scudéry in his *Cid* criticism, and in the Ménage-D'Aubignac controversy on the *Heautontimorumenos*, there seems to me little doubt that

[1] This had been Rapin's argument. Cp. above, p. 128; see also Du Bos, *Réflexions*, I, chap. xviii, p. 139: 'Les Dames Françoises, ausquelles surtout il faut être complaisant, ne trouveroient ces Héros assez gracieux.'

[2] *Op. cit.* p. 66; cp. above, pp. 133 f.

[3] P. 66; cp. above, p. 133.

La Motte's attitude was influenced by Martelli's arguments through the mediation of Riccoboni. The latter states his views on the unity of place in the fourth and fifth chapters of his *Dissertation*, his conclusion being:

> Je ne crois pas que cette vrai-semblance soit mieux conservée dans la severe unité de lieu, à laquelle les Poëtes François se sont si scrupuleusement attachés. Les Spectateurs, à ce que je crois, seroient bien moins blessés en voïant les Acteurs passer d'un appartement à l'autre dans le même Palais, comme l'ont fait les Espagnols, et les Italiens du Siécle passé, que de voir une conspiration concertée dans la chambre, et sous les yeux du Tyran qu'on veut immoler (p. 284)[1].

To the three unities, however, La Motte would add a fourth, without which the three others are useless: the unity of interest. The new unity is discussed in the discourse printed with *Les Machabées*, and, in view of the lack of any very obvious application of it in the dramas themselves, La Motte no doubt arrived at it comparatively late. There is, at least, no mention of it when he discusses the unity of action in the *Réflexions sur la Critique* of 1715[2]. Voltaire was not far wrong in regarding the unity of interest as practically identical with the Aristotelian unity of action[3]; it is, in fact, only the subjective side, the spectator's point of view of that unity, or perhaps merely a new form of Corneille's 'unité de péril.' Here again, I see in La Motte's views little more than a repetition of Martelli's interpretation of the unity of action, as reproduced by Riccoboni. Martelli had said that this unity was necessary in a tragedy because the emotions which tragedy excites lose in interest, if spread over several objects[4]; and Riccoboni's opinion is (p. 299):

> Ce n'est pas la multiplicité des interêts qui rend une Piéce interessante; au contraire elle interesse davantage, quand un seul, et même évenement attire l'attention sans partage.

[1] This goes back to Martelli. See his *Impostore*, pp. 38 f.

[2] *Oeuvres*, III, pp. 37 ff.

[3] Preface to *Oedipe*, 1730.

[4] *Op. cit.* p. 30: 'Se la tragedia fu instituita per muover gli affetti al compatimento delle disgrazie avvenute a chi non tante ne meritava, e per infonder negli animi terrore di que' delitti, che anche commessi con qualche umana, se non divina ragione, si vedono severamente puniti, egli è uopo eccitar l' uno, e l' altro movimento circa ad un solo obbjetto; perchè, se più azioni si rappresentassero in scena, il senso, che tanto è minore, quanto è intento a più cose, divagherebbe o con poca, o senza alcuna movizione.'

When he finds French tragedies so inferior to Greek ones in the observance of the unity of action, it is clearly this unity of interest he has in mind.

La Motte, under the pressure of the demand for 'vraisemblance,' reproached, in agreement with Riccoboni, the French poets for sometimes embellishing a tragedy with 'maximes générales et raisonnées avec étendue.' 'Les Personnages tragiques,' he says, 'sont presque toûjours agités de passions violentes; eh, comment s'étudieroient-ils alors à arranger des réflexions générales, au lieu de sentir vivement ce qui les touche en particulier?'[1] And it is the need for vraisemblance again which leads to the famous paradox of tragedies in prose.

In his first *Discours sur la Poésie* La Motte had warned tragic poets against 'l'enflure...l'excès de l'expression'[2]; and in the *Réflexions sur la Critique* he accepts *Télémaque* as a wholly justified 'Poëme en prose.'[3] But the demand for a tragedy in prose does not appear before the preliminary discourse to his *Oedipe*. He did not himself attempt to write such a tragedy. This is a heresy which finds no support in either Martelli or Riccoboni; although Muratori had not been averse to the use of prose in the drama. Martelli would not hear of prose tragedies at all; and it was Riccoboni's ambition, before he came to Paris, to reestablish verse tragedy on the Italian stage. He deplored the degeneration of taste in Italy which had led both actors and public to prefer prose[4]. But the fact that prose tragedies were popular in Italy could hardly have been unknown to La Motte.

[1] Preliminary Discourse to *Inès de Castro*, p. 300. Cp. Riccoboni's seventh chapter, 'De la Sentence des Tragedies Françoises,' p. 308: 'Les Tragedies Françoises brillent surtout par cette partie, mais elle est aussi souvent l'écueil des Auteurs, qui, se livrant trop au feu de leur imagination, s'éloignent de cette vrai-semblance, qui est le plus solide fondement du beau. Est-il vrai-semblable, par exemple, qu'un Héros dans les transports de la plus violente passion debite les sentimens de la metaphysique la plus rafinée? cette prétendue beauté produit un effet absolument contraire à l'intention du Poëme Tragique.'

[2] *Oeuvres*, I, p. 26.

[3] *Ibid.* III, p. 107.

[4] Cp. his Preface to Giulio Agosti's *Artaserse*, Modena, 1714: 'Il verso, tanto nella Tragedia, come nella Comedia, era creduto mortale, e gli uditori qual' ora sentivan parlar di verso fremevano, e quantunque amantissimi del Teatro lo abbandonavano per quella recita, se mai a Comici fosse caduto in mente di rappresentarne qualch' una di simil sorte.' Even Maffei's *Merope* had been turned into prose for the Italian actors.

And indeed, at the very centre where Maffei's *Merope* was produced, in Modena, there had been played such tragedies—tragedies on classical themes, and otherwise in the traditional classic style—by a Modenese poet, Dr Alfonso Cavazzi. In June 1714, when reporting on the success of *Merope* the *Mémoires de Trévoux* had added (p. 1117):

> Le Marquis Maffei n'est pas le seul Poëte tragique de Modene, le Docteur Cavazzi nous a donné les années passées quatre pieces regulieres et dans le goût François, *Montezume*, *Nise et Euriale*, *Adelaïde Reine d'Italie*, *Pertinax*: elles sont écrites en prose. L'Auteur est persuadé avec beaucoup de Connoisseurs, que la contrainte de la rime et la mesure ôte beaucoup de vivacité aux tragedies, surtout dans les repliques et dans les mouvemens des passions[1].

And 'vivacité' was one of the benefits which La Motte, in his third Discourse, believed would accrue from the use of prose.

Riccoboni, as the leader of the Théâtre italien in Paris, was, unfortunately, a much more influential personage than the Riccoboni who had assisted Maffei to reform and purify Italian tragedy. There is an irony—which may explain the discouragement and embitterment of his later life—in the fact that the services which he rendered in his Italian days to the European

[1] Cavazzi's defence of his use of prose will be found in the 'Esame' of his *Pertinace*, Modena, 1712. 'Per due ragioni,' he says, 'ho io scelto uno stile sciolto per questa sorta di Componimento. L' una; perchè questo è più connaturale a chi parla: L' altra; perchè parmi si renda più intelligibile, e più grato a chi ascolta. Che più naturale sia la prosa, che il verso, a chi parla, egli è fuor di dubbio; o si consideri il metro, che compone il verso; o si attenda la frase, che il distingue dal dire sciolto. Per verità, chi è posseduto da un forte affetto, o d' odio, o d' ira, o d' amore, non conta le sillabe alle parole, e non misura le voci dal suono dell' orecchio, ma da i movimenti dell' animo. Molto poi meno parrà ciò verisimile, se si riguardi la frase propria del verso. In fatti: molte volte avviene, che per sostenere la maestà, e la vivezza del dire Poetico, gli Attori a noi compariscono appunto tanti Poeti, e non que' miseri, o quegli Amanti, ch' eglino sono: Onde non solo togliesi tutto il Verisimile al loro Carattere, ma di più tutta la forza a i loro affetti; mentre in essi più si ravvisa lo studio, che la passione. Altre poi accade (e forse ancor più sovente) che il Poeta, geloso di far parlare i suoi Personaggi con proprietà, e naturalezza, affatto poi si dimentichi di se, e nulla per se ritenga, che il metro; cui tolto, resta il suo dire ridotto a mera prosa, e talor' anche poco felice.' La Motte, too, comments on the want of vraisemblance when a hero of tragedy, under the influence of great passions, has to adapt his language to a definite number of syllables; he points out that the naturalness of characters is sacrificed by putting in their mouths poetic language. Cavazzi translated Racine's *Andromaque*, but in verse (1708). Cp. Tiraboschi, *Biblioteca Modenese*, II, Modena, 1782, pp. 13 f.

drama by discrediting the extempore comedy and expelling from serious tragedy the arlequino, were in some measure undone by the successful French Riccoboni, whose fame depended on the maintenance of those very abuses. In this respect, Germany, with Gottsched, learned a more vital lesson from him than France, although it must in fairness be added that France had not the same need of learning.

IV

Looking back on the higher French tragedy of the early eighteenth century, we may discern several features and developments which were foreshadowed by the Italians. To speak of actual influence may be beside the mark; but the relations of the French and Italian drama in this period still await adequate investigation. This is particularly true of the interesting chapter which is concerned with Voltaire's indebtedness to Italy. Twenty-five years ago Émile Bouvy dealt with the question in his *Voltaire et l'Italie*; but I cannot think in any final way. It is, indeed, a disheartening testimony to the influence of what might be called patriotic motives on literary research to find Bouvy as intent on minimising Voltaire's debt to Italy—notably in the controversy on the question of Voltaire's possible use of Malmignati's *Enrico* in his *Henriade*—as Italian critics are in maintaining the contrary view[1]. Voltaire's most interesting relations to Italy belong, however, to the later part of his life, to a period beyond the chronological limit I have set myself. But of his knowledge of the Italian writers whom I have been discussing, there can be no question[2]. That his *Mérope* was based on Maffei's tragedy, his *Orpheline de Chine* inspired by Metastasio's *L' Eroe chinese*—of which Martelli's *I Tamingi*

[1] E. Bouvy, *Voltaire et l'Italie*, Paris, 1898. Cp. the review of the book by Bertana in the *Giorn. storico della letteratura ital.*, XXXIII, 1899, pp. 403 ff.

[2] Orsi, Crescimbeni, Fontanini, Gravina and Muratori are mentioned by Voltaire in letters of 1745 and 1753 (*Oeuvres*, ed. Garnier, XXXVI, pp. 338 ff.; XXXVIII, pp. 124 f.); Gravina, Martelli and Maffei, in the *Gazette littéraire* of June 14, 1764 (XXV, pp. 191 f.); Maffei, in letters of 1733 and 1738 (XXXIII, p. 364; XXXIV, pp. 374 ff.), in the *Siècle de Louis XIV*, chap. XXXIV (XIV, p. 564), and, of course, in the prefatory matter to *Mérope* (1744, 1748) (IV, pp. 179 ff.); Conti, in a letter of November 14, 1735, and in 1738 (XXIII, p. 69; XXXIII, p. 551).

was an obvious precursor—and that he was deep in Goldoni's debt, are well known facts. But there is, if I am not mistaken, more to be said. The orientalism of *Zaire*, *Mahomet* and *Les Guèbres* had been already cultivated by Martelli; the employment of tragedy as a vehicle of political and religious controversy had been tentatively anticipated in *La Perselide*; and it might be even claimed that Martelli had already realised that fusion of classic tragedy and *tragédie bourgeoise* which Voltaire unsuccessfully attempted in his later dramatic work. There may be no direct evidence that Voltaire was familiar with the theatre of Martelli; but that Martelli was his predecessor in widening the scope of tragedy is undeniable.

The most interesting of Voltaire's friendships with Italians in the first period of his literary life is that with Antonio Conti. Voltaire met Conti for the first time in England; and they were subsequently together in Lorraine. The Italian poet, as we have seen, wrote a *Cesare*, suggested by Shakespeare's *Julius Caesar*; Voltaire a *Mort de César*—sketched at Wandsworth in 1726—of similar inspiration. Bouvy believes that Voltaire was too indifferently acquainted with the Italian language in early years to learn from Italian literature. He demonstrates that the French and the Italian *Caesar* have nothing in common; that Voltaire was not inspired by Conti's *Cesare*, or, 'le connaissant, il a fait tous ses efforts pour que le sien fût tout différent.' He enumerates the differences: Conti's five acts and Voltaire's three; the exclusion of women from the French play; Brutus the adopted son of Caesar in Conti, the natural son in Voltaire; Conti allows Antonius to describe the death of Caesar, while Voltaire shows it all to us, except the final horror. Bouvy does not even find points of similarity in the scenes which are common to both plays[1]. That, however, Voltaire knew Conti's *Cesare* there is no reason to doubt. When, in his *Lettres Anglaises*, he described Shakespeare as 'le Corneille des Anglais,' he was merely repeating Conti's characterisation of the poet in a prefatory letter to his play: 'Sasper il Cornelio dei Inglesi.'[2] I am,

[1] *Op. cit.* pp. 193 ff.

[2] Cp. above, p. 103, and Voltaire's *Lettres philosophiques*, ed. par G. Lanson, Paris, 1909, II, p. 90.

indeed, doubtful whether either *Brutus* or *La Mort de César* would have been written at all, had not Conti led the way. It was all very well for English writers, in their national pride, to make extravagant claims for Shakespeare; but when an Italian—and an Italian who had won Voltaire's friendship and esteem—made such a claim, it had to be seriously listened to.

The relationship between French and Italian comedy in the early eighteenth century was more intimate and subtle than was the case with the tragedy of the two peoples. Actual contact had been established by the Théâtre italien in Paris, and although this concerned, in the first instance, only the cruder aspects of comedy, its influence was considerable on both the form and contents of the plays in vogue in France at the time. But possibly some of the finer modifications of French comedy may be traced to Italy. The origins, for instance, of the delicate psychology of Marivaux have never been satisfactorily explained; and the question might be raised whether the example of Italy—and in Martelli, as we have seen, there was a similar groping after a more subtle psychological technique—might not have contributed to the evolution of Marivaux' delicate art. The more palpable influence of Goldoni in France belongs to a later period than that with which I am concerned.

Apart, however, from the practical domain of the theatre, the influence of the Italian aesthetic ideas in France met with difficulties and hindrances—Cartesian, or merely prejudicial—from the first; and by the time these difficulties were surmounted, it was too late; the Italian theories had ceased to be more than matters of intelligent curiosity. The same forces which were responsible for the comparatively small headway which Addison's ideas made in France, stood in the way of an appreciation of the work of Gravina and Muratori. Thus the real victory in the great French 'Quarrel of the Ancients and the Moderns' was —ironical to relate—not won by France, not won in France at all, but in Italy, England, and even Spain.

Chapter X

Italian Influence in Spain: Ignacio de Luzán

The state of letters in Spain at the end of the seventeenth and beginning of the eighteenth centuries was not unsimilar to that in Italy. Spain, like Italy, had had a great past; she, too, had fallen a victim to that excess of intellectualism over emotion, which was responsible for the extravagances of 'culteranismo'; Marini had his immediate counterpart in Góngora. The Père Bouhours had coupled Spain with Italy, when he deplored the decadence of good taste. The new Italian movement was inspired by resentment at this criticism; it was a revolt of injured national pride. The good taste which Italy attempted to put in the place of the bad taste of Marini, had not been invented in France. On the other hand, the Bourbon accession in Spain encouraged—if it did not actually bring about—servitude to French ideas, thus discouraging a defence of the nation's literary past, at least at this stage. The Spain of Filipe V accepted meekly Bouhours' chastisement as well merited, and looked to French help in banning the evil spirit. Men like Luzán and Feyjóo were not really hostile to the best interests of their nation, or unconditional belittlers of the great literary achievement of the past; they had essentially right and healthy ideas, Feyjóo being, in many ways, a much freer and more liberal spirit than Luzán, a free-lance, whose ideas were in advance of his time[1]. But what one misses in Spain is a healthy militancy: there was no consciousness here of a battle for a worthy cause; no feeling, such as inspired Muratori and Maffei, that the national past was a precious inheritance which had to be defended.

Were it not for the accident of his birth, and the fact that his book is in Spanish, Luzán might have been included amongst

[1] Cp. Menéndez y Pelayo, *op. cit.* v, pp. 11 ff., 156 ff.; also, M. Morayta, *El padre Feyjóo y sus obras*, Valencia, [1916].

the Italians discussed in these pages. As a theorist of poetry, he was, in fact, much more of an Italian than a Spaniard. He repeats with discriminating judgment, but little originality, the views enunciated by his Italian masters. His *Poética*—as an interpretation of the new doctrine, of the first importance for the Spanish literature of his century—is of peculiar interest to us, in so far as it holds up a mirror to the ideas with which the reader is familiar from the foregoing pages. Luzán puts, as it were, these ideas in a new perspective; and, seeing them at a distance and reflected in a foreign temperament, we are better able to judge of their proportions. He thus helps us to sum up the ultimate significance for the eighteenth century of the aesthetic theory of the Italians.

I

Ignacio de Luzán, Claramunt de Suelves y Gurrea[1] was born at Zaragoza on March 28, 1702, his father being Don Antonio de Luzán y Guaso, Señor de Castillazuelo, and at the time governor of the kingdom of Aragón. He should have received an education suitable for a child of such distinguished birth; but the death of his mother and the unsettled political condition of Aragón brought his schooling to an untimely end. His father was obliged to leave the country and settle in Barcelona, where he, too, died. This was in 1706; and the boy was left an orphan at the age of four. When he was thirteen, he was taken in charge by an uncle, Don José de Luzán, who was a church dignitary in Mallorca, and subsequently in Italy. The defects of Luzán's early education were more than made good in the next five or six years at Jesuit colleges in Genoa and Milan. Don José de Luzán was appointed Inquisitor in Sicily, and his nephew accompanied him, first to Naples, and then to Palermo. Having no aptitude either for a military or an ecclesiastical career, he

[1] The chief source of information about Luzán's life is the all too eulogistic *Memorias de la Vida de D. Ignacio de Luzán*, which his son, Don Juan Antonio Ignacio de Luzán, Canon of the Holy Church of Segovia, prefaced to the second edition of the *Poética*, published in 1789. It is reprinted by L. A. de Cueto (Marqués de Valmar) in vol. LXI of the Rivanedeyra *Biblioteca*, and in his *Historia crítica de la Poesía castellana en el siglo XVIII*, II, Madrid, 1893, pp. 335 ff.

took up the study of jurisprudence, and graduated from the University of Catania in 1727. But his study was by no means restricted to law. He acquired a complete knowledge of French, studied Greek thoroughly—he translated and commented on Homer—and Italian was to him a second mother-tongue; he knew many of the greater Italian poets by heart. He even learnt German sufficiently well to speak and write it fluently. Besides languages, he was versed in science, history, music, and especially philosophy; at the age of twenty he wrote a critical compendium of Descartes' philosophy, and, in Italian, a *Rendimento de grazie a nostro Signor Gesù-Christo*.

In 1729 Luzán's uncle died; and he resolved to return to Naples where his brother—it was the time of Spanish domination in Southern Italy—was governor of the castle of Sant Elmo. He continued his studies in Naples and associated with the learned men there—he has even been claimed as a pupil of Vico's—but his state of health warned him that he must moderate his zeal. In 1733 he returned to Spain in order to look after the family estates in Aragón; but he also cherished hopes of a brilliant career. Owing, no doubt, to his studious and retiring habits, the latter were slow in being realised. He did not stay long in Zaragoza, finding the greater seclusion of Monzón more to his taste; later, he lived for a time in Huesca, where he married. Meanwhile the *Poética* appeared in 1737, and at the age of thirty-nine Luzán was elected an honorary member of the Royal Spanish Academy. In 1747, the material reward for which he had so long waited came to him; he was appointed Secretary to the Spanish Embassy in Paris. He seems to have spent more than a year here, carrying on the work of the Embassy with success. In 1750 he was recalled to Spain and entrusted with several important offices, amongst them, that of Treasurer of the Royal Library. About the same time he co-operated with Montiano and others in the founding of the 'Academia de el buen gusto,' in which he took the sobriquet of 'el Peregrino.' He had the prospect of attaining a high position in the service of the state, when he died on May 19, 1754.

Despite Luzán's great learning and industry, he has left little published work behind him. His son mentions an imposing list of writings, which, as set forth by Latassa[1], amount to the total of no less than sixty-one items. Very little of all this ever got into print; a few poems, published in periodicals, the most ambitious of which is *El Juicio de Paris*[2], only prove that Luzán was no poet; and in later years, after his residence in Paris, he published *Memorias literarias de Paris* (1751), a survey of the intellectual life of the French capital as he had seen it, written 'con mucha erudición y buena crítica.' Thus, as far as posterity is concerned, Luzán is only remembered as the author of the first comprehensive Spanish treatise on Poetics.

II

La Poética, ó Reglas de la Poesía en general, y de sus principales especies was published at Zaragoza in a handsome quarto volume of 503 pages in 1737. A second edition in two volumes appeared at Madrid in 1789, long after Luzán's death. The origin of the treatise goes far back into Luzán's Italian period. In the year 1728 he presented to the Academy of Palermo the results of his studies in literary aesthetics in a work comprising six discourses and entitled *Ragionamenti sopra la Poesia*. This, we are informed, was the basis of the Spanish *Poética*. A little later, he laid before the same Academy an ingenious study, *Sogno del buon gusto*, in which he gave 'a fair and judicious criticism of various poets and writers'; possibly this, too, he utilised later. He had been led to these studies by the preparation of a work on Rhetoric, which involved the study of Aristotle and Horace; and we hear also of a criticism of Fontenelle's little treatise on the Eclogue.

The *Poética* is in four books: I. De el Origen, Progressos, y Essencia de la Poesía; II. De la Utilidad, y de el Deleite de la Poesía; III. De la Tragedia, y Comedia, y otras Poesías dramáticas; and IV. Del Poema Epico. Luzán begins by discussing the antiquity of poetry, and the importance of Aristotle and Horace for the criticism of poetry; all that is essential has already

[1] *Biblioteca antigua y nueva de escritores aragoneses*, Zaragoza, 1885, II, pp. 194 ff.

[2] See the Rivadeneyra *Biblioteca de Autores españoles*, LXI (1869), pp. 111 ff.

been said by these two writers. Luzán's object (chapter I) is to provide Spain with a

complete, exact, and perfect treatise on Poetics, from which the public may finally recognise, by the light of manifest reasons, the error and confusion of many things which, for more than a century, they have admired as divine poetry, and which, in the judgment of dispassionate people who know, are very far from being so.

His hope is to 'rejuvenate Spanish poetry and to raise it to such a degree of perfection that it may not have to envy other nations, nor to fear their criticisms, which true merit will convert into applause.'[1] He admits that his intention to establish criticism on a classical basis will bring him into conflict with those who love the old poetry of Spain. Here is the first point of divergence from his Italian masters; for they came forward, not as contemners of the older Italian poetry, but as its defenders against the strictures of the French.

Chapters II to IV are devoted to the origins of poetry, and the differences between Latin and Greek, and between ancient and modern literatures. Luzán discusses these questions with abundance of learning, and generally presents them as they had been presented by the Italians, the discussion of Homer and Virgil—which the *Mémoires de Trévoux* thought could not be improved upon—bearing plain traces of Gravina and even Vico. Chapter V deals with the nature and essence of poetry. After passing in review various opinions, he gives his own definition: it is 'the imitation of nature (de la Naturaleza) in the universal and in the particular, made with verses, for the utility or for the delight of men, or for both conjointly'; a definition which is surely wide enough to have embraced, if not Góngora, at least Lope de Vega. Chapters VI to X deal with the nature, scope and range of poetic imitation. Luzán follows the Italians closely, but not uncritically; he gives 'icastic' imitation, that is, imitation of the universal, a preference over 'fantastic' or 'particular' imitation. Muratori's three worlds are here, and his view that poetry delights by means of the New, the Unforeseen and the Extraordinary ('lo Nuevo, lo Inopinado, y lo Extraordinario'). As to the end of poetry (chapter XI), Luzán

[1] Edition of 1737, pp. 8 f.

holds that it need not be tied down to delight and utility; it may be either the one or the other, or both combined; but this important question is reserved for consideration in the second book.

In that book he discusses first (chapter I) the 'reason and origin of poetic utility,' which he defines on familiar lines, as guiding us to virtue or glory by a pleasant path. The assertion that 'poetry is the daughter or handmaiden of moral philosophy' is a direct translation from Muratori. From the same source is drawn, too, that claim for the influence of climate on customs and their expression in poetry, which, as we have seen, had an established place in Italian aesthetics, and was ultimately to form a corner-stone in Taine's theory. Each form of poetry has its peculiar utility (chapter II); the epic aims at producing great heroes; tragedy is a lesson to princes to moderate their passions; comedy instructs the people; and so on. Like his master, Luzán is not quite sure about love-poets; but they are saved by the Platonic philosophy; in any case, they have a 'utility,' even if that utility is only diversion. The poet (chapter III) has great possibilities of instructing; but he must be careful not to be too didactic; and he must beware of making too pretentious a display of his learning. We get on more promising ground when Luzán discusses (chapter IV) poetic delight. This proceeds, he says, from poetic beauty and sweetness ('dulzura,' which the *Mémoires de Trévoux* characteristically translate 'l'intéressant')[1]. Beauty is the quality that adorns the truth; it pleases the understanding, but has no power by itself to move the heart, whereas sweetness moves the heart and the emotions; this is its chief purpose. He even commends poetry that has incurred the censure of the critics, if it appeals to the hearts of the people. Is there not again a loophole here for the justification of the great 'unclassical' poetry of Spain? Then comes a particularly interesting chapter on the more specific 'dulzura poética' (chapter V). With this conception of the poetic 'dulzura' Luzán has gone a step beyond the Italians; there is nothing of

[1] *Mémoires de Trévoux*, May, 1748, p. 1024: 'Or ce *dulcia* [d'Horace], que l'Auteur appelle en sa langue *dulçura*, et qu'on rendra bien dans la nôtre par l'*agrément* et peut-être mieux encore par l'*intéressant*, c'est là ce qui touche et ce qui persuade.'

it in Muratori. It definitely foreshadows that new spirit of the eighteenth century, which ultimately crystallised into 'sentimentalism.' It has been pointed out that Luzán involves himself in a contradiction in thus appealing to sentiment as a factor in poetry, when, in the following chapter, he sends his readers to the books on rhetoric in order to learn how to compose 'dulces y afectuosos versos.' But may this appeal to the authorities not be a kind of apology for what he felt was an innovation? Whether or no, the 'dulzura poética' forms a serious breach in Luzán's 'neo-classicism.'

From the 'dulzura' Luzán turns to the consideration of 'la bellezza' (chapter VII). Menéndez y Pelayo regards it as an especial merit of Luzán's *Poética* that it contains a chapter on 'Beauty in general and the beauty of poetry and of truth.'[1] But the Italians, as we have seen, had repeatedly busied themselves with such problems. The main difference is that Luzán, accepting the guidance of Crousaz' *Traité du Beau*, comes to closer grips with the definitions of beauty and truth. Five qualities go to the making of beauty in poetry; or rather, it consists of truth accompanied and intensified by the five qualities of unity, variety, order, proportion and appropriateness; and it may be further enhanced by grandeur, novelty and diversity in the object described. This comes mainly from Crousaz; but Luzán does not lose sight of Muratori's definition that poetic beauty is, if not truth, at least the resplendent light that emanates from the truth, illuminating our souls and dispelling the darkness of ignorance. The obscurity of Góngora is the greatest enemy of true beauty. Chapter VIII discusses the two kinds of truth, certain and probable, and is on lines familiar to us from Muratori; as is also the discussion of verisimilitude with its distinction of a 'popular' and a 'noble' verisimilitude (chapter IX). Luzán's method of dealing with the sophistic quibbling of some of his Italian friends, notably Orsi, is a tribute to the clearness of his own thinking. Indeed, Luzán's mind is nothing if not logical; his early preoccupation with Descartes had borne fruit, with the result that he appears in the *Poética*

[1] *Op. cit.* V, p. 28. Taken generally, Menéndez y Pelayo underestimates Luzán's borrowings from the Italians.

as a very level-headed, common-sense thinker with little taste for speculative adventure. Lessing-like, he goes back to the ancients, to Aristotle and Horace, and frankly accuses Castelvetro of explaining obscure things by new obscurities. He puts the whole matter in a nutshell by saying that the poet, unlike the historian, whose aim is truth, seeks the extraordinary and the marvellous; and poetic verisimilitude gives him a better opportunity of attaining his end than simple historic truth.

In the chapters which follow Luzán deals with poetic artifice, the means whereby the poet 'makes the unacceptable acceptable.' Chapter X, again, is pure Muratori; it discusses how new and marvellous matter—'naturalness' not being sufficient—is to be found with the help of genius and imagination, under the guidance of the judgment. In fact, all that follows on the nature of the fantasy, on simple and natural images, on fantastic images and the regulative function of the judgment in holding the imagination in check, that is to say, all in chapters XI to XVIII—and these were vastly important matters for Spain—is merely a faithful reproduction of Muratori's views. The remaining chapters of this book, XIX to XXII, are concerned with the different styles, with poetic locution, and finally metre. There is nothing here that need detain us.

In Book III Luzán first discusses the drama from the historical point of view; he then considers the nature of the dramatic fable and the various problems of Aristotelian interpretation. To the unities he clings rigidly, Aristotle not being strict enough for him; and his definition of tragedy: 'a dramatic representation of a great change of fortune befalling high personages, and serving as an example and warning to all, but especially to princes,' is, as Menéndez y Pelayo points out (p. 188), 'pure Versailles.' On the purification of the passions he falls back on a Spanish predecessor, Don Jusepe Antonio González de Salas, whose *Nueva idea de la tragedia antigua, ó Ilustración á la Poética de Aristóteles* appeared in 1633; this critic held, he says, that the 'katharsis' consisted in the effect which fictitious fear and pity have upon us in accustoming and hardening us to the real miseries of life, in other words, the opinion held by Castelvetro and Gravina. Frankly, all this is disappointing and much inferior to the two earlier books of the *Poética*.

The epic is the theme of the last book, which is even more perfunctory than the third. Luzán seems to have thought that Spain did not need much instruction in this matter; possibly he had himself little interest in it. He deals with the epic in much the same way as he had dealt with tragedy; but he accepts unquestioningly the leading of Le Bossu, and has little or nothing to say of his own. And then, a little abruptly, his work moves to a conclusion. The time has come, he says, to take in all sails, to run the vessel on the beach, and rest from the fatigues of a lengthy voyage. And before grounding on the sand, he recounts briefly the results of his voyage, and enumerates the goods and merchandise that have formed his cargo.

Something remains to be said about the second edition of the *Poética*, which appeared in 1789, more than fifty years after the first. As there seems to be considerable misunderstanding among literary historians concerning the modifications which the work underwent, I have carefully compared the two editions. The circumstances under which the second edition came to be published are explained in the preface. Luzán had left corrections and additions with his intimate friend, Agustino Montiano y Luyando; and from him they passed to Don Eugenio de Llaguno y Amirolo. It has been suggested that the latter was possibly responsible for some of the new matter, and especially for a less tolerant attitude towards the older Spanish writers[1]. But I hardly think that this view can be maintained. The actual changes in the text of the first edition are not extensive; the omissions are, in most cases, due to the introduction of new matter which rendered the old matter superfluous. And it is just the new matter that interests us. The *Poética* is supplemented on the historical side by extending the old chapters and inserting new ones. In Book I the third chapter, 'Del Origen de la Poesía Vulgar,' is considerably amplified in order, not merely to describe the 'origen,' but also the 'progresos'

[1] Menéndez y Pelayo (pp. 175 f.) finds it, for instance, suspicious that a passage of more than lukewarm appreciation of Calderón in chapter xv of Book III has disappeared in the second edition.

of vernacular poetry; and a new fourth chapter is inserted: 'De la Poética de nuestra Poesía vulgar, y reflexiones sobre las reglas y Autores que han tratado de ellas.' In Book II the principal additions are two chapters at the end on metrical matters. The most important new matter, however, is to be found in the chapters with which the third Book now opens. These are: I. 'De la Poesía dramática Española, su principio, progresos, y estado actual,' and II. 'Sobre las reglas que se supone hay para nuestra Poesía dramática,' and they occupy together nearly seventy pages. Here, if anywhere, one would expect to find proofs of Luzán's backsliding; but the impression I gather from these chapters is that he is studiously endeavouring to be fair-minded and objective, even if the old dramatic poets lie outside his personal sympathy[1]. In some respects, indeed, they compare favourably with the uncompromising classical rigidity of the chapters of the first edition which deal with the technique of tragedy. There are no further important additions, and the last Book on the Epic, which stood most in need of revision, is reprinted unchanged.

Thus the second edition bears witness to a considerable widening of Luzán's horizon; he has utilised in it that fuller knowledge of his own literature which he acquired with the years. And not merely his own literature; he shows a knowledge of English writers, possibly as a result of a hint from the critic of the *Mémoires de Trévoux*[2]. He quotes Addison on the imagination, and reveals a quite unexpected warmth for Milton[3]; in fact, his biographer tells us that he translated a considerable part of *Paradise Lost* into Spanish—surely a surprising procedure for a critic who is regarded as an unbending neo-classic. With respect to French critical opinion and French literature,

[1] He opens his survey, for instance, by saying (II, p. 5): 'La Dramática Española se debe dividir en dos clases, una popular, libre, sin sujeción á las reglas de los antiguos, que nació, echó raices, creció, y se propagó increíblemente entre nosotros; y otra que se puede llamar erudita, porque solo tuvo aceptación entre hombres instruidos.'

[2] *Mémoires de Trévoux*, May, 1748, p. 997: 'Il connoît tous les bons Auteurs si l'on en excepte les Anglois; soit qu'il n'ait pas été à portée de lire ces derniers; soit qu'il ne leur trouve pas assez d'exactitude et de clarté, pour les citer dans un Ouvrage qui demande beaucoup d'ordre et de précision.'

[3] Second edition, I, pp. 252 ff.; cp. Menéndez y Pelayo, *op. cit.* p. 29.

a comparison of the two editions entirely disproves the old view that Luzán became more French in his sympathies as he grew older, and especially after his sojourn in Paris. I have not been able to see his *Memorias literarias de Paris*; but I should be surprised to learn that these Memoirs show that Luzán was made more neo-classic by his visit to France; they may even prove that he had sympathy with those advanced elements in the French opinion of the middle of the century, which were more in harmony with the doctrines he had in his youth imbibed from the Italians.

Such then was the work which was regarded as the standard authority on literary theory in Spain for something like a hundred years. With the advent of Romanticism Luzán was dethroned; but in modern Spain his *Poética*, although stripped of its old authority, is again beginning to be regarded with the respectful attention which it undoubtedly deserves.

III

Until the appearance of the fourth volume of Menéndez y Pelayo's great *Historia de las Ideas estéticas en España* in 1890, the most extraordinary and fantastic opinions seem to have prevailed about Luzán's treatise[1]. Few of his critics would appear to have opened it, and none certainly to have read it. And yet it is far from being an unpleasant or tedious book to read; 'I confess,' says Menéndez y Pelayo (p. 175), 'that the reading of the *Poética* has never been tedious to me, but always interested and entertained me, and I have heard the same said by all who have read it with attention.' I am inclined to think that Luzán's

[1] Ticknor put him down as a mere imitator of the French school—an opinion which he also held of Muratori (*History of Spanish Literature*, 1849, ed. of 1888, pp. 307 ff.); Blanco White called the *Poética* a translation of Muratori's *Perfetta Poesia*, and found it so faithful that he used it to learn Italian (J. H. Thom, *Life of Blanco White*, London, 1841, p. 21); still more incredible, Alberta Lista (*Ensayos literarios y críticos*, II, Sevilla, 1844, p. 226) describes it as a translation of Aristotle's *Poetics*! Fernando Wolf (*Floresta de rimas modernas castellanas*, I, Paris, 1837, pp. 3 f.) says Luzán 'hubiera bebido la purisima agua del Parnaso francés á las orillas del Sena mismo'—and this before 1737. A. Alcalá Galiano (*Historia de la literatura española, francesa, inglesa e italiana*, Madrid, 1845, pp. 37 f.) similarly sees French inspiration. I am indebted for these references to Menéndez y Pelayo, pp. 170 ff.

critics have been unduly influenced by that pride of Spanish nationality, which brought down on his head unjust vituperation even in his own century.

The first important critical pronouncement on the *Poética* appeared in the quarterly *Diario de los Literatos de España* in October, 1737. This too short-lived review[1], which was formed on the model of the *Giornale de' Letterati* of Maffei and Zeno, did much to steady Spanish literary opinion in the transition age. Its appreciation of Luzán's treatise, even if tempered by adverse criticism, at once gave it a certain canonical importance for the new critical movement. The very careful and well weighed article seems to have been written by two hands, by Don Juan Martínez de Salafranca and the better known Don Juan de Iriarte; but the critical part is solely by the latter. The diarists recognise that 'of no work has Spain more need than a complete and accurate Poetics,'[2] but they are not in agreement with Luzán's excessive censure of Lope de Vega and Góngora; they hold that Luzán has not understood Lope's *Arte nuevo de hacer comedias*, and claim a place in the theatre for the taste of the people. They have more sympathy for his condemnation of Góngora, but here also they think that Luzán goes too far; there may be absurdities in Góngora's twenty-first sonnet on Babia's *Historia pontifical*, but they have no difficulty in showing that Luzán's criticism is unacceptable. They appeal for the admission of prose as a vehicle of comedy—it had already been employed to good effect by Spanish dramatists—and they bring forward classical justification for tragi-comedy, a form of drama which Luzán rejects. His rigid legislation for tragedy they meet with the wise reflection: 'Many of the maxims which the critics establish as general laws for the drama based on reason, are the particular laws of genius and taste of each century and nation.' Finally, they complain of the omission of a chapter on Satire. As we have seen, Luzán revised his *Poética*; but the modifications and additions in the posthumous second edition are only very partially in accordance with the criticism of the *Diario*. He did

[1] There were only seven volumes: January, 1737, to December, 1738, the final volume not appearing until 1742. Cp. Cueto, *op. cit.* I, p. 165.

[2] See Cueto, I, p. 179; also Menéndez y Pelayo, pp. 149 ff.

not, in fact, take its strictures in good part, and replied, under a pseudonym, in a *Discurso apologético* (1741). The controversy is not, however, worth pursuing.

More significant for Luzán's reputation outside Spain was the series of three articles which appeared in the *Mémoires de Trévoux* for the year 1748, some 120 pages in all[1]. This review is one long, enthusiastic eulogy, to be explained perhaps by the close ties which the journal had with Spain through Blas Nasarre, if there were not even political motives behind it.

> Les François et les Espagnols, says the reviewer (pp. 1002 f.), semblent n'avoir maintenant qu'un seul et même intérêt. Les Littérateurs des deux Nations doivent être aussi unis que leurs guerriers; et si les armes de ceux-ci bravent avec avantage les efforts de l'Europe conjurée, ceux-là peuvent au moins balancer les Littérateurs des autres Nations, et établir sur le Parnasse l'équilibre qu'on cherche depuis un siécle à introduire dans le systême de l'Europe.

The *Mémoires de Trévoux* have practically no adverse criticism to bring forward at all, the only point in which they allow themselves to differ from Luzán being in their preference for the 'genre icastique' over the 'genre phantastique,' for realism rather than idealism. 'En effet, pour instruire les hommes avec succès, on doit copier d'après d'autres hommes les modéles qu'on leur propose' (pp. 1016 f.). The critic regrets that he cannot reproduce in full the précis which Luzán has made of the *Iliad* and the *Aeneid*; 'rien n'est plus judicieux. Personne n'est jamais peut-être mieux entré dans le génie et le goût de ces deux grands Poëmes' (pp. 1466 f.); and he concludes by 'félicitant très-sincérement l'Espagne d'avoir produit un Art Poëtique aussi parfait que celui de M. de Luzan' (p. 1470). As the *Diario* had complained of the omission of a chapter on Satire, so the *Mémoires* regret that no consideration has been given to Declamation. Both defects Luzán had the intention of remedying; but there is nothing on either theme in the second edition.

From my summary of Luzán's work, it will have been seen

[1] *Mémoires de Trévoux*, May–July, 1748, pp. 995 ff.; 1248 ff.; and 1437 ff. There was also a review in the *Journal étranger* of December, 1755 (I, pp. 117–48); but this is little more than a précis of the work.

that much the most vital part of it comes direct from Muratori. Luzán maintained, as fully and frankly as Addison in England, the importance of the imagination as the dominating factor in poetic creation; a doctrine which at once threw open the doors to the appreciation of Shakespeare as well as Milton, and which, had Luzán been able to free himself from the shackles of neo-classicism, might have allowed him to show real appreciation for the glories of Spanish literature. It was the tragedy of Luzán's work, that he was unable to draw from his theory the inferences which Addison drew from his.

But Luzán's attitude towards Muratori is by no means that of the blind disciple; it is true, he borrows liberally from the *Perfetta Poesia italiana*, even to the extent of those illustrations from Ceva, which in Muratori prove so much less than might have been proved by greater poets in the vernacular; but he can at times assert his independence. No doubt his knowledge of what the Italians had written on literary theory was extraordinarily wide and intimate; and his agreement with them—except with what they had to say on the drama, which his own intolerant views prevented him from appreciating—is practically complete. He knew, for instance, Gravina's *Ragion poetica*, towards which his attitude is distinctly critical[1]; and Monsignani seems to have carried weight with him[2]. Most interesting of all, he had felt the spell, as few in Italy itself had felt it, of Vico. His reference to that writer deserves to be quoted as the first indication of the acceptance of Vico as a force in aesthetic thinking outside Italy[3]. Luzán shows a wide knowledge of the literature on Aristotle; he calls practically all the Italian commentaries to his aid. Of these he looked to Beni as the safest guide; this, it is needless to say, meant that he was much less

[1] Pp. 12, 40, 42 f.

[2] *De imitatione poetica* by F. A. Monsignani is quoted (ed. 1737), pp. 33, 35 f., 40, 56. I only know Monsignani's views from his *Lezioni sopra l'imitazione poetica*, Forli, 1714.

[3] In chapter vii of Book IV (ed. 1737, pp. 461 ff.) Luzán accepts Vico's view of the heroic age—the 'dichosa edad'—when kings and princes did the most menial of tasks: 'Y si damos credito á las ingeniosas ideas, y especulaciones del doctissimo Juan Bautista *Vico*, en el segundo Libro de la célebre obra, que escribió *de los Principios de una nueva ciencia....*' It is, as has been mentioned, just possible that Luzán may have come into personal relations with Vico in Naples.

influenced by Castelvetro's break with the traditional Aristotelians than his Italian masters had been.

Luzán's knowledge of the French writers on literary theory was much less complete; indeed, it is safe to say that he learned of them mainly through Italian sources. Lamy's *Rhétorique* he falls back upon with disconcerting frequency, and he knows Rapin; while his unquestioning attitude to Boileau is in keeping with his general mood in respect of the French classic dogma. Du Bos he seems, strange to say, not to have known at all. He learned most from the Franco-German Crousaz, who, as we have seen, helped to supplement in his mind Muratori's aesthetics. In fact, it is just in this fusion of Muratori and Crousaz that Luzán's chief significance—as it was also, to some extent, Conti's—in the history of aesthetics lies. But there are surprising *lacunae* in his knowledge, especially in what concerns the drama. I cannot find that he has ever looked into Heinsius's treatise, still so fundamental for the eighteenth century, on the *Constitution of Tragedy*; nor does he know D'Aubignac's *Pratique du Théâtre*. The only reasonably modern critic who brings a little life into his rigidly Aristotelian treatment of the drama is Dacier, who in his commentary on the *Poetics* had discussed the weak points in Corneille's theory and practice. Amongst the Italian writers on the drama, I doubt whether he knew Gravina's treatise on Tragedy, or Martelli's; Conti's and Calepio's contributions to dramatic theory appeared too late for him to be able to make use of them in his first edition. Again, in the perfunctory section on the Epic, Le Bossu is, as we have seen, practically his only authority. With such limitations, he was but ill equipped to advance the application of aesthetic theory to practice; and he broke down lamentably when face to face with the great dramatic poets of his own literature. He has told us that clear thinking about the drama was principally lacking in his countrymen; but it was just this clear thinking that he proved unable to supply. He did not realise that in Muratori's conception of the function of the imagination in poetry, there lay a justification for Calderón, and even for Lope de Vega, which went far beyond the grudging concessions he occasionally finds himself obliged to make.

Taken generally, however, Luzán's *Poética* possesses a greater intrinsic value than his countrymen have been willing to concede to it. They have regarded it as inspired by French neo-classicism, whereas the only parts of the treatise that matter are neither French nor neo-classic. Unfortunately, Luzán was identified with a group of writers who followed him, eclipsed him, and in great measure sterilised the good seed he had sown. It was not Luzán, but Blas Antonio Nasarre, Agustin de Montiano and Luis José Velázquez, who seriously impugned the great literature of Spain; and it was a misfortune for the good name of Spanish criticism that the writings of Velázquez and Montiano should have been translated into French, while Luzán was not. And not merely into French; for the recommendation of Lessing—which, it is true, he subsequently retracted—obtained a hearing for Montiano in Germany, and the German version of Velázquez' history remained, down to the brothers Schlegel, the chief source of Germany's knowledge of Spanish literature[1]. Thus Luzán, like Muratori himself and, in a greater or less degree, all the writers who are passed in review in these pages, paid the penalty which is inexorably exacted from all who set themselves to stem the tide of reigning taste. The dead hand of the mediaeval Aristotle still lay heavy on Western literatures, and a long period had to elapse before neo-classicism was ultimately vanquished, and the imagination fully recognised as the dominant force in artistic creation.

[1] Montiano's *Discursos sobre las tragedias españolas* (1750) was translated into French by D'Hermilly, Paris, 1754; Velázquez, *Origenes de la Poesia castellana* (Malaga, 1754) into German by J. A. Dieze, as *Geschichte der spanischen Dichtkunst*, Göttingen, 1769.

Chapter XI

The Beginnings of a New Aesthetics in England: Addison

I

In spite of a general disposition in the England of the later seventeenth century to accept the neo-classic doctrines of Boileau and Rapin, a strong obstacle presented itself in the existence of a great national literature which would not let itself be forced into the Procrustes-bed of classic theory. English literature had developed to astonishing splendour on lines directly antagonistic to the Aristotelianism of the classicists. It was consequently difficult to accept the doctrine of a reason-governed poetry which eschewed the miraculous, or pretended that the latter could be brought by a quibble within the bounds of the probable; which hedged round the 'imitation of nature' with reservations; set up laws, and insisted that poetic beauty was one and the same in all times and among all peoples. With all his sympathies for the French ideals, Dryden felt constrained to make repeated concessions to his countrymen's tastes; and Temple took up an attitude quite incompatible with the classic theory. A distinct schism existed in English literary taste; and this schism ultimately found its social basis: the upper classes with their sympathies for and close ties with France, embraced the French classic taste; the nation at large, ignoring the ruling of self-appointed arbiters of poetic excellence, remained tacitly faithful to its untrimmed, unvarnished and unclassic instincts. Thus neo-classicism in England never succeeded in divesting itself of a certain artificiality and unreality.

An important factor in the construction of a new aesthetic theory in England was the sensualism of Hobbes, which, in turn, goes back to Bacon. The latter was, in fact, a pioneer in claiming supremacy for the imagination over the reason in poetic creation, and, as has been seen, he had been read with profit by Italians like Gravina and Muratori. The progressive criticism in Italy from the end of the seventeenth century onwards took its stand with Bacon; it drew vital support from Hobbes, and subsequently from Locke. Here, in fact, lay its real strength; and here, one might have thought, was a very strong reason why it should have been welcomed in England. The significance of this aesthetics lay, however, not in its sensualism and rationalism, which were not ill adapted to link it up with the classic theory of France, but rather in the fact that it admitted the existence of a definite aesthetic sense, which was not amenable to the strait-jacket of classicism. Hobbes, seeking a scientific, empiric basis, stated, as a matter of observation, that man, in consequence of his own self-love and egoism, takes pleasure in certain aesthetic manifestations. His mind is attracted by novelty, and this novelty is the source of his pleasure in poetry. Literary creation he explains empirically on the basis of an association of ideas; he does not consider the question whether the reason or the imagination should be the dominant partner; he only observes that the imagination does play an important part in this association of ideas. The imagination may be an objectionable and even a dangerous faculty; Hobbes merely recognises that it is an essential agent for the discovery of that novelty which pleases, and is thus theoretically an indispensable factor in creative art[1]. With this statement of fact he rests content. From Hobbes these views passed on to Locke; and from Locke to Addison, who was, of course, also immediately familiar with the writings of Hobbes. But the insufficiency of Hobbes' psychology to provide a new basis for aesthetic thinking is to be seen from his reply to Davenant's preface to *Gondibert* (1651)[2], which, admitting the significance of the imagination for poetic creation, yet largely discounts its practical participation. In reality, Hobbes is quite as hostile to the supremacy of the imagination as the classicists of the Bouhours type. *The Faerie Queene* is for him a lamentable example of the evil effects of the imagination when it gets out of hand.

Thus the vital element of Hobbes' thinking, for literary

[1] *Leviathan*, I, chapter viii, 'Of the Virtues commonly called Intellectual.'
[2] There is a convenient reprint in J. E. Spingarn, *Critical Essays of the Seventeenth Century*, Oxford, 1908, II, pp. 54 ff.

theory, remains, not his aesthetic ideas as such, but his determination of psychological facts. There is a very definite cleavage in his thought between the empiricism of such facts and his sympathy with a purely rationalistic interpretation of the aesthetic process; and it was the former, not the latter, that mattered where the preparation of an aesthetics in opposition to classic theory was concerned. In this respect—and in this respect only—his successor, Locke, was furthering, even although he does not use the word 'imagination' at all in the whole course of his treatise on the *Human Understanding*.

In the end, one is forced to admit that the most important of all factors in discrediting the classic theory in England was the irresistible appeal of the older national poetry. Cowley, Temple, Howard and Dryden himself bowed before the cogency of this argument. Shakespeare—and he was only the greatest of many—was the insuperable obstacle to the acceptance of a rationalistic and classic dogma. In the centre of the conflict of opinion stands naturally Dryden. He fully realised that there were elements in Hobbes' thought which made, not for a reason-governed classicism, but for a poetry in which the imagination should hold untrammelled sway; and where Shakespeare was concerned, he made no question of it. But when Shakespeare was out of sight, the tug of classic taste was irresistible. Thus Dryden takes back with one hand what he gives with the other. He was neither a consistent anti-classicist like Howard, nor, on the other hand, an obdurate formalist like Rymer; he endeavoured to maintain a middle course; and thus in his hands the conflict remained undecided, the conciliation of opposing standpoints, if such were possible, uneffected. Dryden never succeeded in freeing himself from a certain distraughtness between his own right poetic instincts and the conclusions to which his intelligence forced him; the claims of realism and the imagination at no time received from him their due. It would almost seem as if the Italian theorists, whose weakness was that they were in no high sense poets themselves, were just in consequence less trammelled, and more able to discriminate the vital elements in the Bacon-Hobbes psychology than Dryden, who had the apparent advantage over them of being a great poet.

Particular importance has been attached by Hamelius, in his suggestive survey of English critical theory[1], to another trend of aesthetic thought in the England of the seventeenth century: the stressing of the religious factor by Milton and his nephew Edward Phillips. No doubt Hamelius is right in regarding this as a new element of real importance for the evolution of English aesthetics. But he is inclined to exaggerate the positive value of Phillips' contribution to the controversy. The *Theatrum poetarum* (1675)[2] is hardly a readable book; nor is it in any sense an exposition of aesthetic doctrine. At most, certain ideas of importance may be extracted or deduced from it. He regards, for instance, the poetic function as the highest activity of the soul, and he demands freedom for genius; but he fails to grasp the significance of these thoughts, in so far as he is unable to separate his claims from an essentially religious application of them. Again, a faint foreshadowing may be detected in Phillips of that substitution of the true classic for the false classic, which was first to become a revolutionary factor in European literature with Winckelmann and Lessing a generation later; and English opinion was, no doubt, influenced by his insistent demand—already voiced by Desmarets in France and Cowley in England—for a poetry, inspired, like *Paradise Lost*, not by heathen antiquity, but by the Christian faith. Dryden was not unaffected by these views; and in his eclectic way, he endeavoured to reconcile them with his other theories; but this with him was only a passing phase.

Such were the gropings towards a modern aesthetic theory in England at the close of the seventeenth century. On the one hand, there was a classical-rationalistic party, who advocated the approximation of English to French taste; on the other, a party which, influenced by religious sentiment and the national achievement of the past, demanded freedom for the expansion of the national genius. The contemporary Italians, whose thought was based on similar premises, may have been at a disadvantage, in so far as their theory had to a large extent no

[1] P. Hamelius, *Die Kritik in der englischen Literatur des 17. und 18. Jahrhunderts*, Leipzig, 1897.

[2] The Preface is reprinted by J. E. Spingarn, *Critical Essays of the Seventeenth Century*, Oxford, 1908–9, II, pp. 256 ff.

living contemporary literature behind it: whereas the English critics could point to the practical realisation of their demands. But the Italians had progressed much further towards a systematic aesthetics. Neither Dryden nor Dennis, nor Shaftesbury at a slightly later date, had, in their attempts to define the instinctive forces of the mind, gone to work so methodically as Muratori; nor were they so closely in touch with the theorising of the earlier time. I doubt even whether they had grasped as clearly the significance of the views set forth by the protagonists of the French 'Querelle.' It is just here that the Italians might have made a valuable contribution to the building up of a modern aesthetic system in England. Unfortunately, however, our critical writers, with, as will be seen, the possible exception of Addison, had no knowledge of their work.

We have never been, for any considerable time in our intellectual history, out of touch with Italy; our older literary theorists were deeply indebted to the Italians. In the seventeenth century the points of contact are abundant; the critical work of that age, from Ben Jonson and Sir Philip Sidney onwards, is, either directly or indirectly, influenced by them; and, as we have seen, our Royal Society was founded on an Italian model. The frequent visits of Italian scholars and scientists to England at the beginning of the eighteenth century might have facilitated the introduction of Italian ideas; Conti and Maffei were highly honoured guests. But in spite of all this, there is practically no evidence that the writings of the new generation of aesthetic theorists were known in England. There were no learned journals, as in France, to give a record of their work. Gravina, it is true, had, much later, an enthusiastic apostle in the person of the Rev. T. J. Mathias, who prefaced the London edition of the *Ragion poetica* (1806) with a eulogistic Italian 'canzone dedicatorio,' and a brief notice of the author drawn from Tiraboschi; and Gravina had another admirer in Bishop Burgess. But I cannot find any trace of his influence on our aesthetic writers. By the eighteenth century England's faith in Italian guidance had waned, and our critics had ceased to look to foreign literatures, other than French, for new ideas.

A knowledge of Muratori is even more difficult to trace in

England than in France; the lack of French intermediaries made it, of course, less possible for us to learn about his aesthetic work. It is true, Muratori was made a member of the Royal Society, but this recognition was certainly not a tribute to the *Perfetta Poesia italiana*. Again, if Maffei was a reasonably familiar name with us, we were only interested in his magnificent books on the antiquities of his native city; we hardly knew that he was a reformer of dramatic poetry. As for Vico, we are told that some Englishmen in Naples bought up the first edition of the *Scienza Nuova*, in order to send it to London[1]; but, this notwithstanding, no mention of the work is to be found in English periodicals, and it has not, even yet, been translated as a whole into English[2].

II

It was reserved for Addison to take the most important step towards a new aesthetic theory, to bridge over, and partly remove the old dualism which had still been apparent in Dryden's compromises.

A laborious analysis of the *Spectator* shows that Addison had something to say on almost every aspect of literary theory and criticism[3]. He discusses the function and methods of criticism and the equipment of the critic. He analyses the productive faculties of the mind, genius—discriminating between natural genius and genius as the result of training and education—imagination, taste and wit. He defines the attributes that go to the making of a work of art, the great, the uncommon, the beautiful and the unpleasant. He passes—and here the shadow of the old Poetics lies more heavily upon him—to the consideration of the rules and limitations of poetry, to questions of probability and propriety, the different kinds of characters, and their relative suitability for literary composition, the matter

[1] Cp. F. Lomonaco, *Vite degli eccellenti italiani*, III, 1803, p. 127.

[2] There is an English translation of Book III, 'On the Discovery of the True Homer,' in H. N. Coleridge's *Introduction to the Study of the Greek Classic Poets*, London, 1830, 2nd ed., 1834, pp. 74 ff. (*Bibliografia Vichiana*, pp. 5 ff.).

[3] Cp. E. Saudé, *Die Grundlagen der literarischen Kritik bei Joseph Addison*, a Berlin thesis of 1908. More discursive is a Danish study, A. Hansen, *Addison som litterær Kritiker*, Copenhagen, 1883.

which a poet may make use of. He discusses composition, the different types of fable, episodes and main actions; he has something to say on verse and the adornment of poetic language with metaphors and similes. The various forms of poetry are all, more or less, dealt with, epic, tragedy, tragi-comedy, comedy, opera; fable, satire, eclogue, ballad. And finally, he discriminates between different kinds of readers. But tolerably complete as all this seems when tabulated, the treatment of the individual items is exceedingly unequal. There is no question of distilling from the pages of the *Spectator* a system of aesthetics; in fact, the inference is rather that Addison's ideas were lacking in any real organic correlation or system. They might, indeed, have been arrived at at widely different periods of his life. We are repeatedly confronted with opinions about poetry which are irreconcilable and mutually destructive. At one time, he seems credulously 'classical,' often merely trivial; while at others, he expresses thoughts which, like a flash, irradiate great tracts of arid aesthetic speculation.

For practical purposes Addison's aesthetic opinions may be regarded as grouped round three chief themes: his criticism of tragedy, of *Paradise Lost*, and the papers on the 'Pleasures of the Imagination.' In the two first groups he is mainly concerned with the traditional reckoning with Aristotle. Here he is, in the main, loyal to the classic dogma; but never so loyal as to exclude a healthy, common-sense outlook on poetry. He may express his abhorrence of the irregularity of tragi-comedy, but, with his master Dryden, he is, at the same time, ready to break a lance for Shakespeare. His criticism of Milton shows perhaps his attitude best; it is a justification of Milton's greatness, but a justification based on the argument that Milton is essentially in agreement with the classic canon. This is precisely the attitude which, a generation later, Lessing took up in recommending Shakespeare to the attention of his countrymen. But the third group belongs to a very different category. It is not too much to say that in the suggestive papers on the imagination Addison laid the foundation of the whole romantic aesthetics in England[1].

[1] It was these papers which provoked W. B. Worsfold's enthusiastic claim (*The Principles of Criticism*, new ed., London, 1902, pp. 51 f.): 'Here

And not for England only; the enormous popularity of the *Spectator* in French translation carried his views far and wide; and they were of very real significance for the building up of a new aesthetic doctrine in both France and Germany. So important, indeed, are these papers, that the rest of Addison's poetic theory may be comparatively neglected. It will not have escaped the reader of the earlier part of this volume that the doctrine of the imagination here expounded shows very considerable similarity with that which Muratori discusses in much greater detail in his *Perfetta Poesia*. Is there any reason to believe that Addison was acquainted with Muratori's treatise?

We still await an adequate investigation into the sources of the *Spectator*. I would not appear ungrateful to the industry and erudition of its commentators; but they are mostly interested in more concrete aspects of the journal than its aesthetic ideas. The *Spectator* is, of course, not a work of erudition; but even if it were, it was not the custom of the eighteenth century to 'document' with scientific conscientiousness the authorities on which opinions were based. This is generally true of all the great critics of that century—of Lessing as well as Addison. It is usually held that Addison's own reading, in literature and literary theory, was very comprehensive; indeed, a remark which he himself makes at the outset of the *Spectator*[1], would appear to favour such a view. I doubt, however, whether it can be substantiated. The impression one gathers from a study of Addison's opinions on literary aesthetics is that, in this field at least, his reading did not extend far beyond the critical authorities who lay in the beaten track of the educated writers of his time. At no time, perhaps, was Addison what might be called a systematic reader; he was—outside the classics—rather a taster of books than a student of them.

The authority of the Greek and Latin critics is, of course,

in England in the opening years of the eighteenth century, the first genuine critic appeared; the first critic who formed a just conception of the duty of his office; the first critic who was able to add anything to the last word of Hellenism, by exhibiting the insufficiency of formal criticism and by establishing a new principle of poetic appeal.'

[1] 'There are very few celebrated Books, either in the Learned or Modern Tongues, which I am not acquainted with' (*Spectator*, No. 1).

paramount with him. Aristotle's *Poetics* and *Rhetoric* are frequently appealed to; while Horace is his constant stand-by. No single work, indeed, is more frequently quoted, either in his text or in his mottoes, than the Horatian *Ars poetica*. Of greater significance for the liberating forces in Addison's thinking is his reliance on Longinus, whom Boileau, followed by English writers, had made a living voice in the criticism of the age. The only criticism of Addison's debt to antiquity that might be suggested, is that he seems to miss the significance of Quintilian for modern literary theory.

We are still strangely ill-informed concerning Addison's relations to his English predecessors and contemporaries. This is due to the fact that, until comparatively recently, no serious attempt has been made to elucidate—apart from Dryden—the basis of critical thinking from which Addison sprang. But now men like Rymer, Dennis and Gildon, whom we used to be content to damn, even without faint praise, have been seriously studied; in fact, there seems a danger of the process of rehabilitation going too far[1]. Addison's dependence on Dryden is sufficiently obvious; but I doubt whether the full effect of the heritage he received from his great predecessor is yet adequately understood; how much he has been, for good or for evil, influenced by Dryden. Of his more immediate contemporaries, John Dennis has good claims to be regarded as Addison's predecessor. In his earlier writings, *The Advancement and Reformation of Modern Poetry* (1701) and *Grounds of Criticism in Poetry* (1704)—and it is obviously only this earlier Dennis with whom we are concerned—Dennis did his best to save what was to be saved of the philosophy of Hobbes for the literary theory of the new century. He showed that just Hobbes' sensualistic psychology provided a basis for defining the function of the imagination in poetry, and its relation to the better understood processes of the reason. He was tempted at many points

[1] Selections from Dennis and Gildon will be found in J. E. Spingarn, *op. cit.* vol. III and W. H. Durham, *Critical Essays of the Eighteenth Century*, New Haven, 1915. There is a monograph on Dennis by H. G. Paul, New York, 1911, and on *Rymers dramatische Kritik* by A. Hofherr, Heidelberg, 1908.

to take up the challenge of the French classicists; but was, unfortunately, content, as a rule, to compromise. He could still regard Le Bossu's *Traité du Poème épique* as an adequate rule of thumb to measure the greatness of *Paradise Lost*. Dennis did not get very far; and his advance was arrested at an early stage, became, in fact, a retrogression. Without him, however, the literary theory of the *Spectator* would certainly have been less distinguishable from that of Dryden.

Of the French critics, Addison expresses the frankest admiration for the Père Bouhours; on him he relies in all matters of taste[1]; and he places, following Dennis, an equally implicit —if not so frankly acknowledged[2]—reliance on the authority of Le Bossu, who is presumably one of the 'greatest modern Criticks' referred to in No. 70 of the *Spectator*. The influence of Le Bossu is naturally conspicuous in his criticism of Milton; in fact, that criticism is essentially an effort to reconcile *Paradise Lost* with the French critic's system. Further, Bayle is a frequent source of information for Addison; and he quotes the opinions of Boileau, Rapin, Saint-Évremond, and the two Daciers.

In view of the obvious parallelism between the treatment of the imagination in the *Spectator* and in Muratori's *Perfetta Poesia italiana*, Addison's writings have to be closely scrutinised for evidence of his familiarity with Italian criticism. In early years he made a lengthy tour in Italy; but the record of that tour is disappointing, if we seek in it an acquaintance with, or interest in Italian books. All that he has to say there of Italian literary matters could be compressed within a page or two. He showed some interest in the theatre; deprecated, as we have seen[3], the encroachment of the harlequin in serious tragedy; he abhorred the buffoonery of Italian comedy, and had some pleasure, not yet coloured by the witty sarcasm of the *Spectator*, in the opera; indeed, he went so far as, after his return, himself to write an opera, *Rosamond* (1707), the failure of which may have

[1] See above, note to p. 11.

[2] Gregory Smith notes the absence of references to Le Bossu in the papers on Milton, except where Addison quotes him to differ from him (Ed. of the *Spectator*, VI, p. 288).

[3] See above, p. 5, note.

lent zest to his subsequent attacks. Our only evidence that he was at this time not oblivious to Italian literary theory, is seen in his reference to the Italians preferring the dialogue to set forth their views on this subject. Obviously, then, not much importance may be attached to Addison's journey to Italy as a formative force on his critical theory; he was still too young and indifferent to the matter; still, too, at the stage when he could discuss English poetry and ignore Shakespeare. Moreover, the new Italian movement, with which the present volume has been mainly concerned, had hardly begun as early as 1700–2, when Addison was in Italy. Of the books that come into question, he might, at most, have seen Gravina's preface to the *Endimione*, and his treatise on the *Ancient Fables*; but Muratori had only just begun to be known as a writer on literary aesthetics.

The *Spectator* shows that Addison continued to interest himself in Italy; but it contains little or no direct citation of Italian books. The faith of English critics in Italian judgments had considerably diminished since the early seventeenth century; even Dryden makes no parade of his knowledge of Italian sources, although it was undoubtedly considerable. Indeed, since Bouhours, it was regarded as little creditable, in England as in France, to appeal to their authority. Possibly this is an additional reason for Addison's silence, if such it was. In an early paper of the *Spectator* he expresses himself about the Italians in a tone which seems an immediate echo from Bouhours: 'The finest Writers among the Modern *Italians* express themselves in such a florid Form of Words, and such tedious Circumlocutions, as are used by none but Pedants in our own Country' (No. 5, p. 22). But from a later sentence it is clear that he was not thinking in particular of the writers of his own day, but rather contrasting Italian writers in general with the 'old Italians,' Cicero, Horace, etc. In the same paper he endorses Boileau's contempt for Tasso; but at the close of the Milton papers he refers to the great Italian poet more respectfully (No. 369, vol. v, p. 198). The only Italian author, actually quoted in the *Spectator*, who is in any way concerned with questions of criticism, is Boccalini, whose *Ragguagli* had long been a familiar book in English translation, and had, in fact, appeared shortly before in a new one[1]. Beyond this, there are a few isolated hints in Addison's journal of further reading[2]; but nothing in the least definite. Thus, as far as actual evidence goes, we have no ground for inferring that Addison was familiar with Muratori's work; but the similarity in the views of the two men is too striking to be lightly dismissed, the more so as it was historically of the highest importance. For it prepared the way for the whole-hearted welcome which the ideas of the *Perfetta Poesia* were to receive in Switzerland.

With Muratori Addison attacks the opera; although his ridicule takes a form very different from Muratori's rather portentous arguments. But the campaign against the Italian opera was originally a French affair, and Addison had source enough, if it is necessary at all to look for a source, in Saint-Évremond's essay, *Sur les Opéras* (1677); or, more likely, it was immediately prompted by his friend Dennis's *Essay on the Operas after the Italian Manner, which are about to be establish'd on the English Stage* (1706). Again, Saintsbury has suggested a possible echo of Muratori in Addison's discussion of True and False Wit. The Italian critic, in his second book, rails against acrostics, anagrams and puns ('bisticce'); he derides the 'wings, eggs, altars,' as Addison does; and his conclusions are similar. But Addison's obvious source for these anti-marinistic sentiments is Hobbes' reply to Davenant's *Preface to Gondibert*[3].

Thus the only serious approximation to the Muratorian doctrine is to be found in the papers on the 'Pleasures of the Imagination.' 'Fine taste' Addison defines in No. 409 (vol. VI, p. 49) as 'that Faculty of the Soul, which discerns the Beauties of an Author with Pleasure, and the Imperfections with Dislike.' 'Good Taste' was, as we have seen, a much debated aesthetic

[1] It had been published in 1656, 1669, 1674 and 1704; and, as *Advices from Parnassus*, in 1706.

[2] In No. 42 (I, p. 157), for instance, he says that the Italians call 'the Art of imposing on the Spectators of a Drama by Appearances, the *Fourberia della Scena*'; and in No. 592 (VIII, p. 128), he refers to 'what the *Italians* call the *Gusto grande*, which is what we call the Sublime in Writing.' So far, I have been unable to ascertain whence comes this information.

[3] Reprinted by J. E. Spingarn, *op. cit.* II, pp. 57 ff.

question at this time. Originating possibly with Gracián[1], whom Addison quotes as saying it was 'the utmost Perfection of an accomplished Man,' it had formed the main theme of Bouhours' two books. But nowhere does Bouhours define taste as a 'faculty of the soul'; it is with him merely a natural ability to discern the 'raisonnable et naturel.' And among Addison's immediate French predecessors, I find no definition at all resembling his[2]. There is no question but that Addison here stands nearest to Muratori. To the latter good taste had been, as we have seen[3], essentially the faculty of discerning the beautiful: 'We understand by good taste the ability to judge what is defective, imperfect or mediocre in the sciences and the arts, and through this judgment arriving at clearness as to what is best and perfect.'

The psychological basis of the papers on the Imagination is Locke's *Essay concerning Human Understanding*. The function of the sense of sight—and the limitations of that sense—in furnishing the imagination with its images, are defined in accordance with Locke's theory, which had been Hobbes' before him. And although Muratori has some excellent pages on the furnishing of the 'arsenal of the imagination' with its stores of images, the parallelism is rather due to Muratori's own indebtedness to the English sensualistic philosophy. Addison's dis-

[1] Cp. K. Borinski, *Balthasar Gracian*, Halle, 1894, p. 39; J. E. Spingarn, *op. cit.* I, p. xcii.

[2] Saint-Évremond (*Oeuvres*, Amsterdam, 1739, IV, pp. 225 ff.) regarded it as a feeling that must be born with us, and he concludes that it is nearly impossible to say what good taste is; the Abbé de Bellegarde (*Lettres curieuses de littérature et de morale*, Paris, 1702, p. 13) was of opinion that 'le goût est exquis, quand il est reglé par la raison; et que ceux qui ne suivent que leur inclination pour guide, ont d'ordinaire le goût mauvais'; the third of the *Entretiens galans*, on 'le bon goût' (Paris, III, p. 117) defines it as a 'raison éclairée qui d'intelligence avec le coeur fait toujours un juste choix parmi des choses opposées ou semblables'; Madame Dacier had said (*Comédies grecques d'Aristophane*, Amsterdam, 1692, Preface, p. [xvi]): 'Le goût est une harmonie, un accord de l'esprit et de la raison. On en a plus ou moins selon que cette harmonie est plus ou moins juste'; and Fraim du Tremblay, although a little late for Addison (*Discours sur l'Origine de la Poésie*, Paris, 1713, p. 120), had identified taste and judgment: 'On l'appelle goût quand il agit par sentiment et à la premiére impression des objets; on l'appelle jugement quand il agit par raisonnement, et aprés avoir examiné les ouvrages sur les regles de l'art et par les lumieres de la vérité.'

[3] See above, p. 70.

tinction between primary and secondary pleasures is a deduction from Locke's distinction between 'Ideas of Primary Qualities of Bodies and Ideas produced by their Secondary Qualities.' Locke does not, however, use, as Hobbes had done, the word imagination; and Addison's contrast of understanding and imagination is rather that of the Italians whose terms are 'ingegno' and 'fantasia.'

The Pleasures of the Imagination, Addison says, 'arise from the Greatness, Novelty or Beauty of an object'; whereas Muratori had proclaimed 'il bello poetico' to be 'la novità, la rarità, il maraviglioso che spira dalla materia o dall' artifizio, o pur da tutti e due.'[1] These two definitions have more in common than is at first apparent; for, while Addison speaks of beauty as an essential quality of the object that pleases the imagination, Muratori is defining, not what pleases, but what constitutes the poetically beautiful. The two qualities which Muratori distinguishes as 'novità' and 'rarità,' Addison includes in one, 'novelty'; for he also describes this as the 'Uncommon' and the 'Surprising.' Again, Muratori's 'maraviglioso' is covered by Addison's 'Greatness' or 'Grandeur'; for he immediately goes on to explain that it is something which causes us a 'pleasing Astonishment...a delightful Stillness and Amazement at the Apprehension' of objects[2].

It is to be observed that both writers restrict themselves to three qualities. Not that Muratori was, by any means, the discoverer of these three qualities; Bacon himself had already, in his *Novum Organum*, insisted on the importance of novelty; and the other qualities had been, long before Muratori's time, evolved from Longinus. But he was the first to group them in this particular way; and he is followed by Addison. That the latter had Muratori's treatise before him, as he had had the *Traité du Poème épique* when he discussed Milton, is unlikely; for, in that case, he could hardly have failed to take a more

[1] *Perfetta Poesia*, I, chap. vii, p. 112.

[2] Gregory Smith suggests that the original draft of the papers on the Imagination, which was published by J. Dykes Campbell in 1864, was a sketch, 'possibly made at college' (*Ed. cit.* VI, p. 305). But this seems to me improbable. The sketch, it may be added, does not bring us any nearer to clearness as to Addison's source.

comprehensive view of the rôle of the imagination in poetry, and to have rounded off his papers with a more positive declaration of faith. But that Addison had at some time looked into the *Perfetta Poesia italiana* seems to me the almost necessary explanation of the striking parallelism in the two writers. Compared with Muratori, Addison gives the impression of having merely dipped into the subject of literary aesthetics; but both men were clearly thinking along the same lines. Muratori and Addison were fellow-workers in the establishment of the new aesthetic theory of the creative imagination; and fellow-workers, who, as the following chapter will show, provided the basis on which the great German poetry of the later eighteenth century was reared. But, whereas the *Perfetta Poesia* was familiar only to comparatively few Italian readers, the *Spectator* was read by thousands in every country of Europe.

Chapter XII

Italian Influence on Aesthetic Theory in Germany

The anaemic conditions of Germany at the close of the Thirty Years' War placed her more at the mercy of foreign influences than any other European country. And of these influences that of Italy was, unfortunately, paramount; literary history has a disheartening tale to tell of the devastation wrought by the imitation of Marini and Guarini on the German literature of the time, then feebly struggling back to life again. What in Italy may have been merely a questionable extravagance of poetic ornament—in the best interpretation, a protest against the dead hand of classic rigorism—became, when transplanted to German conditions, an orgy of tasteless 'Schwulst.' Thus the so-called Second Silesian School, the chief representatives of which were Lohenstein and Hofmannswaldau, touches a very nadir in German poetry.

It was obviously the first business of the next generation to check and discredit this extravagance. But, as in all literary development, there was no sudden change. The influence of Italy persisted. The Germans were readily convinced of the deplorable taste of their own imitations of the 'secentists'; but they were slow to renounce the conception of poetic excellence which they owed to Italy. In fact, one might say that Marinism passed by easy stages from imitation of the Italians to that of the English nature poetry of Pope and Thomson. The gradual transition is illustrated by the Hamburg poet, Brockes, who, beginning as a translator of Marini, became a fervid nature poet, and employed the symbolism of nature in the same extravagant and 'precious' way as Marini's German imitators had employed the Italian 'concetti.' One might even say that—apart from his puritanism, which awakened a sympathetic chord in German pietism—Milton was accepted in Germany, in the first instance, not because the Germans discovered his real greatness as a poet, but because they felt that his language supplied an acceptable surrogate for the striking imagery which Marini had accustomed them to regard as a necessary ornament of poetry. Milton was for them a kind of bridge from Marini to Thomson.

I

The group of writers who set themselves to oppose the ravages of Marinistic extravagance in Germany by reinstating classic taste as formulated by Boileau, is analogous in many ways to the Italian Arcadians. In fact, they had been stimulated to action by precisely the same cause, namely, Bouhours' arrogant refusal to allow any nation but his own to possess taste. His taunt: 'Can a German possess *esprit*?' had created as much bitterness north of the Alps as his attack on Tasso had created in the south[1]. Like the Italians, the Germans combated the bad taste of which Bouhours had accused them, by means of literary societies; and the 'Deutschübende poetische Gesellschaft' in Leipzig, over which Gottsched presided, was more analogous to the Arcadia than to the earlier German linguistic societies, modelled on the Accademia della Crusca[2]. Whether the writings of Gravina or Muratori had actually a share in effecting these reforms, is, however, doubtful. The former's *Ragion poetica* had, as we have seen[3], been briefly noticed in the *Acta Eruditorum* on its appearance in 1708; and it had again been introduced to the German reading public, as early as 1718, by a translation in the Frankfort *Neue Bibliothek*[4], of the lengthy review in the *Journal littéraire*. The French article was also noticed in the same year in the *Neue Zeitungen von Gelehrten*

[1] J. F. Cramer's *Vindiciae nominis Germanici, contra quosdam obtrectatores Gallos*, Amsterdam, 1694, is a direct reply to Bouhours; but Leibnitz's *Unvorgreiffliche Gedanken betreffend die Ausübung und Verbesserung der deutschen Sprache* (1697), and Thomasius's labours to bring the vernacular to honour were also due to the Frenchman's insinuations. See also, C. F. Weichmann, *Poesie der Niedersachsen*, I, Hamburg, 1726, Vorrede.

[2] Bodmer draws the parallel in his *Neue Critische Briefe*, Zürich, 1763, pp. 144 ff.

[3] See above, p. 196.

[4] Cp. A. Farinelli, *Dante e la Francia*, Milan, 1906, II, p. 182.

Sachen, where the critic sums up his opinion of the *Ragion* in words repeated from the *Journal*[1]:

We can point to no book in which there is more sagacity and eloquence than in this; the author, in fact, gives too much. He has often expressed a single proposition by five or six thoughts of which the one is more beautiful than the other and, as it were, smothers them.

In spite of the fact that the Muratorian aesthetics was fraught with such significance for the Germans, it was strangely late in becoming known to them. Reviewing Orsi's *Considerazioni* in August 1705, the *Acta Eruditorum* expressed the eagerness with which it looked forward to Muratori's work[2], and two months later, Muratori presented Mencke, the editor, with a copy[3]. But no review of the *Perfetta Poesia* appeared in the *Acta* until 1711[4], and this was little more than a summary of the book's contents. There are a few insignificant notices and references to Muratori's work in other German periodicals of the time, as the Leipzig *Neuer Büchersaal der gelehrten Welt*. Lastly, Gottsched, who seems to have had a difficulty in keeping Muratori and Maffei apart[5], published a translation of the former's chapter on the opera, ascribing it to Maffei, in his *Beyträge zur Critischen Theorie*[6].

[1] *Neue Zeitungen von Gelehrten Sachen*, No. lxiii, Leipzig, August, 1718, pp. 499 f. Cp. above, p. 197. At a later time J. G. Sulzer quoted Gravina's opinion repeatedly (*Allgemeine Theorie der schönen Künste*, Leipzig, 1786 f., I, pp. 24, 460; II, pp. 470, 504; III, p. 248). Still later, A. W. Schlegel bowed to the authority of Gravina on Dante. Cp. A. Farinelli, *op. cit.* II, p. 183.

[2] Pp. 378 f.: 'Nos, ut et ipse et alii itidem ab Italia Viri docti atque ingeniosi, non suis magis, quam nostris quoque Philologis, calcar at has studiorum amoenitates excolendas admoveant, merito optamus, doctissimique, quem supra celebravimus, Lodovici Antonii Muratorii, cujus beneficio haec ipsa Ursi [Orsi] commentatio, licet serius aliquantulum, ad nos pervenit, quos in litteris, ad Actorum Collectores datis promittit, *duos de Consummata Italorum Poesi tomos* expectamus.'

[3] *Epistolario*, II, p. 782; cp. p. 715.

[4] *Supplementum*, IV, pp. 203 ff.

[5] See below, pp. 254, 284.

[6] Vol. VI (1740), pp. 485 ff.; also *Critische Dichtkunst*, 4th ed., Leipzig, 1751, p. 751. C. A. Teuber's *Critische Abhandlung von der vollkommenen Poesie der Deutschen*, 1738, would appear to recall Muratori only by its title. I know it only from the review in Gottsched's periodical, V (1738), pp. 387 ff. In a letter to Herder of March 4, 1768, J. G. Hamann mentions the *Perfetta Poesia* (*Schriften*, ed. F. Roth, Berlin, 1821–5, III, p. 348). In 1785 Muratori's *Della Forza della Fantasia* was translated by G. H. Richerz, university preacher in Göttingen, under the title *Über die Einbildungskraft des Menschen*.

As in Italy, the movement towards a purified literary taste was not productive of much poetic talent, the so-called 'Hofpoeten,' Canitz, Besser, König, being very modest and mediocre representatives of the art they would reform. In criticism and aesthetic theory their head and spokesman was Johann Christoph Gottsched[1]. Born in 1700 near Königsberg, and educated at the university there, Gottsched early received the stamp of the Leibnitzian and Wolffian philosophies, which remained with him through life. Owing to the accident of his exceeding tallness, he was obliged, in 1724, to flee from Königsberg, to evade the king of Prussia's search for grenadiers. In Leipzig he made a rapid career at the university and was soon recognised as a leader in matters of taste. He was a typical product of the philosophy of Wolff; a scholar of no deep, first-hand scholarship, an indifferent poet, quite unimaginative, but endowed with good common sense and practical judgment. He made up his mind early in life about what he intended to do, and with admirable tenacity of purpose he accomplished it. Imbued with the pedagogic ideas of his master, he assumed the rôle of schoolmaster of German literature. And much as the later poets resented it, it was just such schoolmastering that the Germany of his time stood most in need of. Gottsched's services to theatre and drama were very real, and to these I return later. For the present I am concerned only with his *Versuch einer Critischen Dichtkunst vor die Deutschen*, which appeared in 1730, or rather in the autumn of 1729. A second edition was published in 1737, a

Were it not that there are apparently no points of similarity except the titles, one might be tempted to trace to Muratori's example the extraordinary 'Literary Republic,' which Klopstock tried to establish in Germany in her period of 'Sturm und Drang.'

[1] Gottsched's reputation has gone through interesting vicissitudes. Lessing's animosity and Goethe's contemptuous 'Ganz Leipzig verachtet ihn; niemand geht mit ihm um!' lay heavy on his memory for a hundred years. Then, in 1848, T. W. Danzel published his laborious rehabilitation of him (*Gottsched und seine Zeit*, Leipzig, 1848), which has been endorsed by, among recent writers, J. Crüger (*Gottsched, Bodmer und Breitinger*, in Kürschner's *Deutsche Nationalliteratur*, XLII, 1884). F. Braitmaier (*Geschichte der poetischen Theorie und Kritik*, Frauenfeld, 1888) attempted to reinstate the old opinion of him, while E. Reichel (*Gottsched*, 2 vols., Berlin, 1908–12) has extolled him quixotically as one of Germany's greatest minds. G. Waniek (*Gottsched und die deutsche Literatur seiner Zeit*, Leipzig, 1897) puts Gottsched's case in the most reasonable light.

third in 1742, a fourth in 1751. In the last Gottsched omitted the words 'vor die Deutschen,' thinking that even other nations might benefit from it; and to further this end, he introduced illustrations from foreign literatures. The work arose out of university lectures, and is a strictly practical handbook; it does not profess to give a philosophical theory of literature, but rather, by the application of the Wolffian method to the art of writing, to help the Germans to become poets. Its contents are indicated on the title-page:

> Darinnen erstlich die allgemeinen Regeln der Poesie, hernach alle besondere Gattungen der Gedichte, abgehandelt und mit Exempeln erläutert werden: Überall aber gezeiget wird, dass das innere Wesen der Poesie in einer Nachahmung der Natur bestehe.

It has been a little rashly assumed that Gottsched merely offers his countrymen the undiluted doctrine of French pseudo-classicism; it is true, his faith in the French critics[1]—not, however, so much in Boileau, as in Le Bossu and D'Aubignac; Dubos, if he read him, had not impressed him—is implicit; they have clearly more weight with him than the ancients. But he was not unfamiliar with English books, notably the *Guardian*, which his wife was subsequently to translate. He was in real sympathy with the English development of the classic theory. He also mentions—in the preface to the second edition of 1737—certain Italian authorities, Castelvetro, Riccoboni's *Histoire du Théâtre italien*, Calepio's *Paragone*, and the *Teatro italiano* of 1828, which, however, reversing his previous error, he ascribes to Muratori. But, unless where he condemns the opera, it is difficult to discover any use he made of these works. On the whole, Gottsched's treatise maintains the orthodox classic standpoint, and it held sway as the standard text-book of poetic art in Germany for more than a decade.

Three years before the *Critische Dichtkunst* there had been published, however, a little German book which may, in a higher sense, be claimed as Germany's first contribution to modern aesthetic theory: the *Untersuchung von dem guten Geschmack in*

[1] There is a useful thesis on *Der französische Einfluss im zweiten Teil von Gottscheds Critischer Dichtkunst*, by K. Blanck, Göttingen, 1910.

der Dicht- und Redekunst, by Johann Ulrich König[1]. König's reading was extraordinarily wide; he has an encyclopaedic knowledge of all that had been written on the subject of good taste, French, English and Italian; and it must be put to his credit that he was the first German to introduce Du Bos to his countrymen, the first to quote Shaftesbury. He also knew the *Spectator*, which had been translated from the French version in 1721. With the Italian writers he was familiar as no other of his countrymen. He quotes Pallavicino, Orsi, Fontanini, Gravina and Muratori; and he held out the prospect of a continuation of his treatise, in which he would discuss these Italians in greater detail. Unfortunately, this was never published.

König was, however, rather overweighted by his reading; and instead of striking out for himself, he endeavoured to steer an eclectic course. He was much inclined towards Du Bos' views, but he refused to accept his doctrine of taste as a 'sixth sense.' In fact, he compromised where a compromise was not possible; on one page he tells us, with Du Bos, that taste is an 'Empfindung unserer Seele,' on another that it is a function of the 'judgment'; or he runs the two definitions together as in the following:

> The taste of the understanding is thus nothing but the combined power of the soul to feel and to judge. Through the instrument of the senses it receives a certain impression, and then arrives at a decision concerning this impression by expressing its liking or dislike for it[2].

There was nothing in König's book to bring him into conflict with Gottsched; nor is there in the important aesthetic writings of Johann Elias Schlegel, who was also familiar with the Italian books which Gottsched quotes[3]. Where both he and Gottsched learned from them was in practical matters of the theatre. The real opposition to the Leipzig dictator was being prepared, not

[1] It appeared as an appendix to König's edition of Canitz's *Gedichte*, Leipzig, 1727. Cp. M. Rosenmüller, *J. U. von König*, Leipzig Diss., 1896, pp. 137 ff.

[2] Pp. 257 f. See also p. 292. Cp. Braitmaier, *op. cit.* I, p. 59, and E. Bergmann, *Die Begründung der deutschen Ästhetik durch Baumgarten und Meier*, Leipzig, 1911, pp. 77 f.

[3] He quotes Muratori in his *Schreiben über die Komödien in Versen* (J. E. Schlegel's *Ästhetische und dramaturgische Schriften*, herausg. von J. A. von Antoniewicz, Stuttgart, 1887, pp. 27 f.), and also Calepio (*ibid.* p. 194; but see below, p. 269).

in Leipzig itself, but in Switzerland, by the Zürich writers, Bodmer and Breitinger. It was long, however, before it came to open conflict, or, indeed, before it was clear that there was room for any conflict at all. Not until the end of 1739, ten years after the appearance of Gottsched's *Critische Dichtkunst*, did the literary battle between Leipzig and Zürich open.

This conflict is the first important event in the German literary history of the eighteenth century; from it the whole rapid development of German classical literature takes its origin. In essence, it was a German repetition of the French 'Querelle des anciens et des modernes'; it involved all the general issues of that quarrel, although its scope had been materially widened and modernised by the generation that lay between. Gottsched was an 'ancient,' but an ancient with many 'modern' sympathies; while his Swiss opponents had attained a standpoint, in some respects, considerably more assured and self-confident than that of the 'moderns' of the French quarrel. The battle was fought over again, but fought on a different plane. This affinity with the French—or, for that part, European—quarrel has been rather overlooked by German critics, who have been content to see in it merely a controversy about the respective merits of French and English literature, a quarrel about Milton. Milton took, after all, merely the place which Tasso occupied in the earlier Franco-Italian dispute.

II

Johann Jacob Bodmer was born on July 19, 1698, at Greifensee, where his father was pastor[1]. His early education took place at home, and we know he had, at least, a good grounding in Latin. His poetic imagination was stimulated by the Bible, and he was soon deep in French heroic novels, such as the *Cléopatre* of La Calprenède, and its German imitations. Above all, the beauties of his native land made a deep and lasting impression on his, for the beginning of the eighteenth century, unusually sensitive nature. At the end of his long life he could

[1] L. Meister, *Über Bodmern*, Zürich, 1783; also the life by H. and H. Bodmer in the *Bodmer-Denkschrift*, Zürich, 1900, and G. de Reynold, *Histoire littéraire de la Suisse*, II, Lausanne, 1912, pp. 95 ff. Valuable for the early period of Bodmer's life is the series of articles by H. H. Füssli in the *Schweizerische Museum*, I–IV, Zürich, 1783–4.

write: 'In meinem achtzigsten Jahre schweben mir die Bilder, die sich davon in mein Gehirn geprägt hatten, noch so lebhaft vor Augen, dass ich jeden Hügel, jede Vertiefung, jeden rieselnden Bach, jeden Baum, jeden Marchstein vor mir sehe[1].' His education was continued in Zürich and completed at the Carolinum there. Amongst his schoolmates was his later comrade in arms, Breitinger, although the real friendship was only formed subsequently. Here Bodmer's interest in literature widened; his study of the classics deepened, counteracting the bizarre influence of seventeenth-century fiction. Hitherto ignorant and incurious about the literature of the Germans, he one day discovered Opitz, and for a time was so enthusiastic a champion, in and out of season, of this poet, that he was nicknamed 'Opitz' by his friends. This was Bodmer's initiation into literary criticisms; and it stimulated his ambition to work for the improvement of Swiss literary taste. His disinclination for the Church, the profession his father had desired him to adopt, increased; and it was ultimately resolved to put him into business. In May 1718 he was sent to Geneva and Lyons to be initiated into silk fabrication, brothers of his mother having a factory of this kind in Lugano; here, no doubt, he was to be given his opportunity in life. A new impetus to the development of his literary ambitions came from the chance purchase in Geneva of the French translation of the *Spectator*. He returned to Zürich in July and was immediately sent off to Lugano. His experiences here definitely dispelled the illusion that he was fitted for a mercantile career. He had the opportunity of learning Italian—in one of his letters he even attempts an Italian poem—and of making the acquaintance of Italy itself. He visited Bergamo, Milan and Genoa. This was the decisive event of his young years. He zealously threw himself on Italian books. The manager and his fellow-workers in the silk-factory, says Meister (p. 18), 'lachten des seltsamen Jünglinges, der immer mit sonderbaren Büchern, oder (wie sie meinten) Skarteken umringt war, für die er gerne seinen letzten Pfenning hingab.' Opitz, the *Spectator*, Italy:

[1] H. H. Füssli, *loc. cit.* I, p. I; Reynold, p. 98. The quotation comes from Bodmer's *Persönliche Anecdoten* (written in 1777), published by Th. Vetter in the *Züricher Taschenblatt*, 1892, p. 91.

these were the formative influences on Bodmer's early life; they laid the foundations of his future activity. What books he actually read in Italy at this time, it is difficult to say. Our only information is that he brought home with him a copy of Vida, Tasso's works, towards which he was particularly drawn, and a volume of Beccaria. No doubt, his acquaintance with Italian literature was much wider; but it would be a mistake to attribute to these months, when Bodmer was still only a youth of twenty, too much of the stimulus which was to mean so much to him some twenty years later. The chief thing is that at an impressionable age he came into actual touch with Italy.

He returned home in 1719, quite decided upon a career of scholarship and literature. In 1720 he obtained a position in the Zürich chancellery, and in 1725 he became a teacher of history in the Carolinum; in 1731 he was appointed professor, a post which he occupied for some fifty years. His first flight to Italy remained the only occasion in his long life—he did not die until the beginning of 1783—when he crossed the borders of his native land. Germany he never visited at all.

Of Johann Jacob Breitinger we have less full and reliable information[1]. Born on March 15, 1701, he lived the entirely unspectacular life of a scholar. After a brilliant career at the Carolinum, which culminated with the publication of a commentary on Persius (1723), he settled down to a laborious career of learning. He took holy orders in 1720; in 1731 was professor of Hebrew, in 1745, of Greek. His long list of scholarly compilations and editions bears witness to vast erudition and wide interests; it is said, indeed, that he corresponded with equal facility in four modern languages, as well as in Latin. His death occurred on December 13, 1776. When one remembers that Breitinger began life as a theologian and that his main interest was classical philology, it is something of a surprise that he should have so ably seconded, and more than seconded—for his writing shows, at its best, higher qualities and a profounder,

[1] There are accounts of Breitinger in the older biographical lexicons, Jördens, Meusel, and Ersch and Gruber; but an adequate biography has still to be written. The notice in the *Allgemeine deutsche Biographie*, III (1876), pp. 295 ff., is meagre.

more logical mind than Bodmer's—the latter's efforts to establish a new literary theory; it makes his *Critische Dichtkunst* a very wonderful achievement indeed.

Bodmer set his heart on producing a Swiss *Spectator*; the idea had haunted him ever since his Geneva purchase. Together with a number of friends, chief among them Breitinger, he formed a literary club or 'cotterie'; and on May 3, 1721, appeared the first number of *Die Discourse der Mahlern*, the first important imitation of the English weeklies in the German tongue[1]. All but eight of the ninety-four numbers of the journal were written either by Bodmer or Breitinger, or by both conjointly, Bodmer's share being almost double that of his friend. The idea behind the title came from Locke, whose treatise on education Bodmer had read in the French translation. Locke, Bodmer explained, had said that an author 'painted' what he had to say on the imagination of his reader; and so the members of the club adopted the names of famous painters. Bodmer signed his articles with various names, most frequently, however, 'Rubeen.' The first volume was dedicated 'dem englischen Zuschauer,' and, if Bodmer may be trusted, Steele himself sent him a friendly word of acknowledgment and thanks for the volume.

Die Discourse der Mahlern is very obviously modelled on the *Spectator*, which, however, the 'painters' only knew in the somewhat curtailed French version. Definite borrowings are to be found, as Theodor Vetter showed a generation ago[2], in twenty of the Swiss discourses; and in fourteen others probable borrowings. As in the *Spectator*, questions of literary aesthetics form but a side issue of the *Discourses*; but, Bodmer's purpose being the 'Verbesserung der Sitten,' part of his programme was to purge German poetry of the 'Schwulst' and 'Galimathias' which it had appropriated from Marini; he thus took up the

[1] The minutes of the club were published by Th. Vetter in 1887, as *Die Chronik der Gesellschaft der Maler*; in the same year he also published the first volume—unfortunately not continued—of a reprint of the *Discourses* themselves. See especially G. de Reynold, *op. cit.* pp. 95 ff.

[2] Th. Vetter, *Der Spectator als Quelle der Discurse der Maler*, Frauenfeld, 1887. In the *Bodmer-Denkschrift* (*J. J. Bodmer und die englische Literatur*, pp. 318 ff.) Vetter is obliged to modify, but quite immaterially, his original conclusions, which were based on a comparison with the English text only.

task which the Hamburg opponents of the opera had already begun. Against Hofmannswaldau and Lohenstein were pitted Canitz, Besser, and, above all, Opitz, whom, as we have seen, Bodmer warmly admired. Opitz is the poet who paints nature as she is. In insisting on a return to naturalness in poetry, Bodmer is but repeating a demand which had been made by both 'ancients' and 'moderns'; and he found many sympathetic pages on this theme in the *Spectator*. Addison suggested to him his parallel between the fantastic character of Gothic architecture and the Marinistic taste in poetry; and he writes of the Zürich minster as the English critic had written of Westminster Abbey.

As far as taste and literary aesthetics are concerned, the points of contact between the *Discourses* and the *Spectator* are practically limited to Nos. XIX and XX of Bodmer's first volume, which draw upon Addison's papers on the 'Pleasures of the Imagination.' It is the essence of all the arts to reproduce nature faithfully, and the beauty of nature is perfect. Bodmer is not, however, altogether consistent in defining the process of imitation, at one time apparently demanding complete accuracy, at another insisting that the artist must first form his own idea of the object to be imitated, and then, with his artistic instinct, select what has to be accentuated and what suppressed. The pleasure we receive from art does not consist—following Addison, he refers to Aristotle—in the mere exactness of the imitation, but in the comparison we draw between the imitation and the object imitated. What he has to say about the parallelism of poetry and painting betrays no acquaintance with Du Bos' work, which, indeed, was hardly possible; it rests wholly on Addison, even down to the latter's rather crude view that sculpture is superior to painting in its appeal, because we can *feel* its resemblance to nature. But, again with Addison, he recognises that the poet has a much wider field for imitation than the sculptor or the painter. On the question of taste Bodmer had obviously not yet reflected very deeply; but he speaks of the wise ordinance of providence which does not make all men alike in their tastes—an important admission. His conception of the imagination as a *tabula rasa*, on which objects are painted, originally, of course, goes back to Locke; and, like Addison, he requires the artist's imagination to be well stocked with pictures on which he can draw. He lays, however, particular emphasis on the necessity of the poet being inspired and stimulated by 'passion' towards the objects he depicts[1].

It is interesting to trace in this early periodical the germs of those doctrines which Bodmer and his friend were to elaborate and deepen later; but I doubt whether we may say more than that it suggests where the problems lay. Bodmer was still far from being aware of the real significance of the doctrines he here adumbrates. His reading was limited, and his sources are not far to seek; besides Addison, he relies largely on Boileau and Fénelon. I can find no trace that he had yet realised the importance of the new Italian movement.

Die Discourse der Mahlern had no long life—hardly two years: the Zürich censorship made difficulties, and the 'painters' themselves became tired of their discussions; the club ceased to meet; and the last number of the journal appeared in January 1722[2]. This lack of success tempted Bodmer to attack the more successful imitations of the *Spectator* in Germany; he wrote an *Anklagung des verderbten Geschmackes*; but it was 1728 before he could find a publisher for it. Meanwhile, he had got into touch with König, in partnership with whom he hoped to found a more ambitious periodical; but the plan fell through. The *Discourses* had two important consequences: they cemented the bonds of friendship between Bodmer and Breitinger, and, strengthening Bodmer's admiration of Addison, ripened his resolve to learn English; in fact, he had made a beginning before the first number appeared. Through his friend Zellweger he came into possession of a copy of Milton's *Paradise Lost*, probably, as he said, 'the only one to be found between the Upper Rhine and the Reuss.' Milton was a revelation to Bodmer; here, at last, was the inspired poet of whom he had dreamed. He set to work at once on a translation of *Paradise Lost*, which,

[1] Cp. Braitmaier, *op. cit.* I, pp. 29 ff.

[2] In 1746 Bodmer reissued the *Discourses* in a revised and enlarged form as *Die Mahler der Sitten*.

although completed in 1724, had to wait until 1732 to be printed. His difficulties were ultimately solved by his founding, together with his nephew Conrad Orell and Conrad von Wyss, a publishing house in Zürich. This firm not only issued all Bodmer's works, but it also played an important rôle in German literature in the earlier eighteenth century.

Having a press at their disposal, Bodmer and Breitinger launched out into ambitious schemes of publishing; they planned a systematic work on literary theory and criticism which was to extend to five volumes. The professorial duties of both men delayed the realisation of the scheme, and it was not seriously taken in hand until 1737. Meanwhile, there appeared in 1727, as a first instalment of the work, a treatise of some 250 pages, entitled *Von dem Einfluss und Gebrauche der Einbildungs-Krafft*, for which the two friends assumed joint responsibility. Remembering, however, Bodmer's contributions to the *Discourses*, we shall not go far wrong in attributing to him the major part of the work, and more particularly, that which deals with general aesthetic principles.

It is of significance that this treatise is dedicated to Christian Wolff. Since the *Discourses* the Zürich critics had made a systematic study of the Wolffian philosophy, and it had aided them to bring order and precision into their thoughts. The ground which they cover in the *Einbildungskraft* is not very different from that which they had covered, or at least sketched in the *Discourses*; and there is little or no advance on the views which Bodmer had already expressed. Locke still provides the psychological basis, a basis which the intensive study of Wolff had consolidated; and the Locke-Wolff ideas were, of course, in harmony with those of the *Spectator*. Between 1721 and 1727 Bodmer's reading had enormously widened. As we have seen, he had learned English, and he had now in his possession the original English *Spectator*, from which he quotes. He was thus no longer restricted to the defective French translation. He treasured especially Addison's papers on Milton, which the French translator had not included. These papers he was subsequently to translate as a contribution to the German Milton controversy. His knowledge of English literature included now a first-hand acquaintance with the English drama[1]; for he feels sure enough of his knowledge to offer a comparison of character-drawing in Ben Jonson, Congreve and Cibber. He also compares Lee's *Sophonisba* with French and Italian dramas on the same theme, which again points to Italian reading and the fact that he possessed Maffei's *Teatro italiano*, which included Trissino's *Sofonisba*. He may also have read the important introduction to that work; and he knew Maffei's *Merope*. Of Italian critical writers he mentions in the dedicatory letter Orsi, Muratori and Fontanini. That, however, he had not yet grasped the real significance of Muratori's doctrine—any more than he had grasped that of Du Bos—is made clear by a comparison of the treatise on the *Einbildungskraft* with the later *Gemählde der Dichter*, which covers to a great extent the same ground. Any modification of the views expressed in the *Discourses* is due, not to the Italians, but to Wolff, although in the amplification of these views, I venture to think, Muratori has been of some use to him. It recalls, for instance, the sixth chapter of the first volume of the *Perfetta Poesia* when, discussing poetic descriptions, Bodmer divides these into reproductions of the tangible visible world, and imitations of activities of the mind and soul. He would appear, however, to have been satisfied with an imitation of the physical manifestations of the emotions; such imitations do not thus differ materially from those of his first category. Again, in his last section, he has a description of 'poetic enthusiasm,' which, with due allowance for the contribution of Locke and Wolff[2], owes something to Muratori's seventeenth chapter on the 'furor poeticus.'

Poetic enthusiasm, Bodmer says, is nothing else but the very strong passion for his theme, by which the mind of an author is engrossed and filled. It binds his external senses so that they are not affected by surrounding things; it whips the imagination into an extraordinary frenzy, brings the poet, as it were, out of himself, so that he can no longer distinguish between the ideas which are drawn

[1] On September 23, 1723, he wrote to his friend Zellweger for Addison's *Cato*, Dryden's *All for Love*, Congreve's *Double Dealer* and Cibber's *Careless Husband* (Th. Vetter, *Bodmer und die englische Literatur*, p. 322).

[2] Locke, *Human Understanding*, IV, chapter xix; C. Wolff, *Psychologia empirica*, cap. iii, iv (pp. 53 ff.).

from the objects he has before him, and the objects themselves; he thinks he sees and feels the things immediately. If now a poet in such a situation describes his matter, he speaks of the things which his imagination paints so vividly and sensitively for him, as if they were really present, and he points them out, as it were, to the reader with his finger. He addresses his personages as if they stood before him, and they awaken the same feelings in him as if they were alive[1].

When the treatise covers the old ground and Bodmer is mainly dependent on the *Spectator*, I cannot find much trace of Muratorian influence, although here one might naturally have expected to see it. Poetic description, he tells us, must have the qualities demanded, not by Muratori, but by Addison; it must be great, novel, beautiful. But the nature of this imitation is better defined; it need not, Bodmer now sees, be photographic in its accuracy; it is sufficient that it evoke in the beholder or hearer the same impression as the object imitated; it may dispense with unnecessary details. The question of the ugly and unpleasant as legitimate objects of imitation, is also treated at greater length, but still on the old lines. On one point, however, he claims to have advanced beyond Addison. The latter, he says, had not explained the psychological reason of the pleasure caused by the imagination. Bodmer offers one which, in its phraseology, seems an echo of Du Bos. 'The human mind,' he says, 'is never so satisfied, as when it is occupied with something which gives it a good opinion of its capabilities. Thus our pride is flattered when, in a description, the imitation is compared with the original.' Hence our pleasure is greater—Addison had also said this—when we are in the position to institute such a comparison. The greater the resemblance, the greater our pleasure; and the highest pleasure of all comes from the artist's consciousness that he possesses the godlike power of creating.

Bodmer elaborates his former plea for 'passion' in description and imitation; he discusses its appropriate language; it does not reason, he says, it declaims. And in this connection he discusses the kind of temperament best suited to the poet. The imitation of characters or morals is dealt with at considerable length. Real characters and historical characters are defined; and he demands

[1] Quoted by Braitmaier, *op. cit.* I, p. 77.

from the artist— as Muratori had also done—typical rather than individual imitation of them. Here both the *Spectator* and Shaftesbury are quoted with approval; but it is doubtful whether Bodmer yet knew the latter writer at first hand. The distinctions of national character depend on climate, government and education, an idea perhaps suggested by Du Bos, who may, in turn, have arrived at it with the help of the Italians.

III

An important stage in the development of Bodmer's critical theory was reached in 1728; for in that year he began to see how helpful the Italians might be in furthering his views. His curiosity about them had, no doubt, been stimulated in 1727 by König's treatise on Taste; but their importance was first brought home to him after his acquaintance, which he owed to his friend Caspar von Muralt, with Pietro di Calepio.

There is preserved in the Municipal Library in Zürich a series of some thirty-three letters from Calepio to Bodmer, written between November 1728 and May 1732; a few—unfortunately only a few—of Bodmer's letters to Calepio are to be found in the Biblioteca Civica of Bergamo[1]. The particular significance of this correspondence for Bodmer's views is that it shows his old doctrines in stubborn, but yielding conflict with the more advanced theories of the Italians. In 1732, as we have seen, Bodmer was sufficiently convinced of the importance of Calepio's ideas on the drama to publish for him at Zürich his *Paragone*; and in 1736 he put together some of the letters that had passed between them as: *Brief-Wechsel von der Natur des poetischen Geschmackes, Dazu kömmt eine Untersuchung, wie ferne das Erhabene in Trauerspiele Statt und Platz haben könne*, etc.[2]

[1] I am indebted to the librarian of the Bergamo Library, Signor Locatelli, who kindly sent me, several years ago, a transcript of the Bodmer letters preserved there. Some of them have since been printed by H. Quigley in his thesis, *Italy and the Rise of a New School of Criticism in the 18th Century*, Perth, 1921.

[2] They include, either in whole or in part, and in translation—for Bodmer wrote in Latin and French, Calepio in Italian—those from Bodmer (Eurisus) to Calepio (Hypsäus) of November 11, 1728; March 1729, July 12, 1729; August 30, 1729; from Calepio to Bodmer of January 7, 1729, April 10,

In Calepio's letter of January 7, 1729, he sends Bodmer, in accordance with his request, a lengthy account of the Italian writers on aesthetic theory, and he subsequently helped him to obtain the books themselves. In this account he speaks particularly warmly of Gravina[1], and recommends the study of Muratori's *Della Perfetta Poesia italiana* in the edition of 1724, which contains Salvini's notes. It is, however, possible, as we have seen, that Bodmer already knew the work; in any case, this 1724 edition was in his library.

The theme of the *Briefwechsel vom Geschmack* is whether poetic works are to be judged by feeling, or in accordance with rational principles; whether aesthetic judgment is subjective or objective. Bodmer holds the latter view, that is to say, that taste in poetry is something of general validity, and based on logical laws, or as he puts it (p. 2), may be treated 'in mathematischer Ordnung.' Taste is to him a faculty of the understanding, the function of which is to distinguish between the true and the false, the perfect and the imperfect. There can be only one true taste among all peoples and in all times. A taste that is based on feeling is wholly false, and is responsible for the confusion in men's judgments.

Calepio, on the other hand, pleads for the recognition of a taste based, not on reason, but on feeling; his sympathies were clearly with Du Bos. He points out the distinction, which Bodmer—as König before him—ignored, between taste as a sentiment awakened in us by a beautiful object, and taste as a guide in judging between the good and the bad. A sharper antagonism begins to show itself between the correspondents when they discuss the nature of 'Ergözen,' the pleasure which a work of art causes. This, Bodmer holds, arises from the comparison which our mind institutes between the imitation and the thing imitated: Calepio, on the other hand, maintains with

1729; end of July 1729; September 12, 1729; June 17, 1730, and July 22, 1731. The originals of all these letters, except the two last from Bodmer, are either in Zürich or Bergamo.

[1] There is ample evidence of Bodmer's familiarity with Gravina in his *Neue Critische Briefe*, Zürich, 1749, where he supports his admiration of 'Dantes' by quotations from him; he also repudiates Gravina's excessive praise of Trissino. In Bodmer's writings one often meets with Gravinian phrases and ideas.

Gravina and Du Bos, that our emotions and the consequences of these emotions are in themselves sources of pleasure. We are pleased in seeing a reproduction of some emotion, quite irrespective of any comparison with reality; and this pleasure is distinct from that produced by reflexion. Bodmer would now appear to shift his ground somewhat. He endeavours to show that, if a tragedy pleases us, this is due, not to the emotion represented, but to the admiration—in itself a species of comparison—which the tragic hero awakens in us. Calepio admits that admiration may be awakened, but he insists that the essential pleasure of tragedy consists in its emotional appeal to our own fear, and especially our pity[1]. This view is enlarged upon in the *Paragone*, and finds an echo in German aesthetic theory as late as Lessing's *Hamburgische Dramaturgie*[2]. From the question of admiration the controversy passes to that of the admissibility of the sublime. Here Calepio's conclusion is that the sublime may only be employed in tragedy where it helps to stir our emotions; it may not be an end in itself, otherwise it would interfere with the legitimate tragic effect. Calepio, it will be remembered, takes up the same attitude towards the sublime in his *Paragone*. Thus one might say that, in a vague, confused way, the *Briefwechsel vom Geschmack* is a kind of 'Querelle des anciens et des modernes' in a teacup; and Bodmer, who was the 'modern' in the controversy with Gottsched, is in his correspondence with Calepio distinctly the 'ancient.' It was, as will be seen, the particular mission of the Italians in German aesthetic history, to convert Bodmer and Breitinger to the 'modern' faith.

In estimating Calepio's influence on the Germans, it is important to remember that these ideas are set forth in German in the *Briefwechsel* of 1736, whereas the *Paragone*, although

[1] Cp. also from Calepio's letter to Bodmer of November 6, 1729 (not utilised in the *Briefwechsel*): 'Io dirovvi solamente non essere mia sentenza che il dolore sia assolutamente piacevole; poichè tal proposizione suona male; ma che le passioni della tragedia recan seco an immediato piacere, cagionato in parte dall' interesse che prendiamo ne' funesti successi de' miseri, ed in parte dalla conformità de' sentimenti che secondano il nostro dolore.'

[2] Cp. my article on *Lessing's Interpretation of Aristotle*, in the *Modern Language Review*, XII (1917), pp. 329 ff.

published four years earlier, was only accessible to readers of Italian. And there is no doubt, as Braitmaier noticed long ago[1], but unfortunately did not follow up, that the *Briefwechsel vom Geschmack* had influence on the important correspondence on tragedy, carried on in 1756 and 1757, between Lessing, Mendelssohn and Nicolai.

The *Paragone della Poesia tragica d' Italia con quella di Francia* was fairly well known in Germany. The fact that it had been launched by Bodmer ensured that that writer would do his best to bring it to the attention of German men of letters. He wrote to his friends about it, notably to Gottsched, towards the end of 1732[2]; and about a year later, on January 3, 1734, we find Gottsched hinting to Bodmer[3] that he has undertaken to write an introduction to a translation of the *Paragone*, which was being finished by another hand. This, however, never saw the light.

The *Paragone* is mentioned among the sources of the second edition of Gottsched's own *Critische Dichtkunst* (1737), although there is nothing in the text of that work which suggests the

[1] *Op. cit.* p. 193.

[2] Cp. T. W. Danzel, *Gottsched und seine Zeit*, Leipzig, 1848, pp. 188 f. The letter is interesting enough to quote: 'Ew HochEdl. können die Opern nicht besser wiederlegen, als mit Trauer-Spielen von der vollkommenen Art. Was ich eine volkommene Tragödie heisse, können Sie aus dem Paragone della Poesia Tragica wahrgenommen haben, denn der Verfasser dieser Critik hat mich zu einem Proselyten von seiner Lehre gemacht, statt dass ich von dem Exempel des Corneille und anderer verführt, zuvor gantz andere Gedanken von dieser Art Gedichte gehabt hatte. Als ich ihm einst Addisons Cato als ein Muster der vollkommenen Tragödie angepriesen, gab er mir Folgendes zur Antwort: Io non saprei affermare che il Catone dell' Addison sortisca pienamente il suo effetto, o riguardisi il terrore o la pietà; il primo è inutile perchè patisce un innocente, e rispetto alla seconda quanto il merito della persona e la gravezza della calamità vagliono a muoverla tanto la reprime l' intrepidezza del suo animo: avvegna che non desti perfettamente l' altrui dolore, chi non lo mostra. Nondimeno s' io paragono il labore dell' Addison al labore di M. Deschamps trovo appresso l' Inglese maggiore artifizio nel render compassionevole la calamità di si grande uomo che appresso il Francese perciocche quegli nel dar maggior luogho all esercizio della sua costanza lascia apparir meglio il peso della calamità. Ein Grundsatz meines vornehmen Freundes ist, dass das Trauerspiel poema populare und vor die Bürgerschaft gewidmet sey zumahlen die Zuhörer aus allerley Leuten bestehen.' Donati suggests (p. 263) that there was some malice prepense in Bodmer communicating to Gottsched Calepio's views on *Cato*; but this was hardly likely as early as 1732.

[3] In an unpublished letter, quoted by Donati, *op. cit.* p. 264.

influence of Calepio[1]. I can hardly think that Gottsched would hold him of much account; he certainly did not study him attentively. Gottsched's translation not being forthcoming, Bodmer himself produced a loose and abbreviated paraphrase of the *Paragone* in his *Critische Briefe* of 1746[2], followed by a criticism of his own, in which he took exception to Calepio's view of tragedy as a 'poema popolare,' and to his Aristotelian disparagement of character-drawing, as compared with the all-important invention of the 'fable.' Bodmer also repeats here his former opinion on the place of admiration in tragedy; he still thinks that Calepio underrates the value of this sentiment.

Another German critic of the time who was familiar with Calepio's little book, was Johann Elias Schlegel. The remarkable originality and independence of Schlegel's aesthetic views—it must be remembered, too, that he only lived to be thirty—have never been satisfactorily accounted for. His general 'imitation' theory was largely moulded under French influence; but his views on the drama and the theatre were, to a large extent, of Italian inspiration. The *Paragone* was one of his sources[3]; he was in essential sympathy with Calepio's views. Like him, he demanded imitation of the Greeks rather than of the French, whom he was beginning to recognise as false guides; and he shared the Italian opinion that a healthy dramatic art must appeal, not to the few, but to the people as a whole. From another Italian, Riccoboni, Schlegel learned still more, when he came to devise his remarkable scheme for the reorganisation of the theatre.

Most interesting of all to us now is the possibility that Lessing may have drawn some ideas from the *Paragone* in his great text-book of the theatre, the *Hamburgische Dramaturgie*. That

[1] In an article in his *Critische Beyträge* (v, 1733, pp. 42, 55) Gottsched, however, appealed to the authority of Calepio, in defending his use of 'niedrige Sprache' for his Pharnaces and Porcius in *Der sterbende Cato* (Donati, p. 264).

[2] *Critische Briefe. Auszüge aus Herrn G. von C.'s Abhandlung von der Tragödie*, Zürich, 1746. I am indebted to the State Library of Munich for the use of a copy of this work.

[3] At the beginning of his *Gedanken zur Aufnahme des dänischen Theaters* Schlegel refers to 'i paragoni di teatro' (*Ästhetische Schriften*, *ed. cit.* p. 194). Cp. also the introduction to that edition, pp. lxiv, clxv, clxvii.

Lessing knew and sympathised with the standpoint which Calepio maintains in the *Briefwechsel vom Geschmack*, has already been mentioned; and the influence of the *Paragone* on Lessing's later thought has been tentatively suggested by O. Walzel[1], who rightly argues that it would have been strange had Lessing not been familiar with one of the few treatises of his time, the standpoint of which, especially with regard to Corneille, was so similar to his own[2]. The evidence is not, however, very convincing; at most, we might say that, when Lessing attacks Corneille's interpretation of the disjunctive conjunction in the definition of tragedy, pity *or* fear—the weak point in Corneille's armour which Dacier had overlooked—he may have owed the suggestion to Calepio.

IV

The general plan of the Swiss *Critische Dichtkunst* goes back to 1727, before Gottsched's work with the same title had appeared; and, although the distribution of the Swiss poetic theories over the various parts of their work was subsequently altered, the original place in their scheme of the two volumes bearing the title *Critische Dichtkunst* is clearly discernible. In a letter from Bodmer to Gottsched of July 30, 1738[3], he describes the work as being planned in three parts: a *Critische Dichtkunst* proper, in which 'the probable, the fable and the miraculous' should be dealt with; a part dealing with all kinds of descriptive poetry; and one on figurative language. He also mentions that his defence of Milton's *Paradise Lost*, already

[1] See his review of Braitmaier's work in the *Anzeiger für deutsches Altertum*, 1891, pp. 58 ff.

[2] Cp. my article, already referred to, on *Lessing's Interpretation of Aristotle* in the *Modern Language Review*, XII, 1917, p. 327. It seems to me that it is Calepio—and not, as is usually supposed, Maffei—whom Lessing has in view, when in st. xxxii of the *Dramaturgie* he says: 'Hernach lebte, zu Anfange des itzigen Jahrhunderts, irgendwo in Italien, ein Pedant, der hatte den Kopf von den Trauerspielen der Griechen und seiner Landsleute des sechszehnten Seculi voll, und der fand an der Rodogune gleichfals vieles auszusetzen.' There are also a few minor hints in Lessing's work which may imply familiarity with the *Paragone*. Cp. *Modern Language Review*, XII, 1918, pp. 485 ff. I deal with this matter in more detail in a forthcoming study of the *Hamburgische Dramaturgie*.

[3] Printed by Danzel, *op. cit.* p. 193.

completed, would form some chapters in the work. Instead of a single work, several independent volumes appeared at different times. The defence of Milton appeared first, in 1740; then the treatise on *Gleichnisse*, followed by the two volumes which now are entitled *Critische Dichtkunst*; finally, in 1741, *Critische Gemählde der Dichter*. There is considerable difficulty in affixing the responsibility of the two authors for these volumes; they were apparently, in large part, the result of joint labours, and the names on the title-pages indicate little more than responsibility for the major part of the contents[1]. To emphasise Bodmer's and Breitinger's unanimity, books attributed on their title-page to the one critic were provided with prefaces written by the other.

The full title of Bodmer's defence of Milton against the attacks of Voltaire and Magny is: *Critische Abhandlung von dem Wunderbaren in der Poesie und dessen Verbindung mit den Wahrscheinlichen, in einer Vertheidigung des Gedichtes Joh Miltons von dem verlohrnen Paradiese; Der beygefüget ist Joseph Addisons Abhandlung von den Schönheiten in demselben Gedichte*, Zürich, 1740. Interesting as this treatise is as a document of Milton's rapidly growing fame on the continent, it has small value for the development of the Swiss aesthetics. It is necessarily based on the *Spectator*, and although Bodmer is intent on strengthening Addison's defence of Milton by marshalling classic authority in its support, I doubt if he has added materially to the *Spectator* papers. On the general question of the 'Verbindung des Wunderbaren mit dem Wahrscheinlichen' he has little to say that he had not already said, or which was not to be much better said in the treatises that followed. In fact, the *Critische Dichtkunst* and the *Gemählde der Dichter* made it—unless in so far as it includes a translation of Addison—superfluous.

More important is the first contribution to critical theory which bears Breitinger's name: *Critische Abhandlung von der Natur, den Absichten und dem Gebrauche der Gleichnisse*, Zürich, 1740. Bodmer wrote the preface to it in which he claimed,

[1] As Braitmaier points out (I, p. 153), Breitinger claims the authorship—on the title-page attributed to Bodmer—of the *Gemählde der Dichter*. See his *Critische Dichtkunst*, I, p. 442.

somewhat patronisingly, to have given it 'die letzte Aufputzung, was vornehmlich die Sprache und den Druck anbelangte.' The main interest for us of this treatise, which shows a quite extraordinarily wide reading in French and English authorities, lies in its first chapter. Here Breitinger puts forward a claim, which is also to be found in Muratori[1], for a 'Logik der Phantasie.' The impression of outward things stored up in the imagination are the materials of poetry; and with them the 'logic of the fantasy' has to deal, grouping and comparing them, and thus rendering them suitable vehicles of ideas. The book is a systematic introduction to the use of metaphor, 'Gleichnisse' being really synonymous with what Bodmer calls 'Gemählde der Dichter'; and this, in turn, is the 'dipintura poetica' of the *Perfetta Poesia italiana*[2]. In spite of the fact that the treatise is largely made up of an examination of metaphors as used by the poets, it is by no means the least readable of the Swiss works. Breitinger is clearly here coming to grips with the new aesthetic problems. He has no hesitancy in pointing out the shortcomings of Gottsched and his school; indeed, his excellent chapter on the use of metaphor in tragedy, where he is in sympathy with La Motte's strictures, and does not mince words in condemning Lohenstein and Gryphius, must have given considerable offence in Leipzig. This book, rather than that on the Imagination, which was not reviewed until later in Gottsched's *Beyträge*, is the real starting-point for the literary feud[3]. From now on Gottsched's tone visibly hardens against the Swiss.

Breitinger's *Critische Dichtkunst, worinnen die Poetische Mahlerey in Absicht auf die Erfindung im Grunde untersuchet und mit Beyspielen aus den berühmtesten Alten und Neuern erläutert wird*, published at Zürich in two volumes in 1740, is much the most important of the Swiss contributions to literary aesthetics,

[1] Cp. Muratori, *Perfetta Poesia*, II, chapter i ff., notably p. 71, where the need of logic in dealing with the images of the fantasy is insisted upon. See, however, below, p. 281.

[2] *Ibid*. I, chapter xiv.

[3] Cp. Bodmer's letter to Zellweger, of December 26, 1739, quoted by J. Baechtold, *Geschichte der deutschen Literatur in der Schweiz*, Frauenfeld, 1887, p. 558: 'Ich weiss nicht ob die Freiheit, so Herr Professor Breitinger in den Gleichnissen gegen Gottsched gebraucht, mir diesen Correspondenten abgespenstiget hat; ich bin ohne Brief von ihm.'

and demands careful attention. In accordance with the practice of the two friends, Bodmer provides the preface to the work. He opens with a quotation, not, as is usually stated, from Du Bos, but from Maffei:

> A certain critic has noted that nature existed before the rules, that the best writings have not arisen from the rules, but rather that the rules have been deduced from these writings; since Poetics and Rhetorics have been written, no Homer, Sophocles, or Demosthenes has again appeared[1].

And he proceeds to justify his friend's work by defending the rules. The masterpieces of poetry produced before there were any rules were not, on that account, written without them. It has to be noted that Bodmer, translating the Italian 'regole' by 'rules' ('Regeln'), understands by the word the fundamental laws of poetic activity, not arbitrarily imposed rules for the practice of the art; but a little later he confuses the two things. The rules and that which pleases us in a work of art are not at variance; it is the business of the rules to guide us in discovering what will please. At the same time, he admits it to be 'etwas verwundersam' that the poets who wrote before the existence of treatises on the art of poetry, should have brought their art to a higher degree of perfection than the poets who have written without the aid of such text-books. The works of these early writers were certainly not the products of blind chance. The Greeks arrived at rules by observation and experience, and then applied them to their poetry. In general, the functions of poet and critic are separate, the duty of the latter being to investigate the nature of the human mind and the ideas it expresses. Aristotle was the first of critics; his rules are for all peoples and for all time. Bad taste arises from ignorance and prejudice. The opinion that the judgment of taste depends merely on feeling, or the 'fanatic principle of an internal light'[2] bars the

[1] Review of Calepio's *Paragone* in his *Osservazioni letterarie*, I, Verona, 1727, p. 268: 'Non manca in Italia chi consideri, come la natura fu prima dell' arte; come gli ottimi componimenti non nacquero dalle regole, ma all' incontro furon tratte le regole da i componimenti; e come dopo che si son fatte arti poetiche, ed oratorie, un' Omero, un Sofocle, un Demostene non si son veduti più.'

[2] This refers presumably to Locke.

way to a proper understanding of the laws of art; it induces only blind faith and unthinking obedience. Bodmer, however, hopes much from the general diffusion of the Leibnitzian philosophy. It must be borne in mind that not everything which pleases is good; but all that is good pleases, and must please a correct taste. It is the function of the critic to make these things clear, to show mediocre and bad authors how they may improve themselves. This, it will be seen, is not a very promising or inviting introduction to a treatise, the ultimate consequence of which was rather to strengthen 'the fanatic principle of an internal light.'

Breitinger's first chapter deals with the 'Comparison of the Arts of Painting and Poetry.' It opens with some general observations on the importance of philosophy for the welfare and happiness of mankind, philosophers not being, like the ordinary crowd, at the mercy of their senses. If they will use their philosophy to further humanity, they must, like the doctor, sugar the pill; they must employ the innocent deceit practised by Socrates, and take the arts into their service. Similarly, it will be remembered, Gravina had maintained the didactic function of poetry[1]. Breitinger now passes to the Muratorian doctrine of the interest of men in the new, the strange and the unusual, the doctrine which the Swiss had found first in the *Spectator*, and then in the *Perfetta Poesia italiana*. It is to be noted that Breitinger uses, not Addison's words, but Muratori's. And on to this doctrine he tacks Du Bos' initial principle of the innate need of the mind to be 'moved' ('nichts ist ihm so sehr zuwider, als der Mangel der Empfindung und eine gäntzliche Stille'). Finally, he emphasises, again with the Italians, the function of art as the interpreter of the higher wisdom and the teacher of virtue to the people; the arts must be 'artes populares.' After illustrating this function—he instances Pope's *Essay on Man* as a popularisation of Leibnitz's doctrines—he turns again to Du Bos. He accepts in full the latter's parallelism of poetry and painting, using the word 'Mahlerey' of the poet's work in its widest application ('die gantze Arbeit der poetischen Nachahmung und Erdichtung...die gantze Poesie kan eine beständige und weitläuftige Mahlerey genennet werden,' p. 13). Breitinger

[1] See above, pp. 39 f.

knows the *De pictura veterum* of Du Jon the younger, otherwise Franciscus Junius, Richardson's *Theory of Painting*, which was widely familiar on the continent in Ten Kate's French translation, and, of course, the 'Engelländische Zuschauer,' all of which are duly quoted. It must be emphasised, however, that Breitinger, no less than Du Bos, is clear concerning the essential difference in the nature and methods of poetry, as compared with painting. He shows how far the two arts go hand in hand, how they both learn from nature; but there is no real confusion in respect of their differences. Here, indeed, both the French and the Swiss treatise are definite precursors of Lessing's *Laokoon*. What Lessing opposed was, not the Du Bos-Breitinger theory, which he rather established on a firmer logical foundation, but quite another thing, namely, the abuses to which it led, the objectionable practice of poets, who, misunderstanding the relation of the two arts, deliberately transgressed the limitations recognised by Du Bos and Breitinger, and thus attempted to make poetry do what lay beyond its province. Breitinger has not much to add to Du Bos' comparison of poetry and painting; but at the close of his chapter he cannot resist—as no writer of his age could—reminding his readers that poetry has one emphatic advantage over painting, in so far as its depictions are 'immer mit einem lehrreichen Unterrichte vergesellschaftet' (p. 28).

The second chapter is devoted to an exposition of 'poetic painting,' which is defined as the art of impressing the imagination—we are again on the familiar ground of Locke and Muratori—with pictures as vivid as those received through the medium of the senses. In this way 'die Poesie ist ein beständiges Gemählde.' Like Muratori, Breitinger compares the historian and orator with the poet; in Gravina's phrase[1], poetry seeks, 'als eine kunst-volle Zauberin auf eine sinnliche, und eine unschuldig-ergezende Weise zu täuschen.' Illustrations are now marshalled from Homer, followed by a significant comparison of Homer and Virgil, which, were it original, would enhance our estimate of Breitinger's critical powers; but it has clearly been suggested by Pope's Preface to his *Iliad*. The practical

[1] *Ragion poetica*, p. 15: 'la poesia è una maga.' See above, p. 39.

hints, which follow, on a skilful choice of poetic images, anticipate the fuller treatment of poetic practice in the second volume of the work.

In his third chapter, on the imitation of nature, Breitinger turns again to Muratori, whose exposition of the three worlds available to the poet for imitation he translates almost verbally. This is also the theme of a chapter in Bodmer's *Poetische Gemählde*. The domain of the poet is the real and the possible. Of possible truth, there are, as Muratori had shown, two species, historical truth and poetic truth. Both serve to instruct, but the latter attracts and delights 'durch das Verwundersame,' by bringing things that have no reality before us. And he supports his views, as Muratori had done[1], by quotations from Aristotle, Plutarch and Cicero. Art is a skilful imitation; the more complete the resemblance, the better the imitation. But—and here he is elaborating a standpoint which Bodmer had already arrived at—the aim of the imitation must not be to reproduce the object imitated, but to call forth the same impression on our mind; it must be imbued with a certain 'energeia,' or 'evidentia.'[2] The closer the similarity, again, the greater is the pleasure we receive from an imitation; even the ugly and the repulsive are capable of causing us pleasure, a thought which points to Du Bos rather than to Muratori. An imitation causes us pleasure by adding to our knowledge and surprising us; in this way it arrests the attention in a higher degree than the object imitated.

Chapter IV deals, under Muratori's guidance, with the 'Choice of Matter.' It behoves the artist to make a careful choice from the infinity of objects laid before him for imitation. Not all objects are capable of making the necessary impression upon us when imitated. The two functions of poetry are to amuse and instruct; and Breitinger declines to separate them. He admits, however, that its chief business is to amuse; but the amusement must be innocent, and conducive to virtue and the strengthening of the will. The theme of chapter V is the 'New.' Crüger believed that Breitinger was here a pioneer and discoverer[3];

[1] *Perfetta Poesia italiana*, I, pp. 91, 101.

[2] Muratori, *op. cit.* I, chapter xiv, p. 216, where Quintilian's words are also quoted. Cp. above, p. 80.

[3] J. Crüger, *Gottsched, Bodmer und Breitinger*, Berlin, [1884], p. 155.

were it so, he would be an epoch-making thinker indeed. But he is only building on Gravina, Muratori and Addison. His 'Neues' is Gravina's 'novità,' Muratori's 'vero nuovo e maraviglioso,' Addison's 'novelty that surprises.' The New and the Uncommon, he says, are the sources of the pleasure which arises from poetry. And on Muratorian lines the New is defined; Breitinger merely broadens the definition by drawing on his own wider reading and scholarship. His terms and phrases are often only translations from the Italian. 'Das poetische Schöne,' is 'il bello poetico'; and 'die Neuheit ist eine Mutter des Wunderbaren' recalls Muratori's 'la novità è madre della maraviglia, e questa è madre del diletto.'[1]

It is the first business of the poet to overcome by his imitation the dulling effect of custom; neither the great nor the beautiful can appeal to us if they are constantly before our eyes. It is not enough that the poet gives us a true imitation; the 'poetic true' must be his basis, but he must add to it novelty, which is the mother of the wonderful. Even philosophic truth ceases to arrest our attention, when it has grown familiar. By virtue of this novelty the poetic true must forcibly penetrate into our minds so that we cannot resist it. Nothing can be newer and pleasanter than the miraculous; and nature provides us with inexhaustible means of enhancing the beauty of the truth. Or we may seek the miraculous in the past, in history. In utilising those sources the modern poets are much superior to the ancients. The sublime, again, has the power of arresting our attention in a high degree; but even such sublime things as the rising and the setting of the sun have lost their power over us by their familiarity. There are as great possibilities in little things as in great; for nature is equally wonderful in both. Aristotle underestimates the power of the poet to show us the beautiful in little things. The 'poetic beautiful' includes everything, both great and small, which has

[1] Breitinger, pp. 110, 112; Muratori, I, chapter vii, p. 101. Further examples of Bodmer's use of Italian phrases are quoted by Donati, *op. cit.* p. 301; he calls (*Poetische Gemählde*, pp. 13, 15) the imagination 'die Schatzmeisterinn der Seele,' and the judgment 'der Leitstern und der Compass.' Cp. Muratori, I, chapter xiv, p. 204: 'Regge la fantasia quell' arsenal privato ed erario segreto della nostra anima,' and chapter viii, p. 114: 'il giudizio è la bussola....' I have noted other similarities in phraseology.

the power to charm the mind. What seems strange and wonderful to some minds may, however, have no charm for others; hence the 'verwundersame Neuheit' lies, not in the things themselves, but in the ideas which they call up. What children or uneducated people find wonderful may not appeal to the grown up and the cultured; thus it is impossible to define what is poetically new under all circumstances. Poetry is one of the 'artes populares,' and must aim at giving pleasure to the greatest number; it is the richest source of novelty, and is not restricted either by time or space.

When an idea passes beyond our ordinary range of experience, it ceases to be merely new; it is then called wonderful or miraculous. This is the theme of the most important chapter in Breitinger's work, chapter VI, 'Of the Miraculous and the Probable.' The miraculous is the highest stage ('die äusserste Staffel') of the new. Novelty, it has been shown, may be at variance with our ordinary experience; but it does not exceed the limits of the true and the possible. The miraculous, on the other hand, throws off all pretence to truth and possibility; it appears as frankly false and contradictory of our experience; it disguises the truth in a strange mask in order to make it more ingratiating to our mind. But this falseness is a matter of appearance rather than reality; for the miraculous must always be based on real or possible truth, if it is to be distinguished from pure lying. Were it not so, the most blatant liar would be the best poet. The miraculous is in reality merely a disguised 'probable.' The mind is only accessible to what it can believe; hence the poet must set before it what has, at least, some semblance to truth. He is confronted by a dilemma: if what he describes is too wonderful to be probable, it leaves us cold; if it is too probable, it ceases to be wonderful, and again has no interest for us. Breitinger now investigates the nature of the 'poetic probable.' It must not be self-contradictory; and it must be something that our mind recognises as possible and not outside the power of the Creator; that is to say, it must be in harmony with the plan of the universe, and only differ from what we know, in so far as we have no evidence that it ever existed or happened. It may be based on saga or history, or on popular delusions; or, again, it may represent existing things and attributes in an increased or diminished potency. Breitinger sums up the conditions of the poetic probable under five headings: it may be (i) what is known from trustworthy sources; (ii) impressions conveyed by our senses; (iii) beliefs that have found credence with large bodies of men, and have been handed down by tradition; (iv) what is capable of greater or less perfection; and (v) anything that has ever happened; for what has happened once, may happen again. A distinction has to be drawn between truth of the understanding and truth of the imagination. The false may sometimes be more probable than the true; truth stranger than fiction. It is the business of the poet to represent the true as probable, and the probable as wonderful. This dictum is illustrated and explained by examples culled from a wide range of poets ancient and modern; and the chapter then falls away into a rather trivial discussion of metaphor and allegory.

I have dwelt on this chapter of Breitinger's book at greater length than has possibly seemed necessary; for it has practically no present-day value. But it was just Bodmer and Breitinger's plea for a recognition of the 'wonderful' as a force in poetry that gave their whole theory its dynamic force. Here—and here almost alone—it came into sharp conflict with the views of the dictator of Leipzig; the literary battle between Gottsched and the Swiss was fought over this question: the legitimacy of the miraculous in poetry. The concrete problem was discussed with trivial pedantry by both sides; but it was not the concrete problem that mattered, but the momentous principle that lay behind it, namely, whether the reason or the imagination should be the dominant partner in artistic creation. The victory of the Swiss meant the liberation of poetry from its long thraldom to the reason; the poet was free to soar. Without this liberating idea, and this chapter of Breitinger's *Critische Dichtkunst*, Germany might never have seen more in Milton than an English Marini; there would have been no Klopstock and all that Klopstock meant for the literary revival of the eighteenth century. As to the provenance of the idea, I think I have made it clear that Bodmer and Breitinger's greatest creditor was Muratori, who first clearly and unambiguously mapped out the province of the creative imagination in aesthetic theory. Not that either Bodmer or Breitinger grasped the significance of their doctrine for the future—in fact, their whole attitude to that future shows just how little they understood it; but neither could Muratori have foreseen or approved of what his doctrine became in their hands. This is merely a universal experience in the progress of ideas.

The remainder of Breitinger's treatise need not detain us long. He shows himself as incapable of avoiding the pitfalls of his doctrine of the miraculous as, at an earlier stage of his work, of the relations of poetry and painting. It leads him in chapter VII to an absurd over-estimate of the Aesopian fable, as illustrating the miraculous in its highest potence, and he arrives at the extraordinary conclusion (p. 197) that an epic poem is, in outline, not essentially different from a fable. The eighth chapter deals with the 'Conversion of the Real into the Possible,' which is obviously Muratori's doctrine of the function of poetry being to 'far eminente (or perfezionar) la natura'[1]; although Breitinger is bolder and takes exception to the Italian priest's pious fear that such perfecting of nature might be derogatory to the Creator. Breitinger defines this function of the mind—the heightening of nature's colours and eliminating all that stands in the way of its perfection—as an *abstractio imaginationis*, which —such was the clumsiness of the German speech of his age—he translates 'Abgezogenheit der Einbildung.' The rest of the treatise may be ignored; it deals with 'the art of giving common things the semblance of novelty,' 'the means of improving bad subjects,' and diction; in fact, diction, taken in its widest sense—not merely covering the use and value of words, style, but also the art of translation and metrics—fills the whole of the second volume.

Such then is the most important treatise on literary aesthetics which Germany had yet produced. In spite of the identity of title, there is no overlapping between Gottsched's *Critische Dichtkunst* and Breitinger's; the one is a practical text-book for the poet who can be made and need not be born; the other is a treatise on the psychology of the type of mind with which the

[1] Muratori, I, pp. 115, 155. Cp. above, p. 75.

real poet is born; an investigation of the creative processes of art. In spite of all its limitations, contradictions and pedantry, it has a place beside the other two great European books of its time which laid the foundations of the modern conception of poetry, Muratori's *Perfetta Poesia italiana*, and Du Bos' *Réflexions sur la Poésie et sur la Peinture*.

I have discussed the *Critische Dichtkunst* at such length that it seems unnecessary to consider another volume with which Bodmer—nominally, at least—supplemented the larger treatise: *Critische Betrachtungen über die poetischen Gemählde der Dichter*, published in 1741. There is much here that is also to be found in the *Dichtkunst*; but it is less systematically arranged, possibly a consequence of Bodmer's mind being less orderly than his friend's. It would, however, be as great a mistake to regard it as merely a repetition of the larger treatise, as it would be to describe it, with Braitmaier[1], as merely a *réchauffé* of the earlier treatise on the imagination. In fact, the comparison with the latter is particularly instructive; for one finds in it, often in incongruous juxtaposition—this is true of the *Critische Dichtkunst*, too—old ideas that go back to the Addisonian days of the *Discourses* with the aesthetic doctrines that Bodmer and Breitinger drew, subsequent to 1728, from Gravina and Muratori, from Maffei and Calepio. To us it is not the least point of interest that Antonio Conti succeeds in doing what the eloquence of the *Spectator* had failed to do: he drew Bodmer's attention to the importance of the 'Engelländische Sasper.'[2]

It has not escaped the attention of Breitinger's critics that his conception of a 'Logik der Einbildungskraft'[3] has analogy with that application of logical principles to the aesthetic faculties, which was fundamental for the system of aesthetics erected by A. G. Baumgarten in 1750. The supposition that the latter was indebted to Breitinger on this particular point—there is evidence enough of indebtedness in other matters—is excluded

[1] *Op. cit.* I, p. 154.

[2] *Poetische Gemählde der Dichter*, pp. 170, 594. Cp. my article on *The Knowledge of Shakespeare on the Continent at the Beginning of the Eighteenth Century* in the *Modern Language Review*, I, 1906, pp. 312 ff., and above, p. 103.

[3] See above, p. 272.

by the fact that this logic of the imagination is already discussed by Baumgarten in his first sketch of his system, *De nonnullis ad poema pertinentibus*, of 1735. But the idea would appear to go back to Wolff, or, at least, to his disciple, G. B. Bilfinger[1], and remembering the zealous study which the Swiss devoted to Wolff before 1728, this is the probable source; but I have already shown that it is to be found in Muratori's aesthetics. This suggests another and a wider question: how far might the origins of the new science of aesthetics in Halle not be traced back to the same new forces from which the Swiss drew? The question involves issues, such as the relation of Baumgarten and Meier to Wolff and other predecessors, which would carry me beyond the scope of the present investigations; I only suggest the possibility of another tie between Germany and Italy. Croce has finely distinguished between the aesthetic movement inaugurated by Vico and that of Baumgarten[2], as he has also contrasted Muratori's doctrine, to its disadvantage, with Vico's. But might one not see the real development of the Muratorian idea, not in Italy itself, but in the German aesthetic school of Halle?

V

Although, as we have seen, Gottsched and his followers in Leipzig fought on the losing side in the German 'Quarrel of the Ancients and the Moderns,' he has very positive merits as a reformer of the German drama and theatre. German critics, overawed by Lessing's attacks on Gottsched, have nowhere been less willing than here to recognise his importance. In point of fact, it really mattered little that Gottsched favoured a type of 'regular' tragedy which was anathema to Lessing, and that he insisted on the observance of the pseudo-classic rules in the theatre; the all-important thing is that he succeeded in making the German theatre, which had fallen into—or, rather, never risen from—vagabondage, worthy of the patronage of the cultured and educated. This was a very great achievement; indeed, one, without which there would have been no theatre at all for Lessing in the next generation to concern himself with.

[1] Cp. Braitmaier, *op. cit.* II, p. 14; E. Bergmann, *op. cit.* pp. 2 ff.
[2] *Estetica*, pp. 219 ff.

It is something of a mystery how a writer like Gottsched, who was at no time very accessible to new ideas, and withal a university professor and an autocratic dictator in the world of letters, could have stooped to cooperate with Caroline Neuber and her troupe of actors in Leipzig. He has himself, in the Preface to his tragedy, *Der sterbende Cato* (1732)[1], given the history of his growing interest in the theatre. His attention, he says, was first seriously attracted to dramatic literature by Boileau, and when he came to Leipzig in 1724, he had the opportunity of seeing the performances of the 'privilegirten Dressdenischen Hofcomödianten,' who played in Leipzig during the fairs. 'I hardly missed a single piece which was new to me.' The only good play, however, amidst coarse and tasteless 'Haupt- und Staatsactionen,' was Corneille's *Cid*, *Der Streit zwischen Ehre und Liebe oder Roderich und Chimene*, a translation into prose.

I took the opportunity of making myself acquainted with the then head of the theatre, and of discussing with him the better organisation of the theatre. I asked him why Andreas Gryphius's tragedies, and especially his comedy, *Horribilicribrifax*, were not played. His answer was that he had formerly played the tragedies; but this was no longer possible. People would not now listen to such pieces in verse, as they were too serious, and had no clown in them (Crüger, pp. 43 f.).

Gottsched felt that he was himself still too ignorant to assist, and he set about enlarging his knowledge of the 'wohleingerichteten Schaubühnen der Ausländer.' He read works on theatre and drama, Aristotle, D'Aubignac, Heinsius, Brumoy's *Théâtre des Grecs*, and the *Histoire du Théâtre italien* of Riccoboni. He also familiarised himself with the dramas of the great French writers.

Meanwhile, as I was obtaining increasing clearness on these matters, it happened that the Dresden Court players got a new manager [Neuber]. This actor, together with his able wife, who was certainly in no wise inferior in her acting to any French or English actress, had more inclination and ability to get rid of the chaos that had hitherto reigned, and to establish the German theatre on the same footing as the French (p. 45).

[1] There is a convenient reprint of the Preface in Crüger, *op. cit.* pp. 41 ff.

He induced the company to follow the initiative of the Brunswick court by producing the French masterpieces in German verse; and with the help of members of his 'Deutschübende Gesellschaft,' they were soon provided with a repertory of regular tragedies.

It may have been that Gottsched, like Maffei, was led to take this momentous step in direct imitation of the Richelieu-D'Aubignac reform of the French theatre; but I am inclined to see in Maffei himself the example which Gottsched followed. Maffei's life and work were as familiar to the Germans as to the French; Jakob Brucker had included his biography, with a portrait, in his *Bildersaal*[1], and his works were duly noticed on publication in the German press. His controversy with Pfaff, reviewed in the *Acta Eruditorum*, created considerable stir in theological circles; and his *Merope* had been translated and played in Vienna, before Voltaire's play gained a footing on the German stage, or was even written.

Gottsched's familiarity with Maffei's views on the theatre go back, we know, to the preparation of the second edition of his *Critische Dichtkunst* in 1737; he refers in his Preface to the introduction to the *Teatro italiano*, although, as we have seen, he ascribes it to Muratori, a confusion not unpardonable in view of the fact that the *Teatro italiano* does not bear Maffei's name; and he quotes the same work at length in his chapter on the opera (p. 711). He must thus have been familiar at this early date with Maffei's project to establish a serious theatre in Italy for the higher drama. Gottsched's interest in the reform of the Italian theatre was still further stimulated by Riccoboni's work, which he criticised at considerable length in the second volume —the first to appear—of his *Deutsche Schaubühne* (1741); and it was again the *Histoire du Théâtre italien* which suggested to Gottsched the compilation of materials for a similar history of the German theatre[2].

[1] J. Brucker, *Bilder-Sal heutiges Tages lebender und durch Gelahrtheit berühmter Schriftsteller*, Part II, Augsburg, 1741. The same part contains a life of Muratori. The chief feature of this work is its beautiful portrait engravings.

[2] *Deutsche Schaubühne*, II, Leipzig, 1741, pp. 28 f. Riccoboni had won Gottsched's heart by his praise of *Der sterbende Cato* in his *Réflexions*

It is not, however, until the forties that we find Gottsched taking a warmer interest in Italian plays. His literary organ in the previous decade, the *Critische Beyträge*, did not notice foreign publications, it being definitely concerned with German language and literature only. But the *Neue Büchersaal der schönen Wissenschaften und freyen Künste*, which succeeded the *Beyträge* in 1745, shows considerable knowledge of and interest in Italian literature. In volumes I and II of that journal there are reviews of Guidi's poems, and of new Italian plays, notably, Valaresso's *Rutzvanscad il giovine* and Maffei's *Merope*—the latter 'a tragic piece which has attempted to reestablish good taste on the stage.'[1] Most significant of all is the following passage from the review of *Rutzvanscad*, which I quote at some length, as it shows Gottsched's familiarity with the reform movement in Italy.

> Muratori and the Marchese Maffei endeavoured with great zeal to free their country from this universal evil, to enlighten the debased minds of their countrymen, to purify the extravagant wit and restore a healthy spirit of reason to poetry; and soon they were joined by Gravina, Becelli and others....Tragic poetry, which had completely vanished in the previous century in Italy, was obliged to give up its place on the stage to confused operas ('Singspiele')....This evil Muratori endeavoured to counteract in his *Perfetta poesia italiana* by a sharp condemnation of the opera, and by praising good tragedies, and Maffei by his *Merope*. Both were warmly applauded by learned and other sensible people; especially *Merope* awakened so much interest that it not only appeared in some forty editions in Italy, but was translated into several other languages. Muratori [Maffei] encouraged good taste by publishing in his *Teatro italiano* (Verona, 1727), twelve old tragedies which, more than two hundred years before, had been composed according to the rules and examples of the ancient Greeks. Gravina wrote and published five new tragedies, not to speak of the efforts of others, whereby this end was furthered[2].

historiques sur les théâtres de l'Europe, Paris, 1738. 'Also,' said Gottsched (*Deutsche Schaubühne*, II, p. 9), 'bin ich auch diesem geschickten Manne, für die unsrer Nation erwiesene Gerechtigkeit, destomehr Dank schuldig, je seltner die Herrn Ausländer dazu geneigt zu seyn pflegen.' Riccoboni is further quoted in the *Schaubühne*, I, pp. 13 f., V, pp. 10, 15.

[1] *Neuer Büchersaal*, I, 4 (October, 1743), pp. 327 f.

[2] *Ibid.*, I, 2 (August, 1745), pp. 117 f.

Gottsched is clearly bringing here the work of the Italians into direct parallel with his own. The *Teatro italiano*, with its plays 'nach den Regeln und Mustern der alten Griechen,' suggests the *Deutsche Schaubühne* 'nach den Regeln der alten Griechen und Römer eingerichtet'; and although the latter contained mainly French works, while the *Teatro italiano* was a tribute to the glory of the national drama—a precedent Gottsched, of course, could not have followed[1]—the practical object in publishing the plays was the same in both cases. Further, can one doubt that Gottsched was thinking of his own *Sterbender Cato*—the most successful classic tragedy of its day in Germany—as the German equivalent of Maffei's *Merope*, which had found 'einen vortrefflichen Beyfall bey gelehrten und anderen verständigen Leuten'? The only question is that of priority; and in 1737, at least, when Maffei is cited as an authority in the *Dichtkunst*, the *Deutsche Schaubühne* had not begun to appear.

VI

A knowledge of Conti's aesthetic ideas does not seem to have penetrated into Germany at all. It is a pity, for they would have found a warmer welcome and appreciation, and have been more immediately furthering to German aesthetic theory than to French. Conti's *Il Cesare* was, however, familiar to Bodmer in the 1726 edition. From it he learned, as we have seen, of the 'Corneille of the English,' 'Sasper,' whom he identified, without altering the Italian spelling, with the 'Shakespear' of Addison. He had read the introductory letters to Conti's drama attentively, and he made use of them in his book on *Poetische Gemählde*. He quotes Conti's opinion on the distinction between 'ideal' and 'natural' characters, and he accepts his division of characters into three classes: those based on the universal, on the true, and

[1] The following reads like an apology on Gottsched's part for not having followed Maffei's plan: 'Nun möchte man mir irgend einwenden: ich hätte ja nur unsre deutsche Lust- und Trauerspiele zu Exempeln brauchen dörfen....Allein es ist den Liebhabern und Kennern guter Schauspiele schon aus andern Nachrichten, Regeln, Beurtheilungen, und critischen Anmerkungen bekannt: dass alle diese unsre Schauspiele eben nicht für solche unverbesserliche Meisterstücke zu halten sind, dass man nichts bessers zu wünschen Ursache hätte' (*Deutsche Schaubühne*, II, 1741, p. 7).

those in which the universal is combined with the historically true, the last being the class of which the poets avail themselves[1]. But he opposes Conti's demand that poetry should be established on a strictly historical foundation, quoting Muratori's view that its highest function is to idealise history and perfect nature[2]. I cannot find that the second volume of the *Prose e Poesie* received any attention at all in the German learned press.

In view of the small notice which Vico received in his own country and in France, it is hardly surprising that he should have been equally ignored north of the Alps. The Leipzig *Acta Eruditorum*, which had done much for the reputation of Gravina and Muratori, expressed itself in a very grudging spirit on the first edition of the *Scienza Nuova* in August 1727, and brought upon itself a justified reproach from Vico himself[3]; and in the same year another Leipzig journal, the *Neue Leipziger Nachrichten*, briefly noticed it[4]. But that is all.

Bodmer and Breitinger, no doubt, knew something of Vico, if not directly, at least through the other Italians with whom they were in closer touch. They were, however, interested in more concrete problems of applied aesthetics than are to be found in Vico. There is, in view of what has been already said[5], no ground for believing that, as has been suggested, the 'poetische Logik' of the *Critische Dichtkunst* is an echo of the 'poetic logic' of the *Scienza Nuova*. At a later date, however, we have testimony of Vico having been familiar to two of Germany's greatest writers, to Goethe, who was given a copy of the *Scienza Nuova* by his friend Gaetano Filangieri in Italy, and to Herder, who probably also possessed Vico's works[6]. Another German writer

[1] *Poetische Gemählde*, pp. 392 f., 423 ff.; cp. *Il Cesare, ed. cit.* pp. 70 f.
[2] *Ibid.*, pp. 416 ff.
[3] *Acta Eruditorum, Suppl.*, 1727, pp. 338 ff.; Vico, *Opere*, IV, pp. 345 ff.
[4] Cp. B. Croce, *Bibliografia Vichiana*, pp. 43 f. The *Scienza Nuova* was not translated into German until 1822: *Grundzüge einer neuen Wissenschaft über die gemeinschaftliche Natur der Völker*, aus dem Italienischen von W. E. Weber, Leipzig, 1822.
[5] See above, p. 281.
[6] Goethe's words are (*Italienische Reise, Werke*, XXXI, p. 27): 'Gar bald machte er [Filangieri] mich mit einem alten Schriftsteller bekannt, an dessen unergründlicher Tiefe sich diese neuern italiänischen Gesetzfreunde höchlich erquicken und erbauen, er heisst Johann Baptista Vico. Sie ziehen ihn dem Montesquieu vor....Hier sind sibyllinische Vorahnungen des Guten und Rechten,

who grasped something of Vico's significance, was Hamann, 'der Magus im Norden,' although our only evidence of his acquaintance with Vico's writings is a letter to Herder as late as 1777[1]. But Hamann's ideas on the evolution of human civilisation, of poetry as the 'mother-tongue of the human race,'[2] and many a flash of intuitive thought scattered through his writings, have much more that is Vichian than can be ascribed —as it has been—merely to his study of Rousseau. Again, the fundamental 'Sturm und Drang' idea of the totality of human effort, of the 'whole man working towards a common end,' is also an idea of Vico's; and the conception of 'self-culture' as an end in itself, which lies behind Goethe's personal philosophy, is already adumbrated in Vico's first academic address. When we turn to Herder, we find still more remarkable analogies with Vico's thought. Many of Herder's ideas which mark him out as a pioneer of modern intellectual developments, and make him 'a gatekeeper of the nineteenth century,' are distinctly Vichian. It has been suggested that Herder was here merely building on the foundations laid by Hamann. This, no doubt, was the case in his essay on the origin of language, where the influence of Hamann is admitted; but the whole wonderful conception of Herder's *Ideen zu einer Geschichte der Philosophie der Menschheit* seems to me to be unthinkable without a know-

das einst kommen soll oder sollte, gegründet auf ernste Betrachtungen des überlieferten und des Lebens.' Herder's mention of Vico is to be found in his *Briefe zu Beförderung der Humanität*, No. 115 (1797) (*Werke*, ed. by Suphan, XVIII, pp. 245 ff.).

[1] *Schriften*, ed. by F. Roth, Berlin, 1824, V, pp. 267 f.

[2] Cp. *Schriften*, II, pp. 258 f.: 'Poesie ist die Muttersprache des menschlichen Geschlechts; wie der Gartenbau älter als der Acker: Malerey, als Schrift: Gesang, als Deklamation: Gleichnisse, als Schlüsse: Tausch, als Handel. Ein tieferer Schlaf war die Ruhe unserer Urahnen; und ihre Bewegung ein taumelnder Tanz. Sieben Tage im Stillschweigen des Nachsinns oder Erstaunens sassen sie; und thaten ihren Mund auf—zu geflügelten Sprüchen. Sinne und Leidenschaften reden und verstehen nichts als Bilder.' The analogies between the Italian and the German thinker are made the more apparent by an Italian translation of Hamann: *Scritti e frammenti del Mago del Nord*, trad. e introd. di R. G. Assagiolo, Naples, 1908. Cp. Croce's review in *La Critica*, VIII, 1910, pp. 137 ff. It is characteristic of the German neglect of these problems that in the valuable work on Hamann by R. Unger, *Hamann und die Aufklärung*, 2 vols., Jena, 1911, there is no hint of analogies between Vico's thought and Hamann's. See, however, his *Hamanns Sprachtheorie*, Munich, 1905, p. 125.

ledge of the *Scienza Nuova*. It is the custom to ascribe such collusions to ideas being 'in the air'[1]; but I am sceptical of such hypotheses in the history of thought; and usually, when we probe deep enough, connecting links are discoverable. Could this bridge from Vico to Herder be established, it would justify us in claiming the prophet of Naples—to all appearance unknown to the world outside Italy—as a significant force in the evolution of German thought in the eighteenth century; and even as a precursor, as he assuredly was, whether links are discoverable or not, of the Darwinian conception of evolution in the nineteenth.

With the establishment of the new aesthetics in Germany I have reached the close I had planned for this volume. But it is a close that is but the beginning of a study of much greater magnitude, that of the evolution of the Romantic criticism from the tentative initiative of Muratori, Du Bos and Breitinger, through the critical doctrine of the later eighteenth century—which, perhaps a little prematurely, we in England call Romantic—to the self-assured interpretative criticism of the German Romantic School in the early years of the nineteenth century. From this school the Romantic doctrine spread, largely through the mediation of Madame de Staël, to every literature of Europe, putting the stamp of Romantic individualism on them all, and leaving the nineteenth century to be looked back upon from the twentieth as—in poetry as in science—the most Romantic of all centuries.

[1] Cp. Croce, review of Assagiolo's translation of Hamann, p. 139: 'Tutt' al più è da ammettere nell' Hamann e nell' Herder come un vago sentore dell' affinità di certe loro aspirazioni e attitudini con quelle dell' intelletto meridionale.' Karl Werner (*G. B. Vico*, Vienna, 1879, pp. 290 ff.) attempted to differentiate between the standpoints of Vico and Herder, and Croce has long promised a special study of the relations of both Hamann and Herder to Vico. Since writing the above I have read a dissertation by O. von Gemmingen, *Vico, Hamann und Herder*, Munich, 1918, which materially supports the view I have expressed, although the author seems unnecessarily cautious in drawing inferences. His conclusion may be gathered from the following (p. 37): 'Erscheinen die positiven Einsichten Hamanns noch wie begrenzte Auswirkungen augenblicklicher Eindrücke und zufälliger äusserer oder innerer Erfahrungen, so kommt der umfassende Blick Vicos erst voll zur Geltung, wenn man ihn mit dem Wirken Herders vergleicht, der sein Vollender genannt worden ist.'

I have been concerned only with the genesis of this doctrine. I have shown that it is to the Italians of the early settecento is due the stimulus which resulted in the final overthrow of the tyranny of the reason over the imagination. Here, as four centuries before, as again in the sixteenth century, and once more in our own time, Italy has asserted herself as the leader of European thought in the domain of aesthetics. And I venture to think that the new perspective in which I have placed the beginnings of this world-movement, materially modifies our attitude towards its later developments and, more especially, towards its mode of development.

One deduction from these investigations deserves, I think, to be particularly emphasised, namely, that there is a manifest danger in the ineradicable instinct of our minds to classify and schematise. We love our antitheses: classicism—romanticism; idealism—realism; collectivism—individualism. But with fuller knowledge comes clearness that such antitheses are inherently unreal; the evolution of thought shows no such sharp contrasts, no such hard and fast lines. Nature makes no leaps; and the progress of human ideas, far from being a geometric progression, is an infinitely complicated organic growth, where one thought passes into its antithesis imperceptibly like a dissolving view. The movement which, in the fullness of time, was to culminate in Romanticism, may here be seen dissociating itself from the classic canon by a slow and difficult process. The Romantic doctrine is, in fact, no less a daughter of the Renaissance than the faith of Boileau himself. The Italians whom I have passed in review, have been hitherto known to literary history merely as retrograde 'neo-classicists.' It has been my purpose to show that their neo-classicism was what mattered least, and that, like our own great neo-classic, Addison, they were at the same time—and could at the same time be—anti-classic innovators, and pioneers of a new conception of the poetic faculty. Du Bos, the 'ancient,' still clung to the pseudo-classicism of his century; and he would have been concerned to know that his revolutionary doctrine was to hasten the appreciation of the barbarian Shakespeare. Gottsched's progressive Swiss opponents differed little, if at all, from him as regards the classic precepts he defended.

But, none the less, these Swiss theorists unconsciously set free forces which resulted in the dethronement of pseudo-classicism and inaugurated the most intense period of poetic activity of modern times. Lessing—to Macaulay the 'first critic of Europe'—had, again, the normal type of eighteenth-century classic mind; but, none the less, he materially advanced the progressive movement of literary interpretation. The antagonism of classic and romantic thought, by which we are inclined to set such store, has, indeed, a strangely unsubstantial basis, when it is examined closely. To understand, not the antithesis of classicism and romanticism, but their synthesis, is the way progress lies.

CHRONOLOGICAL TABLE

1668 G. B. Vico born. First *Giornale dei Letterati*. Dryden, *Of Dramatic Poesy*.
1670 Lamy, *Rhétorique, ou l'Art de parler*. J. B. du Bos born.
1671 Bouhours, *Entrétiens d'Ariste et d'Eugène*.
1672 Saint-Évremond, *De la Tragédie ancienne et moderne*. Dryden, *Of Heroic Plays*. L. A. Muratori, Houdar de la Motte and Addison born.
1674 Boileau, *L'Art poétique; Traité du Sublime de Longin*. Rapin, *Réflexions sur la Poétique d'Aristote*.
1675 Le Bossu, *Traité du Poème épique*. Scipione Maffei born. T. Rymer, *The Tragedies of the Last Age*. E. Philipps, *Theatrum Poetarum*.
1677 Antonio Conti born.
1678 Lamy, *Réflexions sur l'Art poétique*.
1681 Gravina (born 1664) at the University of Naples. Sforza Pallavicino, *Del Bene*.
1685 Fontenelle, *Réflexions sur la Poétique*.
1685–86 A. Baillet, *Jugemens des Sçavans*.
1685–94 Vico in Vatolla.
1687 Bouhours, *La Manière de bien penser dans les Ouvrages d'Esprit*. A. Dacier, *Préface sur les Satires d'Horace*.
1688 Perrault, *Parallèle des anciens et des modernes*, I. Fontenelle, *Digression sur les anciens et les modernes*. Saint-Évremond, *Oeuvres meslées*. B. Menzini, *L'Arte poetica*. Gravina settles in Rome.
1690 Founding of the Accademia degli Arcadi (October 5). Locke, *Essay concerning Human Understanding*. Temple, *Essay upon the Ancient and Modern Learning; Of Poetry*. Davenant, *Preface to Gondibert*.
1691 Gravina, *Hydra mistica*. Racine, *Athalie*.
1692 Gravina, *Ragionamento sopra l' Endimione*. Perrault, *Parallèle des anciens et des modernes*, II. Dacier, *La Poétique d'Aristote*.
1693 Locke, *Thoughts concerning Education*. Dryden, *Discourse on Satire*. Rymer, *A Short View of the Tragedy of the Last Age*. Calepio born.
1694 Boileau, *Réflexions sur Longin*. Vico returns to Naples. Wotton, *Reflections upon Ancient and Modern Learning*. J. F. Cramer, *Vindiciae nominis Germanici*.
1695 Muratori in Milan. Dryden, *A Parallel of Poetry and Painting*.
1696 Gravina, *Dell' antiche favole*.
1697 Vico professor of rhetoric in Naples. Perrault, *Parallèle des anciens et des modernes*, III. Bayle, *Dictionnaire*. Leibnitz, *Unvorgreiffliche Gedanken*.
1698 Crescimbeni, *Istoria della volgar Poesia*. Du Bos in London (also 1702). Bodmer born.
1699 Muratori, *Vita del Maggi*.
1700 Crescimbeni, *Della Bellezza della volgar Poesia*. Fontanini, *Dell' Eloquenza italiana*. Maffei, *Osservazioni sopra la Rodoguna*. Muratori returns to Modena. Dubos in Italy (1700–1). Gottsched born.
1701 Fontanini, *L'Aminta del Tasso difeso*. Gravina, *De Origine juris*, I. Dennis, *Advancement and Reformation of Modern Poetry*. Death of Dryden. Breitinger born.
1701–3 Addison in Italy.

1702 Death of Bouhours. Luzán born.

1703 Gravina professor of canonical law. Orsi, *Considerazioni sulla maniera del ben pensare*. Muratori, *Della Repubblica letteraria d' Italia*.

1704 Dennis, *Grounds of Criticism in Poetry*. Death of Locke.

1705 Criticism of Orsi in the *Mémoires de Trévoux*. Bouhours, *Manière de bien penser* translated into English (*The Art of Criticism*). Addison, *Remarks on Italy*.

1706 Orsi, *Quattro lettere alla Mad. Anna Dacier*. Gravina, *Dell' antiche favole* translated into French. Muratori, *Della Perfetta Poesia italiana*.

1707 C. Ettori, *Il buon gusto ne' componimenti rettorici*. La Motte, *Odes* and *Discours sur la Poésie*.

1708 Gravina, *Della Ragion poetica; De Origine juris*, II, III. Vico, *De nostri temporis studiorum ratione*. B. Garofalo, *Ragionamento delle Considerazioni*. Muratori, *Reflessioni sopra il Buon Gusto*. Shaftesbury, *A Letter concerning Enthusiasm*.

1709 F. Montani, *Lettera toccante le Considerazioni*.

1709–10 Martelli, *Teatro italiano; Versi e Prose*.

1710 Vico, *De antiquissima Italorum sapientia*. Maffei, *Della Scienza chiamata cavalleresca*. G. Baruffaldi, *Osservazioni critiche*. La Motte becomes a member of the Academy.

1710–36 *Giornale de' Letterati d' Italia* (Maffei and Zeno).

1711 Muratori, *Vita e Rime di F. Petrarcha*. Shaftesbury, *Characteristics*. Dennis, *On the Genius and Writings of Shakespear*.

1711–12 Steele and Addison, *The Spectator*.

1712 Gravina, *Cinque Tragedie*. Death of Shaftesbury.

1713 Maffei, *Merope*. Gravina, *De Origine juris*, 2nd ed. Addison, *Cato*. Conti and Martelli visit France.

1714 Martelli, *L' Impostore*. Monsignani, *L' Imitazione poetica*. Death of Caloprese. La Motte, *Iliade*.

1715 Gravina, *Della Tragedia*. Conti in England. D'Aubignac, *Conjectures académiques*. Crousaz, *Traité du Beau*. Mad. Dacier, *Des Causes de la Corruption du Goust*. La Motte, *Réflexions sur la Critique*. Terrasson, *Dissertation sur l'Iliade*. Death of Fénelon. Pope, *Iliad*.

1716 Gravina, *Della Ragion poetica*, 2nd ed. L. Riccoboni goes to Paris. Fénelon, *Lettre à l'Académie*. Death of Leibnitz.

1718 Death of Gravina. Martelli returns to Bologna, and Conti to Paris. Zeno in Vienna. Fénelon, *Dialogue sur l'Éloquence*. Voltaire, *Oedipe*. Gildon, *Complete Art of Poetry*. Bodmer in Lugano and Italy.

1719 Conti, *Lettre à Mad. Ferrant*. Du Bos, *Réflexions sur la Poésie et la Peinture*. Voltaire, *Lettres sur l'Oedipe*. Le Bossu, *Traité du Poème épique* translated into English. Death of Addison. J. E. Schlegel born.

1720 Vico, *De universi juris uno principio et fine uno*.

1721 Vico, *De constantia jurisprudentis*. G. Lioni, *Prefazione alla Demodice del Recanati*.

1721–23 Bodmer and Breitinger, *Discourse der Mahlern*.

1721–26 La Motte, Tragedies.

1722 Du Bos appointed perpetual secretary of the Academy.

1723 Maffei, *Teatro italiano*, I, II. Gimma, *Idea della Storia dell' Italia letterata*. Martelli, *Seguito del Teatro italiano*.

1724 Maffei, *Teatro italiano*, III. Martelli, *Il Femia sentenziato*. L. Welsted, *Dissertation concerning the State of Poetry*. Gottsched settles in Leipzig.

1725 Vico, *Scienza nuova*, 1st ed. Hutcheson, *Inquiry into the Original of our Ideas on Beauty and Virtue*.

1726 Conti, *Il Cesare*. Conti returns to Italy.

1727 Muratori, *Vita ed Opere critiche di L. Castelvetro*. Death of Martelli. König, *Von dem guten Geschmack*. Bodmer, *Von dem Einfluss und Gebrauche der Einbildungskraft*.
1728 Death of Crescimbeni. Riccoboni, *Dell' Arte rappresentiva*. Voltaire, *Essai sur la Poésie épique*. J. Oldmixon, *The Arts of Logic and Rhetorick*. Hutcheson, *Essay on the Passions and Affections*. Bodmer's friendship with Calepio begins.
1728–31 Riccoboni, *Histoire du Théâtre italien*.
1729 Gottsched, *Critische Dichtkunst*. Lessing born.
1730 Vico, *Scienza nuova*, 2nd ed. Voltaire, Prefaces to *Oedipe* and *Brutus*. La Motte, *Discours préliminaires sur la Tragédie*. Death of La Motte. Hamann born.
1731 Bodmer and Breitinger professors in Zürich.
1732 Calepio, *Paragone della Poesia tragica d' Italia con quella di Francia*. Conti, *Il Globo di Venere*. Becelli, *Della novella Poesia*. Gorini-Corio, *Trattato della perfetta Tragedia; Teatro tragico e comico*. Maffei, *Verona illustrata*. Maffei visits France. Bodmer, Translation of *Paradise Lost*. Gottsched, *Der sterbende Cato*.
1732–44 Gottsched, *Beyträge zur critischen Historie*, etc.
1733 Saint-Mard, *Lettres sur la Décadence du Goût en France*. Du Bos, *Réflexions sur la Poésie et la Peinture*, III.
1734 G. M. Andrucci (Quadrio), *Della Poesia italiana*. Voltaire, *Lettres philosophiques*.
1735 Bouhours, *Manière de bien penser* translated into Italian. Orsi, *Considerazioni*, 2nd ed. Becelli, *Esame della Retorica antica*. Maffei in England (1735–36). Vico historiographer to Carlo III. Baumgarten, *De nonnullis ad poema pertinentibus*.
1735–40 Baumgarten in Halle.
1736 Riccoboni, *Observations sur la Comédie*. Cartaud de la Villate, *Essai historique et philosophique sur le goût*. Bodmer-Calepio, *Briefwechsel vom poetischen Geschmacke*.
1737 Muratori, *Primo Esame dell' Eloquenza italiana di Fontanini*. Luzán, *Poética*.
1737–38 *Diario de los Literatos de España*.
1737–40 Maffei, *Osservazioni letterarie*.
1738 G. Salio, *Esame critico del Paragone del Calepio*.
1739 Massieu, *Histoire de la Poésie françoise*. Conti, *Prose e Poesie*, I.
1739–59 Quadrio, *Della Storia e della Ragione d' ogni Poesia*.
1740 Riccoboni, *Réflexions historiques et critiques sur les différens Théâtres de l'Europe*. Breitinger, *Critische Abhandlung von den Gleichnissen*; *Critische Dichtkunst*. Bodmer, *Critische Abhandlung von dem Wunderbaren*.
1740–45 Gottsched, *Deutsche Schaubühne*.
1741 André, *Essai sur le Beau*. Bodmer, *Critische Betrachtungen über die poetischen Gemählde*.
1742 Death of Du Bos.
1743 Riccoboni, *De la Réformation du Théâtre*.
1744 Vico, *Scienza nuova*, 3rd ed. Death of Vico. Herder born.
1745 Muratori, *Delle Forze dell' intendimento umano; Della Forza della Fantasia*. Voltaire, *Mérope*.
1745–54 Gottsched, *Neuer Büchersaal*.
1746 Batteux, *Les Beaux-arts reduits à un même principe*. Bodmer, *Critische Briefe*.
1746–48 Lessing in Leipzig.

1747 J. E. Schlegel, *Gedanken zur Aufnahme des dänischen Theaters.*
1748 Montesquieu, *Esprit des Lois.* Gottsched, *Deutsche Sprachkunst.*
1749 Death of Conti. Goethe born.
1750 Lessing *Beyträge zur Aufnahme des Theaters.* Montiano, *Discurso sobre las Tragedias españolas.* Death of Muratori, Zeno and Becelli.
1751 Diderot, *Lettres sur les Sourds et Muets.*
1751–80 *L'Encyclopédie.*
1752 L. Racine, *Réflexions sur la Poésie.*
1753 Maffei, *De' Teatri antichi e moderni.*
1754 Gravina, *Della Ragion poetica*, 2nd translation into French. Velázquez, *Origenes de la Poesia castellana.* Death of Luzán.
1755 Trublet, *Essais sur divers sujets de littérature et de morale.* Death of Maffei and Riccoboni.
1756 Conti, *Prose e Poesie*, II.
1757 Death of Fontenelle.
1762 Death of Calepio.

INDEX

Addison, J. (*The Spectator*), 5, 11, 94f., 124, 199, 204f., 228, 240ff., 257ff., 268, 271, 274f., 286
André, Le Père, 203
Arcadia (Accademia degli Arcadi), 16ff., 24ff., 69, 89, 95, 251
Aristotle, 46ff., 51, 54, 73ff., 126ff., 169ff., 207, 276f.
Aubignac, Abbé d', 158, 193f., 201, 212, 254, 283

Bacon, Lord, 51, 94, 235ff., 248
Baumgarten, A. G., 119, 190, 203, 281f.
Becelli, G. C., 22, 159, 161ff.
Beni, P., 50, 57, 232
Bertana, E., 122, 137, 161
Bodmer, J. J., 130, 166ff., 256ff.
Boileau, N., 6f., 84, 89, 94, 243ff.
Bouhours, D., 6, 8ff., 53, 67ff., 87f., 219, 244f., 251
Bouvy, E., 216f.
Braitmaier, F., 253, 268
Breitinger, J. J., 257ff., 289
Brockes, B. H., 89, 250
Brognoligo, G., 96, 104, 113
Buckingham, Duke of, 100f., 103, 109

Calepio, P. di, 15, 93, 130, 164ff., 201, 206, 254f., 265ff.
Caloprese, G., 8, 25, 52, 180, 182, 192
Carducci, G., 125, 168
Castelvetro, L., 40, 45ff., 50ff., 80f., 91f., 130, 207ff., 254
Cavazzi, A., 215
Cesarotti, M., 104, 193
Conti, A., 44, 96ff., 124, 175f., 199ff., 216ff., 239, 286f.
Corneille, P., 46, 48, 57f., 129ff., 142f., 154f., 169ff., 209, 213, 233, 270
Cowley, A., 237f.
Cramer, J. F., 13, 251
Crescimbeni, G. M., 17ff., 32, 35, 56, 87ff.
Croce, B., 59, 92, 179, 187, 190
Crousaz, J. F. de, 116, 203, 225, 233
Crüger, J., 276, 283

Dacier, André, 51, 170, 176f., 207, 233, 270
Dacier, Anne, 13f., 109, 209, 247
Dante, 28, 44f., 56, 85ff., 185, 194, 197f., 252
Davenant, Sir W., 236, 246
Dejob, C., 105, 138, 141f.
Dennis, J., 239, 243f., 246
Descartes, R. (Cartesianism), 4, 7f., 24, 26, 37, 52ff., 91ff., 97, 112, 182f., 192, 203, 221
Doria, P. M., 8, 166, 182
Dryden, J., 100, 137, 235, 237ff.
Du Bos, J. B., 110, 204ff., 233, 254f., 260, 263ff., 273ff., 289

Ettore, C., 89

Fardella, M. A., 8, 97
Fénelon, 110, 112, 214
Feyjóo, B. G., 219
Flint, R., 179, 184, 186
Fontanini, G., 12, 148
Fontenelle, B. de, 56, 111f., 128, 206, 222
Fraguier, Abbé, 124, 134

Galletti, A., 70, 128, 135, 178
Gassendi, P., 4, 8, 25, 182f.
Gildon, C., 243
Gimma, G., 19, 21
Goethe, J. W. von, 18, 140, 287
Gottsched, J. C., 90, 106, 216, 251ff., 268f., 272, 279f., 282ff., 290
Gracián, B., 89, 247
Gravina, J. V., 14, 17, 21, 24ff., 87, 90ff., 105f., 110ff., 125ff., 182ff., 190ff., 206f., 232f., 239, 274f., 277
Guidi, A., 26f., 90

Hamann, J. G., 252, 288f.
Hamelius, P., 238
Herder, J. F., 288f.
Hobbes, T., 235ff., 243, 246ff.
Homer, 28, 39, 41f., 77, 80, 108ff., 188ff., 209, 275
Horace, 181, 243
Howard, Sir R., 237

Iriarte, J. de (*Diario de los Literatos*), 230

Klopstock, F. G., 167f., 253, 279
König, J. U., 254f., 261, 265

La Motte, Houdar de, 106, 109f., 115, 130, 177, 208ff.

Lanson, G., 7
Le Bossu, R., 56, 174, 210, 227, 233, 244, 248
Leibnitz, G. W., 97, 101, 108, 206, 231, 253, 274
Lessing, G. E., 54, 150, 234, 238, 241 f., 259, 268 ff., 275, 282, 291
Locke, J., 65, 183, 205 f., 235 ff., 247 f., 259, 261 ff., 273, 275
Lombard, A., 204, 207
Longinus, 55, 73, 80, 91, 243, 248
Luzán, I. de, 53, 199, 219 ff.

Maffei, S., 6, 32, 58, 63, 85, 90, 104, 111, 124 ff., 130, 144 ff., 168 f., 176 ff., 200, 214 ff., 239 f., 252, 263, 273, 284 ff.
Maggi, C. M., 6, 12, 63 f., 147
Manfredi, E., 15, 120, 122, 168
Marini, G. B., 3, 20, 23, 71, 74, 83, 85, 89, 251
Marivaux, P. C., 218
Marmontel, J. F., 203
Martelli, P. J., 6, 20, 35, 49, 58 f., 98 f., 106 f., 120 ff., 155, 200 f., 211 ff.
Maugain, G., 4 ff., 10
Menéndez y Pelayo, M., 225 ff.
Michelet, J., 179, 202
Milton, J., 89, 110, 113 f., 137, 199, 228, 238, 241, 244, 251, 256, 261, 270 f., 279
Montesquieu, C. de, 166, 202
Montiano y Luyando, A. de, 221, 227, 234
Muralt, C. von, 165 ff., 265
Muratori, L. A., 12 ff., 54 ff., 60 ff., 101, 113 f., 118, 149, 154, 158, 191, 198 f., 207, 223 ff., 232 ff., 239 f., 244 ff., 252, 263 f., 272, 274 ff., 285, 289

Nasarre, Blas, 231, 234
Newton, Sir I., 99, 101, 107

Oldmixon, J., 11
Orsi, G. G., 12 ff., 62 ff., 88, 101, 198, 252

Pallavicino, S., 55, 74, 76, 92 ff.
Perrault, C., 56, 112, 129
Philipps, E., 238
Pindemonte, I., 144, 146
Plato, 81, 93 f., 107 f., 181, 184
Pope, A., 152 f., 250, 274 f.

Quadrio, F. S., 20 ff., 168

Racine, J., 58, 106, 113, 130, 134 f., 140 ff., 160, 170, 172, 174 f.
Rapin, R., 6, 51, 86, 212
Reich, E., 56, 59
Riccoboni, L., 15, 102, 150 f., 155 ff., 200 f., 211 ff., 254, 283 f.
Rigault, H., 179, 195
Rymer, T., 237, 243

Saint-Évremond, C. de, 157, 244, 246 f.
Saintsbury, G., 10, 21, 92, 246
Salio, G., 177 f.
Salvini, A. M., 96, 101, 124
Schlegel, J. E., 255, 269
Shaftesbury, Earl of, 56, 239, 255, 265
Shakespeare, W., 21, 100 f., 103 ff., 109, 160, 197, 217 f., 237, 241, 281, 286

Taine, H., 52, 224
Tasso, T., 10, 13, 15, 24, 44, 49 f., 55 ff., 82 ff., 156, 167
Tassoni, A., 3, 54 f., 112, 195
Temple, Sir W., 235, 237
Terrasson, Abbé, 109, 170, 197
Thomasius, C., 251
Toaldo, G., 98, 102, 109
Trissino, G. G., 36, 44, 55 f., 156, 263

Velázquez, L. J., 234
Vettori, P., 5, 51, 57
Vico, G. B., 25, 102, 179 ff., 201 f., 221, 223, 232, 240, 287, 289
Virgil, 10, 44, 80, 84, 90, 108, 114, 231, 275
Voltaire, F. A. de, 15, 21, 58, 150, 152 f., 165, 200, 205, 210, 213, 216 ff.

Winckelmann, J. J., 36, 54, 238
Wolf, F., 193 f.
Wolff, C. von, 253 f., 262 f., 282
Worsfold, W. B., 241

Zeno, A., 19 f., 63, 67 f., 147 f., 153 f., 157